Screw the Roses,
Send Me the Thorns

New Milestone in BDSM Literature - Thirteen chapters cover all of the BDSM Basic skill areas, both mental and physical... the authors' irreverent, yet practical attitude is often hilarious, but always useful... [including] fascinating bondage ideas which haven't been shown in books before, the outrageously funny profiles of types of undesirables one sometimes meets in the scene and online, the hilarious cartoons showing the importance of communication.

The Community Standard, Arlington, Texas

The only REAL criticism I have of this book is that it is too big to fit on the back of my toilet. Seriously, it's one hell of a book. I've read most of the introductory books for perverts...this one is absolutely and totally the best.

Yeah, it covers all the regular topics, how to tie up and whack your partner safely, sanely and consensually, and has lots of pics and diagrams and such. There's even bits about building your own equipment with plans and all, from simple cuffs and collars to slings. It's totally jam-packed with information... But that's not why I liked the book. I liked the book for it's treatment of the psychology of dominance and submission. ALL THROUGH THE BOOK there is an awareness of the things I have heard, felt, seen, touched and tasted since I've been in the scene, things I've never seen described anywhere else. The authors are smart-ass and silly throughout, making the book extremely FUN to read.

Jackie Patti, quoted from the Internet newgroup alt.sex.bondage

Brother [Philip's computer "handle"] and Molly did an INCREDIBLE job with this book - which hardly surprises me considering their well-deserved reputation... The book can be considered an "S/M instruction manual" encompassing the physical and emotional sides of the Scene - expressed with candor, clarity and a large serving of wit. It covers everything from gags, different types of bondage including diagrams with specific how-tos, to a drawing showing pulse points to help explain where the pressure should NOT be placed. There are photographs and explanations of whips, paddles, dungeons, scene players and bondage. Also included are instructions on how to make a spreader bar, cuffs, whips and a sling for suspension. All projected with humor and explicit tutorials that make it a book that is VERY difficult to put down.

Quoted from the Majornet's Adult Extremes Forum

It's one of the best manuals I've seen, taking one from beginner to advanced play. It combines the best of Race Bannon's conceptual approach with the hands-on how-to of other texts. And happily, the appendixes alone will be worth the purchase price. The addition of an index is marvelous and more thorough (and helpful) than those found in other books I've seen. It's entertainingly written with the same high good humor I find in the best teachers (and the ones who most love their subjects and students alike). It's beautifully done, and I am proud and pleased to be associated with your excellent work.

Robert Dante, Boudoir Noir Magazine, Toronto

Screw the Roses, Send Me the Thorns... is a gentle and experienced guide taking the reader from the introduction of the principles of S/M to step-by-step instructions on how to apply and receive 'discipline'.

In the recent past, S/M has come out of the closet and is gaining popularity among consensual participating partners as a means to broadening the pleasures of their sexuality. Dominants and submissives practicing within the guidelines of Philip Miller and Molly Devon in this book can find a safe and rewarding way to make reality of their fantasies.

S/M is not for everyone, especially those who are offended by sexual openness and exploration with an eye to finding the limits of their sexuality. But even for these people, I would recommend Chapter two, Sexual Magic, as a prologue to thinking creatively about any type of sexual activity.

Dr. William Granzig, President of The American Board of Sexology

It is an EXCELLENT book. After reading many books, which are all good in their domain, I find this book to be the new, general and detailed S&M scene BIBLE for novices and for advance players. Their writing style is a rare gem to come by filled with humour and good sense. It is a must to have...

Princess Sheeba, Montreal, Canada

It is, simply the BEST book I have read on the topic of BDSM... [Philip's and Molly's] experience, input from others in the scene, and a lot of interviews and research combine to make this THE book to own! You WILL read it, because it's good, and you WILL learn from it, cause it's all there!

'Lite Brite", Rockport, Massachusetts

Your words about 'natural submissives' were wonderful to read after so many years of wondering if anyone would ever understand me. I wish I had been exposed to such acceptance much earlier in my life. Hopefully your book will reach many people who need to hear those words.

A member of The English Palace BBS

Screw the Roses, Send Me the Thorns

The Romance and Sexual Sorcery
of Sadomasochism
by
Philip Miller and Molly Devon

Foreword by Dr. William Granzig

Mystic Rose

Mystic Rose Books

Fairfield, Connecticut

Published by

Mystic Rose Books
P.O. Box 1036/SMS
Fairfield, CT 06432.

We're not lawyers, so we can't say whether any of this stuff is legal or not. In fact, most of it probably is illegal where you live, but laws vary a lot from state to state. Of course, we would never try any of this stuff ourselves, being law abiding citizens, and everything you read here is pure conjecture... we don't even fantasize about any of it. We just eavesdropped, one night, on some sleazy drunks we heard babbling about it behind a bowling alley in Bayonne and our memories are impeccable.

We are not responsible for, and assume no liability for any action undertaken by any person in utilizing this information. We not only think you're nuts to try any of this, you're obviously a sicko too. Any person, relying upon this information does so at his or her own risk. Although the authors and publisher have exhaustively researched all sources to ensure the accuracy and completeness of the information contained in this book, we assume no responsibility for errors, inaccuracies, or omissions or any other inconsistency herein.

We wish to express great appreciation for the articles by Robert Dante, Master Ken and SweetCream, and the fond reminiscences of Janette Heartwood reprinted here by her permission.

ISBN 0-9645960-0-8

First Edition, first printing 1995, sixth printing 1997

Library of Congress Catalog Number 95-79674

Table of Contents

4 "You Want To Worship My WHAT???"
Negotiation and Relationships

51

5 Straight Facts and Bent Phalluses
Sexual Attitudes

69

6 Non-Government Sanctioned Sex and Torture

78

7 Get Them By the Balls; Their Hearts and Minds Will Follow
Bondage Theory

93

8 Of Humane Bondage
Bondage Techniques
107

9 Philip's Philosophy of Phlogging Phun
The Corporal Dimension
132

10 When the Inner Child Deserves a Spanking
Philip's (and Phriend's) Phurther Pheelings on Phlogging
146

Acknowledgements

No one accomplishes anything of value by himself. We are grateful to scores upon scores of people who contributed knowledge, patience, assistance, and support in making this book possible. We can list only a few, but thank you all, dear friends.

For your love, friendship, guidance, and enduring our many moods, thank you: Debbie T., Debbilynn, Lee, Mistress Eva Bathory, Charles Walker, Master Ken, SweetCream, Marie Constance, John, Robert and Mary Dante, Janette Heartwood, Jennifer, Rose, Rana, Mistress Raven, Dane & Leslie Ann <GDG>, Joan, Hans, Josie, Li Chen, Jocelyn, Rebecca, Sara, Ari, Jake, Ali, Jen, Cathy, Robin, Donna, Don, Bob H., both Franks and the patrons of Chez Francesco, Marvin, Pete, two Georges and two Lindas, Doc, Fred, Strider, Kenny, Dr. Wm. A. Granzig, Wendy K., Keri, Remo, Heather, Jerry, Marcia, Jackie, Brenda, Amy, Melissa, Ronii, Laura Antoniou, Adam Selene, Gillian, Roberta, Mistress Sabrina, Kevin Johnson, Bruce, Kayla, Toughlove, Lite Brite, April Greeley, Lynn "Chanti" K., Steve and Eileen Lauer, Princess Sheeba, Veronica & Don P., Andy Anderson, Megan, Doogie John, Songbird Birgit wherever you are, Erica, Tori, Steed, Quirt, Nix, Sharon (C-Pet), Janet, Brook and the Vault denizens, Robert, Morgie, Ruth, Queen Guillotine, Terry L., Michael, Russ, Master Rick, Gregory, Domina Sappho, Shoewolf, Danny, all those plying wanton keyboards on The English Palace, Majornet, alt.sex.bondage, and other cyber-stops.

The Color of a Rose

Different things move us: jeans, uniforms, hoods, tuxedos, leather, lingerie, whips, shoes, silk, latex, corsets, rope, petticoats, cat suits, beards, longhair, crew cuts, tattoos, flannel sheets, feather beds, even knives. Different people move us, too: straights, lesbians, gays, gender benders, bearish men, petite women, heavy and skinny people, the strong-willed and the meek, country, military, and business types, jocks, bikers, hippies, yuppies, techies, and preps. No one suits everyone, but there is always some willing body for every wanting body.

All of the people types and turnons mentioned above represent people we know who practice SM (sadomasochism). Our orientation is heterosexual, dominant male and submissive female and our book represents this perspective. So, if you are gay, lesbian, a dominant woman, or a submissive man, we understand that the context may seem too narrow at first glance. Also, our style of SM is only one of many, even for those who share our basic orientation. Yet, though a tremendous disparity of attractions, orientations, and kinks exists, we are all human and, therefore, the emotional underpinnings of SM apply to us all.

We have learned a great deal about ourselves by reading literature intended for those with sexual orientations that differ from ours. The late John Preston wrote stories about gay SM relationships, but the emotionality and excellent writing within his work offers a satisfying read for everyone. The same can be said of Pat Califia, Laura Antoniou, Guy Baldwin, and many others.

Rather than becoming mired in androgenous pronouns or writing to satisfy everyone's kink, we have written about what moves us, realizing that the emotional core of feelings that draw people to SM is ignorant of gender lines. Regardless of sexual orientation, we all cherish the lovers we choose, our flesh still quivers beneath their touch, and we implore them to penetrate the most forbidden forests of our imaginations.

Foreword

"What can we know or what can we disdain
When error chokes the windows of the mind?"

Sir John Davies (1569-1626)

Philip Miller and Molly Devon have written about scenes, players, playing, toys and playrooms in order to correct the error choking the windows of our minds in our views of bondage and discipline. This comprehensive manual provides an "in the know," how to, understanding of the latest trendy behavior. From Madonna to Versace to 9 1/2 Weeks, sadomasochism appears to be the hip, au courant behavior for the fin de siecle crowd wishing to spice up their sex lives. Oh yes, S/M is sex!

But before embarking on a sexual voyage you must have a map, the proper tools and the knowledge to uses them. This is what Philip and Molly provide to both the neophyte and the experienced player.

Taking the credo of the National Leather Association as their own, that S/M play be safe, sane, and consensual, the authors provide the guide to developing your own scene incorporating their features.

The fourth chapter provides the philosophical framework for the role of the dominant and the submissive and how negotiation is _always_ the beginning of any relationship and establishes the limits that are never to be exceeded. Yes, as in all things, there are limits to what the dominant will do and what the submissive will experience. They provide enough examples for the newest beginner to understand the differences and to abide by them.

S/M is a sexual scene acted out in a significant percentage of the population. According APEX, surveys have listed S/M behavior by as much as 7 to 14% of the population, and is interesting to but not practiced by many more, To see the prevalence, just look at the public's interest in movies, books, and other artistic expressions with S/M as the dominant theme.

And although enjoying a new popularity today, S/M activities have long been performed by many religions and cultures. Early Christian mystics used it (flails and hair shirts). Native Americans continue to uses it for vision quests. Fakirs from India use that same energy that Philip and Molly write about for spiritual journeys, sexual ecstasy, or personal bliss.

While the acting out of bondage and discipline fantasies may look brutal to the uninformed observer, S/M is not as it appears. The uninitiated may believe the dominant does as he/she wishes, without feeling the needs or pain of the submissive, but this is not true. In practice, it is the submissive or masochist that actually has the final say. Philip and Molly write of the process of communicating up front, the uses of "safe" words that will stop the action if the submissive ever feels the scene is not working, and even "rehashing" after the event so that both parties can learn and benefit for the future.

More often the thrill of perceived danger is greater than the actual danger of the process itself. It need not be especially dangerous. Some activities are more physically creative than others. For more strenuous activities the individuals should be in good physical shape, just as for any other sport. In all cases, the players must know what they are doing. This is the purpose of this book.

While the thrust of Screw the Roses, Send Me the Thorns is heterosexual, dominant male and submissive female (or vise versa). I feel that it can be equally valuable as a guide to gays, transgendered, lesbians, bisexuals and any other sexual persuasion.

The authors' explanations of the various forms of play, e.g., bondage, fustigation, mummification, electricity, dominance, submission, humiliation, brachiorectal, brachiovaginal, are clear and enable the neophyte to learn about play from both sides of the equation-- as a dominant and as a submissive. This is an unusually complete volume that will dispel the error in your mind about leatherfolk and their activities.

On a personal note, I met Philip and Molly when we were guests on CNBC's Real Personal, with Bob Berkowitz. In my role as the clinical sexologist "expert" on S/M, I found that this brief encounter gave me a better understanding of this lifestyle and has contributed to my being a better sex therapist in providing comprehensive mental health counseling in my private practice.

Dr. William A. Granzig
President, The American Academy of Clinical Sexologists

Introduction

Marriages of this import deserve an invitation that reflects the uniqueness of the partners being joined. Rather than an engraved proclamation on the finest deckled vellum, we offer a sex manual with a twist.

Screw the Roses, Send Me the Thorns is an introduction and guide to SM for the merely curious, for the novice, and for experienced practitioners with a desire to enhance their exploration of sadomasochism. We use humor and illustration to make it fun. SM is fun and we think that reading about it should be fun, too. It's also hot stuff -- a wild, sexy, funny book that you will be proud to park beside your commode.

Following the emergence of punk in the 1980's, SM has become trendy. The fashion scene, the arts, media, and college campuses are fairly bursting with "fetish-looks" of leather jackets, body piercings, and PVC boots. People everywhere are beginning to enjoy the feel, smell, and look of leather, rubber, and the other fetish fabrics that feed our fantasies.

Some hard-nosed SM veterans loathe the invasion by the fashion butterflies, and they have a good point. Trendiness can trivialize that which we feel at the core of our being. Still, we see it as an opportunity for SM to become known and accepted as a natural aspect of human sexuality. We really have little to worry about; trends pass swiftly and we can learn from the new people we pick up along the way.

Some of the lessons will be profound, others will provide little but entertainment. One young guy we know bought a pair of suede wrist-cuffs to use like a pair of friendship rings; he wore one and his girlfriend wore the other. What the hell, he found the level of fantasy right for him, which is what it's all about. (Still, you have to give him points for originality.)

While we welcome the growing acceptance of SM in society, trendiness has its inherent perils and is one of the reasons that we felt our book was needed. SMers are cast in a bad light based on the mistakes of the ignorant. Misinformation is being circulated as novice players teach other novices practices they have gleaned from fiction. Attempting risky activities without training is stupid and dangerous. Lacking an understanding of the power of SM on the psyche can create even more unfortunate situations.

We want those interested in sadomasochism or any of its subsets including: dominance and submission, bondage and discipline, spanking, erotic humiliation, role-play, and others to understand the importance of having access to the SM community. We discuss safety issues, ideas for scenes, recognizing good and bad attitudes, finding playmates, knowing the difference between fantasy and reality, and learning that techniques are means not ends.

We also reveal facets of SM that have not been addressed in the rather small body of related literature. A few examples: SM techniques are used to achieve altered states of consciousness. Many are aware of the endorphin high, but few have experienced the erotic high called flying. We suggest a four-part framework for using pain to enhance eroticism. We explain how conditioning is another key to advanced eroticism. We offer techniques on whipping, building SM equipment, bondage methods, and pass along the secrets of cultivating a personal sexuality that will quench the most passionate of thirsts.

Allow us to guide you through the rumor, fact, and fancy of Sadomasomythology. Use our book as a source for creative love-making and assistance to help you communicate better in your relationships. We want to welcome you to captivating realms of sensuality, dreamed of by millions, realized by few, and understood by fewer still.

How to use this book:

In the first two chapters we introduce SM and offer a basic explanation of its practice. Some topics may seem fantastic, frightening, or unlikely to the novice. We ask you to read them with an open mind; within are keys that can reveal new worlds of sensation and experience.

Chapters three and four discuss finding partners, forming relationships, and sexual attitudes that work well in SM sexuality.

Chapters six through ten are practical "how-to's." You can skip around these various topics to find tidbits to tickle your fancy.

Chapters eleven and twelve discuss the most paradoxical and elusive elements of SM; the eroticism of pain and humiliation.

We conclude with chapter 13, a survey of dungeon equipment, decoration, and furnishing. Here you will find examples of SM toys and plans for making your own goodies.

As we mentioned above, there is an extensive glossary and several appendices that you may find helpful.

Our qualifications:

While we are not the most noted authorities in human sexuality, Philip can recite the names of every street in Mahwah, New Jersey to the tune of "Misty", and Molly's a whiz on the plant life of Borneo. We also happen to have between us more than twenty years of experience in the kinks so dear to our hearts. Equally as important, we have had the good fortune to have been the beneficiaries of training from people in the SM community with internationally recognized expertise.

On to the Weddings!

We understand that you might be reluctant to join us in our celebration. Everyone has negative impressions of pain and fear, so it is only natural to mistrust someone advocating sadomasochism. Though you may hesitate, you wouldn't be reading this if you weren't just a little bit curious.

Sex has a power over us that none can deny. Most people enjoy the role that sex plays in their lives. The possibility that our enjoyment of sex could be amplified many times if we dared to explore those forbidden urges is hard to ignore. So, even if you would decline in partaking of the consummation of these unlikely unions, we hope you will join us in understanding them.

Black tie is so stuffy. Why not toss inhibition to the winds? Put on those naughty clothes you have always dreamed of wearing, but have never dared to be seen in before. We assure you, all the other guests will be dressed to their fantasy nines, as well.

1 Gee, Toto, I Don't Think We Are In Kansas Anymore!

his way, follow me down the staircase. Watch your step and hold your torch a little higher, that's it. I wish I'd asked you to bring a sweater, it can be quite cold at the very bottom. Don't let the noise distract you, stone walls distort everything. Why, yes, it does sound something like a scream from here. Please ignore it, it doesn't concern you. Let me tell you a bit about our work here.

The inhabitants and customs of the world of sadomasochism are easily as intimidating and confusing as those Dorothy stumbled upon in Oz. Her trip down the yellow brick road taught her that people everywhere have the same needs and feelings. Even the magnificent and terrifying Wizard of OZ turned out to be no more than a lovable old man with a knack for special effects.

Sadomasochists are a lot like the Wiz. We like to project fearsome images and flash fancy toys around, but when you toss us all in the cauldron and boil us down, you find that we are just plain folks having a love affair with fantasy. SM may not be right for everyone, human sexuality can be expressed in so many timbres. We believe that no form of sexuality that nurtures the spirit is less legitimate than any other. Whether you live in an emerald city or dwell in a dungeon, there's no place like home.

Here we are, these are the holding cells. Have a seat on that slab. Now I must leave you in the capable hands of your hosts. Enjoy your stay! Oh, don't be so nervous, we will take very good care of you... and your little dog, too.

Your hosts, Molly and Philip

Hello, I'm Molly. As a maker (and user) of whips, I have acquired some knowledge I'd like to pass on. Besides, I have been a Yenta much longer than I have been a submissive, so I have no inhibitions about throwing in my two cents. In addition to taking the submissive role during sex-play, I am a masochist who adores a good swatting. With some splendid suggestions from our friends and well-placed input from an experienced dominant (Ouch! Thank you, master.), we've gathered these bits of information for your enjoyment.

Hi there, I'm Philip. I am a dominant. You may kneel.

Philip (as usual) giving instructions.

Molly (as usual) making a request.

About this book

Please keep in mind that Molly's contributions are her own opinions. She doesn't profess to tell anyone what's right or wrong, nor does she want you to think she's telling you what to do. Most of the statistics and quasi-scientific sections are Molly's contributions. She loves statistics. She makes them up all the time.

On the other hand, portions written by Philip are absolutely undistorted and accurate. Whatever he says is law. However, as soon as you begin to understand the law, rest assured, he'll change it. Incidentally, Philip is never wrong, and even if it appears as though he is wrong, it's obviously your fault. If you read something here that can't possibly be correct, sit yourself down and write him a sincere apology, and be quick about it or you won't be sitting down for a week!

We will be using male pronouns for dominants and female pronouns for submissives because that's the way it is in our relationship. It also makes the writing go easier. There are, however, at least as many women in the dominant role and men who are submissive. There are also plenty of homosexual SM relationships. While we acknowledge the validity of all gender orientations, this is our frigging book, and we'll do what we want to do. So there.

By the way, we lied. Sadomasochists are in Kansas. We're also in Illinois, California, Mississippi, Alabama, Colorado, Texas, and Alaska. As a matter of fact, we are in Cairo, Osaka, Istanbul, Amsterdam, Buenos Aires, London, and Samoa, too. You see the echoes of our presence in stories and myths from every time and culture.

We are every place where people have the courage and imagination to explore their fantasies. Tens of thousands openly admit their kink. Hundreds of thousands of people do it privately and millions more fantasize about it. We have always been around and we always will be. Why? Because sadomasochism is fun!

What you are about to read is our view of sadomasochism, colored with our experience, opinions, tastes, and preferences. Other experiences, opinions, tastes, and preferences are as myriad as the players in the game. Sadomasochism is a form of sexuality and each person's sexuality is a unique melody. Record those of our songs that harmonize with your sexuality and add your own vibrato when you play them back. No single tune pleases every ear.

There are hints of erotic imaginings in artistic traditions from Greek to Flemish. Here is a kinky floral arrangement by the fifteenth century artist from Phlegm, Heironymus Bosch.

Our society has a marvelous capacity for making the simplest of activities (sex, in this case) an incredibly convoluted affair. Guidelines have evolved specifying with whom you may fall in love, right down to their gender, age, race, and social background. There are also plenty of rules for the "proper" way to make love. This has turned basic instincts into perplexing exercises and normal physical functions into moral and psychological dilemmas. By abandoning society's accepted norms and trying something a little different, one invites social censure, religious sanction, and even legal harassment.

At the risk of ruining our well-tarnished image, we must tell you that the picture of the evil sadist abusing the cringing masochist is not quite the reality. In fact, no sadist we know would pull the wings off a fly unless the fly said that it would enhance its sexual pleasure. Don't let it get around, but compassionate sadists, benevolent dominants, adventurous submissives and wise-cracking slaves are typical. Seem contradictory? Well, paradox is the rule here rather than the exception. This is a world in which the greatest kindness resides within cruelty. This is a universe of illusion, mystery, and supreme delight.

Sadomasochists have stepped outside the norms. Our attitude is, screw 'em if they can't take a joke, but screwing someone who can take a joke is a lot more fun. Some of us really didn't choose SM, it has simply been a part of our sexuality since our earliest sexual memories. We just seem to be wired that way. Then there are the adventurous souls among us who hear about SM, try it, and fall in love with it.

Dominant and submissive attitudes already belong to everyone involved in sexual relationships in one form or another. Lovers establish patterns where one takes the lead for certain activities and surrenders the direction to his partner for others. Sadomasochists simply take this a bit further employing all the creativity and experimentation we can muster.

Sadomasochism (SM) is about spinning sexual yarns, blending threads of fact and fantasy, drama and comedy, tradition and innovation. Twisting and complicating emotions is not recommended practice in daily life, but it can be an opportunity for self-exploration into enhanced sexuality. With a little mischief and imagination, ordinary sexual activity can become a transcendent experience.

What sadomasochism is

> Most people work around their psychological demons, we harness ours up and take them out for a ride.
>   Bob H.

SM employs various techniques to put one partner, the submissive, in a position of helplessness and vulnerability, and the other, the dominant, in a position of command and authority. Bondage, sensory deprivation, flagellation, verbal dominance, behavior modification, and mind games are some of the tools the dominant uses to control the submissive and guide her through an erotic experience.

The dominant gives the orders that the submissive must follow. Sounds simple, right? Any good republican might say, "power flows down from the top." Actually, it works the other way around in SM. The submissive obeys only because she chooses to. There is nothing compelling her obedience except her resolve. The submissive is, therefore, empowering the dominant by her decision. We call a consensual empowerment of the dominant by the submissive a power exchange. Just as she gave her consent, she can take it away at any time. Power in SM flows from the bottom up.

This exchange of power assumes many levels, too. At the lower levels, the submissive gives her dominant a certain amount of control over her physical self. The things that the submissive allows her dominant to do are negotiated before they do anything. She may say it's ok to tie her up, but no whipping, and/or, she may allow him to fiddle around with her breasts, but he can't do anything below the belt... or where her belt used to be when she had her clothes on. Then, after things are neatly negotiated, they do a session.

Assuming things went swimmingly during the first session, and the submissive has gained a little trust, she allows more latitude. If the next session is also a smash (no pun intended), then they negotiate some more. As the partners learn to trust each other, the submissive may begin to give control over her emotional self as well. Now she is giving herself consent to take greater risks. At these levels, the sessions become really intense. The dominant is given a lot more freedom to fiddle, but he is assuming a lot more responsibility and must have mastered many more skills to pull it off.

While it isn't exactly a family sport, we believe that the open practice of SM is a healthy and happy addition to every boudoir. By open practice, we mean freely exchanging fantasies and incorporating them into your love-making. Open communication promotes growth and thaws stagnation. It builds trust, understanding, and acceptance, the three most important goodies in the quest for a more satisfying sex life.

We have a creed that we follow in SM: Everything we do must be SAFE, SANE, and CONSENSUAL. We learn to apply bondage and use our whips or whatever to create erotic experiences without damaging our partners. We don't pull crazy, out of control stunts and we discourage the use of drugs or alcohol during our play as it affects our judgment. We make sure that our partners are willing to participate of their own free will and that they are fully informed as to what we plan to do.

Sadomasochism is spinning a sexual yarn blending threads of
fact and fantasy, drama and comedy, tradition and innovation.

What sadomasochism is not

SM IS NOT ABUSE! Things that make our partners unhappy are bad things and we leave them alone. We don't do things to our partners without their permission or because we are mad at each other. Abusive people do not ask for permission and act out of anger, and they sure as hell don't negotiate a beating. The things we do to each other are done solely in the divine spirit of love and lust.

Abuse is anything but erotic and abusive people mean to harm their victims. Submissives can always stop a session whenever they want to -- abuse victims cannot. Dominants are always in control of themselves in a session, abusers are out of control to begin with.

We've all read newspaper accounts of lunatics who kidnap people, maim, rape, and even kill them. (Some guys just don't know how to treat a date.) In psychiatric parlance these people are called wackos. They are not a part of our friendly, kinky SM community. The most common argument against SM among "vanilla" people (we use the term "vanilla" for people, activities, and things that are not part of SM) is that the things we do to one another are violent acts and are, therefore, abusive.

Philip demonstrates the proper way to treat a date

Some people feel the need to distance themselves from the nuts the newspapers write about so they don't call what they do SM. This is understandable, SM has taken a lousy rap in the press; criminals and abusers are often called sadists. Others just do not understand that what they are doing is really more than a little bondage, some innocent spanking, or a bit of "capture the maiden" role-playing. They are, in fact, applying the basic principles of sado-masochism. The problem with this is that these people may tend to hide what they do and ignore the wisdom and advice of those who openly admit being into SM.

Euphemisms for SM abound in sexual circles. If you have ever investigated the world of sexual alternatives, you may have run into labels like erotic spanking, dominance and submission, guidance and surrender, bondage and discipline, and love bondage. In this book, we dump all these terms into the same basket. Since they all apply the same fundamentals, we call them all sadomasochism. The finer distinctions are simply a matter of taste and degree. Actually, we would rather call it Sexual Magic, because that's what it feels like to us. (This is not our term, by the way; it was the title of a wonderful photo journal by Michael Rosen, written in 1986, and has been kicking around the SM community for quite a while. See our bibliography.)

Simply knowing which end of the whip you prefer does not guarantee that you will know what to do with it when you get one. We have been involved in hundreds of sadomasochistic encounters and have made just as many mistakes. Fortunately, many

The reason for the Mona Lisa's smile is no mystery in this first version of da Vinci's masterpiece. Da Vinci, being understandably entranced by the lady, rendered a more demure version of the painting for a Chinese auction being held at his church. Molly's fastidious research has uncovered the original which has been stored in a dungeon in Sicily for centuries. We acquired it in trade for a Marquis de Sade meat carving set.

kind and patient people contributed their experience to our education. None of our playmates has ever needed a medic on our account. Still, no one is born with the skills to satisfy these fantasies. This book is meant to steer you around some of the pits we have stumbled into so that you may realize your fondest desires with a minimum of calamity. We want to teach you how to do SM safely, to give you a few ideas, and to let you know that you are not alone or psychotic... probably.

Scenespeak, learning the lingo

Sadomasochists' need to share stories, experiences, leather goods, hardware, and the occasional willing body has spawned a subculture with its own kinky lingo and fusion of various fetishes. Decadence is, after all, a social activity. The jargon is used loosely with different meanings to different people.

We have included an extensive glossary at the end of the book where the definitions are short and sweet. Still, it is hard to tell the players without a program, so we're going to sketch a framework for you by defining the vernacular, enriching the definitions, somewhat, to give you a taste of what "the scene" is like. What is "the scene?" We're glad you asked.

Scene

This word has two different meanings;

1) "The scene" takes in the whole scope of the fetish community. Once you begin to interact with others of a similar bent, you have become part of "the scene" and one of the "scene people."

"Scene people" often visit "scene clubs," public places that charge for admission, such as Paddles or The Vault in New York. There are scene events, parties, and gala balls, fashion shows, and seminars. The "Dressing for Pleasure Gala" is an annual New York area event that incorporates all of these elements in a weekend-long frolic attended by hundreds of scene people from all over the world.

There are scene clubs with the structure of support groups. The National Leather Association (NLA) and People Exchanging Power (PEP) have chapters that hold regular meetings all over the country. They do political work, focus on legal issues, hold educational seminars, discussion groups, and throw parties. The Black Rose in Washington, DC, Threshold in California, and Chicagoland Discussion Group are similar local organizations.

When you join the scene, you get to wear lots of funky clothes, hit people who will thank you for it, and toss moderation out the window. Also, under the guise of discretion and protecting the family name, you get to pick a "scene name." Scene names frequently reflect inner fantasies. Female dominants seem uncommonly attracted to the names of goddesses. Diana, the huntress, attracts a hell of a lot of namesakes. There enough of them, in fact, to hold an annual "Goddess Diana" convention.

There are a bunch of Dukes and Duchesses, Counts, Countesses and Contessas, Marquis, Marquesses, Kings and Queens, Generals, Captains, Sergeants, and, of course, Corporals. There's also the full range of deities and scores of literary figures. You have complete freedom of selection; no extra points are given for creativity or originality. Of course, many people use their real names, or just their first names, but isn't it fun to know a place where it is accepted practice to dump the moniker your parents saddled you with?

Coming out of the closet and joining a scene community can help you understand and broaden your experience. Returning to the closet, on the other hand, can be an interesting component of a confinement scene, which brings us to our second definition.

2) "Doing a scene" means performing an erotic activity related to satisfying the perversions we hold most dear. Sessions qualifying as scenes can be as simple as a spanking leading to sex or as elaborate as a weekend spent in thirty bondage positions, each with its own costume, setting, and script.

Binding your lady and tossing her to stew for a while in a cage qualifies as a scene. Tortures such as root-canal, elementary school concerts, and filing income tax returns, though excruciatingly painful, are a part of conventional behavior, and are not considered scenes.

Scenes are often referred to as being "heavy" or "light." Scenes where the submissive is very tightly bound and/or beaten strenuously are called heavy. A light scene will usually encompass more sensual stimulation or, perhaps, just less beating. Remember, these are colloquial expressions. One person's "light" is frequently another's "heavy."

By the way, doing a scene does not necessarily include having sexual intercourse with your partner. Players frequently do scenes without orgasm as a goal. Instead, they focus on catharsis or the sheer intensity, drama, fear, even transcendence as what they want from their scenes.

Playing

To play with someone generally means to have a scene with him, as in: "Do you want to play?" (The question is usually accompanied by a half-lecherous, half-evil grin.)

Player

A player is someone who participates in scenes. This term is commonly used to distinguish someone who actually does SM with real live people from one who merely fantasizes while doing his daily wrist exercises.

Sadomasochism (SM, S/M, or S&M)

The collective term for the activities enjoyed by sadists and masochists is sadomasochism. We don't believe, as do some of our fellow debauchers, in confining the scope of sadomasochism to the merry antics of dungeon denizens. There are as many levels of participation as there are scene people.

We further define sadomasochism as any activity involving power exchange during an erotic scene between consenting adults. This includes bondage and discipline (B&D), love bondage (a term coined by Harmony Communications, publishers of bondage magazines), dominance and submission (D&S or D/S), English culture, corporal punishment, erotic restraint, humiliation, and sexual control. The following are descriptions of the most popularly accepted sub-divisions of SM.

Dominance and submission (D&S, or D/S)

In exchange for obedience by the submissive, the dominant agrees to care for and work toward the pleasure of both partners. Thus empowered by the sub, the dominant takes control of their scenes and agrees to abide by the limits she sets.

Some people extend D/S roles outside the bedroom, often referring each other as "slave" and "master." Generally, these people consider themselves D/S "lifestylers."

Having the submissive set her own limits leads one to wonder who is really running the show. Where people are doing a now and again role-play, this is a valid question. With a "natural" submissive, however, an innate craving to please her dominant is strong and unquestionable. A "natural" dominant also feels an instinctive need to feel in charge, yet neither can realize these parts of themselves without the other. (See "Natural submissives and dominants" below.)

Bondage and discipline (B&D, or B/D)

B&D is perhaps most widely used to describe bondage, the practice of tying and/or chaining somebody in a provocatively compromising position. The discipline part is a little more loosely defined. Discipline within the ropes can take various forms from forcing the bound submissive to provide sexual or non-sexual servitude within mildly restrictive bondage, to heavy, completely restrictive bondage coupled with taking a whip to her backside. When discipline takes the form of whipping or spanking it is frequently referred to as corporal punishment or simply, corporal.

For lazy dominants, the most successful command to issue to a bound slave is, "Stay!" The more innovative master will involve his captive miss in activities such as tickling, sexual teasing, servitude, corporal punishment, and sexual denial.

For lazy dominants, the most successful command to issue to a bound slave is, "Stay!"

The who's who of SM

Sadist

The word is named for the Marquis "Papa" de Sade who wrote lots of wonderfully happy, silly stories about debauchery and torture taken to their utmost limits. The term describes one who gets sexual pleasure from the giving of pain, domination, and/or humiliation.

At this point you are picturing the folks who gave us the Spanish Inquisition. Wrong! Good sadists are really nice guys. The good sadist uses the ability of the human mind to turn pain (and/or the aforementioned humiliation) into erotic stimulation to give his partner panty-loads of pleasure. He never purposely damages his partner, kicks his dog, or abuses his children, and he spends hour upon nauseating hour pondering, researching, and expounding upon safety issues within the practice of SM. The term sadist does frighten some within the scene as much as those outside of it, but then, we do love to scare ourselves.

Masochist

One who derives sexual pleasure by receiving pain, domination, and/or humiliation, so-named for the genteel musings of the Austrian writer, Leopold von Sacher-Masoch. Contrary to popular opinion, the masochist still uses novocaine at the dentist and doesn't proffer her body for vivisection. She will also decline PTA presidential nominations as readily as any non-masochist. It is only pain within the erotic context that she enjoys.

Within the scene, the term is often used to distinguish between those with a higher tolerance or enjoyment of punishment as opposed to those who prefer more sensual activities.

Dominant (dom, domme)

One who accepts control of a submissive. Often referred to by submissives as Master, Mistress, Mommy, Daddy, Domina, Sir, Ma'am, Goddess, God, Lord, Lady, Prince, Princess, Baroness, and Baron.

One submissive we know felt silly calling his female dominant, "Mistress". He asked, "Can I just call you Boss?" She thought that was cute and delightful. We said he was a wise-ass and should be punished severely. He agreed. His mistress said he wasn't good enough to deserve punishment. Confusing isn't it?

Submissive (sub)

A person who surrenders control of herself to her dominant. The submissive, while putty in the hands of a dominant whom she trusts and respects, is likely to be independent and assertive in any other arena. Her sexual submissive nature makes her no more vulnerable to people hawking aluminum siding, encyclopedias or life insurance than anyone else.

Many submissives have a specific fantasy or set of fantasies that they want to enact ritualistically. They will even give the dominant something very like a script, detailing exactly what they expect to happen in a scene. Other submissives live to be surprised, risking the perils of the unknown as evidence of the control they surrender.

Photo courtesy of Dressing For
Pleasure of Upper Montclair, NJ

11

Natural submissives and dominants

Hospitals wrap baby girls in pink flannel blankets, the boys get blue ones. Some of us should have been swaddled in black leather. "Natural" submissives or dominants are people who have felt sadomasochistic yearnings for as long as they can remember. They frequently had fantasies of bondage and torture before they were old enough to read the bathroom walls.

Philip, as a diminutive, seven-year-old sadist, began his descent into deviance by binding his teddy bear (awwwww, isn't that cute). Even with this precocious beginning, it was years before he acted upon his fantasies. In his youth, Philip's secret aspiration to bind his various girlfriends seemed to conflict with his love and admiration for women. (Fortunately, he was well over this by the time Molly met him.)

A precocious Philip binds his bear.

Eventually, he realized that fantasy sex-play was a good and healthy outlet. He learned that domination had nothing to do with disrespect and discovered time-honored methods of using his dominant tendencies to celebrate his submissive's femininity and spirit. People often wonder where SM leanings stem from. We don't have a clue and neither do psychiatric professionals. A leading sexologist we know debunks the common conjecture that sadists and masochists were abused as children. Most of us come from happy, healthy, non-abusive environments.

This sexologist goes on to say that sexual inclinations tend to stay with a person, that if one develops a taste for a sexual practice, it is likely to remain part of his sexuality. This speaks to another common concern: that SM might take over one's sexuality. Since people maintain interests in sexual habits, SM broadens a person's scope rather than supplanting their desires for other variations.

The natural female submissive would seem to have it made. There is, after all, no end of unreconstructed chauvinists who love to control and abuse women. However, being abused is about as close to the loving practice of SM as decapitation is to brain surgery. Unfortunately, natural submissives are frequently unaware of what they are seeking and often end up in exploitative, even brutally dangerous relationships.

Women generally have less contact with sexually oriented reading matter. They are often unaware that they can find the domination they seek in a loving, non-abusive relationship. To satisfy her need, the sub must recognize her natural inclinations. All the "good" doms we know respect and love women. Their views of women are usually quite compatible with feminism. Surprised? These are the guys the submissive woman needs to find.

Tops and bottoms

This is one of the areas where SM terminology is used to mean so many different things that the terms seems to take on a life of their own. Hang on, we're about to take a roller coaster ride.

Some contend that "top" and "bottom" are simply synonyms for dominant and submissive, respectively. Others say a "top" is not necessarily dominant at all, he is merely providing the beatings for a masochist who is not necessarily submissive at all. This is a little confusing, not too hard to understand, but we're just getting started.

In actual practice, a masochist may "top" (a verb) for another masochist who is, at the time, being referred to as a "bottom" (a noun). Our own preference is to call someone who likes to be beaten, but doesn't get off on being submissive to another's will, a "bottom." Anyone who is willing to provide such a beating, regardless of whether they are sadists, dominants, submissives, or other bottoms, we call a "top."

Then again...

Someone who is able to be both a top and a bottom can also be a submissive or a dominant depending upon his or her mood. She or he may be a top who is really submissive, or may be a dominant with a submissive streak. It is possible that he or she is sadistic and/or masochistic regardless of his/her submissive or dominant orientation. In any case, you could call such a person a "switch" (see Switch).

Which is not to mention...

Another common situation is that you find a person who wants to "play" at being submissive but really likes to control the show. In this case you have someone "topping" (the verb, again) from the bottom. Then, there's its sister situation, where a dominant wants his submissive to direct everything that is done to her. In this situation, the dominant is "bottoming" (verb form) from the top and the submissive is "topping" from the bottom.

Understand? If you do, you are already one of us, aren't you?

One lesbian masochist we know says she isn't submissive at all, but once a week she visits her friends to get the snot beat out of her. She says she won't do housework as a slave and if somebody gets pushy about it, or tries to make her call them Mistress, Master or the like, she'll turn around and deck the bastard. We believe her! Mazel Tov!

She introduced us to a friend of hers who likes to start off as a bottom: "...but if someone isn't giving me what I want, or she pisses me off, I'll see if I can make her break the equipment on me, and when she does, I'll get at her ass." We believe her, too! Sheesh!

Switch

In scene-speak, switches are both people and things. Electrical switches have no place in the scene unless the participants are into electro-torture. We'll pass, thanks, but if you are into it, more power to you.

1) Almost everyone has heard of the switch that is a thing. Usually made from willow, ash, or birch, it whistles appallingly on its approach, and stings like a backslap on a sunburn when it finds what it is looking for.

A friend of ours likes switches made from forsythia when it's in full bloom. She loves to watch the little yellow flowers fly all over the room like comets falling among the stars that she is seeing from the last stroke. She calls it her Spring training.

2) The switch that is a person plays both the dominant and submissive sides of the SM game. Seemingly, this guy has the best of both worlds. Often he is paired with another switch. This puts him in a peculiar position.

If he does something particularly nasty to his partner when he's dominating her, she gets the next crack at him. Now, should he do something to her that he knows she's going to like, but he knows it's pushing her a bit? Or, should he back off because he knows damned well the same thing would make him faint?

Molly is always sub, and Philip is always dom; we are glad this isn't our problem.

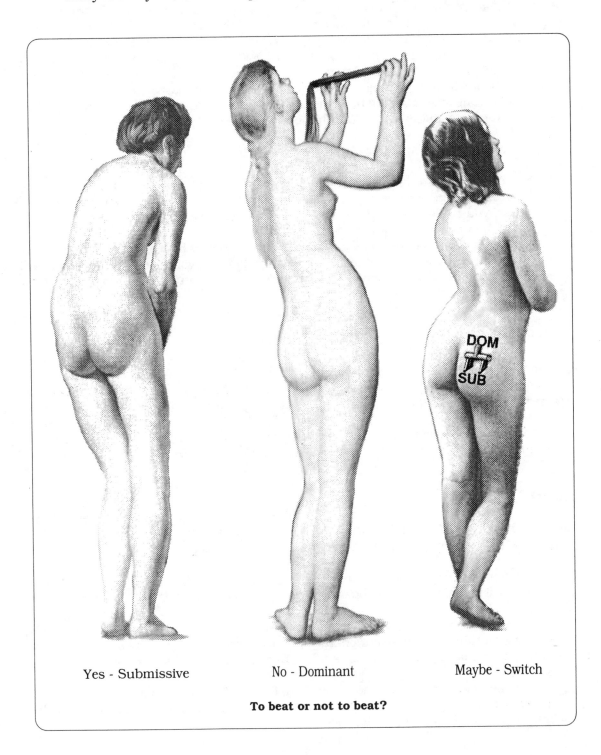

Yes - Submissive   No - Dominant   Maybe - Switch

To beat or not to beat?

Professional female dominants (dominas)

Professional dominas are NOT prostitutes. If you infer that they are, make sure your hospitalization is paid up. Pro-dominas are in the business of fantasy realization and do not have sex with their clients. They are a cross between psycho-dramatist and therapist. A domina, skilled enough to realize a living in the profession, earns every penny she makes. She must be confident enough to intuit and focus on the needs of many different personalities and strong enough pull off scene after scene with expertise and finesse. For any dominant, this is a terrific strain. Having to do so many times each week narrows the field of capable dominas considerably. These ladies deserve a lot of respect.

Much of the best literature on SM comes from professional dominas. Many dominants, including Philip, say they make the best teachers. This makes sense when you consider that they usually have ten times the experience of any "civilian" dom.

Fetishist

A fetish is a sexual fixation on a particular object or sexual activity. Understand that a fixation is quite different from a preference. If inhaling the bouquet from a sweat sock worn by the Dallas Cowboy's half-back is necessary to your scene, or if you only enjoy sex while gagged with your second-cousin's used panties, you have a fetish. The person seeking fulfillment of these quaint needs is a fetishist. Feet and panties seem to generate a great deal of this kind of obsession. The foot-slave is a classic example of a submissive with a fetish.

Sub-chapter XY

He is she & she is he, I am the walrus kookookachu
Gender and sexual orientation

Note from Molly:
Philip isn't sure this section belongs here because most people in the gender community are not into SM. He is undoubtedly right, but I stuck it in anyway while Philip was visiting the Little Master's room. I'll probably be punished for sneaking it in...hurray!

Sexual orientation does not mean a preference for having sex in a horizontal or vertical position. In the scene, you can't take much for granted unless you are a dom (in which case, you can take anything you want). Explaining sexual and gender orientation adequately would fill several volumes, but allow me to offer this modest attempt.

TVs and CDs are not items for sale at Crazy Irving's Discount Electronics. Nope. TVs are transvestites and CDs are cross-dressers. A transvestite attempts to look like a woman. A cross-dresser likes to wear some women's garments.

Let me make this a bit clearer. The big, burly fullback with the satin and lace teddy beneath his jersey is a cross-dresser. The girl that your cousin Norman brought to your parents' anniversary party, who turned out to be a guy (which Norman said surprised the hell out of him, as well) is a transvestite.

Now, if Aunt Edwina used to be uncle or if Cousin Sid used to be Sally Ed she or he is a "transsexual" or TS. Totally different than cross-dressers and TVs, transsexuals are folks who feel they have been born in the wrong body. Unfortunately, Mother Nature screwed up. They are merely correcting the mistake.

By the way, neither the cross-dresser nor the transvestite is necessarily gay or bisexual. Though, if a male-to-female TS still likes women she is now considered gay even though the reverse was true in her past. When the transvestite is also gay this person is also sometimes called a drag queen.

While forced cross-dressing is part of the scene for many submissives, only a small percentage of all transvestites and transsexuals are in the SM scene.

Pronoun, pronoun, who's got the pronoun?

Transsexuals are always properly referred to as if they were the gender they present and should be treated accordingly. Anything else is offensive. This rule applies whether the TS has undergone surgery or not. It's difficult to know what pronouns to use with some of the other gender folk. Some transvestites like to be referred to as "she" only while dressed, others like to be called "she" all the time. If you are confused about what to call someone, just ask what they prefer. Cross-dressers are usually referred to as "he".

The gay SM scene

The SM scene contains people with all the possible sexual orientations. There is also a very separate and distinct Gay SM scene. The contact we have with this scene is insufficient to let us ramble on in our usual authoritative way, so this is all you'll get from us. The principles of loving power exchange are the same.

Simple starts, safe starts

All kidding aside for the moment, while it is a lot of fun, when we're doing SM, we're messing with a person's mental state. That's why it works. It is said that ninety percent of sex is in the head. When SM works well, the joy and loving that are shared have no limit. When we fuck it up, we hurt feelings at best, and create basket-cases at worst. It's easy enough to do it right without having a PhD in psychology if you follow a few basic guidelines.

The first person a good dominant learns to control is himself. Skillful, thoughtful planning, developing complete trust and sincere communication are the secrets to doing SM well.

Contrary to the wealth of sadomasomythology, a submissive is not chattel, a child, nor any less a person than her dominant. She is a real person with rights and feelings, not an object or a pet whose sole purpose is to be trained and controlled for her master's pleasure.

The submissive is also responsible for making her feelings known and maintaining genuine communication. This can be very difficult for a woman (or a man) in a submissive state. She is going to feel a strong resistance to criticizing her dominant at the risk of spoiling the mood. The balance is fragile.

There's a lot more to be said about this and there are a lot of physical safety issues to consider aside from the subjective mental issues and we'll cover those in their appropriate chapters.

The proposition of being tied down and helpless is scary as hell. It should be. Careless bondage is dangerous and the emotional intensity of a good SM or bondage scene is fantastically powerful. We are in the business of pushing limits and sometimes we will push too hard. It happens to all of us. Submissives, learn to be forgiving. Dominants, learn to forgive yourselves and be careful!

The point of SM is to get someone to surrender her physical self to you, and, as surely as whips crack, her heart and mind will soon follow. Please take good care of these three items. People are very, very fragile beings, even you tough-guy sadists. Never be ashamed to drop the roles and the game when the going gets too rough and always be ready to offer a hug and a kiss to remind each other what this is all about to begin with. Be honest, be trustworthy, be kind, and be ever-alert to the condition of the soul you are partnered with, dom or sub. The rewards are extraordinary and very much worth your trouble.

2 Sexual Magic
Why We Do Do That Voodoo

 adomasochists come from every social, economic, and racial background imaginable. No set of experiences typifies their childhood or the sexual values with which they were raised. They represent the full political wing-span, with convictions aligning with every feather from left to right. They are heterosexual, homosexual, and bisexual. They are outspoken and quiet, playful and dry, thoughtful and reckless, adventurous and shy, regal and common. No one has ever found a common denominator among them save for this certain ember glowing amid the folds of imagination.

Some can put a name and a place to the genesis of that spark. A picture, a dream, a scene in a movie, a story, a chance gesture made by a lover, or an intimate conversation overheard on the street that struck the flint and tinder of fantasy and, fostered by the wind of pleasure, grew from fantasy to sexual identity. Others cannot identify that first little fire; for these, it is as though the coals had been ignited at birth, perhaps even at conception.

We frequently keep our fantasies bottled-up within us because sharing them can be scary as hell, even with one as close as a spouse. In exposing these intimate slices of our identity we risk judgment, ridicule, and rejection. Ideally we find partners who care enough to meet our confessions with acceptance, understanding, and even (dare we hope?) inspiration. For in the practice of sadomasochism, clear and free communication is a prerequisite. Without it, one treads on dangerous ground. With it, the possibilities are limitless.

In SM we learn to reveal our fantasies openly, with the understanding that self-righteousness and condescension have no place in our discussions. We gently and gratefully accept our mate's fantasies as gifts, realizing the courage, and often pain, involved in disclosing such intimate details of one's self. We look for a common ground between our two sets of fantasies, acknowledge the differences, and make decisions about those which we will pursue through the process we call negotiation. Then, we take that final, bold step with our lovers. We summon our skills, trust, and knowledge to bring those deep, dark, dream demons to life, discovering that reality can eclipse imagination.

NASA may have its troubles, but in the SM community, the space program is alive and well. Everyday, from bedrooms and dungeons all over the world, people are being launched far beyond the gravitational pull of earth, possibly into other dimensions.

To illustrate our point, we have installed microphones and a one-way mirror in the bedroom of this modern couple. (Voyeurs may take the seats in the first row, but please try not to steam up the mirror. Ladies, fear not, the seats are moisture resistant.)

"I don't want any pain," Terry reminded him.

'Ah, the mating call of every new submissive.' Mark thought to himself, he couldn't suppress a smile. Still, he didn't want her to feel she was being made fun of and covered his amusement with a gentle kiss. "I always go very slowly," he said softly.

Ever since her first adolescent sexual stirrings, Terry yearned to be bound, naked and helpless and ravaged by a lover, but her reveries frightened her. They were just too wild and embarrassing to tell anyone about, lest she be judged unstable. Yet, her fantasies were compelling and satisfying. She gave into them night after night in the solitude of her bedroom, conjuring scenes of torture and rapture while indulging her hungry body in solitude beneath the sheets. And she never told anyone.

As a young woman, Terry was drawn to worldly, self-confident men who assumed the lead in her relationships. Consciously or unconsciously she sought another quality in the men she bedded; they were all a little bit scary. Love and caring were too frequently mingled with turbulence and abuse. The men were bad to her and her self-esteem plummeted.

It wasn't until she discovered people openly involved in sadomasochism that she began to understand her own passion. These people tempered their indulgences with respect. Submissives and dominants were interdependent parts of a whole, a partnership in exploring sexuality. Submissives were revered, not objects of scorn.

Among these people, Terry met Mark. She was immediately drawn to him. Mark's attraction to her was not only obvious, he startled her by telling her exactly what anatomical and personality traits he found so alluring. She'd never met someone so unabashedly forward! Yet, somehow, the charm, wit, and ease with which he made his observations disarmed her. He was not at all pushy and honesty rang clearly from his every pronouncement. Still, he seemed to enjoy hovering a hair's breath away from a slap to the face.

As they spoke, Terry found herself unable to conceal anything from this extraordinary man. In their first afternoon together she had revealed secrets that she rarely admitted to herself. With every confession, she felt a growing trust and affection for Mark. He accepted each as a treasure, never taking her lightly, probing gently for the pieces that lay deeper than others. He was just as open about himself and his sexuality, encouraging Terry to explore whatever caught her interest.

In only a few days, Terry knew Mark better than she had known any man before. She knew, also, that she wanted him. Terry found Mark to be a wealth of information about the dark arts she had dreamed of since childhood. They laughed while trading sexual fantasies and admitting the techniques of SM that appealed to each and those that didn't. This handsome man made seduction such delicious fun! Now she prayed that her attraction had not clouded her judgment. Because tonight, he would plunge her into her most secret and terrifying cravings.

"But, going slowly isn't enough," Mark continued, "you need a safe-word. If what I'm doing is too much, if you become too frightened, or if for any other reason you want me to stop, just say your full name. I will stop everything immediately," he paused watching Terry absorb the idea, "I don't want you to feel the slightest bit self-conscious or embarrassed about using your safe-word. It is a normal part of the game and I won't mind at all if you want to take a break for a while or even stop altogether. It is very important that you understand this."

Terry nodded. His lecture was oddly reassuring and intimidating at the same time. She stretched out on the bed trying to appear relaxed, though she was as nervous as a cat. She couldn't seem to find a comfortable position for her arms. Mark let her struggle for a while, enjoying her little ordeal. Finally he relented, cuddling next to her. "Just relax," he said and placed her hands at her sides, "it is going to be fine and wonderful."

His fingers chased a serpentine path below her ear along the corded muscles in her throat and up over her rising breast to its brown peak, barely brushing it. Terry closed her eyes and sighed quietly. Mark rose on an elbow to view her length: a suntanned, satin landscape of mild-sloped hillocks, rolling one into the next, accented sparsely with fine,

19

sun-blonded down. His took in every detail of her torso, crooning approval in a low, rumbling voice. His hands skimmed across her body softly and skillfully, exploring each knoll and hollow, probing, spiral-like the well of the navel, climbing the furry rise below, drifting down into the crevice to tickle the folds there.

Gentle eroticism wasn't at all what Terry had expected. Then, she really hadn't known what to expect. She came to Mark's apartment in spite of, or perhaps because of his reputed sexual tastes. When he confirmed the gossip, she had been fascinated. His manner was informal, yet commanding. She felt inescapably drawn to his subtle, but firm way of taking charge. This clever, funny, and sensitive man did not fit her image of a self-admitted sadist at all.

A thousand nerve-endings answered Mark's probing fingers. It seemed to Terry that a feverish tide rose in her, following the path of Mark's hands. She shivered and her hips began to twitch beneath his fingertips.

He whispered, "Spread your legs for me, Terry," and she complied. "Now, close your eyes and hold very still... don't make a sound."

Terry became absolutely motionless and quiet. Mark counted off a full minute before moving at all, letting the silence engulf them. Very slowly, from top to bottom, in one endless gesture, Mark's fingers slid lightly over the length of Terry's sex. He began to massage the skin below her slit with one fingertip. The muscles there twitched and churned at his touch. He ordered her to spread her legs wider. Mark's fingers danced up and down the length of her labia, along the outside of the outer lips, smoothly with a fingertip, then scratching with a fingernail. Slowly, tickling every nerve, his fingers worked toward the centers of her lips, crawling ever so slowly over their crest before slipping quickly into the moist inner folds.

There, in the hot, wet center of her, among Terry's slick, sensitive folds of flesh, Mark fingered swiftly, searching out the most responsive points, letting Terry's breathing and involuntary contractions guide his way. There, on the left side of her hooded bud, she gasped as his fingertip found a good spot. That finger stayed there, flicking up and down, up and down, in a steady rhythm that made her flesh seem to writhe. With the fingers of his other hand, Mark explored the lower regions, parting her delicate inner lips, caressing the silken folds, lingering, here and there, to trace tiny circles on the slippery surface. Finally, his fingers found the mouth of her opening and skimmed its circumference, teasing the outer ring without entering. His finger traveled round and round, sometimes softly, sometimes swiftly, often ever so slowly, and always the fingertip above flicked the hooded treasure at the top of her sex.

It seemed terribly important to obey him, but Terry was losing the battle to remain still and silent. She let out a little gasp and her hips moved, she'd swear later, of their own accord.

Mark was pleased. Terry's submissiveness was evident in her effort to obey. He strained with craving to take her then and there. Clearly, she was desperate for it. Yet, her responses were so powerful he knew she could go much further and his pleasure in controlling her was intoxicating. He knew he could press Terry further into submission. As she dove ever deeper, he rose ever higher, riding a tide of god-like omnipotence, reveling in the power coursing through him. His mind seemed to expand, able to absorb the tiniest details with a crystalline precision. For Mark, this was the essence of SM. Uninformed and inexperienced minds had dubbed these sexual traditions sadism and masochism, but giving and receiving pain are only the facade. SM is a mystical union, enrapturing the dominant in a rush of power and dissolving the will of the submissive, granting her, in its place, the freedom to experience pure sensation. SM is sexual magic.

"You seem to be having some difficulty remaining still. Shall I bind you to make it easier?"

Terry's nod and pleading eyes answered for her. In her condition, she would have agreed to anything.

"Tell me your safe-word."

"Terry Catherine MacLean." Simply uttering her name was a tremendous effort. The words sounded thick and heavy.

Mark rolled Terry onto her stomach and drew her to her knees, raising her ass, exposing her sex. He spread her feet far apart and tied her ankles to the corners of the bed. Her arms were drawn back beside her legs and tied by the wrists to the same bed-corners.

"Such a lovely body, such a pretty ass, " Mark cooed over her and fondled her as he bound her, "and so deliciously wet!"

He slipped a blindfold over her eyes and kissed her. She was grateful for it, she couldn't bear to meet his eyes. Mark had reduced her to an object, naked and roped, like an animal, pinned down and positioned for fucking and there was nothing she could do about it, no way of escape. Wonderful!

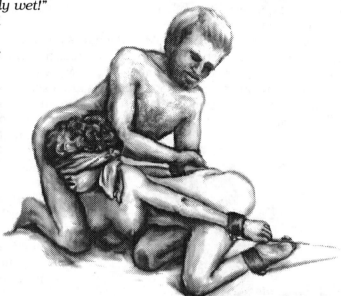

Terry felt utterly vulnerable, embarrassed and flustered, yet happy, secure, and cherished. She did not notice the incongruity, all her feelings fused, saturating and warming her. Her mind was shutting down. Thoughts came slowly, as though through a gelatinous pool. It felt so good just to let them float away, to focus only on Mark.

Mark positioned himself behind her kneeling between her tethered legs. He continued to tease and caress. He leaned over her back to squeeze her breasts. Slipping on the condom, he let the tip of him bob between her thighs, slapping the wetness there. Terry's hips bucked with urgency. She wanted him in her, she needed to be filled. Now! Instead, he slapped her ass.

Though not very hard, it was unexpected. A shock. There was a momentary sting, then a strange heat spread though her. Terry's hips jerked desperately and Mark matched her rhythm with stinging slaps. She was moaning on the verge of orgasm when he entered her roughly, but he halted his attack just in time to deny her that final free-fall. He spanked harder as he moved within her, yet there was no pain, only that delicious heat through her belly.

Terry's moans turned to whimpers. Mark steadied his pace. White-hot pressure swelled within every crevice of her body and she erupted in a pounding series of orgasms. She felt a push that seemed to come from within, driving her mind out of her body. She was beyond reason and beyond awareness of her surroundings, floating, flying free. She felt Mark's soul surrounding her like a shroud, protecting and controlling; freeing her to bathe in the sensations of her body.

Terry came to very slowly. She had been untied without realizing it. Mark was holding her. His face, a sculpture of tenderness, was the first thing she saw when at last she could open her eyes. She'd never felt so warm, so well-loved. Mark's lips curled to a smug grin. Terry chuckled at his gloating, but he had earned it, oh yes, had he ever. She buried her face in his chest.

What differentiates ordinary sex ("vanilla sex" in scene-speak) from the scene Mark and Terry shared? Some of you will say, "Damned little," and to you folks we tip our hats and wish you godspeed. You might notice, though, that there's a certain detachment exhibited by Mark. He has a plan, "He strained with craving to take her then and there... Yet, her responses were so powerful he knew she could go much further."

When people hit the sack together for the first time they typically follow their instincts and begin fucking when they feel the urge. They may even have a plan that includes a little spanking, still, that's not quite SM.

Terry becomes strangely obsessive, too, "It seemed terribly important to obey him..." Women can get very hot while making love, but does passion make them feel compelled to be compliant? Fat chance.

Distinguishing what is SM and what is no more than exuberant boffing isn't easy. Without the ropes anchoring Terry to the bed, this mild scene might be confused with plain vanilla, but for certain elements that SMers will readily recognize.

For one thing, Terry is both anxious and excited that she is about to try SM. Mark recognizes this and sets up the scene smoothly. He maintains an assertive and self-assured attitude. He is in no hurry to jump her bones. He takes his time to find out what he can about Terry and her fantasies. He plays the role of guide and mentor, offering her a "safe word" to use if things become too heavy for her. Then he goes about his business, expertly -- masterfully, if you will. These are all hallmarks of a veteran dominant. Terry readily buys into his attitude; it is exactly what she wants a man to do.

Experienced players learn to relax into bondage.

In making SM work, the dominant introduces a level of discomfort, physical, emotional, or both. In this case, Mark employs conflict. He orders Terry to remain perfectly still and silent. She does her best Buckingham Palace guard imitation while he diddles around with her happy factory. Mark is really good with his fingers and tongue. Terry begins to lose it. She starts building toward orgasm and Mark makes his move, "You seem to be having some difficulty remaining still. Shall I bind you to make it easier?"

Terry really wants to come, but Mark points out that she isn't obeying orders. He offers to tie her up to help her. (What a gentleman!) Mark lets the sexual tension build only so far, not enough to piss her off when he interrupts the action, but enough to unsettle her. She agreed to play the game and she's breaking the rules. Fair enough.

Not accidentally, the penalty he suggests is what she has always dreamed about.

Experienced players learn to relax into bondage. The first bondage experience sets off an internal depth-charge in new submissives and their sexual tension is stepped up another rung. The position Terry is put into plays on another of her buttons. She is forced into a position that leaves her completely helpless and exposed. Mark coos over her naked and excited body telling her how lovely she looks. This isn't idle admiration, he wants to fluster her. And flustered she is, both by his praise of her privates and their vulnerability, but there is nothing she can do -- then, he starts fondling her again!

Terry is struggling to reconcile her embarrassment over her exposed privates, the excitement and fear brought about by her first bondage, the delicious things that Mark is doing to her, and underlying it all, the control Mark is demonstrating over her. She chooses to trust Mark, she focuses only on him and what he is doing. It's not a hard choice to make considering that it all feels so damned good! All these conflicting messages jar Terry's sense of normalcy and she experiences what we call "brain fade." Her thinking slows to a crawl, speech becomes difficult. In brain fade, one feels as if floating in water or that things are happening in slow motion.

Trussed like a Christmas bird, Terry lets herself respond to the sexual teasing as Mark brings her closer and closer to orgasm. Then, all of the sudden, he whacks her. For a moment she is shocked and confused, then she feels a wonderful heat radiating into her from the spank. He spanks her again and now she feels the heat more readily. Mark continues the spanking, emulating a rhythm common to intercourse and it has the same effect. Terry no longer feels the swats as pain at all. The sexual tension is high enough that she feels only a sexy heat from each blow.

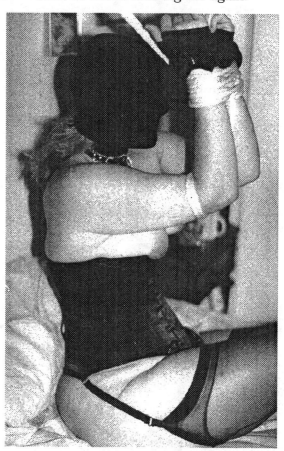

Few can deny that SM is the most intense sexual experience they've ever encountered.

Mark feels her start to come and chooses that moment to enter her, pushing her even further. He continues spanking her and Terry's orgasms start coming one on top of the other. The experience is so intense that Terry is transported. We call it flying, some call it melting away. This, ladies and gents, is SM. (Mark takes a bow, Terry tries to curtsy, but her legs, at the moment, are made of silly putty.)

Sure, it sounds swell, but it's a hell of a lot of work, right? Is there any question, though, as to why we bother?

For some, the ebb and flow of exchanging power is the draw. For others, it's a path toward self-discovery. Along with all the descriptives people use to portray SM: excitement, sensuality, control, adventure, joy, mystery, drama, romance, danger, and fear, almost everyone includes the same adjective: INTENSE! Few can deny that it's the most intense sexual experience they've ever encountered. For us, the intensity ranks first, hands down. There is one more characteristic of SM we adore, it's a good time. It's fun. We wouldn't do it if it weren't.

Although SM is arguably an art, drawing upon one's sensitivity, intuition, creativity, spontaneity, dramatic sense, and so on, one needn't be a Michelangelo to pull it off well. SM employs mental, physical, and strategic techniques that can be taught and learned. With a little thought and a playful attitude, you'll be a class act in no time. In this chapter we'll discuss some of the fundamental elements of the art.

Trust and communication

Making SM work is dependent upon developing honest, sincere communication and profound trust. The thing that sinks most sexual relationships, vanilla, SM, or otherwise, is the inability to let your partner know what is happening inside you. Let him know what pushes your buttons, what you are feeling, and what you fantasize about. It is definitely easier to bare your body than it is to bare your soul, but giving your partner a peek at the real you has a huge payoff. Opening up takes a two level approach; you have to learn to talk frankly, and you have to have a working knowledge of each other's bodies.

"Twust your tweezle! Tell your fwiend what it wants!"

Talking

If you are busy hoping your partner will figure out how to twizzle your tweezle the way you like it twizzled, you will be less able to concentrate on the actual twizzling. Conversely, if you are lying there praying he doesn't tweak your tweezle with the vice-grips the way he did last time, you're going to fight like a hooked salmon every time he reaches for the toolbox.

The remedy is talking about it. It takes a little guts, but it gets easier the more you do it. He loves you and will appreciate knowing what you like. Honest. Show your partner the parts of your tweezle that raise and lower your eyebrows. Let him practice until your eyebrows are zipping up and down like bees' wings. Tell him to deep-six the vice-grips, that it took three weeks before you could twizzle again without screaming. The moral is: Twust your tweezle! Tell your fwiend what it wants!

You have to trust your partner to do what you like and stay away from the things that are too much. Find out what your partner's fantasies are. Share yours. Propose scenes that you would like to try. Make up a sexual wish-list and another list of stuff you can't stand and won't tolerate. Discuss each others' limits and swear that you will absolutely not trespass beyond them. (Don't you dare snicker while you are making this oath, it tends to erode trust.) This is called negotiation. Negotiating your scenes is important enough that we have dedicated a whole chapter to it.

Don't forget that tastes change as horizons expand. Keep the lines of communication open and your creative juices ever-flowing. This sounds easier than it actually is. You may think you already know all there is to know about your partner and for short periods of time this may be true. However, time alters feelings. Tricks and roles get stale. New roles become intriguing. Some of the gimmicks that you used to consider outrageous become indispensable parts of lovemaking. It is too easy to fall into patterns that, while comfortable, become boring shortly.

The important thing to remember when discussing sexual feelings is that most people are very shy about them and that the emotional impact of sexuality is very deeply ingrained in us. We would like to propose a few guidelines for communicating.

Above all, be respectful! No matter how strange your partner's tastes may seem, they are things that he holds very near and dear. Be prepared to bite your tongue in half before you laugh at his fetish.

Listen carefully to what your partner is saying. Many people have trouble saying exactly what they mean. If something isn't clear, be gentle, but ask about it until you are sure you understand. Don't argue. If something becomes too difficult to talk about, or if you are having a misunderstanding that you can't seem to overcome, suggest that you think about the problem for a while and agree to discuss it later.

Accept your partner's opinions about his sexuality and himself. There is no right or wrong in the area of sexuality and emotions. Conflicting opinions are not invalid, but can present a stumbling block. Try to find a way around the hurdles rather than trying to convince your partner to agree with your viewpoint.

Opening up to someone is hard work. Thank your partner for giving you a part of himself. Give him a hug and a kiss to show your appreciation. Then, rip his clothes off and ravage his body.

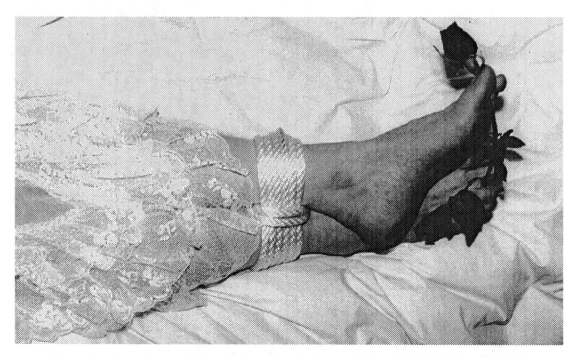

No matter how strange his tastes may seem, they are things that he holds very near and dear. Be prepared to bite your tongue in half before you laugh at his fetish.

Learning the body you want to bludgeon

Everybody's body is different. Gestures and caresses that cause one person to fall in love will make another hurl guts in disgust. A great way to find out some of the things that swing your partner's pendulum is to exchange back-rubs... and then progress to front-rubs. Once you begin to massage each other you'll find out all sorts of amusing secrets.

There are, at last count, 9,234,123,734 books on massage. This is not the 9,234,123,735th one. Pay a visit to your favorite book store, health food store, or new-age center and buy one that tickles your fancy.

Taste and smell are senses that should not be ignored, either. They are every bit as massagable as the average bulbospongiosis muscle (look it up, you'll thank us later). While you're out shopping, pick up some exotic massage oils. You might indulge yourself in a book on aroma therapy, too. Aroma therapy works and there are some essential oils that really do help put you "in the mood." You'll find essential oils in some health food and massage supply stores. Try this one on for size; it is designed to relax inhibitions and warm the heart:

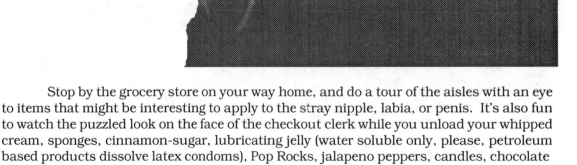

Cuddling Oil

2 fl. oz.	Jojoba or Sweet Almond oil
6 drops	Nutmeg oil
6 drops	Sandalwood oil
4 drops	Lavender oil
3 drops	Tagetes oil

Stop by the grocery store on your way home, and do a tour of the aisles with an eye to items that might be interesting to apply to the stray nipple, labia, or penis. It's also fun to watch the puzzled look on the face of the checkout clerk while you unload your whipped cream, sponges, cinnamon-sugar, lubricating jelly (water soluble only, please, petroleum based products dissolve latex condoms), Pop Rocks, jalapeno peppers, candles, chocolate syrup, clothespins, butter, toothpicks, Oragel, tropical fruit yogurt, Sugar Pops, and fudge-ripple ice cream. If you get a smile from the clerk instead of bewilderment, be sure to take his or her phone number.

Haul all your goodies home and study your tome of massagerie assiduously until your lover arrives. A good dinner is optional depending on the results of your shopping spree (you may opt to feed as you knead). Massage therapists might tell you this is a no-no, but, hey, we're going for grins here, follow your heart.

We find a darkened or candle-lit room with soothing music most conducive to exploration. Find a clean, comfy surface, plop your lover on her belly, and have at it. Try the techniques in your massage book and add a few of your own. Again, we're not going to get mired in the stew of which techniques are better. People and methodologies are just too diverse.

The mind as an erogenous zone

Emotional buttons are hot spots in a submissive's psyche that can be triggered by a dominant. Pushing someone's buttons engenders within them a loss of self-control. In SM, we push each other's buttons to open or expand our partner's sensory and sexual experience. We do this by using one type of energy: embarrassment, anxiety, fear, etc., to spark another: sexual tension.

By agreeing to be submissive to you, your partner gives you permission to channel her emotional reactions into sexuality. As her dominant, your mission is to control the flow and intensity of her emotions. You let her emote sexually as you press the buttons that keep her off balance. With her equilibrium disturbed and you controlling her environment, sensations, and movement, she will look to you for stability and security. Even though you are the one causing her distress, as long as you act confident, keep her safe, and erotically stimulated, your control will increase and the session will become more intense.

Anticipation

It's an interesting paradox. Spontaneity is wonderful for romance, yet, in SM, we often plan scenes with scrupulous attention to detail. We often discuss exactly what we are going to do and why each one wants to do it. This excessive chatter would seem to stomp all over spontaneity, but somehow, it still works!

One key to this is anticipation, a great tool. Keep your submissive nervous as hell. If your scene is going to push her boundaries, the anticipation can be as titillating as the execution (if you'll pardon the expression "execution").

It can have an unnerving effect on the dominant, too. When you're planning to do something a little gruesome to your beloved, there's a certain amount of anxiety to contend with. Keep some Rolaids around for those uniquely scary stunts.

We call this anticipation instead of worry even though the two are closely related. There are two kinds of worrying a submissive can do. (1) She can worry about whether you are skilled enough to pull off the scene; about your adhering to safe-sex practices; about how you feel toward her; and any number of other non-productive things, or, (2) she can worry about the exciting, scary, wonderful things you are about to do to her. It's the dominant's job to see that her concerns are aimed in the right direction. He has to do all he can to quell those other concerns by letting her know she is loved and lusted after, and that he is capable and trustworthy. The following cartoon illustrates a dominant instilling the good, productive kind of anticipation.

Conditioning -- three ways to Skinner a pussy

Why do your genitals tingle when your lover nibbles your earlobe? Is this just a physiologically erogenous zone that all people have in common or is there something else at work here? We think your privates are responding to conditioning and that any area of the body can be manipulated in this way.

Maybe your lover is in the habit of beginning lovemaking by sucking on your fingers. If he does this often enough, and in the same way every time, he can evoke a sexual response anytime. Even if you were sitting in church, a quick nibble of your pinky would set your nether parts to tingling.

People learn to expect sexual arousal through association with prior experiences. Ivan Petrovich Pavlov and B. F. Skinner did some of the initial work in this area of behavioral science. Robert Anton Wilson and Dr. Timothy Leary (yes, the very same, "Tune-in, turn-on, and drop-out," LSD guru of the 1960s) further investigated this linkage, specifically focusing on the sexual realm. Though Wilson and Leary had a broader socio-psychological scope, part of what they worked on were methods of sexual imprinting. They combined techniques of the Hindu Tantra with the use of aphrodisiacs, psychotropic substances, scientific knowledge of the nervous system and human sexuality for reconditioning people away from the repressive sexual attitudes that society impressed upon them. They called these techniques of reimprinting Hedonic Engineering. We use many of the same techniques in SM without the drugs.

Settings, smells, touches, even behavior and gestures become arousing subconscious cues if they are associated with highly sexually charged situations. Carefully linking powerful, erotic stimulation with slightly painful sensation will also evoke erotic stirrings. Conditioning is a facet of what scene people refer to as slave training, or merely, training.

A typical example of this is pinching the nipples while performing clitoral stimulation. Nipples have an erotic connection anyway, but it can be amplified with a little effort and discipline. Eventually, tweaking a nipple will set off an instant clitoral reaction. Heavy spanking while in the advanced arousal of love-making is another common technique of conditioning. Eventually the swats themselves take on the characteristics of a caress.

Conditioning has other interesting and devious uses. Would you believe that you can make someone orgasm on command? Well, you can. Just imagine the possibilities! An amusing addition to quiet strolls in the park, interesting diversions at formal dinner parties, we could go on and on. Once you've become used to responding to each other as dominant and obedient submissive, this is actually relatively simple to achieve.

This technique relies upon the submissive's desire to please, to obey, and her natural craving to orgasm. Again, it is a matter of linking one set of stimuli to another. In this case, the dominant links sexual arousal and sexual release in his submissive to verbal cues. Repetition and taking plenty of time to get it right are the secrets here. If a word or phrase is repeated often as the sub goes through arousal, that phrase will in itself become stimulation. Follow this with a different command to orgasm (at a point where the sub is on the verge, already) and you have a powerful tool.

Visualization -- Scheherazade goes dom

Visualization is transforming fantasies from concepts to mental images through the art of storytelling. It is usually used as a prelude or theme to a scene. Everyone's mental library contains a section devoted to the erotic cerebral cinema. Provocative images and language we garner from books, movies, and both real and imagined experiences become sensual triggers woven into the labyrinthine tapestry of our sexuality. Good dominants are constantly fishing for the sensual buttons that drive their submissives nuts. Rather than concentrating exclusively on what he is doing to his submissive's carcass, her hot-buttons afford access to the woman inside.

There are thousands of personal styles among SM people. We (Molly and Philip) tend toward fantasies combining the textures of velvet and broken glass; very romantic and a little scary...or very scary. But high romance puts a lot of people off. Some like to play correcting the brat, or taming the shrew. Others love to imagine themselves in the service of a liege, taking great physical abuse as proof of their esteem and/or dedication. Still others enjoy villain and hapless-victim scenes. This is one reason that good communication is so important. You have to know where your and your partner's fantasies converge and learn to focus on those crossroads.

Sometimes, things that evoke erotic responses have no intrinsic erotic properties at all, but, through association with a sexual, or even emotionally satisfying experience, they become personal catalysts for sexual stimulation. This is often how fetishes are born. One young lady related how her grandmother always bought her leather clothing and boots. She learned to associate leather with looking pretty and loved the attention she got from Grandma when she wore her gifts. When she grew up, and heard how some people use leather, it was instant fetish-time. Now, just the smell of leather sets her nipples aloft. (GO, Granny, GO!)

Once you have a handle on your partner's buttons, you have the key to all sorts of chicanery. Pick out a few elements of her fantasies and spin a feature-length story for her. Some of the best things to focus on are things she is nervous or embarrassed about. Speaking her fantasy to her, and adding details and colorations of your own invention, helps her blend built-in yearnings with the desire to realize them. Detail makes verbal imagery more vivid and helps one internalize the fantasy. If you carefully develop your story, you can press the buttons that set her mental stage for a very hot time.

Rape fantasies are very common, we'll use an example in this genre. Rape fantasies, by the way, have nothing to do with a desire to be raped. Rape is a heinous act of non-consensual violence. Rape fantasy is a desire to be "forced" to succumb to the sexual will of a lover where both "rapist" and "victim" understand and respect the limits and cravings of the other. No one should feel less of herself for having these fantasies and no one has the right to belittle someone who enjoys them. Please pardon our political digression, where were we? Ah, yes...

Suppose you and your lady are in the mood for an adventure. You are beginning to apply a rather intricate bondage and it occurs to you to fill the time with a story:

"Donna, my love, do you remember when we went to the governor's mansion for the costume ball, and you fell in love with that twin spiral staircase? Do you remember telling me how much you would love to poke around in the rooms upstairs?"

"Well, let's say you did slip away from the party and went upstairs. You thought no one noticed you leaving, but someone did. At first, you just stroll along the hallway looking at the paintings, feigning disinterest in all those closed doors, but your curiosity gets the better of you and you start peeking in this door and another next to it. After all, you can always say you are looking for a bathroom."

"There is a study, a library, and a bedroom, all furnished with the most lovely antiques. You wonder which of them are the property of the governor and which belong to the state. Then you find the master bedroom. You are sure you must be alone, so you go inside and switch on the light. Your nervousness is overcome by the richness in the large room surrounding you."

"A walnut, four-poster bed dominates the room, complimented by a tall chiffonnier and dressing table of the same wood and pattern. The bed is spread with a thick, burgundy comforter of satin...no, it's silk! You reach to run your hand over it and just as your fingers touch its cool, smooth surface the lights are switched off from behind you."

"You wheel around to see a shaft of light, narrowing as the door swings shut with a soft click. You see and hear nothing but a faint beam of light from the heavy, drawn curtains and the pounding of your heart."

"You are terrified, but more terrified to scream and be caught intruding. Still, you realize that someone has caught you and your eyes flit to-and-fro looking for him as they adjust to the all-but-pitch-black room."

"Suddenly, a brawny figure detaches itself from the surrounding darkness, swiftly and silently closing the span between you. He is upon you before you can raise your arms to ward him off, sealing your mouth with his palm. He forces you onto the bed, his large body trapping yours beneath him. You struggle, but cannot move."

"Without the slightest effort, the powerful brute rips open the bodice of your dress and clasps your breast in a painful grip..."

We'll let you finish the story, secure in the knowledge that you will supply your own happy ending.

Sensory relocation

An example of the boundless flexibility of the human mind is shown by sensory relocation. Sensory relocation is a skill related to conditioning and visualization. It is the ability to take a sensation given to one part of the body and experience it in another. Practically, one stimulates one part of the body, say the back, and mentally transfers the experience as a sexual sensation to a more erogenous location, such as the penis or clitoris.

Park your skepticism for a moment. It does work, but it requires some self-conditioning and patience. We use a two stage approach that can take several days to complete. Plan for at least fifteen minutes of quiet, undisturbed time for each session.

The first stage increases your body's awareness of touch and texture. Gather together a few articles that are unique to the touch such as fur, velvet, leather, sandpaper or glass. Close your eyes. Lightly stroke each object with your fingertips and concentrate on fixing each sensation in your mind. Try rubbing the objects on other parts of your body. Notice the difference in feel from one place to the next. Run your fingertips over your body while taking care to maintain the same amount of pressure you used with the other objects. Be aware of the different way you experience the same stimulation on different parts of your body. The object of these exercises is to train yourself to recognize and recall the different sensations and textures vividly. In time, you will be able to remember each one clearly.

The next stage is a bit harder. Rub your fingertips over something with a distinct feel such as sandpaper. Visualize the sandpaper rubbing your left nipple instead of your fingers. With imagination and patience you can develop the ability to transfer the feel at your fingertips to your nipple. Once you have mastered this seemingly silly exercise, have your sweety run his finger lightly over your back, while picturing that touch on your favorite erogenous zone. When you get the knack, you'll know it.

Dominance and submission

Dominance and submission, or D/S, or D&S, is the basic underpinning of all the games that we play. Whether our activities include role-play, bondage, discipline, humiliation, whipping or what have you, our games always involve one person controlling another. Usually this takes the form of sexual control, though sex need not always be a part of our scenes. D/S is an exchange of power between partners, one person submitting to the other's will.

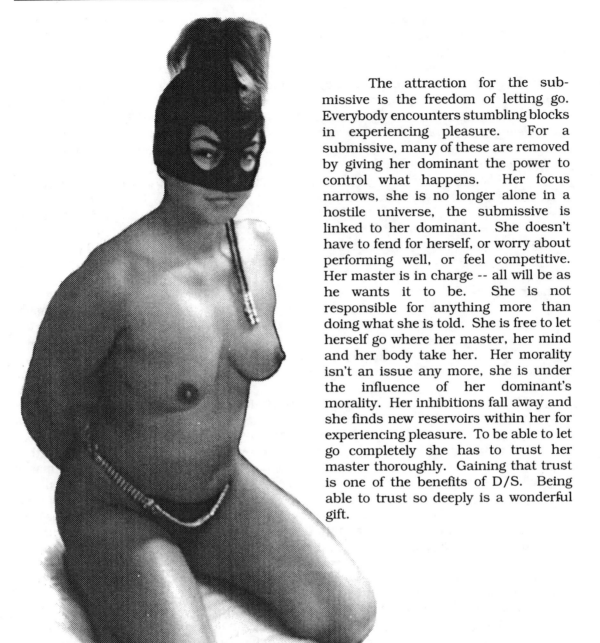

The attraction for the submissive is the freedom of letting go. Everybody encounters stumbling blocks in experiencing pleasure. For a submissive, many of these are removed by giving her dominant the power to control what happens. Her focus narrows, she is no longer alone in a hostile universe, the submissive is linked to her dominant. She doesn't have to fend for herself, or worry about performing well, or feel competitive. Her master is in charge -- all will be as he wants it to be. She is not responsible for anything more than doing what she is told. She is free to let herself go where her master, her mind and her body take her. Her morality isn't an issue any more, she is under the influence of her dominant's morality. Her inhibitions fall away and she finds new reservoirs within her for experiencing pleasure. To be able to let go completely she has to trust her master thoroughly. Gaining that trust is one of the benefits of D/S. Being able to trust so deeply is a wonderful gift.

For a dominant, D/S allows experimentation with a live, willing body. It's a power trip. He tells her to strip naked and she does. He orders her to use her hands, or her mouth, or her breasts, or her pussy and she does. On top of that, he gets to do anything to her that he wants to within the agreed upon limits and she'll willingly, even enthusiastically, put up with it. He doesn't have to ask for any favors. He commands, she obeys, and if she doesn't, he gets to punish her. Life is sweet!

A dominant also gets to exhibit all the creativity his demonic little soul can muster. He sets the mood, controls the action, and employs the props. It is as liberating an experience for him as it is for his submissive, but his is the active role, hers, the passive.

It's his responsibility to take control and stay there, and to make sure that what happens is at least safe and, with luck, hugely successful. Of course, then he can take all the credit for a wonderful session.

How does one dominate? It depends upon what makes a submissive feel submissive. Does she respond to tenderness mixed with force? Try a long, lingering kiss while you pin her arms over her head. Does a smoldering look compel her to drop her eyes? Does she begin to moisten when she's tied to the bed and very slowly undressed? Maybe she needs a little more coaxing to drop her defenses. Perhaps a blindfold would help her focus; that, and the sound of a whip whistling through the air ending in a crack like a rifle-shot. Does that get her attention?

Dominating is a balance of drawing on a submissive's sexual responses and peaking her sense of adventure, while maintaining command of the situation. The trick is knowing what pushes her to the edge, and what pushes her over it. Use fear, anticipation, mystery and menace, but never let her panic. Temper it with love, tenderness, sexiness and confidence. You have to discover what moves and excites her, then plan a scene around it. A dominant has to prepare the scene in his mind and be bold and sure in its execution.

If he is using them, the dominant should be an expert with the props he handles, be they whips, canes, ropes, restraints, or even vibrators. Get the training for whatever you use, and practice until you consider yourself a pro. Aside from being dangerous, clumsy use of toys spoils the moment and makes your sub afraid to trust you. (We'll provide lots of advice on the use of toys in later chapters.)

How does one submit? There are a number of prerequisites. She has to want someone to control her. She must trust her dominant enough to give it all up to him. That takes time, caring, and real communication from both partners. The requirements of a submissive are emotional, internal preparations.

More often than not, submissives have been preparing themselves internally for years before they come to SM. Their sexual fantasies have frequently been of a submissive nature whether they realized it or not. Then, when they discover the D/S scene, they feel as though they'd found a home.

A wise and perceptive dominant once told us, "I can force a woman to do anything she wants to do." Dominants are in the fantasy realization business. A good dominant knows which fantasies will lead in constructive directions and which are best left to the imagination. This isn't always as simple as applying common horse-sense. Some people are prone to fantasies that aren't healthy, others get too carried away with living out their fantasies and end up very unhappy.

One pitfall fantasy is the myth of the "total slave." Nobody can live happily as the live-in slave of another. Nobody who "owns" a slave enjoys controlling her every action twenty-four hours a day. The stress on both partners is just too damned much, even if you both really want to try it. It soon becomes evident that she can't keep the chains on and get all the housework done, because the chains start wearing holes in her skin and the chastity belt with the built-in vibrator is giving her a chronic yeast infection or is just starting to piss her off.

In the end, you make concessions. Pretty soon the fantasy wears on your nerves or the whole thing just gets boring and you end up feeling lousy about each other. Just let your roles develop naturally. You'll find the right level of slaveness and masterness for your relationship if you stay flexible, communicate, and go slowly. There is a hell of a lot to say about D/S: different depths and levels to reach, emotional impact, various methods of control, and so on. It is a complex topic. We'll be covering these other aspects of dominance and submission in later chapters.

3 The Politics of Very Strange Bedfellows
Sensible SM Relationships and Dangerous Liasons

t is easy to drift into a comfortable sexual routine with a partner and too easy for that routine to become stagnant. If you are part of a couple that is still exploring and learning together, good for you. If you are single and have decided to look for someone to share your search for adventurous sex, good for you, too.

Nibbling various morsels from the sexual potpourri is harmless, breaks monotony, and helps you grow. Of course, SM is only one among many choices, but we find that adding Rocky Road to your erotic menu makes vanilla all the more appetizing and can renew the hunger in ongoing relationships. You may be curious about SM and dying to give it a shot, but find that your partner isn't as enthusiastic. Allow us to suggest a few recipes to entice new or reluctant gourmets.

Steering your love-boat into the rapids

Lovers often slip into SM games unwittingly while experimenting with sexual options. Have you ever pinned your lover to the bed and engaged in a little sexual teasing, tried some light bondage, or delivered a few affectionate swats on your sweety's bottom to spice-up your lovemaking? If you have, how did your partner react? Often these simple tactics are all you will need to stir the animal in your paramour. Then again, you may be treading too near troubled waters.

Beginners with a positive leaning toward SM arrive with varied measures of interest. At the ground level are those who are content with daydreams that they would be terrified to put into practice. Go very, very slowly with these people and insist that they set the limits. At the top are people who have always been closet SM'ers and are burning for fate to provide a special someone who shares the dream. With these folks, set your feet deep into the stirrups and wrap the reins around both fists, you are about to have the ride of your life.

Between these extremes are a whole host of motivations and levels of interest. Few people can tell you what motivates the excitement they find in SM. Perhaps the largest group of players had no idea they would like SM until they stumbled upon a player or group of players and decided to give it a whirl. They discover an intensity and degree of communication they never dreamed possible, and boom, instant convert. Some begin playing SM as a counterpoint to the other parts of their lives. A craving for submission may stem from a life fraught with heavy responsibilities; the release afforded by submitting lends balance. A corresponding longing to be dominant may arise in someone who is controlled by others in his or her daily life. Again, these folks are seeking balance.

Then again, people try SM for all kinds of reasons, some more wholesome than others. We have met people for whom SM offers a way to express fantasies of heroism; a low-impact method of dealing with guilt or low self-esteem; an outlet for satisfying an adventurous spirit; a way of proving themselves worthy to themselves and to their lovers; a vehicle for expressing stylishness; an escape from boredom; a way to shock friends and relatives; an ego trip; an unique career path; a means for seeking revenge; a process for achieving self-improvement through catharsis; a way to find a mate; a proving ground for macho challenges; and simply a source of entertainment. There are also vast pools of people for whom SM feels like their natural environment and others who have no idea why they like it, they just do. Come to think of it, these are no different than the reasons people give for going to college.

The point is, people have their own agendas with very diverse and often complex histories of acquiring them. Some are conscious of it and some are not. There is little or no common thread among people who seek SM. As far as we are concerned, if people enjoy what they are doing and their play is safe, sane, and consensual, it doesn't matter why they pursue it. Also, it doesn't matter whether SM is a sexual practice one pursues with a lover or in the privacy of one's mind. The latter, however, may lead to overly developed wrists and/or second mortgages taken out to pay for batteries.

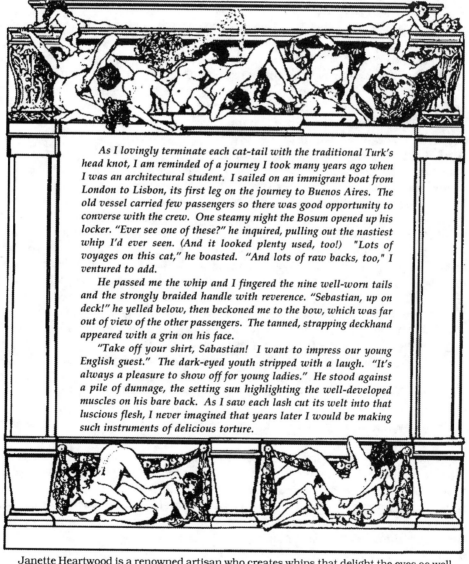

As I lovingly terminate each cat-tail with the traditional Turk's head knot, I am reminded of a journey I took many years ago when I was an architectural student. I sailed on an immigrant boat from London to Lisbon, its first leg on the journey to Buenos Aires. The old vessel carried few passengers so there was good opportunity to converse with the crew. One steamy night the Bosum opened up his locker. "Ever see one of these?" he inquired, pulling out the nastiest whip I'd ever seen. (And it looked plenty used, too!) "Lots of voyages on this cat," he boasted. "And lots of raw backs, too," I ventured to add.

He passed me the whip and I fingered the nine well-worn tails and the strongly braided handle with reverence. "Sebastian, up on deck!" he yelled below, then beckoned me to the bow, which was far out of view of the other passengers. The tanned, strapping deckhand appeared with a grin on his face.

"Take off your shirt, Sabastian! I want to impress our young English guest." The dark-eyed youth stripped with a laugh. "It's always a pleasure to show off for young ladies." He stood against a pile of dunnage, the setting sun highlighting the well-developed muscles on his bare back. As I saw each lash cut its welt into that luscious flesh, I never imagined that years later I would be making such instruments of delicious torture.

Janette Heartwood is a renowned artisan who creates whips that delight the eyes as well as the body. Here she reminisces about an early experience. She graciously allowed us to reprint this piece from her Whips of Passion Catalog.

With 31 flavors available, why serve only vanilla?

Suppose you have a spouse, a lover, or a significant other to whom you have never revealed your fantasies. How do you know your honey isn't entertaining wicked thoughts of a similar nature? Wouldn't it be ironic for the star of your wet dreams to be the man or woman you had been sleeping with for years?

We ran into just such a situation with a handsome young couple we met on the nude beach. The subject SM relationships came up while we were chatting. Molly's pierced nipples and steel collar may have had some small part in inspiring the topic. The young woman took Philip aside and regaled him with nostalgic memories of her previous lover and the bondage games she played with him. Just out of earshot, her husband was confessing to Molly that many of his exotic fantasies included dominating and being dominated.

Though they had been married for seven years, neither spouse dared expose these taboo fantasies to the other, fearing rejection. But given the skinniest chance to make a clean breast without being ridiculed, even to complete strangers, neither could wait to draw aside the veil.

We blew their cover for them when the four of us came together later. At first, they were embarrassed about discovering these secrets about each other, but soon, it was as though the dam had broken and they gushed with enthusiasm. Continuing our conversation, certain things "came up" making it obvious that SM fantasies were very much alive for both husband and wife. (One can curb tan lines on a nude beach, but rarely one's true colors.) We ran into the lovely couple a few times since that memorable afternoon to discover that they had been happily torturing each other ever after.

Is the risk of rejection real or will your loved one value the faith you show by sharing your secrets? There are several ways to minimize the risk.

Movies and books are a way of introducing the subject gently. Pick up a magazine at your local adult bookstore that illustrates a variety of sexual options. On an evening when you won't be disturbed, scan the pictures with your beloved. "I found this magazine in Larry's desk at the office," you'll confess to your lover, "and I stole it so we could look at it together." Leaf through the pages asking her what she finds hot. When you get to a mild bondage shot admit, "Say, that looks sort of interesting. What do you think, Maude?"

The movie *9 and 1/2 Weeks* contains scenes that may elicit some telling responses from your would-be playmate. Mickey Rourke seduces a naive Kim Bassinger into an affair characterized by his probing the limits of Kim's sexual psyche using games of control. During the nearly two and a-half months allocated by the movie's title, Rourke treats Kim to a series of sexy blindfolded interludes. This movie illustrates a classic, low-threat, starter situation where there is no actual bondage or beating. This is a way of introducing beginners to the exploration of domination and submission without terrifying them. What you are doing is merely extending what they are already used to, one step at a time.

For those submissively inclined, try a mildly aggressive approach. Maneuver your lover against a wall, firmly take her wrists in your hands, pinning her wrists over her head. Plant a world-class kiss on her mouth of the kind that lasts until the following Tuesday. If she melts under your mellow attack, you've got yourself a submissive. Still, take things slowly and carefully. Follow up with a moderate performance of your dominant artfulness and let her proclaim you Lord and Master.

A submissively oriented lady trying to get her vanilla boyfriend into SM might prepare a surprise for her lover by donning her most seductive dress, then binding her hands to the headboard of the bed. Wear enough clothing to allow your would-be dominant to unwrap his present at his leisure. A blindfold and/or gag are interesting additions to the enterprise, but use discretion so as not to invoke too great a shock.

Are you a good storyteller? You might try snuggling in bed with your flame and beginning a tale with a spicy SM theme.   Some people are very quiet during a story-session, but their breathing will tell you a tale or two.

The key to unlocking the secret gates of lust in your cherished one is finding the right imagery. Is your lady looking for a stern daddy? A wise, but kinky mentor? A knight in shining armor? A sinister villain? A naughty doctor? Does she star in her sacred fantasies as a princess? A lowly slave? A priestess of carnal rites? A heroine enduring the ravages of her captor? A savage huntress needing to be tamed? A virginal maiden? A barroom slut?

On the other hand, perhaps your honey needs a mommy to paddle the bad boy out of him. Or a strict governess devising nasty little chores for naughty little boys. Or a goddess to worship and put him through his paces. Or a bitch queen to keep him quaking in fear from torture to torture.

Once you know how to cast each other, let the fantasies fly! You can set an elaborate scene with props and costumes, if you like, or simply set the stage in your imagination and let nature do the rest.

Catching a live one

It takes (at least) two to play in the realm of control, fantasy, and pain. But, if you are single, how do you find the right co-conspirator? Here are several safe and sensible methods for finding SM partners.

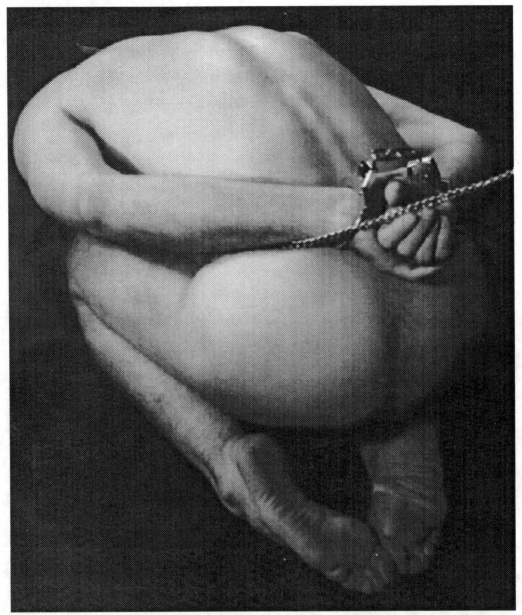

Submissive males represent the largest group one finds in the scene. (photo: Steve Lauer)

The law of supply and demand

If it is better to give than to receive, why are there so many more willing submissive bodies than people willing or knowledgeable enough to properly abuse them? Submissive males represent the largest group one finds in the scene.

There is a tremendous shortage of women in the fetish community. This is due to our society's sexual double standard. While men are more or less expected to pursue and develop their sexuality, society still encourages women to reject theirs. So, fewer women present themselves in sexually liberal environments than do men. Since SM is not only a sexual taboo, but a social one as well, the number of women is decreased all the more. This diminutive figure is further split between submissive and dominant leanings.

So, what's a subby guy to do? To begin with, he has to hang out where the dominant women hang out. He should find the clubs, organizations, and/or computer bulletin board systems (bbs's) that cater to SM and start to make friends (covered in more detail below). Being extremely charming, devilishly handsome, and fabulously wealthy will not hurt his chances or, if he already has a mate, he may be able to teach her to play dom for him. Some men are so frantic to find a dominant Ms. Right that they attempt to whine, cajole, and annoy the nearest female into topping them. This creates a situation where even an unskilled or cruel mistress will have hoards of desperate slaves begging to slobber over her boots. This might seem humorous were the risks of abuse not so substantial. Safe, successful domination is an art that relies on instinct, research, education, and practice.

The competition for ladies able to assume the dominant role is so stiff, however, that the submissive seeker frequently resorts to the services of a professional domina. Competent dominas may work independently or in a reputable house of domination.

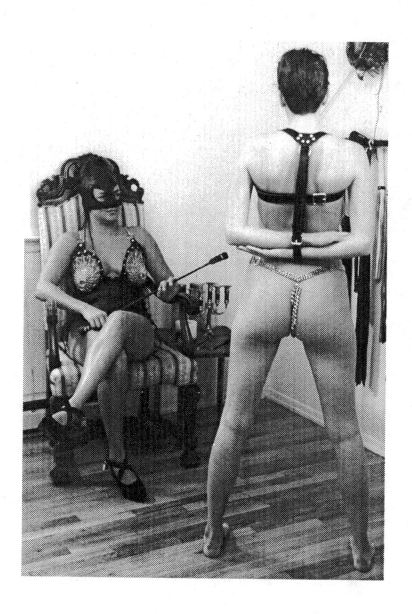

Scene people love to talk about who they know and how good they are. Becoming involved and making friends in the public scene will help you find the reliable professionals.

Another way of locating that special lady is through ads in the several SM newspapers and magazines. Any adult bookstore will have a few. Among them, look for *Corporal*, The *Dominant Directory International, Dominant Mystique, House of Horror*, and *B&D Pleasures*. *Screw Magazine* also has a small SM section as do some of the swingers' magazines.

Just as there is an abundance of submissive men in the scene, there is no shortage of men claiming to be dominant. The notion appeals to the traditional male fantasy, yet loving, dominant men who practice their art with skill and sensitivity are rare. Submissive women are forever angling for their attentions. This dearth creates a condition whereby the typically slutty, but worthier dominant can control a stable of subs. (Adam Smith be proud, the law of the marketplace works!) Of course, these guys must constantly perform for their harems or lose them. Vitamin companies are thrilled by this.

What to look for

So, how do you find a safe, sane partner with compatible kinks? Dominant, submissive, master, slave, sadist, and masochist are intriguing labels exotically bestowed on people for their preferred sexual roles. But, people, however they label themselves, are complex and far more than players in a sensual theater. The qualities you want in a SM partner are the same things you look for and admire in a lover and friend: honesty, sincerity, warmth, integrity, mutual respect, and, of course, the requisite that he or she shares fantasies that are compatible with yours. The ability to be open and to give and to receive love are far more critical than skill with a whip or a high pain tolerance. Technical proficiency can be learned; the basics of human nature are difficult to change.

The people you play with should be careful and reliable. It isn't enough that he dons a leather outfit that makes you melt, or that her eyes glaze over and her nipples turn to stone at the vaguest allusion to handcuffs. A sense of humor is also helpful in getting though the hard times. Fundamentally, a playmate must have the characteristics you require in an intense personal relationship and possess compatible fantasies.

Looking for Mr. Good-dom

Besides all the warm and wonderful character traits found in your ideal lover, here are a few additional requirements for a dominant with the right stuff. He should be:

- someone with whom you communicate well. You may be a regular motor-mouth with your friends, but seal up tighter than a clam when you are with a lover. SM requires a solid, steady stream of communication to keep your relationship safe and satisfying. The guy you find may be hotter than a rocket, but if you cannot find a way to tune into the same wavelength, find yourself another, more well guided missile.

- someone who is careful. His first concern is always safety.

- someone who respects your limits. It is fine to gradually broaden your submissive's horizons or to coax a hesitant sub into some experimentation. The good dom will not push or coerce his submissive into anything she really doesn't want to do.

- someone who knows his own limitations. He won't attempt to carry out that which is beyond his capabilities. He must be willing to take the time to plan, research, practice, and seek training when needed.

- someone who values his submissive and considers her his equal. In role, do what makes you happy. When it is time to drop the fantasy, each of you is a full and equal partner.

- someone who considers the enjoyment of his partner on a par with his own pleasure.

- someone who knows the difference between fantasy and reality.

- someone willing to try everything that he intends for his partner on his own body first. While he may not enjoy a whip stroke he still must understand its feel.

- someone who is patient and kind. He will take the time to understand his submissive.

Seeking suitable submissives

Care for a game of Capture the Flagellant? While the dom is nominally in charge, the characteristics of a good submissive are no less important in making a SM relationship work. You want a partner with whom you can communicate, a person willing to risk telling you something that she thinks you may not want to hear.

Communication from your submissive is important on another level, too. She has a responsibility to tell you if you are going too far or if something is wrong with her. This is particularly difficult for a submissive. It is one of the paradoxes of SM. In the fantasy, she is yours to do with as you will. Yet, you are both playing for mutual pleasure. She must find a way to say that this or that turns her off without feeling like she'll break the spell. You want her to share her whims, also, so that you can satisfy them. Beyond this, your perfect submissive will be:

- someone who respects herself.

- someone who doesn't want real abuse.

"Submissive", a sculpture by Molly.

- someone who has a good sense of reality versus fantasy.

- someone who is not looking for you to take over her life, but to enhance it.

- someone you can trust not to blame you later for dominating her. For example; avoid someone who might ask to be "taken" sexually, then cry rape.

- someone wise enough to let you learn who she is, what pleases her, and what she wants. Good communication is a critical factor in any relationship, but in SM a lack of it can be devastating.

- someone who does not make demands. Pushiness on the part of a submissive or a dominant is a turn-off. There may something your submissive wants that you are not prepared to give her because you cannot bring yourself to do it, are not trained for it, don't like it, or feel that it's not safe and sane. On the other hand, you do want a submissive who will tell you what she wants, enjoys, and expects.

The hunt

Now that you can identify the prey you seek, it is time to load your ammunition and go after the beastie. Among the approved methods of capture, leghold traps are acceptable, but lethal means tend to yield rather unresponsive partners. Here are some suggestions for where to look and how to flush out the game:

Organizations & support groups

We live in a truly wonderful time. You can find support groups and societies for everything from left-handed, underwater basket weavers to disciples of Milliard Fillmore. SM is no exception.

SM support groups are found in most major cities. The National Leather Association (NLA), The Janus Society, People Exchanging Power (PEP), The Power Exchange, and The Black Rose are some of the names you might run into. These groups hold seminars and meetings to exchange ideas, learn new techniques, show off their toys and to socialize with people who share their interests. This is an excellent way to meet potential partners. (See our appendix for a list of organizations and their addresses.)

Public clubs

A few cities have public SM clubs and more are popping up all the time. Two we have visited in New York are the Vault and Paddles. On any given night, curiosity seekers will be able to witness spankings, whippings and a variety of bondage techniques. These are also good places to perform publicly, if that is your thing.

Clubs are risky places for a novice to seek a partner, though they are excellent places to begin acquiring a new circle of friends. Be wary of people who want to play as soon as they meet you; impulse shopping can be dangerous in SM. Playing with someone new on the premises of a club diminishes the risk considerably. Clubs generally employ people to make sure that scenes do not get out of hand. Staff members are usually receptive to a request to keep an eye on you while you play with a new partner. Taking that new person home with you is extremely dangerous. Unless you have the recommendation of someone you know and trust about a prospective playmate, don't take the chance.

Magazine and newspaper ads

One can see and place ads in the "personals" of almost any newspaper. *The Village Voice* and *The Aquarian*, in New York, are publications catering to younger and single crowds and all have very lively personal ad sections. So do many of the mainstream papers in larger cities. You will find ads from people looking for SM partners under the "alternative life-styles" or "anything goes" sections. In the early days, when people were still being coy, French meant oral, Greek meant anal and English meant discipline, bondage, or SM. The ads are usually more explicit now, though they still may be "coded" in the mainstream press.

There is definitely an element of risk here. You would not believe some of the stories we have heard, yet ads can be fruitful if one is careful. See the section on meeting safely, below.

Kink goes electronic

In the beginning of the information age, when the computer was the sole domain of the technically inclined, lonely programmers discovered how to pass messages from computer to computer over telephone lines. One lonely programmer, Arnie, worked deep in the bowels of IBM's research and development department in Spokane. Having little to do (IBM doesn't invent new things, they borrow other people's ideas and market them), Arnie started calling distant computers to see if he could find a friend. After only 3,278 phone calls, Arnie struck pay dirt.

Beth worked for an idle GM plant in Duluth. The union kept her at her terminal even though not a single car had been produced in two years. One day, Beth was happily creating a picture of Richard Gere on her screen when her terminal's modem began to ring! Though she was finally getting Richard's nostrils just right, she instantly switched on her communications software to answer the phone. You guessed it! It was Arnie!

Well, to make a short story longer than it has any right to be, Arnie and Beth got along swimmingly, though they had never met in person. Beth uploaded her incomplete picture of Richard Gere to Arnie and Arnie insisted that if the nostrils were stretched out just a little, the picture would look just like him.

Arnie called Beth every day. In fact, they both started putting in a great deal of overtime as their cybernetic love burned up the phone lines and hours of long-distance charges (using safe computing to avoid viruses, of course).

Late one night, Arnie dialed a wrong number and found himself connected to Lois at an Atomic Energy Commission site outside of Albuquerque. Arnie downloaded Beth's drawing of Richard Gere to Lois, claiming it was a self-portrait. Thusly were born both the electronic bulletin board (BBS) and the cyber-slut.

Personal computing now allows even vaguely computer literate people to access public bulletin board systems. Public BBSs, InterNet, CompuServe, America On-Line (AOL), Prodigy, and GEnie, have "open chat" areas of the network where one can "talk" via keyboard to hundreds of people at one time. People type to each other to share technical information or just to socialize.

People have a delightful knack for perverting the most innocent of technical devices. They soon discovered that chatting by type was an ideal media for swapping sexual fantasy and making friends. For a few thousand dollars, a private network operator (sysop) could start a multiple phone-line chat system. There are now literally thousands of private BBS's around the world. Most are available to anyone, regardless of age, but many of them cater exclusively to the lust of their adult membership.

For free or for a nominal charge, the sysops of these adult networks will give you access to their chat areas, their libraries (containing lots of dirty pictures and stories), and they'll provide you with an alias (or "handle") by which you will be known to other members of the BBS.

The beauty of BBS'ing is that you can try out your fantasies from the comfort of your home with real people and you are protected from face-slaps by the distance and anonymity of the network. Be warned, though, creating a phony persona is a double-edged sword. Arnie was eventually caught out by Lois and Beth as a two-timing nerd whose only resemblance to Richard Gere is that he also has two nostrils. After ruining Arnie's reputation, first nationally and then internationally, Lois and Beth met Steve and Mark and were married in a double-ring ceremony in Silicon Valley.

Most chat systems cater to general lust. You may find a few users on these systems who will admit an inclination to B&D or SM, and many of them will have special sections dedicated to our kink, but there are also BBS's just for us. At this writing, the biggest and best SM-oriented BBS is The English Palace in New Jersey, (908) 739-1755. This is a good places to find potential partners, exchange information and get support from others who share your interests.

One downside of the bulletin boards, particularly for a woman seeking a real partner, is the number of people who are only into the fantasy, but pretend otherwise. There is an especially large number of male doms that we call "wannabes.' Wannabes have distinctive mating calls that go like this: "What do you look like?", "What are you wearing?", and "What are you into?" The woman reading these familiar refrains soon understands why the typing at the other end is so slow. (Try typing with one hand sometime.) On the alt.sex.bondage newsgroup on internet they are sometimes called CHDW's (pronounced chudwah) for clueless-het-dominant-wannabe.

Would-bes, Wannabes, and other forgettable characters

They come in various flavors ranging from amusingly absurd, to truly annoying, to downright dangerous. We would love to see a few of these scene animals make the endangered species list.

The Virgin
(Novis Incognito)

These people are embarrassed about their lack of experience, which they cover with bravado while they pretend to be very experienced. The operative term here is pretend. They think that acting severe will make them seem competent. So on the BBS they type a lot about punishing and grabbing hair. While these fellows are boring, they can sometimes be taught to act like a mensch over time. These guys are the most forgivable of the wannabes.

You can find them at the clubs in freshly purchased leather duds. They will be brandishing a shiny new $40 whip with a plastic handle purchased from their local adult boutique. Should they carry off the masquerade well enough to convince a submissive (usually another novice), they will whip all the wrong places as they have not bothered to take time to learn how to use it. Damage is minimized when the cheap plastic handle disintegrates and the thongs go flying off into a pitcher of martinis behind him.

The Celestial Princes$$
(Divina Nolo Mentis)

This Goddess has always been aware of her divinity; finally the world knows, too. She never concerns herself with learning the skills to be a top. After all, a goddess is infallible. (Oops... oh well, submissives come with two kidneys, don't they?)

The discovery of her interest in SM came when a girlfriend explained that guys would pay to worship her. She only had to abuse 'em a bit (something she had done all her life). Thus she was saved from the ignomy of a real job. America is still the land of opportunity!

Hobby: shopping at Bloomingdales
Favorite scene: shopping at The Pleasure Chest.

The Peter Pan
(Autoerotico Fabula)

These guys have lived in fantasyland so long, they need a passport to visit reality. They read, read, read, porn, porn, porn. Unfortunately, they don't know what is possible and what isn't. One Mr. Pan we know yearns to bind a girl so she is forced to stand for hours on her tiptoes. Another Patricia Pan claims to enjoy whipping her submissives into unconsciousness, then continues the whipping! She says she can tell when her subs have had enough, even while semi-comatose. Golly, don't these guys tickle your erotic fancy?

While annoying on a BBS, they are actually dangerous if they ever try to play "for real." Fortunately, most of them are scared to death of reality.

Favorite vacation shop: Roissy
Favorite drink: Paga

The TRUE Master (or Mistress)
(Equis Dorsum Primus)

Too often one runs into the dominant who says he wants total control of his sub at all times, together or apart. This individual really believes a submissive should live solely for the pleasure of her master. They have a penchant for referring to themselves as "True Masters." Some of them believe that subs who set limits are not "true" submissives. Another type of True Master believes that a sub wants precisely what she says she will not tolerate.

These are lovely fantasies. At best, these fellows have little experience; they are confusing what they have read in stories for reality. The correct scene term for them is "asshole." At worst, they truly behave in this manner, in which case they are referred to as "dangerous assholes".

Favorite Book: *The Q-letters*

Very Married, but...
(Semper Infidelis)

These guys want to cheat on their wives, but lack the courage, so they live out their fantasies by hot-chatting on a BBS and phone sex. They frequently lie and make promises they cannot or will not keep.

Eventually, some of them do play for real, making things worse. They usually forget to mention to their partners that they are married and always forget to mention to their wives that they are fooling around.

Favorite sex toy: telephone

The Performer
(Barnum Maximus)

He (or she) loves to demonstrate his skill in public. Quite a few female doms seem to fall for this trap. These clowns are so busy trying to impress their audience that they pay little attention to the sub under their whips. Amusing as these entertainers are, they are also dangerous. Image is so important that they will never admit there is anything they can learn. Narcissism is the real kink here.

Favorite sex toy: mirror

The Macho-man
(Neanderthal Vulgaris)

These are unreconstructed male chauvinist piglets who confuse submissiveness with inferiority. As they do not recognize women as human, they do not feel any requirement to deal with their needs.

SM to these buffoons means "owning" a female who will serve beer to him and his friends while they watch a football game on TV, then give them all a good blow-job during half-time. Basically insensitive, they will never understand the difference between exploitation and SM.

Favorite game:
Bowling for submissives

Favorite beverage:
Brewski

Crude, Lewd and always Horny
(Erectus Perpetua)

If they know you are sub, they are dom, and vice versa. They see SM as just another opportunity to "get some" (another opportunity that they usually blow). They never experience the deeper intensity possible in SM because they are really just looking for a compliant female to boff. To them, SM is merely delivering a few whacks as a substitute to foreplay.

Favorite sex toy:
Hey, we aren't fussy!

While these doms want subs, there are three things they never do. They never treat a submissive with respect, make friends before attempting to play, or are honest. This is why these guys are usually alone and chronically horny. Unfortunately, because of the shortage of women in the scene, female dominants with the same flaws easily find subs willing to live with their abuse.

The downside of the subside

Some submissives give us the willies, too. Here are a few to watch out for:

The Cinderella
(Odalisque Calamatus)

Her life is a mess. This is no surprise because she has taken no responsibility for cleaning it up. She is broke because she can't (or won't) hold a job long enough to support herself. She doesn't have (or won't acquire) the skills she needs to get a decent job. She has endless excuses for not seeking work or getting the education she needs.

Often her excuses date back to her awful childhood or some other more recent experience that has left her too emotionally traumatized to be self-sufficient. She is waiting for her prince Charming in the shape of a dominant to take charge of her life. Many dominants, being nurturing and romantic by nature, fall prey to this lady.

The True Slave
(Tedium Varitas)

She (or he; lots of male subs seem to go for this one) is the counterpart to the "True Master." She desires to lose herself in the fantasy. Looking for total control at all times, she exhibits very little personality of her own. Since she is offering what so many say they want, she is baffled that her potential suitors find her boring so quickly. Wouldn't these two make a nice pair of bookends?

Favorite game: Who is the more submissive?
Favorite beverage: You don't want to know

The Wonder Woman
(Vexata in Adversum)

She wants to be controlled by someone stronger than she. The catch is, no one stronger exists. She challenges any show of authority. She puts down those who find her not worth the energy expenditure as wimps. People frequently break toys on her out of sheer frustration.

Favorite game: Who's on top?

The Wanna-mate
(Femme Desparata)

Having grown up on a TV diet of "Leave It To Beaver" and "The Donna Reed Show," she is certain life begins with marriage. Having failed to snag an appropriate male by any other means, she is now trying the scene. She answers ads looking for live-in slaves, viewing obedience as a decent trade-off for security. She is the female counterpoint to the macho-man.

Newsflash: the fifties are gone, ladies, Nick-At-Night not withstanding.

Favorite scene: Serving dinner

Safety suggestions for meeting through ads or BBSs

1) Get a post office box for correspondence, or use the system set up by the newspaper for maintaining confidentiality. Never list your name, phone number, or address on a bulletin board or in a newspaper ad.

2) Check out a person you are interested in by getting references. You don't need a note from his clergyman, but you do want names of other people who know how this person plays. If the person has played in the local scene for a while, others will know him.

3) Customarily, women should be given the men's phone numbers. Ladies should not offer their numbers, especially if they live alone.

4) Start by corresponding through the mail (or "e-mail", if you are using a BBS), then progress to phone conversations. A genuinely interested party will understand the wisdom of going slowly and will stick around for the payoff. (Doesn't this sound like something your mother would approve of?)

5) Exchanging photos is a good idea and avoids embarrassment before you meet. Some people don't care much about looks, but to others it is critical. Hopefully, both people have realistic expectations. Let's face it, few women are going to look like Madonna and few men are going to be a cross between Tom Selleck and Kevin Costner.

6) Arrange to meet first at a public place for coffee or lunch. Make sure that play is not on the schedule for this first meeting. This is safer AND less embarrassing if you don't hit it off.

7) Trade some privacy for safety. When you finally get together with your potential Prince or Princess Charming, make sure a trusted friend knows exactly where you will be, with whom, and for how long. Your safety-buddy should have the real name, address, and phone number of the person you plan to meet. Most importantly, make sure your new play partner understands that you are doing this.

8) Make a plan with a friend for emergency measures. One of the best "silent alarms" to use is a phone call to your friend, planned for a specific time. If the phone call is not made on time, your friend calls in the police or takes whatever action you deem appropriate. By the way, the police in most towns are familiar and cooperative with this procedure. If an emergency does arise, just tell the cops that you made this arrangement with your friend because she is on a blind date. Tell them that in all likelihood, nothing is amiss, but could they please send a car around to the fellow's apartment just to make sure. Philip has been "safety man" for a friend who forgot to call him on time and he found the police very understanding and cooperative.

Obviously these are only suggestions, but we do want you around to buy our next book. The following example is typical of what you are likely to run into:

The charming dom wants to meet you at a hotel to play. You love his letters, full of promising hours of delight and exertions that would tire a star athlete. He swears that he can part his hair with his tongue. But, he won't give you his number and he can't give you references.

Does this mean you have a Hannibal Lechter just dying to sink his teeth into you? Not likely. You probably have that most common of rogues, the married man cheating on his wife. But can you afford to take the chance? Well, if you're the kind of woman who dives into empty swimming pools, go for it. It's been nice knowing you.

Even supposing its only a married man, not some wacko out to get his jollies and send you to the emergency room. You've got a serious problem. The morality issue isn't the only question in this case. Lots of people in the scene have open marriages or complex arrangements. The lack of honesty is the point. Trust is the backbone of an SM relationship. Can you trust someone who is lying to both you and his wife?

Mistress Manners

Perhaps you are under the mistaken notion that having freed yourself from the sexual conventions, you are freed from social conventions as well. Not so; while SM etiquette may vary from that which your mother drummed in to you, there are rules of polite behavior.

Many of the baby-boomers, remembering the rebellions of their youth, find formal rules of behavior stultifying or inhibiting. Shared expectations, however, can help avoid misunderstanding and preserve people's feelings. Once you've demonstrated boorish behavior it is difficult to turn that impression around. Manners are the oil that keeps the social wheels turning.

Mistress Manners has kindly accepted our invitation to answer a few frequently asked questions and to offer a few guidelines to make things flow easier. It may prevent some unmeaning gaucherie.

Mistress Manners

"My kink is okay, but yours is not." One of the strangest, yet most common phenomena is the newcomer to the scene who, after winning a struggle many years long to accept himself for his own kinky desires, puts down those of others. It becomes particularly humorous in retrospect, when, as happens often, he later he finds he enjoys these activities himself. Be tolerant of others and open-minded. You may have a broader range than you thought.

Public scenes are invitations to watch, not to join in. If the top wants assistance, he'll ask for it. Never interrupt a scene by talking to a dom while he's working on a sub. It breaks his concentration and can spoil the mood of the scene. Never talk to the sub who is doing a scene. Besides spoiling the mood, the broken concentration can set back the sub to a level where pain is pain once again... ouch!

It is considered a courtesy to ask the person who appears to be in charge before talking to his collared submissive. Asking a dom you do not know to allow you to use his submissive is tacky, and in most cases, resented.

Deciding who pays the expenses of the evening is no easier in the scene than elsewhere. Generally it is the man unless some other arrangement is negotiated in advance. We are a community that thrives on romance and fantasy; this includes some archaic conventions. The submissive male pays for everything out of respect for his mistress. The dominant male pays as part of the controlling and nurturing role. There are a few dominant men who expect the female submissive to pay for things, but this is rarer.

Yes, it's unfair. If you still believe life is fair you are far too naive to be playing with the grownups. When two people know each other well, they make whatever arrangements suit their circumstances. If a couple decides to go "dutch" they should have enough class to not haggle over the check.

Most gifts are forever. Collars are an exception. The collar "given" to the submissive usually remains the property of the dominant to be returned when "forever" turns out to be a little shorter than anticipated. Unlike other gifts of clothing or jewelry, a collar is most frequently bought by the dominant to remind you, symbolically, of your submission to him. It remains his collar.

A collar can engender deep emotional responses from both submissives and their dominants. If the collar was purchased or made for you alone, he will not use it on his next sub unless he is totally gauche. Collars that are used casually as part of bondage equipment are treated like ordinary toys. The collar that a male sub is directed by his mistress to buy for himself belongs to him.

Most good manners here, as elsewhere, are handled best by laying back and observing how others around you behave. People are also amazingly eager to answer questions and smooth the entry of newcomers to the scene. If you aren't sure, ask. You are the greenhorn, having entered a new country and having yet to learn the customs. People tend to gravitate to those with similar values, so it is likely that you will find shared behaviors among compatible people. Be considerate of other people and apologize when you goof (even if you are dominant, mistakes happen).

Photo of Mistress Sabrina by Jerry

4 " You Want To Worship My WHAT???"
Negotiation and Relationships

n a quiet Cleveland cafe, a couple absorbed in intimate conversation lingers over coffee amidst the ruins of a completed meal. They have the look of lovers. Josh is doing most of the talking in a steady voice not much above a whisper. His focus is on the reactions of his companion to the word pictures he paints for her. His eyes, islands of intensity in the calm sea of his face, reflect his studied attention on the girl who would be his lover.

Cheryl's visage is a turbulent ballet of changing expressions as her emotions are manipulated by his words. The steady sound of his voice is broken, occasionally, by her gasps, sighs, and embarrassed giggles. When she can gleefully add to the fantasies being woven, the interruption to his storytelling is longer. Cheryl's trepidation is undisguised. She stares down at the table to avoid his eyes during a momentary blush and attempts to regain composure with a drag on her cigarette.

She listens intently as he describes in great detail the scenarios and bondages that might be done to her. She adds detail at times to scenes that appeal to her. Other ideas are curtly dismissed with an "ewww," a "yuck," or a "No way!" If she is too embarrassed to admit to liking a hot idea, that, too, is betrayed by a deep silent swallow. When her responses are clear in meaning, both by expression and words, Josh makes a mental note. Those times when she seems almost overwhelmed or when it appears difficult for her to talk, he relentlessly pursues the topic until her feelings are unmistakable.

"Gee, that's something I have always wanted to try." "Wow, I don't think I could do that." "You want to WHAT?" "Ummm maybe, but..." Cheryl is voicing phrases that Josh has heard often. Buried amidst the many ideas he is testing on her in fantasy, are those things he may someday carry out. He is not concerned about ruining some future surprise, nor is he creating a blueprint or game plan that he must follow slavishly in the future. There are so many possibilities, that there is not enough time in the world to do even a fraction.   He is now getting her consent, her agreement, making her a co-conspirator in the process. Her likes, dislikes, what scares her, and what makes her hot are filed away for future reference. Meanwhile, they are enjoying the process. She savors the anxieties and expectations. He loves the effect he is having on her.

This is negotiation. The excitement playing over Cheryl's features, the sparkle in her eyes, the frequent blushes, her shy giggles, his whispered propositions and the wetness they evoke will become the basis for an intense sexual encounter. Any loss in spontaneity is more than made up for in anticipation.

Exchanging fantasies with a potential playmate is frequently the beginning of the negotiation process.   Reaching this agreement does not lock one into anything. Negotiation is an open-ended process. As likes, needs, and desires change they are constantly renegotiated.

"You want to worship my WHAT???" is a quote from Mistress Eva Bathory, a professional domina from New York City, and is used here with her permission.

There is a huge diversity in style of play and expectations among scene people. Only the basic premise that SM play be safe, sane, and consensual is shared by all. Everything else is open to interpretation. So, to attain consensus regarding expectations, intentions, and safety, we negotiate.

Outside the scene it is common for people to learn their partner's likes, dislikes, and eccentricities gradually, over time. They often verbalize their erotic preferences solely in the language of grunts, groans, moans, and the occasional, "Oh god, please don't ever stop." This process of learning in mid-frolic is haphazard at best, and it is totally unworkable in the practice of SM.

As Jay Wiseman put it in his book, *SM-101*, "When two people are alone together, and one of them is naked and tied up, and the other is standing over them holding whips and other torture implements, this is not the time to have a serious mismatch of expectations."

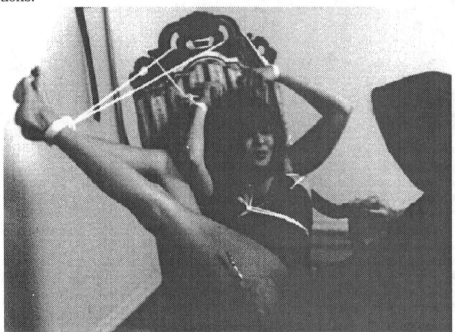

Compatibility

The mystery of sexual attraction has been doing its job since the dawn of the species. Certainly, sexual attraction reigns supreme in our selection of lovers. Yet, as we mature we learn that looking through the world through lust-colored glasses alters our judgment and perception significantly.

Eventually, we discover that there is more to building a relationship than a set of tight buns, a terrific pair of melons, a baritone that can melt steel, a sultry whisper that can singe eyebrows, a slink, a swagger, a bounce, a bulge, shoulders of granite, or legs that go way up to "here." We learn to glance above, below, and to the sides of our hormonal lenses to focus on qualities and attitudes that will be compatible with our own.

But, what makes a dominant and a submissive compatible? Everyone's fantasies are complex, personal, and unique. It is often helpful to write down the qualities of your ideal fantasy partner. This exercise can help you understand your own attractions, limitations and tastes. If you can swap ideals with a prospective partner, you will see the areas that will require compromise. The following are two romantic expressions reflecting idealized styles and values.

The ideal dominant

The ideal master controls himself, so that he might control his submissive. He will, as stern dominant, cause tears to flow, and, as lover, kiss them away. An unashamed romantic, he cherishes his submissive lady. Yet always, he remains aware of the difference between fantasy and reality. When there is need he is ready to leave the roles behind to be a friend.

He understands that to own a woman, one must court the mind with intelligence and humor; win the spirit with compassion and warmth; and take the body with determined strength. He is old-fashioned enough to be gallant and chivalrous. Naturally protective, he would fight for his lady's honor. He understands and accepts the differences between men and women, but is modern enough to know there is no inferiority to it.

He is the honorable sadist who uses pain to extend the bounds of pleasure, vigilant that no harm comes of the hurt. He is the mentor and guide who takes his lady into flight, the wind beneath her wings and her tether to the earth. Enveloping the submissive in his strength, he lends her the courage to reach new heights.

The good dominant is not lazy, mentally or physically. He researches carefully his toys of choice. He seeks out those having the skills and knowledge to teach him to use those toys properly. Then, he practices each skill he would have, whip to cane. Trusting nothing to chance, he tests everything first on his own body.

He is patient enough to learn his submissive well. Aware of the fragile nature of the human mind and spirit, he would not violate those entrusted to his keeping. He knows that submission to him will deepen as trust grows and control will extend as affection increases.

Confident in his dominance, he has no need of silly posturing. He accepts titles as tokens of respect and kneeling as outward expression of genuine feeling. He has no desire to cheapen these by compelling as ritual. He understands that the compliance that comes out of fear of punishment is weak at best. While the obedience engendered from real submissive feeling and the desire to please one's master is unequivocal.

He is secure enough to laugh at himself and the absurdities of life, courageous enough to accept assistance, open-minded enough to learn new things, and strong enough to grow. His tools are mind, body, spirit, and soul, with assistance from whip, chain, and blindfold. He understands that each partner gains from pleasuring the other. Most of all, he knows love as the only chain that truly binds.

(photo: Jerry)

The ideal submissive

My ideal submissive will know the difference between strength and stubbornness, preferring the former to the latter. I don't do brats. Still, I want someone with a solid sense of self-worth. Someone who is happy being who she is and can communicate what it is that she wants.

What she wants, naturally, will be the complement of what I want. She will treasure romance and be thrilled by heady, perilous, dramatic fantasy.

We will be desperately in love with love and in love with each other. We will never be able to get enough of each other, foregoing food, family, and fortune in order to stay in bed together. She will find me completely fascinating and I will find in her humanity's most beautiful, elegant, and delightful creation.

Outwardly we will appear as doting lovers, even sickeningly so. Because between us there will be such easy communication as to leave no room for argument, such dedication that one never wants for affection from the other, such commitment to each other's happiness that one never thinks to manipulate the other to satisfy personal needs. Easy communication, dedication, and commitment are just manifestations of the intimacy we will share. The driving force beneath it all will be a common need, one so primal that it cannot be defined by words, it can only be alluded to by metaphor.

For at the core of my ideal beloved's sexuality will be an urgent longing to surrender to and be thoroughly consumed by a sexual beast. It isn't important for her to realize, at the outset, that she is half the beast's body and I am its other half. It will be all the sweeter when we discover that together.

Because, if she is the right one for me, and I the right one for her, our coupling will be like locking in battle to get outside of ourselves and into each other, always searching for the beast. With each coupling, I will lead her further along a path of discovery guided by a beacon of pain. She'll submit happily each time as I show her how to transform the pain into pleasure, using each stroke of the whip to take another step in our quest.

Then, while our passions find ever stronger release, surging and melding, drawing strength from deeper and deeper sources within us, the beast will at last rise between us, creating itself of raw intensity, heat, and obsession. It will hover over us, surround us, suffuse our every straining, groaning fiber while we spit our lovers' rage from between clenched teeth. It will take control of us, tearing away the layers of virtue and morality that define us as individuals, laying bare two aboriginal souls, merged as one in a combat of primitive heat. This is the fire that feeds the beast, and in giving it life, we will bask in the light of its power. But the beast lives only as long as our bodies can sustain the tempest and when we reach our final gust of fury, its body is ripped again in two, the halves sucked back into each spent lover.

No, it isn't pure, honorable, and chaste love that I seek from my ideal submissive, though I cherish this, too, and have been lucky enough to find an exquisite love with more than one. But my ideal submissive, my perfect lover, will be the woman who can, time after time, become the mother of our bastard child, a beast of unfettered lust.

The ideals stated above are individual expressions. There are a multitude of other styles. What is silly to one individual is an essential ingredient in another's fantasy. Sometimes in the negotiation process, it becomes overwhelmingly clear that your fantasies or concepts are too far apart for an SM relationship to work. This shouldn't be looked at negatively. It saves months of frustration and unhappiness. The two of you may decide that while the SM relationship is unworkable, you can enjoy limited play together.

Finding a good match for your styles, roles, and desires is only the beginning of negotiating. Next you discuss where, when, and how you will play. Which fantasies do you really want to pursue and which would you prefer to remain grist for the masturbatory mill? Will dominance and submission be limited to the duration of a session, will it be part of the overall way in which you relate to each other, or do you relate to each other more as top and bottom than dom and sub?

Some people may have fantasies of switching from top to bottom. If you and your partner like to switch, it is a good idea to agree on a rule of no retaliation. Otherwise, your scenes can deteriorate to little more than "tit for tat" sessions because of mistakes that are best forgotten.

Negotiating sex in SM

> I just don't feel like having sex anymore unless I know somebody is going to get hurt.
> **Mistress Eva Bathory**

It is essential to discuss sexual intercourse regarding your SM relationship. To some it is an important part of the scene relationship while others absolutely do not want it. If you haven't reached agreement here, someone will end up very unhappy. As one women who has been a long time in the scene explains:

"Submissive feelings seem to be a natural part of my sexual response. I submit to my lover which reinforces and intensifies the feelings of lust and affection that are already there. When I am between relationships, I occasionally bottom to friends just for the physical enjoyment of bottoming, but it lacks the magic of real submission. I tend to see a dominant who wants to control me outside of a sexual, romantic relationship, as just another asshole who wants order me around."

Another scene person has the opposite opinion:

"It's very simple really. I enjoy giving erotic pain and domination to masochists who desire it. They may have boyfriends or others in their lives who fill their other sexual needs. It doesn't really matter, the need for pain and control is a separate thing."

Both of these attitudes, while dramatically different, are common to the scene. Clearly, they are incompatible with each other. Levels and types of commitment within SM relationships are infinite in their possibility. Whether seeking a casual play partner, a deep romance, or a potential spouse, sexual goals must be verbalized.

You must also concur on multiple partner, same gender involvement, and the various types of sexuality you would like to pursue. Please, please, please always discuss and adhere to safer sex practices.

Explaining one's feelings completely is important. What one person views as a "light" scene may have his lover pressing assault charges. For example, does a "group scene" mean getting a public spanking or does it include sex with the entire defensive lineup of the Cleveland Browns? Be clear and thorough.

Levels of dominant and submissive power exchange

As with the roles of dominant and submissive, many people have developed a fairly clear idea of what they want and expect in an SM relationship. For many people, dominance and submission are not a part of SM play, but to those for whom it is, we offer the following formula for linking levels of power exchange with the depth of a relationship.

The specifics are less important than the concept of mutual give and take in a D/S relationship. One of the most common types of psychological abuse we see is by the dominant who demands submission without being willing to assume the responsibilities that domination entails.

The following schema is based on certain assumptions:

1) Everything done is in SM is safe, sane, and consensual. A lot is said in that little sentence. Safe is pretty clear. Sane means we don't do things to screw up each other's heads and we don't pull stunts that will land one of us in a loony-bin, intensive care unit, or grave (though, sometimes you have to pray and keep your fingers crossed). Consent, though, needs some discussion. Full disclosure is required to achieve this, because uninformed consent is not true consent. More importantly, most of us can't be certain that what we think our partner thought was meant, is really what our partner thought we meant until we have elaborated it. If you barely understood that last statement you have an idea how hard some thoughts are to convey.

2) There is no inherent inequality in the roles of dominant and submissive. Both people are equally deserving of respect. Everything done is equally for the benefit of both people involved.

3) The exchange of power is a truly balanced exchange. One cannot receive more than one is willing to give. The prerogatives are commensurate with the responsibilities willing to be assumed. Imbalances in the desires for depth of relationship must be addressed. Continued imbalance, when one partner wants to get more than he or she is willing to give, will be met by resentment and anger.

4) Human beings are capable of a vast range of emotional responses to each other. Loving responses can range from being honorable as a reflection of feeling toward all mankind to deep romantic love.

Love is not linear. Between honor and romantic love exist warmth, fondness, and affection, plus types and degrees of love for which English lacks the appropriate words. Love is not a single thing that can be boxed and labeled. Each loving relationship is as different as the people feeling it, both in type and in depth. Human beings have an infinite capability for loving. One type of relationship detracts from another only while the people involved exercise limited imagination and emotional flexibility.

The level of intimacy in a relationship depends upon the degree to which two people are willing to become vulnerable to one another. While wading through the murky swamp of a loving relationship, questions of trust, commitment, communication, and differing life objectives thrash about your legs like so many hungry alligators. Dominant and submissive roles are intended to enhance passion. Sometimes though, the roles can interfere with honest expression of self. Few of us survive the stroll without acquiring a few "gater hickies". It is important to set aside time to take off the masks of mysterious dominant and selfless submissive to express our real feelings.

Power exchange level one: conditional compliance

This is an agreement to play casually (do a scene, or a set of scenes during a weekend), the SM equivalent of a one night stand. The playmates are agreeing in a spirit of mutual respect to perform limited physical activities or role play together to the satisfaction of their own needs. Neither person is expected to perform any activity that does not give him/her pleasure or that does not enhance his/her own fantasy.

Trust level: One person will not physically injure the other.

Dominant: The prerogatives of the dominant are limited to those expressly given by the submissive. The dom should not expect or encourage deep submissive feeling, and should not attempt any pushing of limits. He remains responsible for maintaining safety.

Submissive: The submissive is responsible for clear communication of limits. The sub should endeavor not to allow herself to sink into a depth of submissive feeling that makes them overly dependent on her partner's judgment.

This is more of an encounter than a relationship and its success is measured solely in terms of immediate gratification. (How fun!)

Power exchange level two: restricted ongoing acquiescence

Here, the agreement to play casually is extended. The playmates are agreeing in a spirit of mutual respect to continue to perform limited physical activities and/or limited role play together to satisfaction of each person's own needs. Neither is expected to perform any activity that does not give him/her pleasure or does not enhance his/her own fantasy. As an ongoing relationship, the partners know each other better and should attempt to give a moderate level of satisfaction.

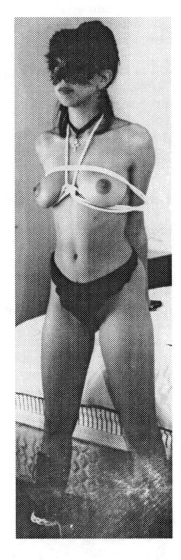

Trust level: Some elements of psychological as well as physical safety can be considered. The submissive will not have any real emotional dependence upon the dominant except during the course of a scene.

Dominant: The basic prerogatives of the dominant remain the same as in level one. The dom should refrain from assuming greater power while the other person is psychologically vulnerable. He may assign small tasks, only if it enhances the shared fantasy. He may do "play punishment" only if both agree that it enhances the fantasy. The dominant may only "force" the sub into acts requested by her. Any suggestions to the sub not directly related to her own scene activities are advisory in nature (as a friend).

Submissive: The basics remain the same as level one with the following additions: the sub may agree to accept small tasks or minor "play" punishments if it enhances the fantasy and may also agree to act in a requested style for the other's fantasy, but she is not expected to internalize this.

As in level one, the success of this relationship is measured solely in terms immediate gratification. Any activity not fun for both people should be abandoned.

Power exchange level three: provisional submission

This relationship is characterized by sincere concern for the other's welfare and genuine fondness. Each partner is willing to devote some time and energy to satisfying the other's emotional and sexual needs.

Trust level: Each partner has made a genuine effort to understand the needs and motivations of the other. The submissive will not have any real emotional dependence upon the dominant except during the course of a scene.

Dominant: Often, the submissive gives the dominant the right to make a few minor restrictions. Very minor penalties for violations may be agreed upon. Real punishments or deep humiliation is inappropriate at this or any other level. While the dom can expect deep submissive feeling in the submissive at times, he is careful not take advantage of this psychologically vulnerable state. The dominant should not seriously push limits. He may assign tasks, but nothing that requires significant time or resources from his submissive. The dominant may only "force" the sub into acts requested by her or where reasonably dependable knowledge of the submissive indicates a given act would be welcomed and appreciated. In these cases, the dom must be prepared to back down quickly, if he is wrong. Suggestions to the sub not related to their scene activities may become advisory in nature; here the dominant is becoming accepted as a mentor or guide.

Submissive: She is responsible for good communication of her limits and for helping the dominant to understand them thoroughly. The submissive may allow herself to sink into submissive feelings that make her temporarily emotionally dependent on her partner's judgment. The sub may agree to accept tasks, instructions, and accept minor play penalties. The sub will now make an attempt to behave in a style for the dominant's approval with minor internalization of theses norms. Respect for her dominant's desires and opinions can usually be observed by the submissive's behavior.

The success of this relationship is measured in terms of emotional satisfaction as well as immediate gratification. Each partner will have made some effort to modify his behavior to please the other.

Power exchange level four: The covenant of dominance and submission

This relationship is characterized by deep emotional involvement and mutual devotion. Each partner desires to satisfy the other's emotional and sexual needs. Frequently, the dom and sub have fallen in love. They have entered a symbiotic relationship. In some relationships, daily life retains some, or quite a bit, of the dom/sub flavor of the bedroom. "Master" is no longer merely an honorarium, but is deeply felt title by the submissive. "Lord" or "Master" and "slave" or "pleasure slave" and the like are appropriate and respectful terms of endearment. The bond felt by dominant and submissive is characterized by feelings of belonging and responsibility to each other. At this level SM partners may feel a desire to have a concrete symbol of their bond by body modification such as piercing, tattooing, or branding, or the submissive may wish to be collared by her dominant.

Collaring is often observed at lower levels of commitment, too, depending upon the potency the players attach to the symbol. For some, a provisional "training collar" is worn from the outset of the relationship with the understanding that it will be replaced with a more resplendent one once the slave's "training" is completed. Some dominants and submissives feel as strongly about their collar as they would about a wedding ring.

Trust level: Each of the partners loves and understands the other. Things not immediately enjoyable are done for the long-term good of the relationship and each other. The submissive will develop some emotional dependence on the dominant, which the dominant welcomes and accepts responsibility for.

Dominant: The submissive gives to the dominant the right to make restrictions and give instructions. Deep submissive feelings will characterize sessions, and the dom is careful with this psychologically vulnerable state. Seriously pushing limits is often a common goal. There is more responsibility for maintaining safety as the submissive is less capable of decision making. The dominant may ask that which takes significant time or resources (but will also devote significant time and resources to the relationship). As the dominant is now a respected loved one who is deeply concerned about the sub's welfare, the submissive may welcome advice and assistance in non-scene areas of her life. The dominant feels deep respect for the submissive and a desire to protect, help, and care for her.

Submissive: The submissive remains responsible for helping the dominant to understand her well. She must make a sincere effort not to allow submissive feelings or the intense desire to please the dominant interfere with honest communication. She may sink into submissive feelings that make her temporarily dependent on her partner's judgment, but must continue to maintain her integrity as an independent person. The sub will have a strong desire to please her dominant, frequently defer to his judgment, and will agree to obey some orders. She will usually internalize the dominant's style. She has deep respect for the dominant's desires and opinions.

Power exchange level five: absolute ownership

This relationship is characterized by the submissive's total adoration and obedience to her Master. The Master is the most important person in the slave's life. The desire by the sub to give obedience, deference, and deep devotion is absolute and constant.

Trust level: The slave maintains the conviction that decisions made by her Master are never to be questioned. There are no limits, as the slave is the property of the dominant.

Dominant: The Master may do as he sees fit with his property, to the point of selling her when she no longer pleases him. All errors and disobedience will be met with punishment, at the Master's whim.

Submissive: The slave has been trained not only to obey, but to anticipate the desires of her Master. She welcomes correction when she fails to live up to this expectation. Her pleasure comes from pleasing him and she has no relevant needs of her own. She is freed from the burden of considering her welfare as her only concern is the pleasure of her Master. She lives to serve.

This is the realm of the "True Master" and the "real submissive" who live in the pages of novels by Anne Rice, John Norman, and in the true confessions of John Q's *The Q-Letters*. This is fantasy-time, folks. We might belabor the point of how damaging this kind of relationship could be, were we not already certain that those attempting this are already pretty psychologically damaged.

Ownership and lifestylers

To be serious for a moment, we are not putting down the slave-master fantasy. There are wonderful relationships that center around this special kind of bonding. It is an important component in SM life. We have, however, seen enough abuse justified by the ownership concept to make us wary.

It may appear obvious as to why a dom would wish to "own" a slave. Yet, the strongest desire for this element in the SM relationship frequently comes from the submissive. Why would an adult wish to be treated like a small child, unable to make decisions on her own?

The first thought that comes to many minds is a desire to escape from responsibility. There is an ingredient of this in the recipe for slavery. A person with a life full of responsibility may need a break from being in control. This alone is not usually the foundation of the desire for ownership.

Most women in our culture still function within traditional roles. Acting as mother, nurse, teacher, social worker, or secretary they are the nurturers, care-givers, and protectors of the children and men (sometimes they find it difficult to tell the difference) in their lives. Seldom does anyone perform this function for them. In exchange for service and obedience, a slave is nurtured and protected. Something is being done "for them," rather than, as usual, by them for someone else.

Being a slave may seem preferable to being a housewife as it acknowledges her services rather than taking them for granted. In fact, it is a running joke in the SM community that the major difference between a housewife and a slave is that slavery is consensual.

Slavery is an intensely romantic notion. What greater gift to give a lover than oneself? And how affirming is it to have your lover accept that control! When told how to dress, to talk, or to behave, a person becomes the focus of attention. The feeling of being owned is a feeling of being wanted, belonging, being cared for, and being loved.

There are people in the scene who refer to themselves as lifestylers. Most lifestylers have the same views and feelings about the practice of SM that we have outlined in our writing. They believe that SM must be safe, sane, and consensual. They advocate negotiation, limits, and safe words. Most of all, they understand that SM must sustain and nurture the physical and spiritual needs of both partners equally.

The lifestyler differs from the average person in seeing SM as a way of life rather than as role play or a sexual orientation. They think of dominance and submission as a philosophical belief system that they have integrated into their daily existence. Still, they remain aware of reality and make the adjustments required to function within our society.

Successful long-term relationships formed in this model between a male dom and a female submissive tend to resemble marriages of an earlier era, but with better communication. The master is titular head of the household, but there is mutual respect and the opinions of the slave are extremely important to her master. Call it what you like, this is Donna Reed with whips and chains.

We don't want to lose sight of the fact that there are also plenty of lifestylers for whom the woman is the head of the manor. In fact, there are probably more Don Reeds than there are Donna Reeds. Obviously, same sex relationships avoid many of the traditional hurdles and stigmas associated with heterosexuality, yet they encounter a wholly different set of problems. You can run, if you like, but you just can't hide from yin and yang.

Paradoxical though it sounds, personal codes can be worked out to allow the philosophy of total control to co-exist with actual sharing of decision making. Sometimes this is done by declaring certain areas of the submissive's life "out of bounds." Other times there is tacit acceptance that certain things will be decided by the submissive with the dom's agreement being nearly automatic. There are no hard and fast rules about how to make such a relationship work other than the maintenance of mutual respect and good communication.

The flip side of absolute domination is complete dependence. A responsible person taking unlimited control will have answers to the following. What happens to a dependent slave when her keeper is too ill to control? What happens if the relationship ends? What is to be done with a helpless sub if her partner dies? In other words, who cleans up after the elephants when the circus show is finished? Resurrecting the custom of *suttee* and having the slave throw herself on the funeral pyre of her master is extreme, but tidy.

Abandoning conventional patterns and reinventing the structure for relationships is a tricky endeavor. A manifesto proclaiming freedom from vanilla standards will not alter human nature. Constructing a relationship that better meets the personal needs of the individuals than a conventional coupling is an ambitious undertaking. When layers of reality and fantasy intertwine this can become very creative.

We knew a lovely lesbian woman who fantasized about being a small boy. When she submitted to a bisexual male dominant, her little boy persona appealed to his gay persona. In their imaginative imagery they were involved in a gay male relationship. Outlandish as it sounds, it worked for them.

The three biggest lies

Everyone knows the three biggest lies: "the check is in the mail," "I will love you forever," and "I'm from the government and I'm here to help you." Every person involved with the SM scene has heard his own version of the three biggest lies. (A drum roll, please maestro). They are: "my only need is to serve," "real submissives don't have limits," and the ever popular, "I am only giving my submissive what she wants." With minor modification by Milton Bradley they can furnish hours of amusement for the terminally bored.

"My only need is to serve," is the classic line of the new male submissive, but a few fems grab this dream line as well. It is usually either followed by a script specifying, often in exquisite detail, exactly what is meant by serving or, it is the opening round of a game that we call "Guess My Fantasy." When Goodman and Toddson puts this on during prime time, we'll know that SM has gone mainstream. Few dominants will tolerate being told exactly what to do and how to do it, and they are not a class of mind readers, either. Let's find a middle ground, shall we?

"Real submissives don't have limits," is a bit of fancy misused by those at both ends of the whip. The sub-text is that limits are not needed with a true master, who, by definition, is a caring and knowledgeable dom. Basically, there are two types of dominants who don't want limits.

One is dangerous and the other is quite benign. Since they both refer to themselves as true masters, the trick is in telling them apart. The first kind really doesn't give a damn. To this wretch, the submissive is a toy that can be replaced if broken.

True master type two (we will dub him TM2 for brevity) is conscientious and caring, but for obscure internal reasons, needs to maintain the illusion of unlimited control. This fiction is preserved by some not-so-clever camouflage. This master, being conscientious, will insist on having complete knowledge of his slave's (true subs prefer being called slaves) values, fears, medical history, and an annotated biography.

| Suppose, for example, TM2 learns that his new sub is an orthodox vegetarian witch with a spastic colon, who gets vertigo standing on a phone book. The dom, godlike in his perceptiveness, will declare, from on high, that dinner at Barney's Barbecue, burning-at-the-stake scenes, enemas, and suspension from high places must be ruled out.

There are several types of submissives who don't want to set limits, as well. There are the self-destructive ones who want real danger. There are the inexperienced subs who really don't know what limits to set. There are also submissives who prefer to rely solely on careful selection of a dominant, carefully seeking one they can trust not to harm them. The macho submissive may want prove her devotion and submissiveness by not setting the rules of play. All but the self-destructive sub (who must be avoided) is a good match for 'ole TM2. They can work out the boundaries together, and never once will either use the hated word -- limit. The only problem with the TM2s and their slaves is a tendency to put down others who don't subscribe to their mythology. But, what the hell, for the most part they aren't hurting anybody so we'll just hand them top prize in the "How To Convolute Coherent Communication Competition."

"I'm only giving my sub what she wants," is, unfortunately, heard most often as a defense after someone gets injured. Destructive or unhealthy fantasies by the submissive never justifies poor judgment by the person in charge. We know a dom who is fond of saying, "There is nothing as sincere as a wet pussy or a hard cock." This may sound astute on the surface, but so what? A dom must know that, though "activity X" makes his sub hot, it is just too dangerous and must be avoided. He must also consider the current and long-term psychological effects of his actions. A dominant who justifies abuse by saying, "I am only fulfilling fantasies," bears a striking resemblance to the Nuremberg defendants who claimed, "I was only following orders." Control always carries responsibility.

Abusive relationships

Within any group of people, no matter how noble the aspirations of the pack, are the ignorant, the abuser, and the occasional psychopath. Within the group of SM lifestylers is a very small group that we, in our kinder moments, refer to as the "hard-liners". It is here where the major abuse takes place.

"I do not role play master, I am a master," is the way the typical hardline dominant will draw the distinction. Whether this is a harmless conceit or a formula for abuse depends on his interpretation of this nuance, though this statement should be enough to make one suspicious. The abuser does not believe that he is empowered by the consent of the submissive to his control. He believes that the power derives from some mysterious personal source within him. It is a kind of birthright, not unlike the divine right of kings.

The most serious danger to those who engage in this style of SM is psychological. The abuser believes that his needs totally supersede those of his slave. In a common bit of sadomasomythology, once initial consent is given, the submissive loses the right to leave the relationship until formally released by the dominant. The submissive can, of course, be dismissed on a whim. This ignores the reality that submissives can always vote with their feet.

Only consent by the sub allows the dom to maintain control. Every order obeyed is a decision to submit. This paradigm gives the submissive too much power for the insecure dominant. Hopefully, early in a relationship, negotiation will unmask the butthead ... errr, dominant who does not believe he is empowered by the submissive.

Skillful dominants are good at identifying emotional triggers. It is very easy, even tempting to use these buttons destructively or to keep an abusive relationship going. Guilt buttons are a favorite among the unclued. To suggest that a submissive is being a bad sub or not really submissive because she disagrees is a common way of pushing the guilt button. To imply that a submissive is selfish for considering her needs is an attempt to employ guilt to avoid dealing with real issues. It is a way of diverting the subject under discussion from the success of the relationship to the worthiness of the individual.

When a dom or a sub feels that a relationship may not be meeting his or her needs, it is time for straight, serious, out-of-role talk. The dom who, rather than discussing the problem as an equal, attempts to "straighten out" the sub needs some straightening out himself.

A relationship is abusive when it works for one person to the detriment of the other. No sane adult wants a relationship to continue if it is harmful to his partner. Now is the time for talk, talk, and more talk. Some seemingly severe problems are merely the result of misunderstanding. Frequently, people have incompatible needs. Less often, people are deliberately abusive.

Everyone makes mistakes. It is easy to get caught up in emotions and involved with a person whom we only later identify as destructive to our well-being. If you feel that this is the case, regardless of commitments or affections, there are actions you should take. SM is emotionally intense. The pain of ending a relationship may be magnified significantly.

First, get away from the destructive situation. If you are living together, physically leave. If you are involved, but living apart you may need to reduce contact. A clear mental space helps as you rethink the relationship.

Next, talk with a scene-friendly therapist or supportive friends. When a relationship fails, people often feel some blame. You may need bolstering or reassurance that your choice was correct for you.

Ending a relationship where you lived together long enough for property to be accumulated, may require legal advice, even for the unmarried. Feelings of guilt and painful associations frequently have people ready to abandon all, to move on with their lives. Right now you are not in a good head space to make objective decisions alone. A few years down the road you may very much regret a hasty choice to abandon property.

Limits - The lines never to be crossed

Things that are beyond your limits are things that you would absolutely, under no circumstances, never, ever, even consider doing - FEH! Subs must relate the existence of phobias to their doms. The moronic dominant who locks a claustrophobe in a dark closet is a whiz compared to the submissive who neglected to mention her fear of confinement. During the opening-up process of negotiation, minor fears and uncertainties must be revealed for the safety, sanity, and happiness of both partners.

Things that create sexual tension and excitement need to be explored carefully and slowly. Submissives always seem to find a way to furnish the means for their own torture. This is just one of the inherent delights of SM.

There are physical issues to discuss, too. The dominant would rather know about your weak ankles before he spends a fortune on five-inch spike heels with locking straps. Knowledge of the lacrosse injury that makes bending difficult should be verbalized before you are bound-up like a pretzel.

Establish safe words and signals well before the scene begins. A word to stop everything and another to slow things down are common (see the section on safe words, below). "If you do that again I will throw-up" will generally stop the action, but a singularly stalwart dom may merely throw down a plastic sheet before proceeding.

Safe words

Always use a safe word or a safe signal when playing no matter how skilled you are. A safe word is a prearranged verbal signal for use by the sub to tell her dom to stop the scene immediately and release her from bondage. A safe signal has the same use, but is a non-verbal signal for times when m'lady is gagged. Safe words and signals are most commonly used to let the dominant know that his submissive is experiencing a problem that he may not be aware of such as a muscle cramp, numbness caused by bonds, excessive pain, extreme fear, or imminent nuclear attack.

Choose your safe words carefully. Words like NO, DON'T, STOP, and HELP are unacceptable. In the heat of passion, lots of people say these words and don't mean it. As often as not, NO, DON'T, and STOP, really mean, YES, and PLEASE DO, and DON'T STOP!. HELP frequently means, "I'm coming like a bus load of Scarsdale housewives at a Bloomie's half-off sale!" Of course, they can also mean, NO, DON'T, STOP, and HELP. See what we mean? You just can't bank on them.

People also become suddenly religious when the going gets really hot, so safe words evoking various deities and religious figures, or proclaiming things like "Holy Shit"and "Oh my God!" aren't going to cut it either.

Many people use what has come to be called the stop light method. YELLOW means "This is getting very difficult, ease up, buster," and RED means "Cool it immediately! This scene is officially over! Get me outtahere, NOW!" Some people also use GREEN too, to indicate, "Hey, this feels really good, please don't stop!" We like these safe words; they are clear, easy to say, and easy to remember.

Another common practice is to use the submissive's full name. Chances are, she won't easily forget it. If neither of these appeals to you, find a word that will be so out of context in a scene that the dominant will recognize the situation immediately. "Safe word" itself is becoming a popular for use as a safe word. People often declare it as the official safe word for use during play parties.

If m'lady is chomping on a gag during your scene, it's important to devise a non-verbal signal. Have her hold a ball or bell in her fingers. She drops the ball or continuously rings the bell to tell you something is going on that's definitely uncool. You might want to accompany the ball-drop or bell-ring with a predetermined series of short grunts. Even if the gaggage is severe, at least some sound still escapes.

Gagged people can also choose the safe signal of repeatedly squeezing their dominant's hand or whatever body part presents itself.

Whichever safe word or signal you choose, be sure that it is clear, unmistakable, and thoroughly discussed. Every time you include another element to your scenes, be it gaggage, bondage, or what have you, you are increasing the likelihood for error and danger. Insist that the submissive practice it a few times as the scene begins. It may seem silly, but hearing yourself verbalize the word a few times actually makes it easier to say it when you need it. When it's clear that she knows what to say or do if she finds herself in trouble, it's okay to let the subject drop and get on to happier business... like twisting her nipples!

<u>IMPORTANT NOTE FOR DOMINANTS: DO NOT DEPEND UPON THE SUB</u> to say the safe word if she's reached her limits or is having a problem! As a dominant, you are responsible for knowing your submissive's condition at all times. A safe word is simply an additional safety valve. Remember that if you are successful with your technique, your submissive will be leaving earth's orbit in a way that would make NASA envious. While in this state (traveling somewhere in the vicinity of Jupiter) she cannot be depended upon to know if she is being damaged.

Under very stressful times, submissives can forget their safe words because they are panicked, too spaced-out, or confused. We find that safe words are more commonly used during less stressful times than reaching outside limits of endurance. While in bondage, for example, too much pressure may be exerted on her shoulders, a beating may be progressing too quickly to be enjoyable, or she simply doesn't feel right about what you are doing. Small irritations like these will distract your submissive from being able to place her focus where you want it to be. It is much better to stop for a minute, correct the problem, then resume the scene.

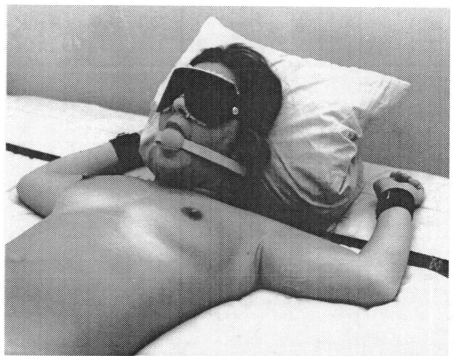

A safe signal for a gagged submissive can include a predetermined series of short grunts. Even if the gaggage is severe, at least some sound still escapes.

Submissives do not like to use their safe words. It may feel to them as though they are criticizing their dominant, that they are being wimpy, or that they just do not want to stop the scene. A safe word is just like a seatbelt, it isn't there because you don't trust the driver, it is there because things happen accidentally that are nobody's fault. Accidents DO happen; always use safe words or signals.

Contracts and agreements

Slave contracts giving total control of one person over the other can fuel a fantasy. They have no force in law except, perhaps, as evidence. We've seen ones that even include arbitrary body modification as a right of the dominant. To be more than a prop for sexual psychodrama they need to be realistic in scope. Creating a document together, reflecting real needs, goals, and aspirations can be a wonderful exercise. The process of writing can help you define your relationship more clearly. Elaborate contracts make sense for longer term relationships. A brief document may be appropriate for a weekend or a new relationship.

The following is a sample contract of submission:

Agreement of Service

I, _____ with a free mind and an open heart; do request of _____ that he accept the submission of my will unto his and to take me into his care and guidance, that we may grow together in love, trust and mutual respect. The satisfaction of his wants, desires, and whims are consistent with my desire as a submissive to be found pleasing to him. To that end, I offer him use of my time, talents, and abilities.

Further, I ask, in sincere humility, that, as My Master, he accept the keeping of my body for the fulfillment and enhancement of our sexual, spiritual, emotional, and intellectual needs. To achieve this, he may have unfettered use of my body any time, anyplace, in front of anyone; to keep or to give away, as he will determine.

I ask that he guide me in any sexual, sensual, or scene related behavior, both together with, and separate from him, in such a way as to further my growth as a person.

I request of _____, as My Master, that he use the power vested in his role; to mold and shape me; assisting me to grow in strength, character, confidence, and being, and that he continue to help me to develop my artistic and intellectual abilities.

In return, I agree:

To obey his commands to the best of my ability.

To strive to overcome feelings of guilt or shame, and all inhibitions that interfere with my capability to serve him; and limit my growth as his submissive.

To maintain honest and open communication.

To reveal my thoughts, feelings, and desires without hesitation or embarrassment.

To inform him of wants and perceived needs, recognizing that he is the sole judge of whether or how these shall be satisfied.

To strive toward maintenance of a positive self-image and development of realistic expectations and goals.

To work with him to become a happy and self-fulfilled individual.

To work against negative aspects of my ego and my insecurities that would interfere with advancement of these aims.

My surrender as a submissive is done with the knowledge that nothing asked of me will demean me as a person, and will in no way diminish my own responsibilities toward making utmost use of my potential. In recognition of my family obligations, nothing will be required of me that will in anyway damage or harm my children, nor interfere with the performance of my duties as mother and as wife.

This I, _____, do entreat, with lucidity and the realization of what this means, both stated and implied, in the conviction that this offer will be understood in the spirit of faith, caring, esteem and devotion in which it is given.

Should either of us find that our aspirations are not being well served by this agreement, find this commitment too burdensome, or for any other reason wish to cancel, either may do so by verbal notification to the other, in keeping with the consensual nature of this agreement. We both understand that cancellation means a cessation of the control stated and implied within this agreement, not a termination of our relationship as friends and lovers. Upon cancellation, each of us agrees to offer to the other his or her reasons and to assess our new needs and situation openly and lovingly.

This agreement shall serve as the basis for an extension of our relationship, committed to in the spirit of loving and consensual dominance and submission with the intention of furthering self-awareness and exploration, promoting health and happiness, and improving both our lives.

I offer my consent to submission to _____ under the terms stated above on this the _____ day of _____ in the year ____, _____

I offer my acceptance of submission by _____ under the terms stated above on this the _____ day of _____ in the year ____, _____

Negotiation Questionnaire

To give people an assist in starting the discussion process, we've come up with a questionnaire that while admittedly doesn't cover all the possible activities and questions,

Pre-scene Negotiation Questionnaire

This private information will not go into a government file, on your permanent school record, or be given to your mother, so be honest.

Part I: General information - check all that apply:

1) SM scene experience:
   a) novice   b) experienced

2) Sexual orientation:
   a) heterosexual   b) bicurious   c) bisexual   d) gay

3) Gender orientation:
   a) male   b) female   c) crossdresser   d) transsexual

4) Dominant:
   a) always   b) often   c) rarely   d) never

5) Submissive:
   a) always   b) often   c) rarely   d) never

6) Masochistic:
   a) very b) somewhat c) hardly d) no, those people scare me

7) Sadistic:
   a) very b) somewhat c) hardly d) no, those people scare me

8) Main interest:
   a) sensual - physical (bottom/top)
   b) psychosexual - mental (dominant/submissive role play)
   c) both are equally important

9) Will play at:
   a) anywhere!
   b) my house/apartment
   c) outdoors
   d) parties
   e) at SM clubs
   f) public - near my home
   g) public - a safe distance from home
   other places: _____

10) Who can know of your activities?
    a) I'm so discreet I don't even know what I am doing.
    b) Private play - only my partner needs to know.
    c) A few very trusted friends.
    d) Other scene people can know.
    e) Willing to be in Madonna's next book.

11) How do you feel about other people in your scenes?
    a) I only play with myself.
    b) just me & my partner.
    c) threesome.
    d) small groups.
    e) the more the merrier.
    f) pre-approved people only.

12) How do you feel about service (cleaning, errands, etc.) ?
    a) I live to serve!
    b) Helping my dominant in little ways makes me feel good.
    c) It is part of the fantasy, but don't overdo it.
    d) Exploitive nonsense, I will do what is fun.

13) How do you feel about punishment?
    a) It is part of training and a right of the dominant.
    c) Penalties for "disobedience" enhance the fantasy.
    b) It can be okay as an excuse to have fun.
    c) Pointless; mutual pleasure needs no justification.

14) What bruises or body marks are acceptable?
    a) Leave my body as is or I call my lawyer.
    b) Temporary redness - gone in a few hours.
    c) Occasional accidental bruises are okay.
    d) I expect to carry souvenir bruises for a week.
    e) My ass should look like a road map of Chile.

Sample roles: Amazon * Baby * Barbarian * Bitch-Goddess * Boss * Burglar * Child * Clergy * Cowboy(girl) * Daddy * Doctor * Evil Priest(ess) * Femme Fatale * French Maid * God(ess) * Hooker * Indian * Ingenue * Inquisitor * Interrogator * Hero * Kidnap Victim * Knight * Leather-Macho * Master * Mentor * Mistress * Mommy * Nun * Nurse * Rapist * Role Reversal * Perils of Pauline * Pet * Pimp * Pirate * Policeman * Ponygirl(boy) * POW * Prince(ss) * Principal * Prisoner * Puppy * Sage * Savage * Scientist * Secretary * Sex Object * Sissy * Slave * Slave Owner * Slut * Student * Suspect * Teacher * Teen * Torturer * Victim * Warrior * Wild Beast

Roles I want to play (using above list & own ideas):

_____

Roles I want a partner to play:

_____

Fetishes (example: foot worship, body types):

_____

Wants & perceived needs:

_____

Medical, physical, or emotional concerns (past breaks, sprains, chronic conditions, or phobias):

_____

Limits:

_____

Part II - Preferred Activities

A list of some scene activities with typical responses. Pick the closest response and use the answers to generate embarrassed giggles and discussion. dom (D) and sub (S) enter number (or symbol) indicating their level of interest.

(**1**) Yes!! (Pant, drool)
(**2**) Mmmmmmmm, I like this
(**3**) Doesn't excite me, but I'd do it for you, darling

(**4**) Absolutely not, I will call the cops
(*****) Intriguing, but scary; would push my limits
(**!**) Embarrassed to admit wanting/force me, please!

S D Corporal:
1. spanking (hand)
2. leather paddle
3. wooden paddle
4. belt /strap
5. switch
6. deerskin cat
7. leather cat
8. braided cat
9. rubber whip
10. knotted whip
11. single lash
12. taws
13. cane (rattan)
14. fiberglass/plastic rod
15. riding crop

Bondage:
16. mental bondage
17. silk scarves
18. nylon rope
19. cotton rope
20. chains
22. leather bonds
23. spandex bonds
24. plastic wrap
25. body bags
26. gags
27. leather cuffs
28. steel shackles
29. arm sleeves
30. straight jackets
31. breast bondage
32. genital bondage
33. infibulation
34. spreader bars

S D
35. ceiling/wall hooks
36. cages
37. slings/swings
38. stocks/pillory
39. crosses
40. suspension (on toes)
41. suspension (full)
42. outdoor setting
43. indoor setting
44. public setting
45. semi-public setting
46. private setting
47. 1-3 hour duration
48. 3-6 hour duration
49. overnight duration

Torture & Sensory Deprivation:
50. blindfolds
51. hoods
52. headphone/ear-plugs
53. tickling
54. feathers & fur
55. sexual teasing
56. sexual denial
57. chastity belt
58. pinching
59. hair pulling
60. nipple clips
61. clothes pins
62. genital torture
63. weights
64. cock rings
65. ball stretchers
66. water torture

S D
67. ice
68. oils, lotions, spices
69. hot wax
70. fire & ice
71. needles
72. cuttings
73. abrasion
74. electric torture

Sex:
75. digital sex
76. directed masturbation
77. vaginal sex
78. oral sex
79. vibrator/dildo
80. strap-ons
81. anal sex
82. anal plug
83. multiple penetration
84. anilingus
85. vaginal fisting
86. anal fisting
87. fantasy rape
88. directed bisexuality
89. threesome
90. group

Humiliation & Exhibition:
91. foot kissing
92. kneeling
93. crawling
94. lead on leash
95. dirty words
96. verbal abuse
97. pub. embarrassment

S D
98. face slapping
99. cross dressing
100. secret sex in public
101. public display
102. public sex
103. public whipping
104. infantilism
104. golden shower
105. enema

Dress & Adornment:
106. innocent
107. slutty
108. prim & proper
109. ultra-feminine
110. official domina goddess uniform
111. french maid
112. child/baby
113. slave
114. macho
115. biker
116. leather
117. spandex
118. rubber/latex
119. masks/hoods
120. costumes
121. lingerie
122. garters/stockings
123. corsets/cinches
124. boots
125. high heels
126. tattooing
127. body piercing
128. branding

Comments & added items:

How do you like it ? (use all that apply):

(**N**) never
(**T**) thuddy
(**S**) stingy
(**L**) light
(**M**) medium (ouch)
(**H**) heavy (hurts)
(**?**) unsure

Part of body:	bondage	corporal	torture
back & shoulders			
bottom & thighs			
breasts & chest			
genitals			
feet & ankles			
wrists			

Part III - Checklist (we have discussed):

__Limits and safe words
__Exclusivity and depth of relationship
__Sex and birth control
__Safer sex - current health (infectious diseases, HIV, STDs, herpes), testing, preventative measures (condoms, dental dams)

5 Straight Facts and Bent Phalluses
Sexual Attitudes

"I love oral sex, I can do it for hours and hours."

"I always make sure my woman has an orgasm before I enter her."

"The most important thing to remember about sex is to satisfy your lover."

"No woman wants to have sex with another woman after she's been with a good man."

"Women like their sex hard and fast."

very woman playing the dating game endures these manifestos with cynical amusement. Half of all women experience math anxiety because they are always told that "it" is eight inches long.

Sex is a powerful issue beset by mythology, stigma, and repressive attitudes. It's strange, isn't it, that sex plays such a large and wonderful part in our lives, yet we have so much trouble talking about it. Still, for a sexually tongue-tied society, we sell every product imaginable by insinuating that buying them will improve our sex lives. Sex is implicit, if not blatant, in every novel printed and every movie made, fashion is based on it, hell, you can't even buy a tube of toothpaste without being promised that Brand X will get you laid more often. We arm ourselves with sparkling teeth, disarm our underarms, and make our crotches as inviting as an April shower, but we're still left clueless about handling our love affairs.

Nice people simply don't talk about sex unless they are degreed in psychology. We couch our comments on sexuality so guardedly that our meaning is often misconstrued. Some regard sex as a necessary evil for procreation, others use it as a weapon or device for getting ahead. We teach our children next to nothing about it and what we do teach them is almost entirely designed to scare the crap out of them. Sex is fun, yet we castigate ourselves and others for making light of it. Is it any wonder that we have so little understanding of sexual technique?

Rather than expound upon why our society is so puritanical, we are going to assume that you are reading this because you have cast off the shackles of sexual repression and are ready to snap on the shackles of sexual expression. We want to alter some of the attitudes that keep people from realizing their sexual potential. Let's see if we can assess the issue as it stands.

Thought on sex has long been dominated by a male perspective. This is not only injurious to women, men end up shortchanged by this kind of thinking, too. Kinsey, Masters and Johnson, Nancy Friday, and many other sex researchers found certain presumptions commonplace.

Most men who adjudge themselves sensitive, considerate lovers, engage in foreplay lasting from ten to fifteen minutes, while the sex act itself lasts only a few minutes more. Typically, the goal of foreplay is to get a women to the point where she is wet, warm, and ready for penetration. Most men don't think that they have had sex unless they ejaculate into or at least on, a woman. The man who makes sure his partner also has an orgasm is thought to be a good lover. If he can withhold his orgasm long enough to make his lovemaking last more than thirty minutes he is considered fantastic. It is assumed that men will have (or take) all the pleasure they need from women, so we needn't worry about teaching them ways of enjoying themselves. The most crucial issues addressed are methods of getting a woman into the sack, even if the woman is already your wife! Women's pleasure seems to be discussed as an afterthought; in fact, some men treat women as though they are no more than facilitators or receptacles for a man's sexuality. Frequently, men are threatened by women who openly admit their sexuality. They are suspicious of a woman whose fantasies do not exclusively involve her mate or they feel that if a woman has to fantasize, her man is not satisfying her. Women have just as much right to their fantasies as men do; or perhaps more accurately, women cannot refrain from fantasizing any more than men can. Because of societal pressure, women often buy into this quagmire and try to deny their fantasies. It cannot be done. It is impossible to hide from your own sexuality.

Too often, men and women approach sex as rivals. By doing so we needlessly create anger, distrust, shame, and humiliation. David Steinberg, in his book, *The Erotic Impulse*, said it as well as we have ever heard it expressed:

> **...what we often experience in erotic connection between the genders is more of a tug of war--the battle of the sexual marketplace. Men trying to get sex from women. Women resenting the sexual preoccupations of men. Men angry that women have sex and won't give it to them. Women angry that men try to take something from them through sex.**

> **We become embroiled in elaborate sexual power games, overt and covert. As Wilhelm Reich pointed out, sex becomes a commodity, whose value is inflated by induced scarcity. As with all commodities, a primary question becomes who gets what from whom and at what cost. Implicitly and explicitly, sex comes to be exchanged for money, financial security, attention, personal favors, the illusion of affection. Instead of a dance of love and mystery, we too often experience the erotic as an arena of manipulation...**

What a tragedy, what a senseless loss, to reduce genuine affection to an illusion that we trade upon. But it is easy to slip into this spiral, isn't it?

Another self-defeating aspect of approaching sex as a rivalry is feeling that we have to prove ourselves to each other. We compete to give better or more than we get from the other. Competing to give, isn't that pointless? Let's stop keeping score, it just makes us uncomfortable and discounts the pleasure we get from the gifts we receive. People are not equal, some can do one kind of giving better in one area than in another. It doesn't even matter if one gives more than the other as long as it feels good, whatever the balance is. Let's just enjoy what we get and give what we can.

Orgasm, also, has been too long the focus of sexuality. The word foreplay, itself, is indicative of this. Foreplay is what you do before orgasm, or so that you can have an orgasm, right? Well, what if we were to consider non-coital play an end in itself? What if we abandoned the expectation of intercourse and orgasm every time we feel sexual toward each other? What if each kiss and caress were regarded as complete sex acts instead of preliminaries to copulation? What if orgasm played a part in a session of lovemaking only if it seemed appropriate? How much anxiety could we avoid if we didn't approach sex with predefined expectations?

No goals, no roles

What we're suggesting here is dumping goals of conquest, duration, performance, achieving simultaneous orgasms, etc. We are suggesting that we reject sexual goals altogether. We're also suggesting that we renounce traditional sexual roles and learn to listen to our inner role-models; that we learn to identify those desires that are authentically our preferences and not those which we think we should have. How about just learning to take things as they come (so to speak)? Just as dwelling on the past or on the future leads to despair, focusing on the way sex was or the way you want it to be diminishes the delights of the now. Learn to savor the moment. Don't worry about getting her/him to orgasm or plan for your own. It will happen all on its own. The biologists planned it that way, the clever bastards.

There are a few issues we would like to get out of the way first, though. Guys, Philip would like a word with you alone.

Ladies, will you kindly excuse us men for a while? We have some cigars to smoke, some digestive gasses to expel, and some other manly business to conduct. You would just be bored, so if we may beg your pardon...Molly will be conducting a quilting bee to keep you occupied until our return. Cookies and punch will be served.

Philip's tree house
!!!No Girls Allowed!!!

Men, I'm about to impart to you civilization's most closely guarded sexual secrets...

HEY! Is that a women in the back there? Get out of here, can't you read the sign? Oh, you're a cross-dresser. All right, then. Hey, great hat! (You have to like a guy who knows how to accessorize.)

Now, as I was saying...To obtain these secrets, I have traveled to every continent, seeking the most respected, the most wise, and the most exhausted men in each community.

Now right off the bat, I'm going to tell you that there's nothing I like better than the feeling of that old trouser worm spittin' his load. It's the best three or four seconds of the day, am I right or am I right? But, fellas, if that little squirt and a few provocative poses of a naked lady are all you're expecting from sex, you have been ordering from the kiddie menu.

OK, I'm going to lay it on you straight. Men, you have to learn to make love like women. Don't go getting your jaws all tight, now. I'm not saying that you have to become women; I'm not here to have you pluck off your chest hair. But, there is a lot we can learn from the way women do sex that will help us to get more out of sex than we're getting.

A lot of women are capable of having multiple orgasms to our measly one, and if that ain't enough for ya, some of them say they feel orgasms all over their bodies. Not only that, but they get no end of pleasure out of every kiss and hug you give 'em! Is that fair?

They are having more fun than we are! Is that right? Hell no, it ain't right! (Gary, use the goddamned spittoon there, will ya? Thanks, ole pard.)

Check it out. The next time you're doing the mattress mambo, watch every move she makes. Give her a kiss, one of your best, and watch how she reacts to it. You are going to find that she's enjoying the son-of-a-bitch! That's right, she's enjoying the hell out of one stinkin' kiss! And if that don't beat all, give her back a tender caress from the tippy-top of her neck all the way down across her butt. Same damned thing'll happen, I swear it. There you are, pecking and stroking, not even getting to her tits yet, and she's already having a good time! What the hell's shakin' here?

Now don't get yer shorts all bunched, let me tell you how she's doing it. Whether she realizes it or not, your lady is focusing on what is happening to her right there at the moment. She's not thinking about what it is going to feel like when you have her skivvies down around her ankles, or about how happy she's going to be when you finally shove that power muscle into her sugar-shack, or even about how fine that first puff of the cigarette is going taste when the whole fiesta is over.

Nope, she is sucking that kiss for all it's worth. She feels your arms holding her and she relaxes into them, she feels the heat from your chest pushing against her boobs, she looks into your eyes and feels the attraction in them, she looks at your lips and feels your lust, she feels your lips nibbling at hers, feels your tongue sweeping over hers...

Have you got the picture, boys? Do you know what I'm driving at? Our ladies have more fun because they are know how to take pleasure in every little thing we do to them. A kiss goes right through them. They use their whole bodies as sex organs and guess what, guys, so can we.

Women use their whole bodies as sex organs. A kiss goes right through them.

What we have to do is learn to slow down and enjoy the dance. We have all the same nerve endings they do in our backs and butts and thighs and throats and fingertips. All you have to do to use them is slow down and let it happen. Let the sensations go as far inside you as they will. With a little practice, you'll feel sensations you never thought about before.

The key to this whole sex-thing seems to be about attitudes. You and I have been raised to ignore a big part of ourselves that Mom and Dad thought was only for girls. We were taught to stomp out our emotions. Somehow, our society got the notion that emotionalism stood in the way of being a successful man. So, Mom didn't play with us as much as she did with Sis, and Dad showed us how to be strong and let a lot of our feelings slide off our backs.

All of the sensual stuff was reserved for the enjoyment of the lady-folk. Cooking, flower arranging, etiquette, dancing, art, and decorating were for girls or sissies. We were supposed to pursue the macho endeavors of building things, working on cars, playing ball-sports, hunting, fighting, business, and publicly scratching our crotch. Well, a lot of that is changing for kids, and it's high time it did. All people have both masculine and feminine characteristics, and all those sissy activities help develop an appreciation for pleasure.

Women learn as girls to take pleasure in something as simple and innocent as a gesture. Fictional romance is full of eyes being cast upward, downward, and sidelong -- of breath being drawn sharply, sighed wistfully, and snorted angrily. Actions and deeds, concrete, swashbuckling, and well-defined, were the parlance of our adventure fiction, excluding most of the subtleties so important to girls' literature.

Yes, I am grossly exaggerating the differences between bringing up boys and girls, and sweeping generalities about with an industrial-sized broom. My point is that women have been trained to communicate subtly and, therefore, have been privy to a lot of fun of which we have been robbed.

OK, now listen up. We don't have to put up with this shit one second longer. I have a sure-fire plan here that's gonna get us even-steven on the fun barometer. We have some catching up to do and it's going to be a lot easier than you might think.

The next time you are fixing to haul the old lady into the sack, cut yourself short of slamming her on her back and banging away in the usual way. Stand her up on her feet again, let go of that fistful of hair, and help her straighten her dress just like it was when you spotted her. Oh, and take your finger out of your nose, we're going to do this real sophisticated-like. It will confuse the hell out of her and that's ok. It might even scare the pants off of her and that, obviously, is ok, too.

A word about approach

Don't be pushy. No one reacts well to being pushed into sex. The more you push, the more you will encounter resistance that leads, ultimately, to revulsion. If something is going to happen between the two of you, it will come naturally. If nothing happens, let that be OK with you, too. Let her know that you are happy just being with her and enjoying her company. If she's not ready for closer contact, anything you do to push the matter isn't going to work. A "no" may simply mean, "not yet." You may be being tested to see if you'll walk away when you are refused or stick around for the long haul.

Sign language

People communicate with each other by exchanging messages that follow cycles. Romantic encounters operate on messages that are primarily non-verbal. The pattern runs something like this: signal, action, comprehension, reaction/response, and then the cycle starts all over again with the next signal. What I want you to do is learn to recognize and savor each step of the cycle. Yeah, I know this means you'll have to slow things way down. And yeah, all this extended lovemaking might make you miss Letterman's top-ten list, but you have to suffer if you want to sing the blues.

Let's assume you are out to dinner for the first time with a lady you met at the office. She works in another department so she is a relative stranger. Dinner went well, conversation was warm and pleasant, the check is paid, and question of the rest of the evening is hanging in the air. You could pop a question, "Would you like to have a drink at my place?" or "What shall we do now?" You could simply gather your things and suggest, "Shall we go?" These are the moves of a man of action, but they lack subtlety. They demand a response.

Try instead, establishing a mood by more subtle, non-verbal means. Indicate your feelings for her in a friendly, non-suggestive, non-threatening way. Catch her eye (signal) and give her a warm, friendly, "You sure are a nice lady," smile (action). Watch how she receives your gesture (comprehension). How does she return your smile (reaction/response)? Is she emoting at all? Does she smile back the same way? Is she confused or shy about it? Does she reject your smile and look away?

You never know how your partner will respond and it is often unclear (particularly with new partners) what her response means. That is half the fun of the game. Don't rush, and be playful, but sincere and easy with your signals and the way you respond to hers. Learn to enjoy the game, enjoy the way she reacts to you, and notice the way you react to her.

There are so many variables and various ways to react to them that following all the possibilities would fill volumes. The point is, whole conversations take place without words. I want you to become more aware of that language and how to use it in your relationships.

Rediscovering the joys of the flesh

When things go well the semaphore leads to fleshly adventures. Take your time. Play some games. How hot can you make her by caressing every part of her except her genitalia? Which of you can withstand teasing the longest? Undress her slowly without letting her touch you at all. When she is entirely nude, and you are still dressed, pose her in various lewd positions. Nibble, suck, and caress your prize, observing her reaction to your sensuous scrutiny. If she is embarrassed, offer to blindfold her. If she cannot be still, offer to bind her arms for her. See how easily you can begin to dominate her?

As you make love, remember that she is using her whole body as a sex organ. You can, too. You just have to unlearn a few things that have been socialized into you. A typical male touch is deliberate and direct; men commonly solicit specific reactions from touching here and prodding there. I want you to try to develop a new tool.

By defining sensuality as less intense or at least less important than sexuality, we limit our experience. Women touch without expecting or trying to extract a specific reaction. Their touch is more exploratory, touching and waiting to see what the reaction is, then exploring some more. You have to alter your attitude a little bit. Instead of trying to get her "ready" for the old plunge, let her responses guide you. When you find something that works, licking a place in a certain way, at a certain speed, play it out. If she heats up from what you are doing it means she likes it. Don't accelerate to match her reactions by speeding up or licking harder, keep doing just exactly what you are doing. She may come to orgasm or she may simply rise through a peak and begin to relax. As she is on her way down you can begin to vary your activity and try new things.

As you are relishing each of her curves and dimples, take her on a guided tour of yours. See which parts of you she enjoys playing with and "force" her to play with them the way that most excites you.

Always be a gentleman, even while you are being a barbarian. In other words, stay in control of yourself while you are controlling her. Never stop regarding her reactions and take care not to go too far. You can push a little, but be prepared to back off and regain her confidence in an instant.

There, now we've grown from shit-kickers to suave sexual animals. Wasn't that easy? Let's rejoin the ladies, shall we? (Gary, take the spittoon with you as you leave; I don't think we'll have any further use for it.)

Molly's notes from the quilting bee

It often shocks men how open and graphic women can be when discussing sex with each other. They will discuss failures as readily as successes. Women don't see sexual prowess as proof of feminity. They actually share their experiences with each other while trying to gain information and understanding. We aren't angels though; there is a bit too much levity at the expense of our male partners. Can you imagine how much better our sex lives would be if we could talk to our lovers as freely as we talk to our girlfriends?

Society, in denying women the right to be sexual beings (nice girls don't...), has thrown the burden for good lovemaking onto the male. But ladies, rather than challenging the taboos, we frequently hide behind them. We fear appearing to know too much about sex. We want men to be the teachers, while we remain the coyly reluctant students. We don't risk honesty with men because of their sensitivity to what might be criticism of their lovemaking ability. Part of this is our fault, ladies; we must assume more responsibility for what happens between the sheets.

Men are applauded when they show sexual expertise and criticized when they lack it, while sexual experience in women doesn't seem to be desirable. Ignorance (feigned or real) shouldn't be a virtue. Can we as women open up and be honest with men about our wants and desires? Women are honest with each other because we all share the same dirty little secret, that we are at least as sexual as men. It might help us to open up if we felt secure that men appreciat our knowledge rather than fear it.

Another sticking point in opening up is female perception that males value newness too much. Men seem to adore the near virginal female, and love the excitement of a new partner, while women often feel that sex gets better as people know each other well. It is only after some of the mystery has ebbed that we feel really comfortable about opening up to our partners...just about the time we fear that men get restless and ready to move on.

We worry that men enjoy the chase more than the capture, so we try to make ourselves more mysterious rather than less. Man the hunter versus woman the builder. These are not issues with easy solutions.

Really, we women worry too much and dare too little. If we don't trust men enough to be honest about ourselves, can we reproach them for not understanding us? Should we chide them for hanging on to outmoded views while we do nothing to counter those notions?

It has become almost too easy to make fun of men. We joke about the insecurities they show in their angst about sexual performance. Yet we still generally wait for them to make the first moves. Isn't this the feminine equivalent, allowing them to take the risk of rejection so we will not be vulnerable to that same stress?

I really became aware of this foible when I began exploring my bisexuality. A male friend asked me how I approached a women in whom I had an erotic interest. I laughed,

"I approach women basically the same way I approach men. I use the hint and pray method. I make vague hints and pray for divine intervention." This is a very safe technique, but not terribly effective.

It appears we suffer from insecurities just as the guys do. It merely takes a different form. Instead of performance anxiety we have approach angst. Uncertainty is basic to being human.

So, ladies, this is an area where we can learn from men. We tell them to make their moves and continue their seductions without taking negative responses personally. Perhaps we could listen to our own advice?

One of the draws of the submissive role for women is the seeming resolution of this conflict. Gee, it makes life easy. He orders and she obeys. No risks, no conflicts and no responsibility for assertive action. This is an illusion, a submissive woman need not be passive. We can contribute more to the relationship if we are willing to take a risk. Suppose you and your dominant lover are taking an evening stroll though the park. It is dark and you are on a seldom-traveled path that takes you through a copse of trees and shrubbery. It occurs to you that you are well-screened from the casual observer. A bit of fun here might be exciting with little real risk of exposure. Your choices are a) hope it occurs to him, b) make obscure hints and later explain what you were babbling about, or c) seize the moment and demonstrate how hot he makes you.

Good girl, you picked c! You knelt quietly in front of him and unzipped the little beast. When your mouth has engulfed that familiar part of his anatomy, you look up and your eyes meet his seeking approval.

Honest communication includes the possibility of letting your "fingers do the walking." There are many guys who adore the woman with a direct approach. They enjoy the certainty of knowing their partner's desires. They may see the typical demure feminine approach as part of a game they would rather not play.

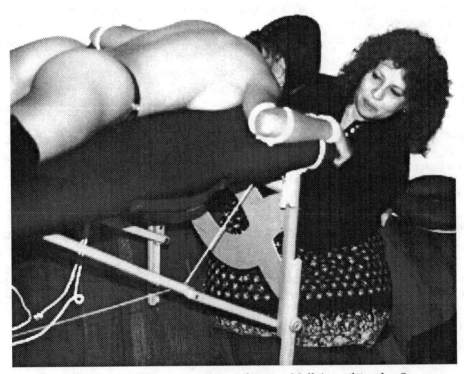

Did anyone really believe we were quilting at Molly's quilting bee?

Other men, many dominant males included, are turned off by what they see as aggressive behavior in their female partners. Still, men enjoy being shown they are desired as much as women do. The behavior in the example above was assertive rather than aggressive. Most fellows would view this as feminine, submissive, and utterly charming.

The worst pitfall you may encounter when initiating sexual activities, particularly in a relationship where your partner is at least nominally in charge, is giving the impression he must respond in a particular way. Your actions might be better received if given the flavor of a request rather than a demand.

We mentioned this earlier in regard to approach with a potential partner. It remains equally valuable to remember in an ongoing relationship. It must be okay with you if he is too tired, too busy, or just not in the mood.

It is positive and affirming to express "you really make me hot." It is not kosher to say "I need sex now!" This requires that equally crucial part of communication -- listening. Listening is more than auditory phenomena, it means paying attention to a response be it verbal or body language. It means being sensitive to the other person's needs, not only expressing your own.

It can be very difficult for a women to accept sexual rejection. Even the temporary rebuff can feel like a strike at the core of our femininity. Hey, aren't men supposed to always want it, while we imperiously decide whether to grant their petition?

For centuries women otherwise subject to the whims of men, have drawn power from controlling an artificially created shortage. We have reinforced the myth that men always want what we could live without. Our unwritten bargain has been, "Men, be really nice to us and we will give you sex." Withdrawal from this position is painful. Revising our sexual attitudes with our male friends is something we can suffer through together if we support rather than combat each other.

Busting barriers

Superb sex is realized by challenging traditional attitudes and scrapping the relics of old mores. Above, we have discussed abandoning traditional sex roles and learning to tune in to our inner sexuality. We have seen the folly of using sex to manipulate each other and of trying to out do one another's performance. We have discovered methods of increasing our sensitivity and improving our skills in touching and non-verbal communication. OK, all of these things are good, solid foundations of healthy sexuality, but why have we included them in a book about SM?

Most people look to achieve honesty, communication, trust, and intimacy in their relationships. These are the ultimate goals that great majority of the vanilla world is striving for. Little is sought, nor perceived seekable, beyond them. Yet, having these aspects of our relationships in place is necessary BEFORE we start playing with SM. SM pushes the limits of trust. Without good communication skills and honesty, much of what we do can be dangerous physically and/or emotionally. Without intimacy, our little tricks will ring hollow.

SM is advanced sexuality. This chapter was How to Have Groovy Sex: 101. There is a lot more that could be said, but you can find hundreds of books, courses, and lectures, even video tapes about good, basic, sexual techniques. It would be well worth your while to explore some of these before donning your leathers. Neither of us did, and in many cases, wished we had. You can play the game without having learned the fundamentals, but a lot of the magic will pass you by.

6 Non-government Sanctioned Sex and Torture

 here's torture, and then there is sex and torture. Raising kids is torture. Sadomasochism isn't anywhere near that cruel. Our version of sex and torture can involve a lot of things; tickling, giving sensual pain, playing psychological games, administering contrasting sensations, depriving the senses, and/or overloading the senses. We might make our submissives come repeatedly until they beg for it to end, or bring them to the edge of orgasm for a long while and deny the final release.

There are few tricks dominants will not use to accomplish their ends. Dominants strive to understand and control sexual energy. They are even willing to take their own bodies to task. For example, they will develop an ability to delay their own orgasms or learn to focus on building their submissives' sexual energy while completely denying their own. Dominants often set themselves up as merely props in their submissives' fantasies, seeking no pleasure for themselves. They also use more toys than you can find in F.A.O. Schwartz in pursuit of their basic goal, which is to leave their partners a limp, exhausted, quivering mass of happy flesh.

Dreaming up new and nasty nightmares is a major pastime for both dominant and submissive. The following techniques are a few of SM's best-selling sexual torments. If we miss any of your favorites write us, we'll try anything at least once.

Clips, clamps, and clothespins

The nipple, pretty in pink or tantalizing in a tawnier hue, ascends saucily from its enchanting orb when inspired by the barest nibble. This brazen jewel seems to beg for attention and it rewards our efforts by expanding and growing taut. There are few activities in life as simple, yet, as satisfying as pinching a nipple.

There exists an enormous array of devices designed to deliver that gratifying tweak. Adult boutiques carry the standard pair of alligator clamps joined by a chain. The adjustable alligator clamp with a screw to regulate pressure, and the Japanese clover, or butterfly clip, are nearly as common. These are flesh-crushing types.

Less universally available are the "Clinging Claws." These sound and look more fearsome than they feel. They have four stiff, but flexible wires gathered in a small metal tube on one end and extending outward on the other end, like long pistils in a flower. The ends of the wires are bent, claw-like, and fit over four sides of the nipple, then are squeezed together over the nipple by movement of two rubber O-rings sliding toward the ends of the wires. Their form was inspired by a tool for electronics. They restrict circulation far less than the above mentioned flesh crushing types.

There are also many other types of clamps devised for torturing nipples, some that tighten by twisting, some that look like cute, miniature wine presses, and some that are nothing more than 1960s-style roach-clips perverted...oops, converted for sexual use..

Your Mickey Mouse watch has been promoted to an indispensable piece of dungeon equipment. Five minutes can seem an eternity to a novice sporting her first pair of clamps and is the longest we recommend for a first session. Fifteen minutes in clamps is safe. The placement and tightness of the clamping, the skin type, experience level, and sensitivity of the clampee are a few of the variables that make it impossible to recommend a longer duration. Restricting blood flow and squashing delicate flesh for too-long a period is not healthy for the afflicted part.

Chronic pain can fade into the background, becoming a dim counterpoint to a more acute and intermittent pain such as spanking. This is another reason to rely on the position of Mickey's hands rather than depending solely on feedback from the sub. Tolerance is highest at the peak of sexual arousal. A clamp that "hurts so good" before an orgasm may be overwhelmingly painful after the climax.

Distress peaks when a clamp is removed and normal circulation returns. Exploiting this farewell factor by synchronizing removal for maximum effect tests the dominant's skill. Removing a clamp at the wrong time can present a real problem as noted above.

The "right" time to remove a clamp from a nipple varies from person to person and depends on what you want to achieve. If you want the ensuing pain to push your masochist over the edge into orgasm, it isn't likely that you will achieve success the first time. This requires precise coordination and cooperation between partners. Melding this intense pain with pleasure can be very hot, though, and you should be able to master the technique with a little practice and perseverance.

Clothespins and binder clips are a few of the common household objects used to deliver an erotic pinch. A clothespin may need to have its spring loosened. Test the feel on yourself first. Binder clips are very tight and are for the experienced clampee only.

Breasts, cocks, labia, and most any part of the anatomy, even the clitoris, can be confined in a clip's painful embrace. (You will be very careful when clamping genitals, though, won't you?) When positioning a clothespin or clamp be aware that less is more with pinching; the smaller the area being squeezed, the greater the pain given.

These are a few of the many nipple clips sold by Leather Masters of San Jose, CA.

Weights can be added to the clips or clamps as tolerance builds. Bowling balls are pretentious and considered overdoing it. Small lead weights for fishing is more in the realm of the possible.

The daisy, created by encircling a bound breast with clothespins as petals, is soul-satisfying art. Removal of the clothespins by knocking them off with a riding crop is theatrical and intensely painful.

For dramatic torment the "zipper" ranks high on our list. You create a zipper by running a string between the jaws of a series of clothespins. Pull on the string and enjoy the staccato chorus as the clothespins pop off one after the other.

Fire and Ice

The "Fire" in "Fire and Ice" most commonly refers to molten candle wax; the "Ice" is, yup, ice. Both of these are applied to breasts, fannies, tummies, arms, genitalia, you name it. The trick to doing a good fire and ice scene relies on timing, dramatic sense, and knowing how fire and ice will feel on your partner's skin. To a blindfolded lover, the sensation of ice can feel as hot as melted wax.

Test the temperature of the candle by dripping the wax on your inner arm, just as you would check the temperature of a baby's formula. Drop the wax from the same height as you would drop it on your victim. This test will help to prevent leaving burns on your submissive, though the yummier parts that we favor dripping on, like nipples or labia, are more sensitive.

Molly, on rare occasions, tops to demonstrate a technique. An ad hoc request for a waxing demo caught her fancy. Testing the white dinner candle she was given raised a surprisingly large blister. It is affirmation of the care we exercise in SM that someone who subs ninety-nine percent of the time acquired her only scene-related scar by taking the dominant role.

Wax comes in two basic flavors, beeswax and paraffin. Beeswax burns at a much higher temperature so we recommend paraffin. Candles are made of more than wax. Hardeners, coloring, and scent added to wax generally raise the melting temperature.

We are fond of Shabbat candles. They contain no additives (by Kosher law), are a good size to work with (about an inch in diameter and 4 3/4 inches long), and come in large boxes that are cheap to buy. Shabbat candles are usually found in grocery stores catering to Jewish populations. If you cannot find Shabbat candles, hunt for emergency or utility candles of about the same dimensions.

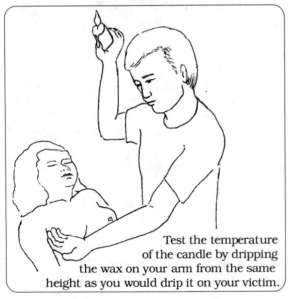

Test the temperature of the candle by dripping the wax on your arm from the same height as you would drip it on your victim.

Start dripping wax from a height of several feet above the body and gradually bring it closer. Retest on your arm periodically as you reduce the drip height. As always, you want to begin with relatively less sensitive areas (like the back or chest) and work up slowly. Not only does this give the sub a chance to get used to the feel, but it gives them plenty of time to contemplate what a drip of hot wax might feel like on her clit. Anxiety is useful!

If you keep an ice cube handy during your hot wax scene, and you blindfold your submissive, judicious, well-timed applications of the ice can yield dramatic surprises. Blindfolded, your sub won't know what you will use next, nor where it will land.

Candles are not the only way to serve Submissive Flambe. Fire sticks burn alcohol and are a quick way to remove unwanted hair less painfully than with an Epilady. Flash powder is another dramatic method. Get an expert demo before trying either of these techniques.

Ice can be used imaginatively on and in your partner. There are ice molds you can purchase in the shape of a cock. A popsicle is merely flavored ice with a convenient handle, however, the chemical balance inside a vagina is delicate and some people are highly prone to infection. Still, you might find a couple of less dangerous orifices to receive a popsicle harmlessly if you look hard enough. Inserting a square peg, the ice cube, in a round hole is safer after you melt the edges by putting the cube in your mouth first. Be aware that excessive amounts of ice in the anus can cause cramping like a cold enema.

While playing with ice, make sure your partner's shivers are properly motivated. A submissive, especially bound, is engaged in less physical activity than her dom. A room temperature that feels comfortable for the active dom may be too cold for the passive and exposed sub.

Electro-torture

Electric shock can disrupt the rhythm of the heart causing death. Is that clear enough? The dangerous element of electricity is called current or amperage. According to several sources, it only takes one-third of an amp to stop the heart. Common sense and the following rule of thumb about electro-torture should help you stay clear of homicide charges. Never use a device above the waist that passes any current (amperage) through the body.

There are, however, a few electrical devices that have the coveted Philip & Molly seal of approval for safe sensuality. Unfortunately, none of these toys comes cheaply.

TENS units (transcutaneous electrical nerve stimulation units) are used by chiropractors to stimulate the nerves. TENS units pass current through the body, so don't use them above the waist! Two or more wires extend from these little battery operated boxes. The wires have electrodes on their ends with adhesive that sticks to the skin above the muscle(s) you wish to stimulate. A small current passes through the skin causing muscle contractions. It is a most peculiar sensation. You don't feel a shock. The electric stimulation makes the muscles move independent of the subject's control. It is very weird to watch as well as to feel. In the United States, these units sell for up to $700 as of this writing, but we know people who have bought them for as little as $100 overseas.

The violet wand is a device that gives a mild-to-wild shock with no amperage. Violet wands are static electricity generators with various attachments to tickle, tingle, and delight. Have you ever walked across a woolen carpet during winter and felt a static electric shock when you touched a friend? Then you already have some idea of the feel of this device. There is a buzzing sound, eerie violet sparks, and the smell of ozone in the air when the wand is in operation.

Among the violet wand's multiple attachments is an interesting accessory that lets you use your body to conduct the energy. This is power at your fingertips. Imagine giving an electrifying kiss. Now consider the effect of a light nibble at a more sensitive part of the anatomy. The ability to pass the juice from person to person makes for a nifty party game.

Our violet wand with six attachments set us back about $425. There are, no doubt, vendors offering a better deal as the wand's popularity is growing by leaps and bounds...no pun intended.

There is yet another electrical device that stimulates the nerves and muscles from a company called Paradise Electro Stimulation. Again, this toy passes electric current and, therefore, is for use below the waist only! They do not have a catchy name for their toy, but it consists of a DC base unit to control various attachments: an anal plug, a vaginal plug, a vaginal shield, an intra-anal probe they call the "sparkler," and a cock ring that you purchase separately according to your hopes, desires, and individual tastes, and the size of your wallet.

The attachments all have conductors to stimulate muscles they are meant to contact. The vaginal plug, for example, directly causes muscular contractions that simulate fucking in a much more realistic manner than a vibrator. You can actually see the clear Lexan plug move slightly in and out of the vagina, yet the sensation is anything but slight. Ten minutes with this toy is usually sufficient to induce a state of blithering, euphoric idiocy.

The control unit has four knobs that regulate pulse, frequency, and current (coarse and fine controls). With a little practice, one can simulate the perfect fuck -- and the PES unit doesn't snore! It does, however, demand something of a commitment; we paid about $750 for our unit with the box, vaginal plug, vaginal shield, and butt plug.

The cutting edge

The use of a knife in a scene beyond the cutting of rope or being left in view for ambiance needs thorough negotiation. Some people are absolutely terrified of knives. Approaching a bound submissive with a knife you have not discussed may cause justifiable panic.

Residual fear of knives can add a real thrill for the submissive if she is fairly certain you don't plan to disembowel her. Philip has a fearsome-looking hunting blade that he uses more for its psychological effects than its keen edge. Carefully scraping the wax off a body after a fire and ice scene with a large sharp steel blade is both terrifying and sensual (one of our favorite combinations). There is hardly a thing we can think of hotter than disrobing your darling piece by piece. The feel of cold steel against a warm skin is a sensation to be savored.

We do not advocate play that breaks the skin in any way. There is just too much risk of infection, accident, and scarring. However, cutting, branding, and piercing are becoming more and more common. These are techniques for experts. If you intend to try them yourself, find a pro to train you. We understand the draw to this kind of play; both of us are pierced. Blood sports can be very dramatic and satisfying, but you don't want to mess with it without knowing what you are doing.

Anal play, general considerations

Any sexual play in or around the anus carries with it the hazard of infection from a variety of organisms, notably, hepatitis and staph infections, and HIV. Poop is dirty stuff. Some people go for scat play. We don't recommend it. We're not passing judgment here, but we think it's dangerous.

Aside from ca-ca catastrophes, the tissues of the anus and rectum are prone to abrasion and tearing and are very sensitive to touch. Also, the lining of the rectum is porous and thin. It is one of the most disease-vulnerable parts of the body. But, if this kind of play still appeals to you, use the safety precautions of a latex barrier and plenty, plenty, plenty of water-soluble lubrication. Latex responds to petroleum like a witch to water: it melts. Don't use Vaseline on condoms.

Safety barriers used for hand-to-anus play are usually disposable latex finger cots or gloves. Both are readily available in boxes of 50 to 100 in most pharmacies. Of course, condoms are the barrier of choice for covering penises, dildos, butt plugs, and so on. A dental dam or plastic wrap will allow you to give that most intimate kiss safely.

Aside from the physical aspects of anal sex-play, one must consider the mental. We like anal sex, but it isn't for everyone. After all, we don't understand why some people ruin a perfectly good pizza with anchovies. Fish on pizza? Yuck! Still, what is disgusting to one person is another's delight.

Some of us are taught to be embarrassed about our bodily functions. It's almost impossible to reconcile the fact that we burp, sweat, break wind, and have body wastes. It betrays our pristine self-image. (Molly has an advanced degree in this school of thought. She doesn't perspire, she merely becomes "dewy." She doesn't fart either, she "poofs.") Whereas it is undeniably true that, "even queens and great ladies defecate," we are taught to do so abashedly and with the utmost of discretion. Therein lies the important key.

When anal sex is proposed, it is a potential tinder-box of residual emotions that can be productive or disastrous. Letting a lover play with that most personal, private, dirty little part of you is a ticklish proposition that includes elements of humiliation and of losing control. It's a risky business; be sensitive and go slow.

MOLLY'S NOTE: We learn from infancy that eating is the only activity related to digestion that is not private. Fellas, did you ever notice that when you go out with two or more couples, the women always retreat to the restroom as a group? Well, discharging bodily by-products is low on our agenda. We use restrooms to re-coiff our hair, to freshen our face paint, to distribute colored condoms to match our outfits, and to decide which, if any, of our guys is going to get lucky. But, if we must also use the facilities, we keep those stall doors securely fastened. Most women just don't like to open up about elimination. (I hope you appreciate being let in on this secret; I had to request permission to expose it from The International Women's Council on Stuff We Let Men Wonder About. Permission was granted only after months of deliberation. Thanks, ladies!)

Why are we blown away by these normal, common bodily functions? Negative attitudes toward our bodies are remnants of religious and cultural beliefs that have nothing to do with common sense or current concepts. We tend to blame mothers for continuing to instill these attitudes. Consider, however, the mom who is confronted by a wall displaying her two-year-old's artistic talent with you-guess-the-media. If she can restrain herself to a comment as mild as, "Oh, nasty," she is exhibiting the height of restraint. Ultimately, it is the feelings that are important whether the reasons for having them make sense or not.

Anal sex

Clumsy vaginal sex may be boring, but inept anal sex is likely to be agonizing. Anal sex tends to give extreme pleasure or extreme pain. It is rarely neutral. Most of us prefer pleasure so it is important to understand the ins and outs of this sex act. Even a submissive who enjoys moderate pain from a spanking may not like this pain in the ass.

Understandably, a painful episode with anal sex will deter many people from another try. It's hard to separate the act from the skill of the actor. Women who continue to have bad experiences are even harder to comprehend, but feel it is an ordeal they must endure for their partners. A message posted on a computer bulletin board gave a chilling example of this. The note was written by a woman complaining of her lover's "Greek obsession." Her letter ended with the sentence: "Well, at least I don't bleed anymore. " Sexual martyrdom gives us the willies.

Sensitively executed anal sex doesn't hurt. A twinge or two of discomfort are acceptable if it feels good overall. No wait... forget good, sex should feel great! The acutely sensitive nerve-filled anus is a nest of erotic feelings. Between a woman's two lower apertures are only thin tissues, so stroking here is often felt in the vagina as well. Most pain is caused by scanty lubrication, inability to relax, or by the actions of an ignorant or selfish partner.

Step one in anal play is hygiene. Simply leave an offering in the porcelain altar and then wash well. Some people advise an enema or even two enemas. The penis should be covered by a condom, of course.

The sphincter is a bit like a cop at the end of a one way street. When the traffic flow is in the wrong direction it is natural to constrict this muscle. To loosen things up, this instinct must be resisted. We have some control, but relaxation is key. You slacken the muscles by bearing down as if you were having a movement. If fear of an embarrassing encounter with an odious substance is a source of anxiety a pre-scene enema may help. When apprehension about pain is the problem, a slow approach with lots of reassurance is the solution. A nice back-rub helps to dispel tension, as well.

"The handsome hero wets his enormous cock in his hot slut's dripping slit, then plows full throttle into her unprepared ass, eliciting screams of delight." That, dear readers, is pure bullshit. Well, there may be a scream, but there will not be much delight. In the real world, this "natural" lubrication is nearly always insufficient. There is not enough of it and it is absorbed too quickly.

It is best to use a water soluble lubrication such as KY jelly. There are commercial products made just for this purpose. Some have names that advertise their intent like "Analease™." Read the ingredient list carefully. A few contain a numbing agent such as benzocaine. Do not use a product that masks pain. Where there is pain, there is potential damage and a need to modify technique.

Prepare your penis for entry by bagging and lubing. Prepare your lady by using your fingers to grease and stretch her nether entrance. Anointing each other can be foreplay. Titillate her so she wants you inside her. If you can't make a finger or two feel good in her bottom, she isn't going to enjoy the greater onslaught of your penis.

Even when your paramour is ready and begging for sexual release, continue to reign in your steed. Entry is a slow trip with frequent stops. A pause after entry of the head of the penis is vital. This allows the muscles to relax and adjust. In fact, if your lady says, "no" or, "stop" at any point, freeze rather than withdrawing or proceeding. Count to ten before asking if she wants you to stop and abide by her wishes. Often, all she needs is a little break in the action for her anatomy to adjust. If she wants to continue, do so slowly with frequent pauses until you are fully inside her. Move gently at first, allowing her reactions to guide you. Eventually, you will feel her sphincter relax. Now you can increase the pace gradually. Relube frequently as you are fucking; lubricants are quickly absorbed in the rectum.

We began with cleansing and we end with it. A complete washing after anal sex is de rigueur. A fresh condom is always required before you enter the vagina, whether you came or not. Bacteria normal to the digestive tract can create havoc in the vagina causing vaginitis, cystitis, or other uncomfortable maladies.

Anal training and object stimulation

Penetration causes stretching that makes subsequent entries easier. Relaxation is a learned process that becomes effortless with practice. Anal training is a deliberate strategy to prepare a submissive to accept larger objects in her anus. Training begins with insertion of small objects (a dildo, a vibrator or a butt plug) usually under an inch in diameter. Larger toys are brought into play when they can be comfortably accommodated.

Butt plugs come in all kinds of material from hard plastic to soft vinyl. The soft ones are better because there is less chance of damage to the delicate anal lining. Never insert anything breakable or that has sharp edges. The most common shape is a cone that narrows again after reaching its maximum diameter, with a flared bottom to prevent the need for a search and recovery mission.

The typical adult store seems to carry butt plugs in just three sizes: too small, too big, and almost right. The beginner, or too-small size, has a maximum diameter of three-quarters of an inch and is four to five inches long. The medium sized plug's largest diameter is about an inch and a half, just slightly larger in girth than the average penis. The large is fully three inches in diameter and five to six inches in length. This is the "oh my god" or the "no way Jose" size. A much wider variety of sizes and shapes can be found in mail order cat-

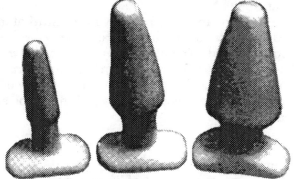

Typical butt plugs in three sizes; too small, too big, and almost right.

alogs. Dildos and vibrators for anal intrusion are more slender than those for vaginal play and narrower at the tip, and they usually narrow again near the base.

European devices often have a chain for retrieval should you lose them inside. If you do lose something inside, don't panic. After all, you were designed to empty this area. Try nature's way first. If unsuccessful, emergency room personal are very experienced with this type of redemption. Don't be too embarrassed to seek their help (unless you enjoy being embarrassed). If you do have exhibitionist tendencies, you will find their matter-of-fact manner disappointing. Trust us, they have seen many stranger things.

There is an amusing, but bizarre practice called tampon training. A few mistresses "force" their male subs to wear tampons while they (the mistresses) are menstruating.

This quaint ritual is justified as way to teach men to understand the discomfort and inconvenience women regularly undergo. We know several subs who reluctantly complied even though they found it non-erotic and uncomfortably annoying.

A tampon in an ass is nothing like wearing one in the vagina. The vagina is self-lubricating -- the anus is not. Molly feels that being around her during PMS is punishment enough, so penalizing men for not being female is gratuitous. The exception to this may be the cross-gender sub who actually enjoys the practice as part of the feminization process.

If you really must do this, guys, lubricate the tampon very well and change it often. Tampons are meant to absorb; a dry one can easily adhere to the wall of your rectum. Rectums, being also absorbent, can easily adhere to the tampon. Removing a tampon that has been glued to you this way gives new dimensions to the phrase, "tearing a new asshole." Enjoy, we'll forgo this little pleasure, thanks.

Self-training for anal play

If your first experiment with anal sex is unsuccessful, don't worry about it. If, however, you would like to try it again in the future, there is some practical action you can take to make things easier next time.

Repose in a tub of warm soothing water. If you wish you may add bubbles or your favorite scented oil to the bath. All comfy? Good. You are alone now so there is nothing to embarrass or inhibit you. Insert a soapy finger into your rear entry. Now practice contracting and relaxing the muscles as the pressure on your finger gives you feedback. You can gain conscious control of these muscles this way. Once you learn controlled relaxation try inserting two fingers. Use your fingers to gently stretch the area. After the bath, rub body oil into your nether parts and allow yourself to the enjoy the sensual feelings.

Make anal play part of your masturbatory repertoire by adding butt plugs, dildos, and vibrators to your usual maneuvers. Try small ones at first, covered with a condom and well lubed, of course. Covering your toys with a condom facilitates cleaning the items. It is important to keep insertion toys like vibrators and dildos very clean especially if you want to use them vaginally. When a small one is comfortable you should try a slightly larger one. When you enjoy using a dildo the size of a penis, you are ready to enjoy the real thing.

Enemas

The very thought of liquid being pumped into one's behind sends a lot of people screaming for cover. Many of these folks share that reaction to any kind of anal play, but there are still plenty of plucky people for whom a warm, sudsy flow flooding their rectum is quite a turn-on. However, anal play is abundantly laden with emotional reflexes, so if your partner shows some reluctance, tread lightly and slowly and be prepared to abandon the idea altogether. He or she may be simply too embarrassed or grossed out to consider the option openly or freely.

In an SM sense, surrendering to an enema can trigger submissive buttons. They range from being humiliated and violated to being lovingly cared for as an infant would be by Mommy or Daddy. In any case, administering enemas within a fantasy scene can supply a richly voluptuous experience.

Enema equipment consists of a rectal tube with a smooth, rounded tip, an enema bag, and tubing that connects the rectal tube to the bag. These can be easily found in most pharmacies and are safe to use if you follow the directions.

There are a couple of optional tube tips available, chiefly the single and double Bardex™. The single Bardex™ has a "balloon" that can be inflated inside the anus to help keep the tube from slipping out while the enema is being administered. The double Bardex™ has two balloons. One is inflated inside the anus and the other on the outside. This keeps the tube from slipping out and from being pushed further into the anus. Single and double Bardex™ tips might not be as easy to find as the standard enema tube-tip, but most medical supply stores carry them.

In addition to the basic bag and tubing, you will need a good supply of water-soluble lubricating jelly to ease the passage of the tube into the anus, an enema solution, and a pair of latex gloves. Optional, but handy equipment includes: a water-proof pad or sheet; an extra pillow; a large bowl; a thermometer; toilet paper; a bedpan or toilet; and a washcloth and or towel. You will also need a place to hang the enema bag while the fluid is being infused. Hospitals have rolling racks for the job, but these cost plenty. A nail in the wall will do, and should be placed a foot to a foot and a half above the level where your lady's anus will be.

The procedure is simple, but remember you are pushing a stiff object (the enema tube) into tissues that are very delicate and tear easily (the rectum). Regardless of the cruelty of the fantasy, adopt the inner attitude of a care-giver.

Assemble your enema kit and fill the bag. It's best to use a warm (never hot) saline solution, tap water, or clean, soapy water. One quart is as much as an adult should hold according to common nursing practice. You can fill the enema bag and let it heat up in a bowl or sink of warm water until it is just right. One or two degrees over body temp is warm enough, 100 degrees (F) starts to be too hot. Hot water can burn the mucosa of the rectum. Cold water, on the other hand, causes cramping.

Lay your "patient" on her left side on top of the rubber sheet with her knees drawn forward a bit. Her sigmoid colon takes a left turn inside; positioning her this way lets gravity help the enema flow easily.

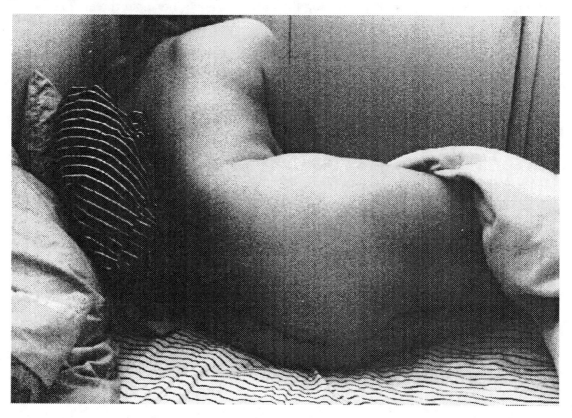

Wash your hands and don your rubber gloves. Place the enema bag on a pillow behind your patient. The pillow is to raise the bag slightly above the level of her anus so that the fluid will flow into her gently. Take a moment to let your lady relax before you plunge in. Massage her ass and fondle her nether parts and while you're doing so, think through the entire procedure to make sure all will go smoothly.

Lubricate the enema tube and the patient's anus well while coaxing her to relax. Separate her buttocks and insert the tube pointing it towards her belly-button. Insert the tube very carefully and slowly, about three inches. You want to be careful not to scrape the rectal wall with the tube which can damage the mucosa. Also, avoid pushing it in too far. Pushing the tube past the rectum and into the bowel can tear the bowel.

Hold the tube in place while the fluid is being administered. Involuntary bowel contractions can cause the tube to slip out of the anus. Open the clamp on the enema tubing and allow the flow to begin slowly. Letting it flow too quickly can stimulate the bowel to contract and evacuate.

Raise the bag slowly to the nail or hook and secure it there. While the enema is flowing, be ready to lower the bag or clamp it off if your patient starts to cramp or if the fluid starts to leak. Pinching the cheeks together can stop leakage. A few moments' pause can relieve cramping. The rate of flow you want to achieve is about one quart in ten minutes.

When the bag is empty, clamp it off immediately; you do not want to let air inside her. She will have a distended, full feeling. This is normal and if she's worried, tell her so. Wad some toilet paper around the tube and slowly remove it. Be careful not to change the angle of the tube as you withdraw it.

Medically, enemas are used to induce defecation for patients who are constipated and to administer certain kinds of medication that are best absorbed through the colon. The longer the fluid is retained, the more the colon will be stimulated to evacuate. Anticipate "accidents" and decide when you will let your lady expel. You can hold her butt-cheeks together or insert a butt-plug if you want to help her hold the enema.

You may hear of people using a little wine in an enema solution. Wine enema fans, we're sorry to be killjoys, but there are lots of people with allergies to sulfites and many people don't have a very high tolerance for alcohol. [We don't drink much, and Philip, though he has considerable body mass (he's chunky, but cute!)], gets plowed on only a couple of beers. Can you imagine what even a three-parts water, one part wine enema would do to him? Alcohol enemas force very, very deep intoxication very, very quickly. We think the practice is too dangerous to screw around with; besides, we never advocate mixing scenes with drugs.

Length of retention time depends on the scene you are playing and your patient's ability to hold the fluid. Do you want her to kneel in front of you begging to be allowed to go to the toilet for relief? Should she perform fellatio on you before she is granted reprieve? Does she have to come before she can go to the bathroom? (Be ready for some messy waterworks in this last scenario.)

Feeding the pussy syntho-meat

Moving forward, so to speak, we have the vagina. Just as nature abhors a vacuum, so do many in the scene regard emptiness here. Dildos are objects imitating the shape of an erect penis that are used in much the same way as the item they are fashioned after. They range in size from "poor little fella" to "in your dreams" and are usually made of rubber or plastic.

Some dildos have mechanical innards to produce vibration and/or gyration. These active monsters are vibrators. Clever name, huh? These can be manually or electrically powered, the latter being energized by batteries or standard household current. We are going to assume that our readers will figure the basics of these toys without detailed instruction.

Having a lover sensually distracted from her mundane realities by constant fullness in her lower parts is a charming notion. To fulfill this romantic ideal, some subs strive to keep their interior nooks well furnished. The constant sexual arousal is supposed to maintain their submissive status and their good master always in their thoughts. This is another bit of sadomasomythology that transfers to reality poorly. We have known submissives who complied with this for days or weeks before being stopped by discomfort or infection.

Take good care of the sweet lil' pussy. She purrs when she's played with and stroked, but she also needs to rest, breath freely, and have her juices flow unhampered. Keeping toys in the vagina for prolonged periods interrupts the natural cleansing process. The fullness here may also create pressure that curbs urination which can lead to bladder infection.

An anal plug will get dry, irritating, and finally painful if not frequently relubricated. We suggest limiting the wearing of internal devices to a few hours, maybe a half-day. Find a non-biological site for long term toy storage.

Fisting

The brutal thrust of an enormous fist bruising and possibly tearing delicate tissues is the fantasy. The reality is a careful, slow, and sensual procedure. Most women (virtually all mothers) can take a fist into their vagina without damage. The vagina was designed with enough flexibility to allow the passage of a baby's head. The analogy breaks down somewhat when you know that hormonal changes during pregnancy increase the elasticity of these tissues; still, the vagina has quite a bit of give. The trick is maintaining a patient approach.

Sexual arousal increases elasticity and relaxes the muscles. Tension constricts muscles, increases pain, and reduces suppleness. Know your lady. If she is the type who is turned on by danger (perceived, not real) raise her anxiety by telling her you are going to fist her (perhaps even exaggerating the supposed brutality you will use). Otherwise, you can leave this as a surprise. With the proper approach she may not realize you are doing more than finger fucking her until your whole hand is inside and you have shown her in a mirror or by having her feel with her hand.

Fold your hand to make it as narrow as possible.

Fingernails should be short and filed smooth and you should wear a latex glove. There is little danger of HIV transmission, but even well washed hands carry many germs. Lubricated latex gloves also reduce friction which makes insertion easier. Cover your hand liberally with lubrication. The pussy outdoes the butterball turkey as a self-baster, but this is one time that more is called for. Your hand should be a gooey mess. If the process takes a long time you may have to add more lubrication as you go.

Start by moving two fingers in and out of the vagina. Keep your darling hot with desire. Try to keep her on the verge of orgasm with her natural juices flowing. Then use three fingers and finally four. The vagina will become looser and looser as she wants more and more. If it does not becomes loose enough to proceed, stop and move on to other activities. Never force any hard object into the soft tissues of the vagina.

Fold your hand as in the picture. Bring the middle two fingers together, the first and little finger on top of them and the thumb in the middle. After the entire hand has been inserted into the vagina above the pubic bone, just fold in your thumb, relax your hand, and it will naturally form a fist. Some women love the feeling of fullness. Others also enjoy movement of the inserted hand. Beware of contact with the cervix, it can be painfully sensitive.

Though we have no personal experience, we understand that anal fisting is accomplished much the same way, though it is slower and more difficult to achieve. There is more chance of failure as it is harder to stretch the anus to this extent. So don't get upset if you can't achieve this. The size of the fister's hand is a variable over which you have no control. An enema before attempting anal fisting is advised. Most importantly, you must never consider an activity a "must do," and remember, NEVER FORCE ANYTHING!

Forced sex (never say never)

There are submissives who list "forced" oral sex as a favorite activity. Only in the "through the looking glass" world of SM does calling an activity both forced and desired make sense. What the sub really enjoys is pretending that she is being forced into oral service. A dom can foster this illusion in several ways.

"Suck me!" issued as a command is often coupled with dire threats about what will happen if its not done well. The dom may chose not to cum (if he is able). Uh oh, the wench failed in her duty! Now he has an excuse to inflict some play punishment.

Some submissives absolutely melt when their hair is locked in a firm grip while their mouth is engulfing an erect organ. The dom may relax and enjoy ("Gee, its good to be king!") or he may take charge of the timing and depth of the strokes. Perhaps he may try forcing the penis deeper than is easily accommodated. Trust us, many people love this and the sounds of gagging and choking are music to their ears. Determine whether your sweety falls into this group or if she will just get pissed off by what can seem like callous selfishness.

Forced vaginal or anal sex is similar. Real rape is a violent assault. It is a terrifying, traumatizing experience that has nothing in common with a forced sex or play rape scenes. Some submissives enjoy the fantasy that they are innocent victims as all sorts of nasty, naughty, fun stuff is done to their innocent and helpless bodies. This may be motivated by the archaic notion we learned when we were young that good lassies said no, while girls who enjoyed sex were worthless sluts. This is a way to be the "good girl" while enjoying all the lovely kinks that naughty sluts enjoy. Being "taken" reinforces the feeling of being deeply desired and supremely feminine. Sex in bondage is a type of forced sex. The tied victim is helpless and at the dominant's mercy.

Smoke and mirrors

Tendrils of fog cling to the ancient granite alter and embrace the lithe form of the helpless maiden lying chained and terrified. OK, we confess the satanic miasma was created by the dry ice machine we borrowed from the special effects department. Practitioners of sexual magic are wizards of wow. We perform our sorcery while the victim is left wondering, "is it real or is it Memorex™?" Admittance to the guild of sexual magicians is dependent on knowing where to place the mirrors and imaginative sleight of hand.

Fantasies too perilous to act out can be fulfilled by clever subterfuge. You have an advantage an illusionist would envy and an audience with a deep desire to believe. Feats of prestidigitation can be simple tricks or elaborately constructed scenarios requiring long range planning and numerous props.

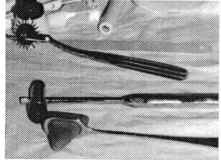

The Wartenburg pinwheel is normally used to test nerve response. Items found in medical supply stores can be given creative uses.

A branding fantasy can be satisfied very neatly without any permanent damage to the "branded" slave. A dear friend had success with the following ingenious scenario. We found it too cute and clever to keep to ourselves, but don't divulge this trick to more than thirty or forty of your closest friends.

The ingredients include a bound and willing subject, a blindfold, a hibachi (or a skillet and hotplate; hibachis are more dramatic, but indoor ventilation is a problem), a bit of raw hamburger, a can of frozen juice, and a branding iron. The branding iron is not absolutely essential, but it does add a lot to the atmosphere. These wrought irons props are nifty to have anyway. They inspire interesting thoughts and conversations when left hung on a wall.

Proceed as if you were going to really brand your partner. Bind her so that she won't move. Show your lady the hibachi and the branding iron (if you have one). Get her consent to proceed with a branding. Talk about the pain that is to follow and how to care for third degree burns to help build your victims anticipation. Now comes the blindfold.

When the person has reached the right frame of mind, and when hibachi the is very hot, it is time for the moment of truth. Push a frozen can of juice hard against your victims skin while simultaneously tossing your hamburger onto the hot coals. The cold of the can against the skin will feel like burning, while the hamburger produces the sounds and smell of searing flesh. Optional screams are furnished by the submissive.

Millions of tricks and tortures to torment and delight your lady lay dormant in nearly every object you own. All you have to do is stroll through the house in a wicked frame of mind. For helping us perform our magic, we cannot be more grateful to the lowly blindfold; it allows us to pull off the most delightful of ruses. A bound and sightless submissive will believe you have pricked her with a needle when a body hair is plucked by a tweezer. A toothpick pressed into soft tissue feels like the flesh has been pierced while skin is actually unbroken. A dominant can act out a very convincing piercing on a blindfolded victim using a toothpick if he sets the stage with meticulous attention to detail. Here are a few more examples just to leave you in a properly devilish frame of mind:

Feathers are standard and delightful sex toys. How many ticklish spots can you find?

Metal and glass objects are usually cool to the naked skin, but, of course, they can be refrigerated, too. Come to think of it, they can be warmed, too.

Glance through your kitchen drawers to see what might be effective under the right circumstances. Off hand, all silverware, salad tongs, cast-iron pans, spatulas, wooden spoons, and so on can be useful.

Covertly refrigerate a damp bath towel and flop it on a bound, blindfolded submissive.

Generously coat several strings with liquid soap, then drag them haltingly over the body of your lady. Can you make them feel like worms or snakes?

Guessing games with common objects are fun to play with blindfolded submissives, particularly if she has to pay a price for each wrong guess. Everyone knows what a toothbrush feels like in the mouth, but how many can guess what it is if you use it elsewhere on the body? How about a sponge? A piece of silk? A comb? A shot glass? Don't forget sounds, smells, and tastes in this game and don't forget to have fun.

7 Get Them By the Balls; Their Hearts and Minds Will Follow

The Basics of Bondage

adies, imagine--

You've lingered over an elegant supper. A warm, summer night's breeze blends the bouquet of lilac from the garden with that of the cognac remaining on your lips. Your lover leads you by the hand from the table to your bedroom. The bed's covers are drawn. He stops at its edge and moves behind you. A candelabra with five tapers is the only light, flickering waves of golden glow over bed sheets of navy-blue satin.

Your ear tingles as your lover's lips move against it. He whispers, "Put your arms behind your back."

He ties your wrists behind you with silk scarves. You test the scarves, but cannot free your hands. They are expertly bound, held tight, yet comfortably. He gathers your hair in one hand and cups your breast in the other, gently pressing. He nibbles and licks and kisses your throat and your head yields into his shoulder.

He folds his arms around you. The buttons of your blouse come undone and the fabric glides across your nipples. The blouse slides from your shoulders, falling loose at your waist. Your skirt is unzipped and left hanging on your hips.

Your lover's fingertips flirt with your skin, slithering downward, echoing the curve of your upturned throat. Downward; swirling, curling over the swells of your breasts, lingering there; kneading and teasing each nipple as if he were fashioning knobs of porcelain for the lids of teapots. Pulling, rolling, squeezing, scratching the tips with fingernails until the clay is cured and hard.

Your nipples ache and feel a shivering warmth spreading...downward. Downward, his hands flow following the heat, flat palms on your belly, fingers splayed, downward, until they reach the furry patch. He nuzzles you there further fueling the furnace glowing just below -- then he takes his hands away!

Loosely rolling another silk scarf, he blindfolds you tenderly, but securely. Slowly, and with great ceremony, your clothes are completely removed and you are bound face-up on the bed, arms and legs stretched wide open, wrists and ankles fastened firmly to the four corner-posts. The satin sheets are cool and slick on your backside. You wriggle as much as your pinioned limbs will allow to feel the satin sheet glide beneath your shoulders, ass, and thighs. Much movement is impossible and, though your trust in this man is complete, a thread of anxiety floats within you. Chills and gooseflesh swarm wavelike across the surface of your chest and belly.

A tattletale, kitten breeze licks between your legs, chilling your naked sex. It whispers to your lover, "she's so wet!" feeding him your hot scent. He listens to the vulgar little breeze and chuckles. He dips his head, loudly filling his lungs with the perfume. He smears some on his lips. Your hips jump involuntarily and your cheeks blaze in disgrace.

In the blackness of the blindfold, your whole world becomes what he makes of it. Every sensation is magnified, nerve-ends and imagination replacing vision. The heat of his hand and cool air pushed before it. Sound and silence. Pressure and none. Tingling slap and tender caress. Rhythm and chaos, a kaleidoscope of tones, tastes, textures and temperatures. Intensity grows with each passing second, his every touch is electric!

Immobile and defenseless, naked and vulnerable, you soon surrender mind, body, and emotions, gladly and gratefully. Trust surges from its hiding place, deep within your helplessness, almost too keen to bear. Your ragged breath announces your gift; breasts, belly, sex, and soul, all are his for the taking.

Still, the whole night lies before you.

Imagine!

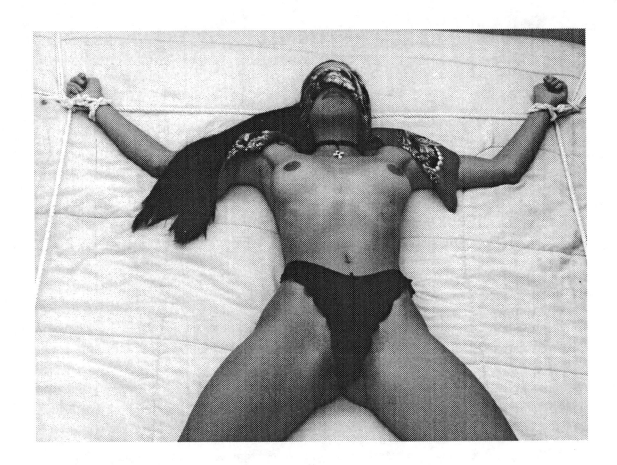

Hey, everybody needs a hobby, right? Call us deviant, call us shameless, obsessed and sick, but you can't call us dull. We love bondage. Done with a flair for high romance, creativity, and a touch of drama, bondage can send you both sailing away on clouds of ecstasy.

Bondage is a perfect foil for a thousand fantasies. Be a salty pirate capturing a luscious island girl. Be a wicked schoolboy cornering the young teacher he's always lusted after. Be a corrupt jailer, disciplining his hapless charge. Or just be yourselves, experimenting with lust, sensation, and surprise.

First, you need a plan

Bondage is a blast, but it adds a few elements to lovemaking that you need to be aware of. So, before you lash your lass to the mizzen mast, indulge in some preliminary planning to make the scene go smoothly.

Drug the kids, put them to bed early, and bolt their doors shut. Better yet, send them to camp two states away. Then bolt and lock your own bedroom door. Daddy will have years of explaining to do and lots of analysis to pay for if the brats pop in and see a naked Mommy dangling from hooks in the ceiling. If you decide to advance beyond this chapter, and Mom's also sporting a few crimson hand prints or rosy stripes on her fanny, it's real hard to explain to the children how she's actually having a good time.

Bondage scenes take a lot of time. You'll be amazed at how quickly the hours go by; set aside lots of them. Consider everything that goes into a bondage scene. You have to choose and lay out your equipment. You'll want to set an appropriate mood, so you will be fiddling with lighting, music, clothing, food, wines, surgical instruments -- oops, those were for the last chapter.

When everything is ready, it will take some time for the two of you to become absorbed in the fantasy. You'll proceed with a secure and attractive job of tying, which you will want to do without marring the surface of, or dislocating pieces of your darling.

Once your spectacular scene is in full swing you'll both become incredibly horny. With fate smiling upon you, that is going to eat up another hour or so. Lastly, you'll need time to relax and cool off while your submissive packs up the toys and puts clean sheets on the bed. (Philip: "Right, honey?" Molly: "Grumble.") We recommend that you plan to spend at least three hours, which, by the way, we consider a quicky.

Bondage safety

Dozens of people have told us that they disavow any association with sadomasochism because, "that's how people get hurt!" and they'd never hurt anyone, and "All we do is a little 'love bondage'." The dangers of bondage are one of the least understood, even by long-term practitioners of the art. Reaching into Molly's stack of inarguable and unsubstantiated statistics, we find that 89.3779% of all SM accidents are bondage related. OK, we made up the number, but rest assured, far more injury is done by bondage than by whipping and smacking.

Ropes have only so much give and chains have none at all. Both are a lot stronger than a body's parts. Guess which is going to give first, when push comes to shove. The following are suggestions for maintaining normally accepted anatomical order:

Three-eighths inch cord is the minimum thickness we recommend for direct contact with the skin. Skinnier cord can abrade or cut too easily. Of course, lacing fingers together with a thinner cord or string may be used, but the hazards of circulation loss and tendon strain are more probable, even if the bondage is not load-bearing. Never use direct stress on shoulders, soft organs, throat, pulse points, or fine bones.

Suspension is the art of supporting a submissive's body, partially or totally, by bondage devices. Suspension is an activity for experts only. The likelihood for serious injury is increased a thousandfold. Our advise is to stay away from suspension until you are well experienced in other forms of bondage and can find someone competent to train you. If you absolutely must subject your victim to suspension, various slings and harnesses are commonly sold in SM shops. These are generally safer than devising your own suspension with ropes, but remember, there is no Underwriter's Laboratory in the bondage trade. Caveat emptor. The responsibility for your lady's safety and well-being rests squarely upon your shoulders.

Many people are so taken by bondage that they commit themselves to a regimen of stretching exercises that they may endure stringent bondage positions. We think that it is a good idea to do some stretching before a bondage session. You can avoid a lot of injuries by doing so and it never hurts to limber up before an exhausting session. Molly is the original loose goose. She has kept herself so limber that she can slip out of almost any bondage. Of course, when she does, Philip is always more than willing to punish her for it.

Every conscientious dominant is always concerned for his victim's well-being. We have compiled the following guidelines for basic bondage safety.

Ten rules to be bound by

1) Be skilled at every bondage you undertake.

2) Bondages should be snug, not tight. Make sure you can easily slip a finger under the ropes, chains, scarves or what have you.

3) Determine how long each bondage can safely be endured and watch the clock. Begin testing new bondages with fifteen to twenty minute durations before working up to longer periods.

4) Submissives, never let anyone you don't know and trust very, very well tie you up. You are literally placing your life in his hands.

5) As with any SM practice, negotiate the bondages that will take place during the proposed session and clearly outline the submissive's limits.

6) Agree upon and practice your safe word before each scene.

7) Never cross pulse points with direct pressure from ropes.

8) NEVER, EVER use a length of rope or chain around the front of a submissive's throat and make sure that all bondages avoid putting any pressure there!

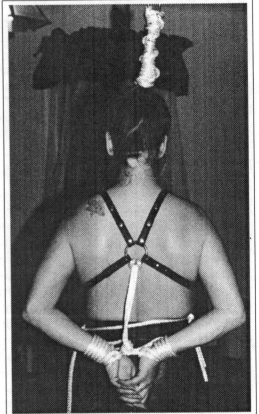

Hair bondage is fun for a short scene. The hair of this woman is tied to a ring above her, but her weight is completely on her feet. Never suspend anyone by the hair!

9) Keep a heavy pair scissors or a knife handy to cut your submissive loose in an emergency.

10) Always keep watch over a bound submissive!! Check constantly for numbness, discoloration, and cold skin as signs of circulation loss.

Let us expound on the rules for the bound:

1) Be skilled at every bondage you undertake.

Risk is unavoidable, however basic the bondage. Keep this in mind and stay sharp while you are doing your scenes; you will avoid a lot of unforeseen accidents.

All kinds of things happen in bondage scenes that you just can't predict beforehand: beds break; submissives squirm into very unlikely positions; cramps develop where they never did before; ropes get twisted and/or loosen; wall mounts fall out; blindfolds begin to hurt; neighbors call the cops (this has happened to us, really!); landlords, UPS drivers, meter readers, mothers-in-law, kids, and girl-scouts bearing cookies come pounding on the door hollering, "I know you're in there!" You never know what to expect.

Beginners should start experimenting with very simple bondages and take note of obvious hazards. Chumming around with other people who lash their lovers is a great way to build a list of do's and don't's. Still, you are going to make mistakes. Trying to anticipate the perils as much as possible helps you dodge anything really serious.

Joint and muscle flexibility varies widely from person to person. This is an important point to cover while you are still in negotiations. Hold her arms in positions you would like to try and ask her how it feels. How far behind her back is too far? Bondage books are filled with models who have been doing yoga since they were two. Just because they can touch their elbows together in six positions doesn't mean your honey can. Even if she claims to have joints made of elasticized pasta, check it out for yourself. Making a game of it by wrestling around with each other can lead to some spicy encounters, too. Carefully test each submissive's ability to remain comfortable within every bondage you want to try.

2) Bondages should be snug, not tight. Make sure you can easily slip a finger under the ropes, chains, scarves or what have you.

If your bondage is too easily escapable, do not make it tighter, re-evaluate your technique. A few extra turns (windings) of rope will usually cure most ineffective bondages. So, you have to spend a few more bucks at the hardware store; who said domination was going to be cheap?

3) Determine how long each bondage can safely be endured and watch the clock. Begin testing new bondages with fifteen to twenty minute durations before working up to longer periods.

It is preferable to suffer a groan of disappointment than a torn muscle. While you are a novice, we recommend changing bondage positions every fifteen to twenty minutes to avoid problems. It is easy enough to make the change a part of your scene. Frequent changes in position will help to keep your submissive's muscles from cramping or overstretching. Still, you may be inclined to experiment with long-term or overnight bondages.

Tying someone for a long time is fine if you follow a few common sense guidelines. Remember that everyone is different physically and mentally. While your submissive may be able to handle being bound overnight without physical problems, she may get freaked out by the duration. Your presence, frequent attention, and reassurance may solve this problem.

Always do long-term bondages on a bed or thick, soft padding to avoid pressure ulcers (bed sores). Pressure sores are serious injuries to the skin caused chiefly by pressure of bones against the skin when someone remains in one position for a long time. When this happens, the skin loses blood circulation at the pressure site and begins to suffer from lack of oxygen. The affected area is commonly numb, so the person doesn't often know that a problem is occurring.

Moisture on the skin will soften and therefore weaken the skin, making it more prone to damage. For this reason, you will want to make sure that your submissive is lying on an absorbent surface. Rubber sheets are not a good idea for long-term bondage.

To avoid pressure ulcers, let your lady move about or change her position every couple of hours. Check for redness, too. Check every place where bones are near the surface of the skin, and around the area where you bind her, even if you are using the softest of restraints.

People vary greatly in their susceptibility to pressure ulcers according to age, skin condition, nutrition, and other factors. If redness persists longer than fifteen minutes after the pressure is relieved from a given site, you may have the beginnings of a problem. Decrease the interval for moving your charge.

Always bind your honey in a natural position and remember that even the most comfy position can become torturous and, therefore, dangerous in as little as an hour. One solution to this problem without ruining the fantasy is planning an "exercise" period every hour or two. This exercise can take the form of sexual "use" of your captive slave-girl, with her immediate return to bondage. Make sure to flex all her joints and check her skin for red spots.

For example; let's suppose your sweety has been bound on her back in a classic spread-eagle position. Release her, check her wrists, and re-tie her hands at her sides or behind her back. Then take her doggy style. This changes her position completely, flexes her joints, and the abused prisoner fantasy is not only intact, but you have both been laid!

4) Submissives, never let anyone you don't know and trust very, very well tie you up. You are literally placing your life in his hands.

Dominants, the trust issue is just as important for you. Don't tie anyone up unless you; (a) feel sure she can handle being helpless without freaking out, (b) are absolutely confident that the bondage you will use is safe, and (c) know your potential lover well enough to know that she won't cry rape after the scene. This last possibility has happened more than once and cannot not be blamed entirely upon the submissive. SM is powerful emotional fuel, best experimented with by people who know each other well. Misunderstandings are frequent, even between people who are well acquainted with each other.

5) As with any SM practice, negotiate the bondages that will take place during the proposed session and clearly outline the submissive's limits.

Don't accept, "I'll do anything you want," as an answer. Say, "OK, but what if I want to do this?" Then move her into the proposed position and ask how it feels. Ask her where she feels the most stress. Remember that simulated bondage is looser than real bondage. Also, when you move a bound person from lying to sitting, from sitting to standing, or from face down to face up positions the stresses on the bound body parts will change. For example, bondages applied to straight legs will become a lot tighter when you bend the legs. If you're planning to have sex with your lady while she's in bondage, keep this compression factor in mind.

6) Agree upon and practice your safe word before each scene.

We don't have to explain this, do we? Just do it! (We'll send you a pair of Nikes.)

1 Neck & Throat

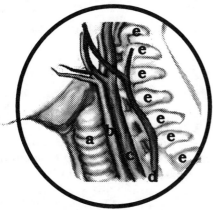

Anatomy for Safer Bondage

Circled areas are locations to avoid pressure or to use great care. Never put pressure on a pulse point.

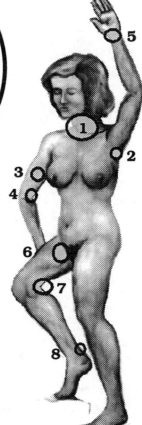

5 Wrist - Palm side

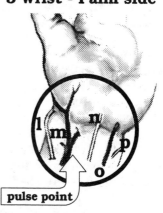

pulse point

1) Neck & Throat

Pressure on the throat can cause loss of consciousness, brain damage and death.

a) trachea
b) carotid artery
c) internal jugular vein
d) external jugular vein
e) cervical vertebrae

Release from suspension by a sudden drop can cause spinal injury (whiplash) or even break the neck.

5) Wrist - Palm side

l) radial nerve
m) radial artery
n) median nerve
o) ulnar artery
p) dorsal br. of ulnar nerve

3 Upper Arm

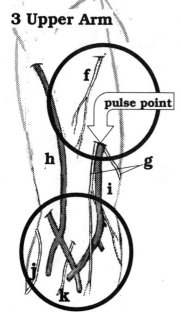

pulse point

6 Upper Thigh

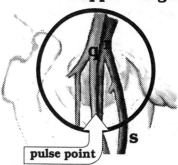

pulse point

2) Armpit

intercostal-brachial nerve
brachial vein and artery
Pressure on this pulse point is dangerous.

3) Upper Arm

f) medial cutaneous nerve of arm
g) medial cutaneous nerve of forearm
h) cephic vein
i) basilic vein

4) Inner Elbow

j) posterior cutaneous nerve of forearm
k) lateral cutaneous nerve of forearm

6) Upper Thigh

q) femoral artery
r) femoral vein
s) great saphenous vein

7) Back of Knee

8) Achilles Tendon

Be aware of how position changes put stress on this tendon.

4 Inner Elbow

99

7) Never cross pulse points with direct pressure from ropes.

Several major veins and arteries are close to the surface of the body: at the insides of the wrists, inside the tops of the thighs, inside the upper arms near the armpits, and all over the neck (See next rule, below!) You will probably encounter the need to pass a rope over some of these points, but there are techniques we will cover for shifting the load away from the pulse points.

8) NEVER, EVER use a length of rope or chain around the front of a submissive's throat and make sure that all bondages avoid putting any pressure there!

Necks are tricky to bind. Many submissives use their throats for breathing, swallowing, and screaming. A majority of subs also store their brains in the bulbous growth above their necks; therefore, a lot of their biological functions depend upon keeping all the tubes, cables, and wires in the neck in good repair. If your submissive has developed similar neck habits, encourage them by being very careful with what you wrap around them. Your relationship will last longer than a few minutes this way.

The safest way to secure a neck is to leave it alone, but if you really want to do it, use a collar designed for the purpose and bind her in such a way that any pressure will be on the back of the neck, avoiding the throat. A better alternative is to use a hood with a bondage ring attached to the top or sides of the head. This bypasses putting strain on the neck and throat altogether. Don't get nutsy, though, and try to hang your lady by hood rings. Her head may pop off and the ensuing goo will stain your dungeon floor.

Bondage collars usually come with one or more metal rings attached to them. A wide, stiff, dog collar will do, but there are dozens of bondage collars available that are made with safety and function in mind.

9) Keep a heavy pair scissors or a knife handy to cut your submissive loose in an emergency.

Is your sub afraid of knives? Hurray! Leaving a ten-inch Bowie in plain sight without an explanation can have a delightfully chilling effect! If she asks what it is for, just say you might be using it later. Just let her wonder what you mean by that, it's good for your scene. Scissors with dull, rounded ends, such as bandage scissors, are preferable to knives as they are less likely to poke a hole in your honey. Whatever you plan to use, make sure it's going to be more than sufficient to cut through whatever you're using to bind her. (See emergency quick release, below.)

10) Always keep watch over a bound submissive!! Check constantly for numbness, discoloration, and cold skin as signs of circulation loss.

Ask her how she is doing, frequently; submissives tend to ignore problems they are having because they do not want to interrupt the scene or break the mood. They are much more likely to answer a direct question than to volunteer the information.

Emergency quick release

Be sure that any bondage you attempt can be released in thirty seconds or less. No, no, no, this does not mean planting plastic explosives beside intricate knots, that would be overkill...literally. There are several quick-release knots, such as a few links of chain plait (same thing as a crochet stitch), that will hold very securely until you pull the rip-cord. Single and double-looped bows work well, too.

As mentioned above in rule 8, keep a good pair of scissors or a sharp knife around for cutting through ropes and scarves even if you are using only quick-release knots. Any knot can become snarled during play and hold fast at the wrong time. Be fully resolved that you might have to destroy your toys in an emergency. You don't want to be nervous about cutting through a $90 silk scarf while your lover is in a panic or hurting. Letting her catch you hesitating while you measure her safety against the value of even the finest of hand-tooled leathers tends to have a corrosive impact on a relationship.

Resign yourself to it now -- all toys are expendable.

If you are using padlocks and chains, or anything else that locks: stocks or pillories, collars, chastity belts, harnesses, etc., keep the keys close at hand and make sure that all the keyholes are easily accessible throughout the scene. Keep all locks well lubricated; stash a small bottle of graphite lubricant in your toy bag and use it frequently.

The lock is jammed.

But honey, that body harness cost me a fortune.

Then cut me down!!

Paul, eunuchs have no need for bondage toys.

Novice bondage

Some folks get downright fidgety when the topic of sexual bondage comes up. Others drool in anticipation. Most people fall somewhere in between, knowing little or nothing about it. Still, we've rarely run across an active libido without at least a passing curiosity.

Simple, safe bondage is an easy way to begin playing with power and trust. Explaining the allure of power and trust games, though, is a little like trying to describe an orgasm to a virgin. You have to try it to understand it. If you are wondering whether bondage will float your boat, but either you or your partner is nervous about it, we recommend trying the following gentle progression.

The first session

Take your novice to bed and have her lie on her back with her hands over her head or behind her neck. Her manner of dress is up to you, but you will want her wearing something that will afford access for intercourse. By now you may have surmised that we are of the "slow and sensual" school. Starting a session naked is nice, but we love to generate all the anticipation we can. Exotic lingerie helps set her mind in the right place and gives you something engaging to play with while you tease her along. Tell her that she must keep her eyes closed and that she may not move a muscle, nor make a single sound unless you tell her otherwise (to help you remove her panties, for example).

It is important to get her to agree to this. By agreeing, she is taking the first step toward surrendering to you. Reward her with delightful sensations. Begin slowly: cuddle with her for a while, then start doing whatever she likes best, but stop short of intercourse. This exercise is entirely for her pleasure, not for yours. Summon your best cunnilingus style, if that's what she likes, play with her breasts, use your fingers on her genitals, or do whatever pushes her buttons. Work her over slowly and methodically. She'll be straining at the bit in a few minutes.

At some point, she will almost involuntarily move her hips or begin moaning and wriggling about. This is good. You want her to lose control so that you can remind her of her promise to remain still. If she is really getting hot, a simple verbal reminder might not keep her quiet. This is even better! Stop touching her. She'll get the message plenty quick.

When she regains her composure (and don't you dare touch her again until she does!), reward her by resuming your loving maneuvers. Take your time by bringing her up to another frenzy. Stop again. Tell her that you will let her finish when she calms down. This time, keep at it until you sense that she is about to orgasm.

This is a critical moment, and often, a difficult one to judge. Before she comes, but not until she is very close to falling over the edge, give her a sharp command to come. She is going to come anyway, but, by issuing the command, you are both giving her permission and reasserting your control over her.

This scheme has two goals in training your submissive. Firstly, it demonstrates the joys of controlled sexual response. You generated a very strong orgasm by building sexual tension from one plateau to a higher one, then to an even higher one before allowing her a final release. Secondly, you are teaching your slave-girl the rewards of obedience through positive reinforcement; she gets to feel good if she behaves well and does what she is told to do. Positive reinforcement is a subtle and very compelling technique for beginners. There is no punishment involved that might scare her away, only good stuff or nothing at all.

Settling down time is a wonderful time to cement this new part of your relationship. Snuggle next to her under the sheets and tell her how good she was. Tell her that you are proud of her. She is going to be happy and grateful that you took such good care of her.

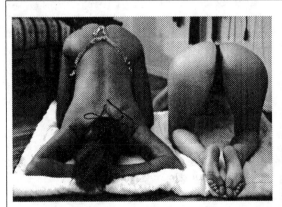

Mental bondage is an alternative to physical restraint. The submissive is trained to take and hold a position.

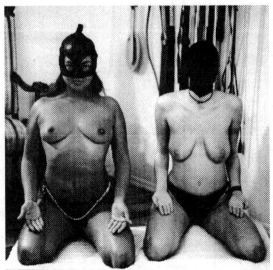

Now, let her pleasure you. Give her a gentle order to make love to you, give you an oral release, or whatever you are in the mood for.

By the way, some dominants prefer to go a route other than bondage at this point. You may, too. Some dominants, upon asserting their control, prefer a type of "slave" training with little or no bondage. They may want their submissives to learn special positions (kneeling, prone, sitting, standing) that they will assume on command. We call this mental bondage. Others may prefer to train their ladies to perform service or to dress in a special way. It all depends on the fantasy that you both decide upon, but this is, after all, the bondage chapter, so we'll proceed in that vein.

The second session

The next step introduces two new elements: a non-threatening bondage and sensory deprivation. You will need two silk (or silky nylon) scarves about three feet long from corner to corner diagonally. If you do not have these, find a substitute that will be comfortable for her keeping in mind that one of the scarves will be a blindfold. Also, assemble a small collection of things you can use to tease and surprise her with, but keep these things out of sight.

Pick things that will stimulate different senses and provide contrast. From the pleasingly sensual category you might collect: a feather, a piece of bunny fur, perfume, massage oil (terrific if it is heated before you use it), a rich chocolate truffle, a glass of wine, a heating pad, a swatch of velvet, some fruit pieces, whipped cream, a bell or pretty-sounding chime, headphones attached to your stereo or a walkman with sensual music, and a vibrator. For contrast, you might select a broken popsicle stick (to prick her lightly with a sharp point, it is safe, but will feel like a needle), an onion or clove of garlic, a piece of sandpaper, an ice cube, ice water and an eye dropper to apply it, a clothespin or two, a smelly sock, a joy-buzzer (the kind you use for "shocking" handshakes), and so on.

All of these items are to be a surprise to her; she is not to see any of them or know about them before your session.

Again, order your lover to close her eyes and remain still and silent. Repeat your instructions from the first session in exactly the same words, if you can. This reinforces the conditioning you initiated in the first session. Again, reward your lady's compliance to your commands. Pet her long enough to stimulate her, but not enough to make her really hot.

Stop teasing her and blindfold her with one of the scarves. She may be surprised (remember, her eyes have been closed) and wonder what you are up to. She may even object strongly.

If this happens, you have encountered one of two situations. You have either uncovered a deep-seated fear or your submissive is testing you. Do not try to cure a phobia in a scene, that's not safe play. Making someone panic is not safe either. If she objected to using blindfolds during your negotiations, then you have no business using one and this scenario is not for you. She set blindfolds as beyond her limits and respecting limits is an inviolable trust. But if she is testing you, or what you are doing scares her and gives her a thrill at the same time, the activity is worth pursuing.

It is easy to find out whether she is testing you or if she is really having a problem. At her first objection, stop what you are doing and ask your lady if she remembers her safe-word. Have her repeat it out loud. Remind her that it is perfectly acceptable for her to use her safe-word if she needs to and that you will stop the scene immediately. Reassure her that there are a million things to try in SM, no one thing is indispensable, but that this is something you would like her to try. Proceed. You will have your answer shortly.

The tournament of wills, or...

"You wouldn't!" she said, "Oh, but I would," he replied.

You are blindfolding her for the first time, or embarking on some other evil task and she shouts, "No!" You remind her about using her safe-word and she doesn't use it, she's not on the edge of panic, and she's not catatonic, she's responsive. But she says she doesn't want you to go any further.

Dominants always have to prove their mettle at some point; it is a normal development when you assume the roles of dominant and submissive. A dominant has to win his lady's submission. Your submissive is not necessarily testing you out of spite or just to be a brat. She may simply be frightened by the unexpected and unaware that she is testing you at all, or, she may be playfully objecting as a part of the fantasy she is living-out. In either case, you are being tested. Here is how to pass the test.

Let's stick to our example of the blindfold. Don't be touchy about her objection or ridicule her for being babyish about something as benign as a blindfold. Calmly ask her if she will agree to trust you. It is important not to go any further unless and until she does agree. If she doesn't, be supportive, loving and understanding, but tell her that you will continue her training only when she can trust you enough to allow the blindfold.

Assure her that you will not let any harm come to her, that you will never exceed the limits she has agreed to, and that you will not hurt her. If she still will not agree, quietly let the issue drop and suggest that you make love and forget about training for a while.

She will not be able to forget about it for a second. The longer the idea festers in her mind, the more profound will be her capitulation... if it ever happens. Your job is to stay cool and not give her an inch. Do not ignore her either; you don't want to deprive her of sex or affection, but she may not tell you how to administer her training. Let her rant, let her rave, if it comes to that, and you will remain calm, friendly, and loving and willing to do anything she wants to do except bondage or SM.

Curiosity is a sinister master. The odds are overwhelmingly in your favor that she will finally agree to the blindfold. This is only an example of when your test will arrive. She may have no problem with a blindfold, but balk at some other devious torture you have dreamed up. Be certain, though, that your submissive will put you on trial, usually more than once.

People are rarely aware of all of their limitations before they begin experimenting with SM. Re-negotiation is a continuing part of the game. Following our example, your lady may discover that she panics when blindfolded only after you try it. She may never have been blindfolded before. Allowing, even encouraging re-negotiation between scenes is very reassuring to a submissive, affords her a deeper level of trust and admiration for the care and concern you are demonstrating.

Tested or not, your next step is to tie a silk scarf around one of your lover's wrists leaving the one end as long as possible. Tell her to lay on the bed with her hands over her head. Instead of tying the loose end to her other wrist, just loop it around the headboard and tell her to hold the loose end in her free hand. (In case your headboard doesn't have a place to loop a scarf, we have some attachment solutions for you below.) Make sure she doesn't peek while you are tying her. Ask her if she is comfortable.

If she gets uncomfortable or frightened, all she has to do is let go of the end she is holding and she will be free. You'd be amazed at how many people will wail and scream for release while holding on to that scarf for dear life.

Now the fun can begin.

While she is blindfolded, fetch your collection of goodies and place them within your reach. Be quiet about it, though, you don't want to give her any advance warning.

Begin stroking her body gently. Use your hands in the most sensual manner you can muster; lightly scratching her skin from her armpits to her breasts, circling there, then transversing her belly and navigating about her hips. Move your palms, finger-tips, and finger-nails in tiny circles close to her nipples, but never touch them. Nestle your fingers among her belly hairs, but leave the more sensitive flesh below unattended.

Relax and take your time no matter how she pleads, you can draw out this scene for hours. Enjoy the variation in the textures, flushing colors, and scents of her flesh. Let her pleasure flow through you. Discover where she is ticklish and where your touch electrifies her. Pinch her, sometimes softly, sometimes harder.

Control the building and waning of her arousal under your caresses. Imagine a silent movie of a car traveling over a smooth road in a hilly terrain. Slowly excite her as the car climbs a hill, sooth her as the car descends.

Let her feel different parts of you as you direct her arousal. Give her your lips between her thighs, but only your hot breath near her sex. Give her your flickering eyelashes against her throat, your tongue around the outline of her lips. Let her smell your cock while you stroke it against her cheek. Move your mouth to her hair and sigh quietly.

Now stop and move away. Let silence and stillness fill the room. You have awakened all the nerve-endings of her skin. Let those tingling nerves reach out to find you from behind the darkness of her blindfold. Let her wonder what you are up to. Let her wait a while.

Turn on some sensual music and let it play. Fill an eye-dropper with ice water and drop a single drop on her nipple. Wait for her to process the sensation. With the sharp end of a broken stick, prick her other nipple. Again, let the sensation ripple through her. Move your mouth close to her ear with the stealth of a thief and whisper that you love her.

Plan the use of your toys to stimulate her senses one at a time. Crush a clove of garlic and wave it under her nose. Then break off a small piece of chocolate, place it on your tongue and feed it to her with a lingering kiss. Use the bunny fur to massage her breasts. Tickle her ribs and armpits with a supple feather, then use the eye-dropper to coat her lips with sweetened cream. Nuzzle your cheeks between her thighs scratching them with your beard. Prick her labia lightly with a pin, then lick away each small pain from it.

Be aware of everything in the room, the music, the warmth and smells of your bodies. Let your own arousal and her responses foster your creativity and guide you. Work to bring both of you to new levels of intensity. Use the toys in your arsenal to ignite, to tease, to amuse. Cause her little pains and smooth them away with your mouth and fingers and cock and chest. Let her feel your arms surrounding and loving her. Be playful. Be dramatic. Be scary. Fuck her deeply and violently. Leave her breathless.

Afterward, untie your lover and let all your tenderness flow into her. Remove her blindfold and let your eyes communicate your love for her.

We don't know about you, but we need a shower. We seem to have become a little... um...sticky.

The third and all the rest of your sessions

Now you are ready to try more restrictive bondages. Re-negotiation is in order. What did she like, so far? What fantasies did those first two sessions elicit? What do you want to try next?

Remember to take your time, introducing only a couple of new elements during each session. Too many new things at once dull the effect of each part. Soon, you will come to understand the levels of bondage with which you are comfortable and can begin mixing your bondage with other elements of SM.

Is corporal intriguing to you? Experiment with spanking and paddling. Does torture hold a special appeal? Surprise her with the delights of fire and ice. Has she always held a secret fantasy of humiliation? Strip her naked, bind her arms and crotch. Then cover her with a full length coat and take her shopping in the mall. Let your imaginations soar!

photo by Jerry

8 Of Humane Bondage

Bondage Techniques

ou are visiting your neighborhood hardware store. For the last twenty minutes, you have been standing in front of a pegboard display offering three dozen kinds of rope. Your eyes settle on one plastic bag after another as you visualize each rope wrapping around your true love's naked, tawny body. Finally, a sweet, grandmotherly clerk saunters up beside you asking, "May I help you?"

Realizing the spectacle your absent-minded behavior must have created, every cc of your blood quits nourishing whatever part of your body it was busy feeding and rushes to your face, which is now glowing brighter than a river of molten lava. "No, thank you," you manage to stammer.

"I like the nylon, three-eighths inch, twisted strand stuff, m'self," the hardware matron offers, "it marks my skin some, but it makes a lovely vibration when my husband draws it over my nipples."

Battling to hang onto your cool, you cock an eyebrow and thank Granny Fixit calmly, and reach for a polybag of nylon, three-eighths inch, twisted strand. Unhappily, the polybag snags on its hook and the whole display crashes merrily over your head. Even more unhappily, the accident doesn't kill you and now every eyeball, forefinger, and mouth is glaring, pointing, and laughing right at you and they don't stop until you melt into a puddle of mortified slush.

Bonds that tie

To help you avoid this scenario of social suicide, we prepared a brief look at the kind of ropes to use in your bondage scenes. Wandering into your hardware store you find rope in sisal, hemp, manila, nylon, cotton, the poly family (Ester, Ethylene, Propylene, and Amide), and cousin Kevlar. For the most part you can toss out every one of these but cotton and nylon. Toy with the others, if you will, but we predict a short and unsatisfying affair.

Both nylon and cotton ropes are constructed in two styles, braided and twisted strand (or cable-laid). Braided rope is what we usually think of as the type we use for clothesline. Six or eight bunches of fibers are braided around a core. Twisted strand is made from three strands of rope laid right-handed (twisted to the right). Each strand is made from three to nine smaller strands of yarn, twisted left-handed. Both kinds of rope can, of course, be found in a plethora of thicknesses.

To pare down your options, we suggest you keep a few goals in mind. You do not want the rope to be too abrasive, nor to be so thin that it becomes deeply imbedded in the skin over the length of time you anticipate keeping your lady bound. Also consider the types of bondages you want to do. Three-eighths inch is a good, all-purpose bondage rope, half-inch and thicker is fun for wrapping (semi-mummy style) but it is more difficult to handle and the knots may be more cumbersome to deal with. Philip prefers a thicker rope for threading through a lady's crotch because it covers more flesh and feels more formidable than three-eighths inch rope. Still, tastes and crotches vary considerably. You just have to resign yourself to experimenting with different textures and thicknesses until you find the right combination for you and your sweety.

People continually debate the merits of cotton versus nylon ropes. We prefer nylon; you'll have to make your own decision. The arguments usually include the following: Cotton is more abrasive than nylon. Nylon is soft and silky against the skin. But, if cotton is laundered with a fabric softener it can be as soft as nylon. Nylon doesn't hold knots as easily, nor as tightly, as cotton. A half-decent knotsman has little trouble with nylon. Cotton shrinks as it dries, causing tighter bondage and knots that are difficult, if not impossible, to untie. Knots that are difficult to untie are good. Knots that are difficult to untie are bad. Nylon is more expensive than cotton. Cotton is more expensive in the long run because you ruin more rope by having to cut people out of bondage.

A similar unending debate flourishes between braided and twisted strand rope. Braided rope fans insist that twisted strand unravels too easily. Twisted strand devotees are willing to go to the extra effort to finish the ropes properly in order to enjoy the bumpy ride afforded by the twists as they are slowly dragged across the skin.

Again, make your own choice; we prefer twisted strand nylon for its sensual feel. If you are inexperienced, start with nylon, braided or twisted; we feel that it is much more forgiving than cotton.

Finishing the rope

The ends of every piece of rope you use in bondage should be bound (whipped), melted (this works only for nylon rope), taped, or knotted to keep them from snarling during your scenes. Finishing a rope helps prevent difficulty in releasing bondages and makes it more attractive.

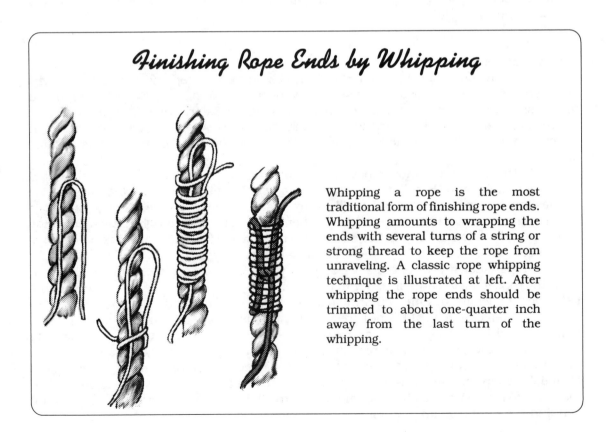

Finishing Rope Ends by Whipping

Whipping a rope is the most traditional form of finishing rope ends. Whipping amounts to wrapping the ends with several turns of a string or strong thread to keep the rope from unraveling. A classic rope whipping technique is illustrated at left. After whipping the rope ends should be trimmed to about one-quarter inch away from the last turn of the whipping.

Melting the ends of a nylon rope is easily accomplished using the heated blade of a knife. Be sure to melt all the fibers together into one lump so that none are free to unravel. Melting tends to leave a few sharp points on the rope end which can be easily sanded smooth.

Taping is a quick method of rope finishing which can, with a little planning, be a great help to you in performing your bondages. Any strong tape will do, but if you use colored, plastic or electrical tape, you can color code your ropes by length.

When choosing the colors to code the lengths of your rope, keep in mind that you will often be doing your scenes in dimly lit, romantic settings. Therefore, choose colors that will contrast sharply, making it easier to select the right length at a glance. We suggest white for six-foot lengths, red for ten, yellow for fifteen, blue for twenty, orange for thirty, black for forty. An alternative to the color scheme is to draw rings around the ends with indelible marking pen to signify length. Use one ring for six-foot lengths, two for ten, three for fifteen, etc.

Knot books offer a number of ways to create round or cylindrical finished ends. Though knotted ends look great, this is our least favorite method of rope finishing. The knotted ends, being thicker than the rope itself, are a hassle when executing bondages. Still, making a simple overhand knot in the end of a rope to keep it from fraying is a handy quick-fix.

Knots

There must be sixteen squizzillion knot books on the market, so we're not going to spend a lot of time teaching you what you can learn better elsewhere. Philip's favorites are the square knot, the half-hitch, the overhand knot, the figure eight knot, and the chain stitch. He applies almost all his bondages with combinations of these simple knots.

Overhand or Thumb Knot

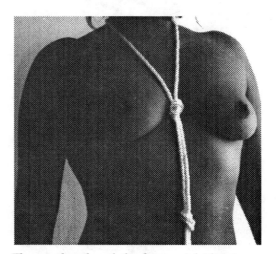

The **overhand knot** is the simplest knot to tie. It can be used as a stopper to keep a line from slipping through an eye, ring or hole, or it can be used as a simple method of keeping a rope from fraying. Some call this knot a **thumb knot**. Overhand knots are also good for creating loops as in the photo at right.

The overhand and the figure eight knots are also used for creating strong, non-slipping loops. This photo shows an overhand knot used to make a loop for the beginning of an oriental rope dress. Using a figure eight knot in place of an overhand would yield a more decorative knot that will also lay flatter.

109

Figure Eight Knot

The **figure eight knot** serves the same purpose as the overhand knot. Its advantages are that it is large, so it will not slip through a ring or eye as easily, it can be considered more decorative, and it is easier to untie.

Bowline

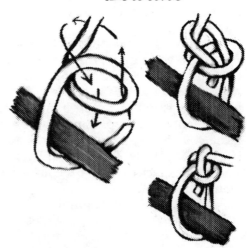

The **bowline** makes a very safe, non-slip loop. We don't use this knot very often, but it is an essential for suspension bondage where loops that can be relied upon not to tighten are critical.

Square or Reef Knot

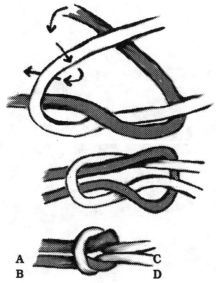

The **square**, or **reef knot** is the workhorse of most of our bondages. It is a quick, easy knot to tie and holds well for most purposes. This knot is generally used to join two ends or pieces of rope that are the same size. To break the square knot, simply hold the two adjacent ends (A&B, or C&D), and pull them apart sharply.

Surgeon's Knot

The **surgeons's knot** is similar to the square knot, but each step includes one extra twist between each of the two steps in tying it. This helps to keep the line tight between steps. This knot is useful when you are joining two lines together when they are under tension.

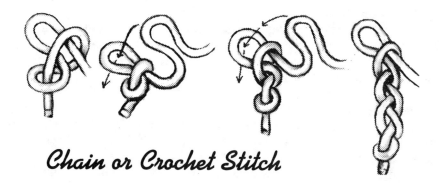

Chain or Crochet Stitch

The **chain** or **crochet stitch** is an attractive and useful knot. When binding the ankles, several "links" can be tied between each ankle to create a decorative and effective hobble. The chain stitch can also be used as a spacer between the elbows to anchor them behind the back without stressing the shoulders. For either of these uses, tie as many links as desired for the length of the hobble or spacer, then pass the loose end through the open loop to fix the chain so that it will not unravel.

One of the more interesting features of the chain stitch is that it unravels instantly by tugging on the loose end. This makes it perfect as a quick-release knot. The illustration below demonstrates an elbow bondage with a chain stitch spacer and extending one of the links, using it to bind the right elbow. We locate the finishing stitch where the submissive cannot reach it. Using the chain stitch as an instant release provides both a safety factor and can add to the drama of releasing your lady from an intense scene by popping the ropes off with a single tug.

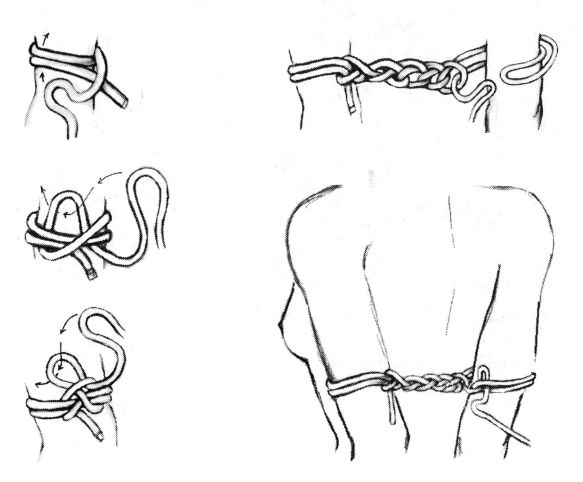

Releasing your victim

At the end of a bondage scene it is considered polite to untie your submissive. Generally, submissives object to being left to die in bondage and it has been known to annoy religious societies, local law enforcement agencies, and close relatives. Since it is the only acceptable etiquette, why not make untying your submissive a fun part of a scene?

You have played the villain so far; now you can become your lady's hero, slicing through her bonds and gathering her up into your arms! Or, you can stay in thug mode, adding to the torture by slow, ceremonious unraveling of your physically and emotionally spent victim.

If you are using twisted strand, you can untie a rope and slowly draw it from under another rope that is still under tension. This sets up an intriguing vibration that is particularly taunting if the taut rope passes over a nipple or a vagina that has already orgasmed about thirteen times.

Also, many submissives are very nervous around knives. You can squeeze from her a few more ounces of fear as you abruptly (but very, very carefully) slice away her bonds affording her both the glorious sensation of instant release and the thrill of being so close to a razor-sharp blade.

(Photo: Jerry)

If the knife is just too scary, or you are too worried about cutting your honey, you can still give her the quick release by using safety shears. You should always have a pair of safety shears around, anyway, for emergency situations. These shears have blunt ended blades and are tough enough to cut through coins. Safety shears cost only a few dollars and are widely available in variety and hardware stores.

Better still, give your lady love an instant release by incorporating the chain stitch or bows at key points in your bondage. This takes a great deal more planning, but the magic of tugging on a few loose ends and having all your ropes magically fall to your submissive's feet will delight her and earn you no end of respect. This is no easy feat, but it can be done. If it all works the way you plan it to, you deserve to be fed peeled grapes while having your genitals attended to most tenderly.

A Simple Wrist Bondage

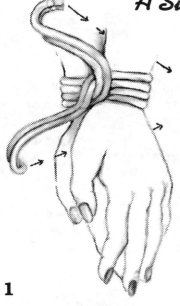

1

Place the lady's palms together. Fold the rope in half and wrap it around the wrists twice. Don't pull it tight, just make it snug. If you cannot easily stick your finger under the rope, it is too tight.

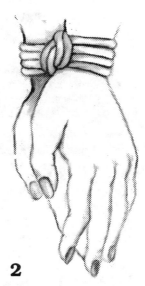

2

Bend the loose ends across each other, pass one end between the hands and the other between the arms above the double wrap.

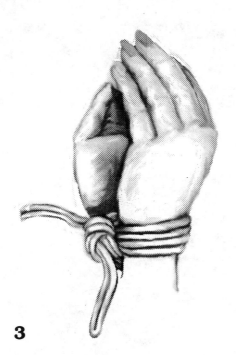

3

Secure the loose ends with a square knot, and torture away!

Use a six- to eight-foot length of rope. We recommend a three-eighths inch braided nylon, commonly found in hardware stores. Twisted nylon works fine too, but the ends tend to unravel more readily.

Always try to use a "palms together" bondage to avoid putting pressure on the veins and arteries inside the wrists. This bondage is effective because the knot is below the wrists, a difficult place for the submissive to reach.

This bondage also works well for ankles and knees where you want the limbs to be bound in a parallel fashion. For ankles, start with a ten-foot piece of rope, for knees, you may need fifteen feet. You may wish to add more stringent bondage by adding more turns around the limbs or more cinch knots. You will need twice the rope for every two extra turns you choose to add and about one third of the original length for every two cinch loops. Select a longer rope accordingly.

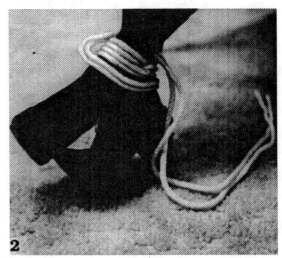

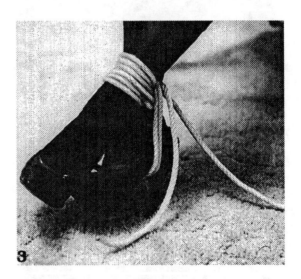

Crossed Ankle Bondage

Positioning your lady in high heels with her ankles crossed makes an ankle bondage more difficult to escape and increases her feeling of vulnerability.

This example incorporates the heels of the shoes into the cinch loop. This adds to the visual effect and helps to keep the shoes on during play. We use a ten-foot length of three-eighths inch twisted nylon here. The rope is folded in half and looped around the ankles (fig. 1). Pass the rope a single turn around the ankles, than pass it between the legs above the turn to begin the cinch loop (fig. 2). The cinch loop hooks under both ankles and is passed again between the legs (fig. 3). The loose ends are then wrapped around the ankles in opposite directions and the bondage is finished with a square knot (fig. 4).

For added stability, you may want to increase the number of turns and use a couple of cinch loops instead of one. This will require doubling the length of the rope.

Crossed-legged ankle bondage yields a delightful dilemma for your lover. In this position, it is very difficult to keep the legs together which affords easy access to the treasure between them.

There is a running controversy about the safety of winding rope around each breast or binding breasts tightly. Some feel that tight breast bondage may cause the skin to stretch and/or encourage the growth of cysts. Women who are prone to developing cysts should avoid breast bondage or use a low impact bondage such as illustrated here.

Breast Bondage

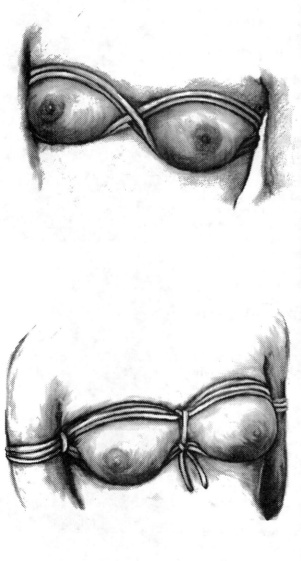

Oriental rope dress

Rope dress is a most attractive and versatile bondage. There are two traditional styles of oriental rope dress, the diamond and the box. We will be illustrating the basic diamond style. It looks like an intricate web of rope which enhances your submissives shape by covering her with symmetrical diamond patterns.

Once you master the principles of the basic style, you can begin to experiment with doubled ropes, overlapping diamond patterns, and various configurations for attaching the arms and legs to the rope dress. The rope dress can also be useful as a harness or for attaching the person to furniture, whipping benches and the like.

Rope Dress

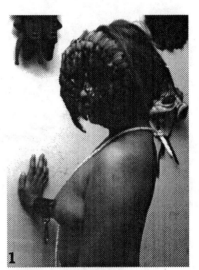

1) You will need a length of one-quarter inch or three-eighths inch rope from forty to fifty feet long. Fold the rope in half and tie an overhand knot in the middle, leaving a three to four inch loop. Your lady will have to be standing up to apply this bondage.

The overhand knot is placed behind your lady's neck with the ends draped over her shoulders and hanging between her breasts (fig. 1).

2) Make sure your lady is standing up straight. Tie three more overhand knots placed so that the top one is directly between her breasts and the second at or slightly above her navel. Placement of the third knot is critical to maximize her enjoyment of the bondage. The third knot should be tied so that when the rope is brought under her and up between her butt-cheeks, the knot rests directly on your lady's clitoris. The knot will stimulate the clitoris with her every movement (fig. 2).

Now pass the two rope ends between your lover's legs, between her labia, and upward between her ass-cheeks, then thread the ends through the loop at the back of the neck. Pull it slightly taut and adjust it as necessary to ensure a snug, but not tight, fit. Do not make it too tight, we are going to be putting more tension here shortly.

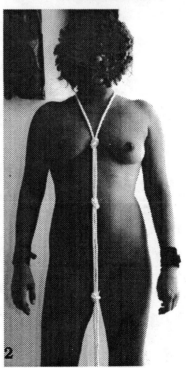

NOTE: An attractive substitute for the overhand knot is the figure eight knot. As the ropes are doubled, the figure eight should be tied taking care to form a flat, even knot serving as a decorative focal point.

ANOTHER NOTE: Clitorises, as do any of nature's gentle creatures, vary greatly in size, shape and sensitivity. If your lady's clitoris is very sensitive, you may opt to tie the bottom knot so that it rests just above the pubic bone. You don't want it pressing against the pubic bone, so aim for the top line of her furry triangle. If she shaves, come see us, we'll find it for you. (Aren't we gracious?)

Now, instead of passing the rope ends between her labia, pass them to the outsides of her labia majora, in the crease between each thigh and the outer lip. Then you may bring the ends together and proceed as directed above, threading the ropes through the loop at the nape of the neck.

3) Now bring each end of the rope around to the front, passing them on either side of her and under each arm and above her breasts. Thread each end under the ropes descending toward the knot between the breasts and tug each end outward, slightly, to separate the midline ropes (fig. 3).

4) Pass the ends back under the arms again and around to the rope running along your lady's spine. Loop each end around this doubled, midline rope, passing them under the arms again toward m'lady's front (fig. 4).

5) This time the ends will go beneath your sweetheart's breasts, in fact, try to place the rope just beneath her rib cage, following the line of her ribs to where it meets the descending rope in front. Again, thread each end through one line of the double rope and tug outward to create a diamond shape in the midline ropes (fig. 5).

6) Repeat the process of step #4 in back (fig. 6) and make the bottom diamond as you did in step #5. Finish the rope dress in the back with the knotting of your choice.

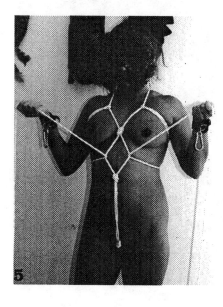

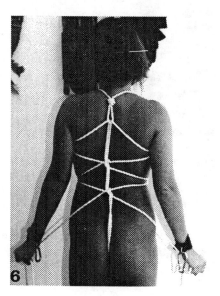

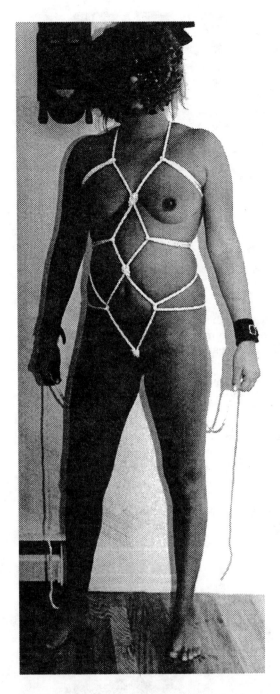

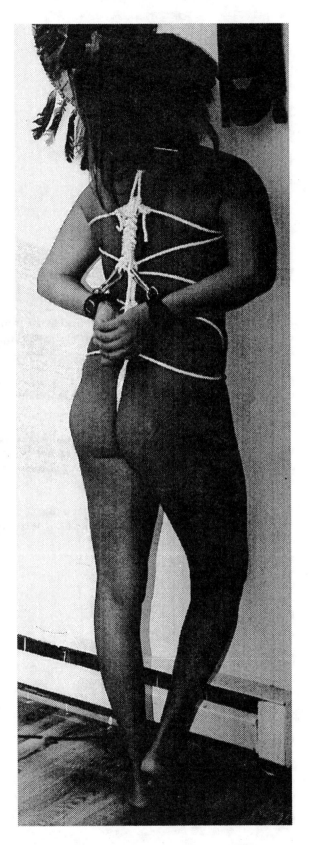

The finished product from the front is shown above. Notice that she is holding the two, rather long ends of the rope left over after the operation was completed.

One possibility for finishing the rope dress is making a decorative attachment for the wrists by braiding the remaining rope around the midline rope (right).

118

Hints

Creating rope dress takes time, relax and enjoy the process. Hurrying will only snarl the ropes and cause frustration.

As you are threading, you will find that there is a lot of rope to contend with. Pull slowly to avoid rope burn; the friction builds up very quickly.

Always maintain tension on the ropes to retain crisp diamond shapes. Each time you thread the front rope and pass the ends around back, give them a little tug to pull apart the two parts of the front rope yielding the diamond patterns that makes this bondage so pretty and creating a nice snug bondage. Allow your submissive to hold the ropes under tension as you work from front to back.

Variations

There are a million ways to add your own signature to an oriental rope dress. Use various colors, sizes, and textures of ropes. Macrame a star in the center knot and attach ropes to radiate from it creating all kinds of patterns.

You may choose to use thinner parachute chord, which comes in many bright colors or a thicker, half-inch rope which can also be found in a fair array of colors. We have seen some in a soft gold nylon that would make a stunning rope dress.

Thinner rope affords a sleeker look to the rope dress that subtly enhances the body. Thick rope makes the bondage look more formidable and intimidating. We like them both.

Instead of winding the rope around the midline rope in the rear, you can add two additional knots to the midline, one at the small of the back and one-half way up, between the one at the small of the back and the loop at the nape of the neck. Then, as you are winding from front to back, you can create diamonds in the back the same way you did in the front.

You can attach a shorter rope, about twenty-five to thirty feet long, to the front, bottom knot to create a diamond rope dress for the legs. Similar attachments can be made starting at the hips or shoulders to make rope dress for the arms.

The box style rope dress, mentioned at the beginning of this section, utilizes two midline ropes in much the same fashion as we wound the wrapping ends to the midline rope at the back of the diamond rope dress. This can cover your lover from head to toe, wrapping her as you might a long package.

Rope alternatives

There is a camp of bondagers who enjoy using anything but rope to secure their charges. When these folks poke around in their closets and dresser drawers, scarves, belts, bandages, and neckties all begin to assume erotic dimensions.

You can create some stunning bondages using several brightly colored satin or nylon scarves. Belts make terrific bondage straps, but get yourself a leather punch; the holes seem never to be in the right place. Bandages, both gauze and elastic, can provide endless memories of dear old mummy, and neckties, well, we've always thought they look much more appealing around her wrists than around his neck. Yet, these are only the most obvious of bondage treasures to be found laying around the house. Erotic play toys are indigenous to every room of the house.

We find ourselves drooling over rolls of plastic food wrap. (It comes in colors, shoppers!) Philip is fond of using an entire roll to encase his ladies from shoulders to toes. Once she is helplessly gift wrapped, he takes his time with his sexy packages, carefully cutting holes through the plastic to tease, torment, and have sex with various pieces of the lovely dish inside.

Wrapping   (photo: Jerry)

Our plastic wrapped lady looks like a mermaid.

Plastic Wrap Bondage

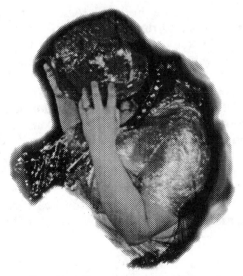

Breaking free (photo: Steve Lauer)

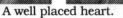

A well placed heart.

120

We know people who can find lascivious uses for a staggering array of common items: large bath towels; layer upon layer of thick sweaters; parkas; sleeping bags; laundry sacks; duct and electrical tape; bed sheets, blankets; throw-rugs; curtains; and all manner of industrial packaging products. Aside from beds, they also make use of other furniture, exercise bars, ladders, stair railings, doors and door frames, and closet poles.

While scavenging through the house looking to convert ordinary objects into sex toys, don't overlook unusual combinations of things. The spreader bar below comprises an ordinary man's belt and a foot-long length of PVC pipe left over from a plumbing repair. It can be used to manacle the wrists, the ankles, or elbows. For a longer spreader bar, use two belts linked, chainlike, inside a longer piece of pipe. The surface of PVC pipe takes spray paint very well, so it is easy to cover over the black stenciling.

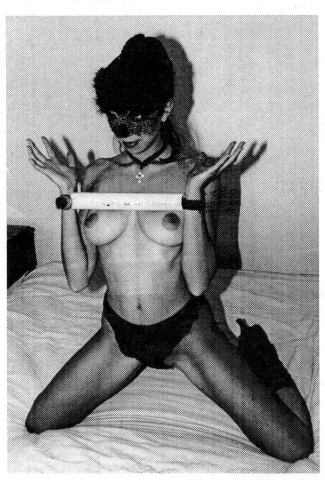

Wrist and ankle cuffs

The bondage community has spawned a cabal of craftspeople engaged in designing traditional and innovative devices for imprisoning themselves and others. Chief among this clique are the leathercrafters whose wares can be found in erotica and SM shops around the world. (See our appendix for a list of vendors.)

Though the primary materials for handcrafted wrist and ankle cuffs are leather, metal and cloth are becoming more prominent as vegetarians and the politically motivated turn their interests toward bondage. Handmade cuffs are often lined with fur and sheepskin, or the synthetic versions thereof.

There are so many designs available that it is impossible to describe all the types available. There are cuffs designed for light play to full body suspension. Some lock with padlocks and others have simple buckle or velcro closures. There are cuffs made to be easily foiled (for self-release) and cuffs that can outwit the budding Houdini.

Look for materials and construction that suit your bondage style and purpose. Avoid cuffs that are cheaply made, narrow enough to cut off circulation (wide bands of leather spread stress over a larger area, thus reducing the likelihood of constriction), or that have hardware that might injure you. Rivets should be strong enough to suit the task. The strongest are called keyposts. These have two pieces that screw together as opposed to the common rivets which are hammered together. Buckles also come in a wide variety. Don't buy cuffs with buckles that are stamped from sheet metal; the finishing of these is often poor and they can have rough or sharp edges.

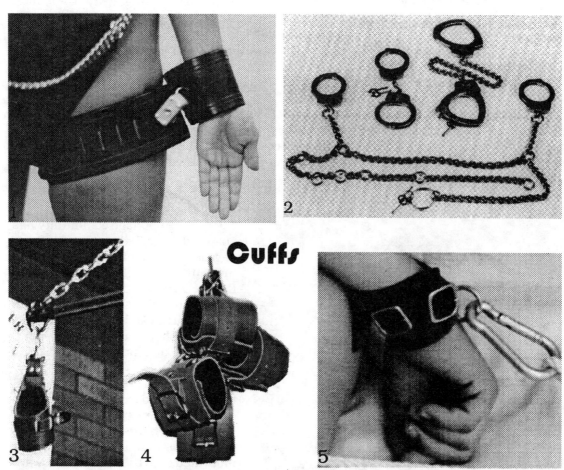

1) Thigh-to-wrist cuffs are locked with a common padlock. 2) Steel handcuffs, leg irons and belly chain made by Smith & Wesson from the Leather Master's Catalog, California. 3) Suspension cuffs used on a trapeze and 4) comfortable wide leather cuffs are from Fantasy Isle, a fetish boutique in Danbury, Connecticut. 5) Our favorite double-wrap suede cuffs.

The signs of a better leather cuff include beveled, cleanly cut, straight edges and rugged hardware. Also check for uniformity in the leather used to make them. Hides are not uniform in thickness or finish; better craftspeople are willing to waste some leather to make a good, uniform product. Only you know the stress to which your cuffs will be subjected. Choose carefully; it is easy to waste your money and spoil your fun on the cheap stuff.

Police supply houses are learning to turn a blind eye to their customer base as handcuff orders abound from individuals without security credentials. We're not big on steel handcuffs. If you struggle in them, they hurt. Steel cuffs are usually made with squared edges that dig into the skin to make prisoners struggle less. This is exactly why some people prefer them. The rounded-edged cuffs made by Fetters of England are less punitive, still these are also uncomfortable after a while.

If you like steel handcuffs, though, be sure to get a good pair with a pin that allows you to lock them in a position so that they will not close tighter than you set them. Expect to pay from fifteen dollars for a generic brand and up to fortyfive dollars for brand names like Smith and Weston or Hiatt.

A leather buckling collar, a locking steel style, and these creatively outrageous models in a glass case display are just a few of the many collars found at Dressing For Pleasure in New Jersey.

Bondage harnesses and collars

Harnesses and collars are typically made of leather, but we have seen some crafted from nylon webbing, fur, even stainless steel and wrought iron. Collars are less useful for bondage than body harnesses because of the fragility of the neck, but they carry a heavy emotional influence. Bondage harnesses fit over the shoulders, around the torso and often around the upper thighs. These are usually outfitted with steel or brass D-rings for attaching the legs and arms to the harness or for attachment to fixed furniture, hooks in ceilings and floors, etc.

As with wrist and ankle cuffs, look for quality and fit. Most harnesses are not designed for suspension (hanging the body in mid-air), they are designed for simpler bondages. Unless the craftsman specifically builds a harness for suspension, do not presume that it will suffice for that purpose.

Many collars have D-rings built-in that look solid enough for bondage purposes. We recommend treating them as decoration only. Because of the potential for danger, use collar rings only from the front and only for very SM practices, such as attachment to a leash. Never attach a collar ring to a suspension bondage.

Blindfolds

Blindfolds are wonderful beginner's toys. Scarves, sleeping masks and cloth diapers all make very serviceable, inexpensive blindfolds. Make sure not to tie the blindfold too tightly. Pressure on the eyes causes that ageless, anti-erotic excuse, the headache.

A naked, blindfolded lady is not only a vision of loveliness, she's going to feel more vulnerable. She'll feel even more so if bind her, hand and foot, in a classic spread-eagle position. This is, of course, assuming you have progressed to light bondage. Prepare a nice tray of goodies to tease her with while she's sightless. Ice cubes, feathers, silk, fur, sandpaper, pins, scented oils and perfumes, chocolate, fresh fruit, champagne, and whipped cream are the kinds of things you're looking for.

Get the picture? What you're trying to do is awaken all her other senses while her sight isn't available. You can pipe some of her favorite music through stereo headphones, too, to keep her from hearing what you are cooking up next. Stealth, surprise and creativity are your allies here. Take your time between introducing each new sensation. You can perform a virtual symphony of tastes and textures on m'lady's delicate parts. Her juices ought to be flowing like the mighty Mississippi in no time and you can follow up with whatever comes naturally.

Once you have successfully hooked your lady on these antics, let her know there is a whole world of bondage fun you can share.

With newcomers, the best rule is always: GO SLOW! Better to be too easy than to scare her away or face an assault charge. If going too slowly pisses her off a little, you can always say it's your way of getting her to beg for more. (Philip has been known to pansy-out this way.) Don't introduce more than one or two new techniques during a scene. More than that can be confusing and the new things will lose some of their impact if you toss them all in together.

Talk in detail about things you'd like to try before doing anything. Don't worry about spoiling your scene by being open about it beforehand. There are always plenty of surprises that happen in a scene that neither of you counted upon. As you get used to a person's reactions under stressful situations, you can try new and more intricate stuff.

Start with simple, non-threatening bondages and progress carefully. It's not at all uncommon, even for veteran bondage fetishists, to experience panic. You may find that one bad scene throws your partner into mental tailspin that will ruin anything you want to try in the future.

When you set out to do a scene, you are giving a performance. Your every action is under your lady's scrutiny and you can be sure, she will be paying attention. She is, after all, entrusting you with her body. You must be bold and sure with each technique. There is nothing more nerve-wracking and confidence-shattering than hearing a dominant say, "Oops!" while you are blindfolded and helplessly bound.

Gags

Gags increase feelings of helplessness, but are ostensibly for keeping a person from talking, yelling or crying out. In that sense alone, they are inherently dangerous to bondage players. Whenever you use gags, you must use extreme caution and pay strict attention to what your submissive is going through. Never, ever leave her gagged and unattended.

You must devise a sure safe signal to replace your usual safe word. No gag can stop all sound; one can always hear a grunt even if it is muffled in the throat. One safe signal you might use is a repetitive series of grunts, e.g., "Uh, uh, uh..." followed by a pause, then repeated, "Uh, uh, uh..." until the dominant gets the message -- which had better happen pretty quick. A better safe signal is one that does not rely on the submissive to make noise.

Holding a ball in the hand, and releasing it as your safe signal is a popular technique. Holding jingle bells or a buzzer is another. Which ever you use, do not rely on it as the only method of stopping a scene that gets out of hand. A safe signal, like a safe word, is only an additional safety measure; nothing replaces attentiveness as your first and most critical safety rule.

Now, with the proper nod to safety out of the way, let us present the mad, carefree, zany world of gaggage. For your mouth stuffing pleasure, we have elicited the expertise of our dear friend and cloth gag virtuoso, Master Ken, and his lovely assistant, Sweetcream.

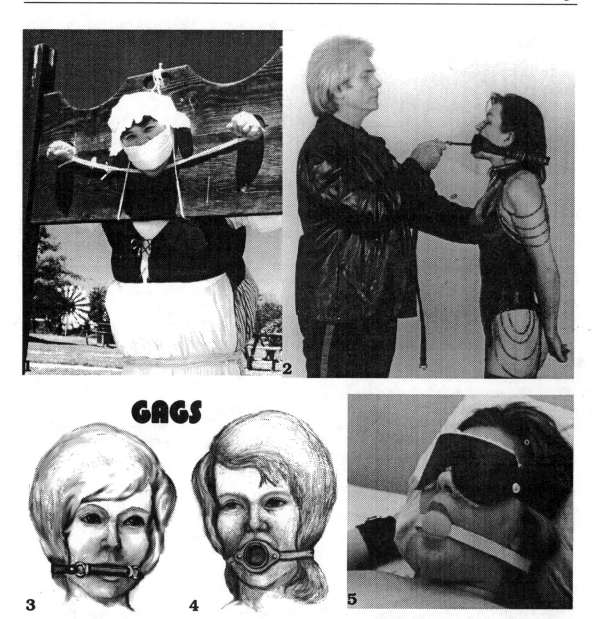

GAGS

1) A historical setting augments the fantasy for this muffler gagged lass. (gaggage and photo of SweetCream by Master Ken) 2) A gag with leash attachment. (photo: Jerry) 3) A bit gag is less rigorous than a ball gag. 4) A pipe gag muffles speech, but allows mouth access. 5) The classic ball gag. If the submissive has breathing problems a perforated practice golfball works well.

We know of no person more qualified, nor anyone with a greater fetish for cloth gaggage than Master Ken. The tricks he lovingly performs with bandannas, scarves, and ordinary flour sack dish towels will leave you speechless. The flour sack dishtowels Ken likes to use measure from twenty-nine to thirty-six inches square and can be found in any variety or discount department store for about a dollar a piece.

The gags he will be demonstrating here are graduated in severity from mild mufflers to major mouth packers. Few people can endure the more potent gags without a real love of the medium, so don't feel as though you have to try them all.

Master Ken is precise and fastidious in his gaggage. Neatness counts! We think you will come to appreciate a well folded gag for the beauty it lends to the wearer. If you leave too many corners untucked, we'll tell Master Ken where he can find you.

A cloth gaggage primer

The muffler

Mufflers are applied as a reminder to be silent, to annoy, and to mildly humiliate the wearer.

Fold clean or used dish towel to a four inch width. Tie this over the mouth, knotting it at back of neck. If your are also blindfolding your submissive, there is a trick you can use to keep the knot from slipping down the neck. Tie the gag knot on top of the blindfold knot. The natural curvature of the head holds the overlapped knots in place.

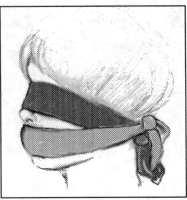

muffler

The bit gag

Bit gags are applied to cause discomfort and annoyance while stretching the jaws and mouth.

NOTE: Packing the mouth with wadding

Some of the following gags include packing the mouth with cloth. Such wadding in the mouth makes a gag more silencing and punitive. Care should always be exercised to see that no loose corners of fabric face rearward. These could conceivably work their way into the throat and cause choking.

Packing the mouth with dry wadding allows more sound to escape and can, over time, cause the mouth to dry out as cloth is usually absorbent. For greater silencing, saturate the mouth packing with water. Two purposes are served: the liquid clogs the fiber of the cloth, further preventing the passage of sound, and the dampened wadding will not stick to the lining of the mouth as sometimes happens when the mouth becomes too dry. Rubbing the wet wadding on clean bar soap increases the degree of displeasure, as does saturating in lemon juice, vinegar or unsweetened Kool-Aid.

First variation:
1) The dish towel or scarf is folded to one and one-half inches, pulled between the teeth, then tightly knotted behind neck, drawing back corners of mouth.
2) A bandanna is wadded into mouth.
3) A second bandanna, folded to a three inch width, is then brought forward from the back of the neck and knotted tightly between the teeth, forcing the wadding deeper into the mouth.
4) A third bandanna, also folded to three inches in width, is then tied over the gaggage and tightly knotted behind neck.

Second variation:
1) Lay two bandannas atop each other, fold them to their smallest wadding and place them into the mouth
2) Hold them in place with a dish towel or scarf, rolled to a one inch diameter tied behind the neck.

Third variation:
1) Use bandanna wadding in the mouth as in the second variation.
2) Roll a flour sack towel and tie a knot in the center of its length. Place the knot over the wadding and tie the towel behind the head. The effect of this is to push the wadding deep into the mouth, and hold jaws wider apart.

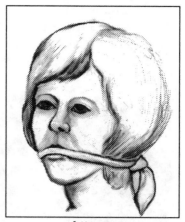
bit gag

Knot gags

Knot gags are an expansion on the bit gag design. Knot gags, depending on size and material, are less comfortable than many other gags. They prevent intelligible speech and can be used punitively, to stretch mouth and jaws.

Knot gags constructed as below are used in a variety of sizes and are referred to as RKG's (regulation knot gags). A knot gag is an excellent choice for long-term discipline such as overnight wear since there is virtually no danger of choking or suffocation.

To create the knot, a large square or rectangular cloth (the flour sack towels or large scarves will suffice) is folded once on the diagonal. Starting at the point, roll tightly toward the long, folded edge of the cloth, forming a rope-like affair. Tie a single overhand knot beginning just off-center of the cloth so that the ends are equal in length when the knot is tightened. Obviously, the dimensions and thickness of the cloth determine the size of the knot created. We tie and keep several sizes and styles on hand for instant use.

Regulation knot gags

#1 - Most women have large head squares available and flour sack towels are available at many variety stores. Either of these rolled as above create a fairly small knot. These are excellent for use on a novice. A mouth-filling bandanna packing may be used before the knot is thrust between the teeth and tied off behind the neck.

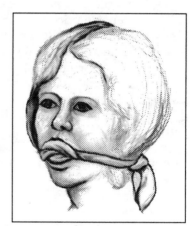
knot gag

#2 - Number two regulation knot gag is formed of a larger cotton cloth (a twentynine inch square flour sack) or a head scarf in which a bandanna has been laid out and rolled into the "rope." The additional bulk provides greater mass and the knot holds the jaws wide apart. The ends should be tightly tied, draw-ing back the mouth corners when used punitively. Wadding may also be inserted to acquire the desired silence.

#3 - A cotton or muslin square of thirtysix inches or so is large enough to form the giant knot tied to spread the jaws most uncomfortably wide. The number three is punitive for long wear though not silencing. Add dry bandanna wadding and it becomes a "consuming" type of gag to wear when tightly drawn back and tied off.

In order to insert the larger knots in the mouth, place the knot on the captive's lower teeth, pressing downward as you "roll" the knot into the mouth. Much like a well fitted ball gag, the knot is nearly impossible to expel with the tongue and tying the ends tightly behind the neck complete the appliance.

Silence is golden...and FUN too !

Thank you Master Ken! When this man speaks, it's always a mouthful. Master Ken further advises us of a technique to avoid snarling your lady's hair in the knots you tie behind her head. He always ties the knot downward in the direction of the hair's growth and frequently uses an ordinary kerchief and ties the knot over it.

   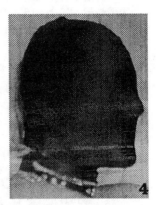

1) Leather hood and 2) Head harness from Dressing For Pleasure in New Jersey. 3) Latex hood from Fantasy Isle in Connecticut. 4) A submissive in a spandex hood has an other worldly appearance.

Hoods and Sensory Deprivation

Hoods made for SM play come in a blinding variety, if you'll pardon the pun. Some are meant only to enhance fantasy, others serve to combine the features of blindfolds and gags, as well. Leather hoods necessitate a great deal of detail work which is reflected in their expensive price tags. Spandex hoods, being far simpler to make, cost much, much less. Rubber and PVC hoods vary greatly in price from one manufacturer to another.

A hood is basically a covering for the head. People use them to consummate a extensive spectrum of effects. The executioner's hood is made for its looks and the way one feels wearing it. Hoods incorporating gags and/or blindfolds move into a realm we call sensory deprivation.

Four of our five senses, sight, hearing, taste, and smell occur in our heads. Interfering with or blocking one or more of them has a disorienting effect and makes one feel more vulnerable. This can also lead to panic; test which mode(s) of sensory deprivation appeal to you and you submissive before running out to buy a $350 hood.

Spandex

Spandex is a wonderful fabric for bondage. When it is stretched over the body it feels smooth and silky and it holds tightly. We list a few vendors of spandex bondage equipment in our appendix or, if you're handy with a sewing machine you can create your own hoods, body bags, single arm sleeves, and straight jackets.

Philip has a black spandex hood that works wonderfully, but the submissive can see though it in strong light. This is easily remedied by folding a cloth napkin over the eyes before slipping on the hood, or by tying a kerchief blindfold over the hood.

A submissive, struggling inside a sleek spandex hood and body bag, makes a strangely seductive, other worldly sight. We highly recommend this mistreatment of your loved ones.

An inexpensive alternative to spandex for binding the legs is to force them both into a single nylon stocking. The effect is similar to spandex, and perhaps not as versatile, but it will give you an idea of what this kind of bondage feels like before investing yet more of your children's college funds in erotica.

Specialty items

Give the same consideration to choosing quality bondage gear that you would to selecting a fine suit. Details such as even stitching, consistent material, be it leather, fabric, or metal, and hardware all have an impact, not only on style, but also on safety. Dyes should not rub off easily, zippers should be well attached and strong enough to handle stress, and closures should operate smoothly.

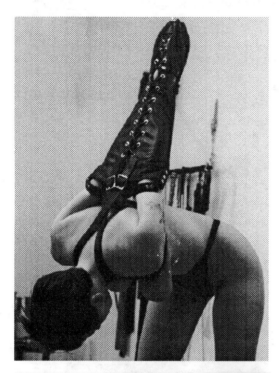

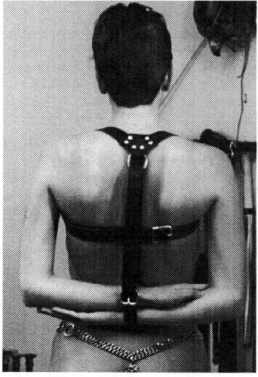

This single-arm sleeve was made by Northbound Leather of Toronto, Canada. Though they look great, most people are not flexible enough to wear a single-arm sleeve.

A friend of ours crafted this clever shoulder harness and wrist restraint. We were most impressed with the simplicity and utility of his design.

Three Common Knots for Securing Ropes to Stationary Objects

The single **half hitch** (left) is rarely used by itself; more often, another half hitch is tied below the first for stability. Several half hitches, tied one below the other will yield an attractive spiral pattern.

The **lark's head** (right) is often used to secure the middle of a rope to a bedpost leaving two equal lengths of rope to secure ankles or wrists.

The **clove hitch** does much the same work as a half hitch, but is easier to untie. This is both an advantage and a disadvantage as the rope can become loosened more readily.

Lark's Head

Half Hitch

Clove Hitch

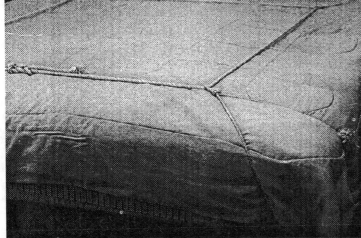

Simple solutions for attachments

Preparing the bed for bondage fun does not require sawing holes in the headboard or even screwing eye-hooks into the frame or box springs. Any mattress and box spring can be fitted with anchor points by looping rope around the corners and tightly weaving the rope together from corner to corner.

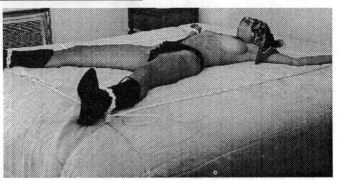

Another unobtrusive toy for making a bed bondage-ready is a tarp "tie-down" or come-along made for securing cargo to a car roof or inside the bed of a pickup truck. This is usually a two-piece affair found in any hardware store: a long, soft nylon strap with thick metal hooks on either end and a ratchet with a take-up reel to tighten the strap.

 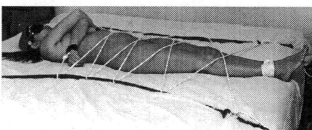

This is a favorite of Philip's for several reasons. It is cheap (a fifteen-foot model sells for about ten dollars). The nylon strap is very soft, but very strong, typically rated to support fifteen hundred pounds of stress. It can be affixed tighter than any rope web you can fashion and is quick and easy to attach to a bed.

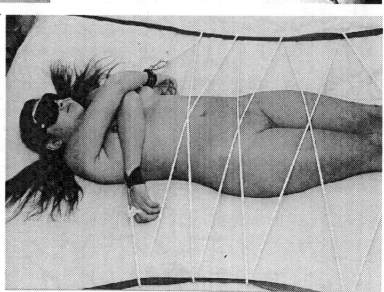

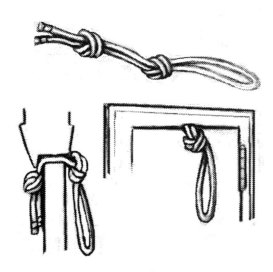

A door can also be outfitted for bondage as easily as a bed. Start with a three foot length of quarter inch rope and fold it in half. At the folded end, tie an overhand knot, leaving a three inch loop in the end. Approximately six inches away from the first knot tie another one. Simply position the rope on top of a door with a knot on either side, and close the door. On one side, your will have a fixed loop to which you can attach your lover's bound wrists.

If the rope is too high, you can tie additional knots to make an adjustable length bondage toy.

All three of these "bondage fixtures" are among the easiest to hide from prying friends or relatives. You simply coil the rope or strap and stash them when you're finished playing.

9 Philip's Philosophy of Phlogging Phun

The Corporal Dimension

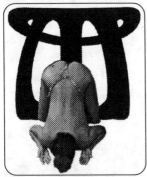

y name is Philip Miller. Philip Miller is an idea, it isn't really me, but I have bought into the idea and have told all my friends that this my name and they bought into the idea, also. Philip Miller has been a serviceable idea for a lot of years, though my uncle once told me that pronouncing my name bears all the excitement of chewing a mouthful of Lima beans.

Sometimes, though, I tire of citizen Lima Bean. Sometimes I would rather foster the idea that I am Torquemada, the Grand Inquisitor of Spain. Or a mercenary knight from Camelot, on a quest to uncover a plot against the throne. Or I become an executioner dwelling deep within the bowels of a medieval castle, master of all the pain and suffering that transpires in my lightless domain. Torquemada, the knight and the executioner occasionally run into a lady who has likewise discarded her daily identity, adopting some unusual ideas of her own.

Maybe she has an idea that she is a vile sinner, caught in a heinous act of heresy and brought to me to beg for absolution. Or maybe she wants to be my captive princess, the daughter of a king at war with Arthur. Or perhaps she has an idea that she is a high-born lady, falsely accused and convicted of some loathsome crime, then, sentenced to suffer at my hands...somewhere at the bottom of dozens of stone stairways, far from the gay and the frivolous, far from the safety and loving protection friends and family.

Sometimes she and I share our ideas with each other and take off on a romp in fantasy together. More often, though, we keep our ideas quietly churning away in our thoughts; one of us binding and slapping and moaning and fucking while the other struggles and cries out and moans and fucks back.

My ideas, my fantasies, often change in mid-scene. Torquemada, the knight and the executioner give way to a demented scientist, an evil priest (he's a real prick), a stalking rapist, a cultured slave-trader, and a wild-eyed beast-man in hormonal overload as easily as changing channels on a TV. Then again, I spend a lot of scene-time as plain old me, lover and sadist.

Underlying all these shifting personae, whenever I am involved in scenes, are my own practical guidelines for making SM work. Morality, rationality, creativity, and caring are parts of them that Molly and I have burdened you with elsewhere. Here, I would like to offer the simple nuts and bolts that make up my brand of SM.

Environment

It is usually up to the dominant to select the environment for playing -- the scene of the scene, if you will. Suitable scene environments are indoors and out, upstairs and down, private and public, morning and night. In other words, anywhere and any time will do depending only on how you feel and where you spot an opportunity. In fact, there is such a wide range of possibilities here that I will only mention a personal observation. People prefer to take their clothes off when they are warm. 'Nuff said?

People react differently in private than they do with others around. Some love to find themselves on display, others can't stand the idea, and still others hate the idea, but love to be forced into exhibitionism, anyway. I have done a lot of both private and public scening. Generally, I'll do a lighter scene in public because having people around watching is not just a distraction, it adds an element to the scene that might affect my control of the situation. Privacy is a point that should always be a part of negotiation.

Environment is the sum of all the elements of your setting. Sound is an element that is often overlooked. I like to work with music. I choose music that compliments the mood and tempo I want to set. Music is my background, I don't want it to be a distraction. Sorry, headbangers, I'm an ass-whacker, most rock won't do. Even my beloved Janis Joplin can't cut it when I'm about to deliver a whipping, but hey, to each his own. I like scene music to be a combination of spooky, moody, soft, and spacy. Gregorian chants are great, they fit in with my evil priest bit perfectly. Certain Reggae pieces aren't bad either. Bach organ music or other baroque pieces are fun, too.

A group named Enigma recorded an album that has become such a scene classic that many cringe at the thought of having to listen to it again. Still, you have to use it in a scene at least once to earn your whipping merit badge. Peter Gabriel is one of my personal favorites and a sweet lady recently introduced me to an Andreas Vollenweider album named, "Caverna Magica" that has wonderful possibilities.

If possible, I like to make tapes for a scene. One pattern that I find practical will include a long, quiet, sort of eerie buildup, settle into something with a steady beat, build further to some drawn out crescendo then settle down abruptly, changing to something very soft and soothing. This, of course, is an ideal that I've achieved rarely. Usually, I'll settle for a couple of good, all purpose tapes or load up the disc changer and make do. The New Age artists are providing a wider variety of good scene music these days and there are a few candidates from the Gothic movement that can be used for accent.

Beginning a session

When I'm happy with the room and the musical score, I'll turn my attention to the body before me. What I do depends mainly upon what we both want. During negotiation, I watched my partner to learn what excites her and began formulating possible scenes. Before we start I have an idea or two that I'm going to try, often involving a bondage that I'm fond of and that I think will work well for her. The first thing I do is take control. If I want her naked, I'll tell her to undress while I watch. If I am in the mood to undress her myself, I might bind her arms behind her and strip her at a leisurely pace. I don't let her direct me. Submissives often try to assume control for several reasons.

She may be nervous about giving up control. She may like playing the part of a brat and be expecting me to "correct" her. She may be testing me, or she may be acting out of any combination of these things, but she is not going to run the show. That's my job. My job description says, "dominant" or at least, "top." That means I am responsible for what happens. So, if I am accepting that responsibility, we'll do things my way or not at all.

I want to delight and surprise my submissive. I want to move her in ways she isn't expecting. I hate to be told what to do during a scene and I will not argue about it, but one has to be sensitive to a submissive's feelings. Saying, "NO!" and being bratty may be a part of your submissive's fantasy. It is best to be clear about this during negotiation to avoid hurt feelings, confusion, or panic in your scenes. If you find your lady getting mad, or very insistent, if she uses her safe word, or if she becomes panicky, something is really wrong and you should stop the scene. Then it is appropriate to sit calmly, step out of role and discuss the problem.

One submissive I play with loves to object to what I am doing to her. In her fantasy she is being forced to commit all kinds of atrocious sex acts and since she voices her disapproval she need not feel guilty about enjoying them so much. I wasn't entirely sure when she was acting and when she really needed me to stop when we first started playing together. Of course, I wanted to please her, not upset her. Consequently, I was always stopping the action just when it was heating up for her. She finally straightened me out before one of our scenes. Now when she tells me to stop caning her, unless I see that she is really serious or hurting, I simply say, "OK," and keep stroking. Since our little conversation we have been deliriously happy with each other.

Be aware that having a group watching your scene can disguise what your submissive is feeling. She may be trying not to embarrass you or herself even though something is really bothering her. It's a good idea to check with her often in the beginning to see that she is OK with what you are doing. For this reason, I usually do lighter scenes in public than I will with the same person in private settings.

Positioning

My favorite way to pose a floggee is lying down, face-down or face-up, depending on my intended targets, or kneeling, presenting ass and back for a whipping. Any of these positions can include bondage or not, as fantasy and whim dictate. I am not fond of whipping a standing slave for three reasons: 1) The angle of attack is better in the above mentioned positions. 2) My victim will tire faster if she is standing. 3) Lastly, a standing victim cannot let her body relax completely which diminishes her attention to my whipping. For the same reason, I like my victims on a soft surface like a futon or mattress as I want them to concentrate on the discomfort of my strokes and not on the discomfort of a hard floor or grating carpet.

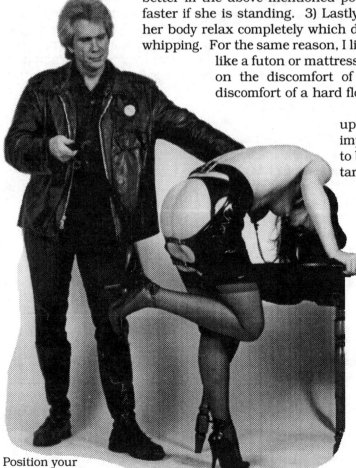

The height of the surface upon which my floggee rests is important, as well. I don't want to bend over or kneel to reach my target, I want to stand upright, in a comfortable stance. Having to bend over is bad for the lower back, and, if you are whipping, it shoots your accuracy all to hell. As a rule, I like to position my quarry at about the level of my crotch because my hands hang around that level; that's where each stroke naturally concludes. Also, crotch-height affords excellent access for fondling and penetrating genitalia without having to stretch or stand on a stack of books.

Position your target for easy reach without bending and take a comfortable stance. (photo: Jerry)

One of the best "whipping benches" I have used is a massage table. The height is adjustable and I can move all around my prey, whipping, paddling, spanking, pinching, probing, and petting where I will. Most massage tables are also well-padded and comfy for m'lady and one can easily bind her in a number of positions. (A massage table is also ideal for torture! My table becomes a part of my fantasies as a laboratory bench or doctor's examining table.) Massage tables are expensive, though. Mine is a sturdy portable weighing in at thirty pounds.

A bed is a fine surface, too, if it isn't so low that you have to bend down to deliver a whip-stroke. It also has the added advantage that you can join your lady after her punishment for some snuggles, cuddles, tickles, or a round of hide-the-salami.

The arm of a sofa is great if it's a butt you're aiming to whack. Hand spanking and paddling lend well to the classic over-the-knee position. Both of these positions put stress on the submissive's tummy and the organs therein, and, as her head will frequently be below the level of her heart, blood will flow to her head which can give her a headache. Headaches, as we mentioned earlier, are hardly erotic. If you want to use these positions, move your girl around a little bit during the session to relieve undue pressure.

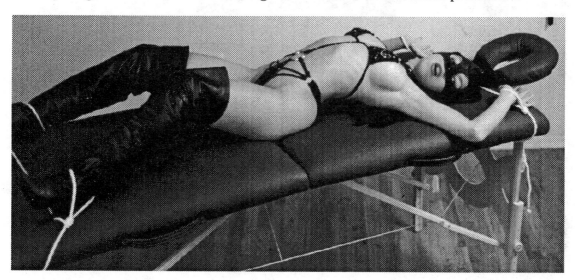

Bondage and whipping

It is particularly difficult to hold still while one is receiving a whipping. If you were ever spanked by your parents you might remember trying to cover yourself with your hands to protect your fanny from the stinging blows. An unbound submissive, ordered to hold still for a whipping, is under a certain amount of stress having little to do with the whipping itself.

Alex Comfort, author of the classic, *Joy of Sex*, quotes Havelock Ellis as saying, "Any restraint upon muscular and emotional activity...tends to heighten the state of emotional excitement."

A whipping is usually easier to take if one is bound. Also, the bound submissive can let herself experience the sensations involved easier when the choice of escape or hindering the assault of the whip is removed. On the other hand, it may be useful to leave a submissive unbound while training her to surrender control to you. She will hold still, then, by choice. It is a chance for her to prove her devotion and progress in submissive skills.

Generally, bind a beginning submissive and give her a whipping that builds very slowly in intensity. Fondle her a lot during her beating so that she comes to expect sexual gratification with the feel of the lash. From time to time, leave a more advanced submissive unbound for her whippings and focus on the training aspects of your relationship, praising her for her accomplishments.

A whipping is usually easier to take if one is bound. (photo: Jerry)

Beginning

I'll assume that the stage is set, the mood established, and my plan is under way. Before flailing away without mercy, I want to wake up my beloved's senses.

I often begin a corporal scene in one of two ways:

I may want to throw a bit of a scare into my lady so, she'll be blindfolded and tied so that she can hardly move. Then we'll be still and let the silence sink in for a while. I've often waited as long as five minutes before doing anything at all. This might not sound like a long time to you, but try setting an alarm clock to go off in five minutes. Blindfold yourself (or better still, force yourself to keep your eyes closed) and wait without moving for the bell to ring. It can feel like an eternity. I have even walked to the door, opened and shut it to give the illusion that I have left the room. (Of course, you would never really leave the room where you've bound a submissive.) My first touch is given without warning and is usually very soft. I know it worked well when she jumps like a bomb just went off beside her.

Alternatively, I might start by caressing and lavishing affection on my submissive. I have grown fond of sweeping a large silky scarf or satin sheet into the air above her and letting it drift over her body, then slowly pulling it across her skin. This is a lovely sensation. Then I'll use a pin or something sharp and prick her slightly to let her experience the contrasting sensations.

Both of these techniques offer the same result: they get her attention and help her focus on skin sensations.

My next goal is to establish a link between physical punishment and emotional or sexual response. I'll alternate between soothing sensations, sexual fondling, and slapping, scratching with my fingernails, or whipping with a light whip. Occasionally, I'll deliver a sharp, stinging blow and follow it immediately with gentle rubbing of the spot I just hit. This gives a quick, painful sensation that is "erased" or eased right away. While this is going on, I will commonly be whispering to my partner or in some way let her know that all my focus is with her.

Very gradually, I build the intensity of the whipping or spanking along with her passion. It is important to remember that not touching and withdrawing touch can be as devastating as a sharp crack of the whip and that arousal is achieved from plateau to plateau. Learn to develop a dramatic sense of timing that will enhance this period of sexual tension building up. It isn't something that can be taught and every person you will be with responds differently. With practice and becoming familiar with your submissive's responses, you can send her soaring by using a wide range of sensations and blending loving feeling with anxiety and surprise.

Ending a scene

Before we get into the various techniques of demolishing bodies, remember that you'll want to end a session on a happy note. You'll both be tired and in need of a cuddle, so allow enough time for a good one before the kids wander in or before the boss comes back from lunch. Untie your lady-love and hold her tight for a while...hell, hold her for a month if you have the option to. For me, the end of a scene is the sweetest part of it.

After a scene, your submissive may be in a very spacey frame of mind. All sorts of body chemicals have been flowing through her blood that aren't usually there, and scenes can uproot deep and unfamiliar emotions, so be patient and loving. She may withdraw, or she may cry uncontrollably, but don't panic, just stay close and be sensitive.

Submissives, if you are reading this, show some appreciation for all the work your top went through for you. Topping really is a tremendous effort that requires juggling a lot of emotional and physical balls aside from all the planning and training he or she undertook to give you pleasure.

Kneeling before the lash

Beating or whipping is perhaps the most menacing aspect of sadomasochism. Thinking about it provokes the prettiest range of green skin tones in the tenderfoot which become brilliant red upon honest initiation. Kind of Christmassy, isn't it?

We refer to beating and whipping as "corporal" techniques from the term corporal punishment. We really don't hit each other for punishment, though. We do it for fun. We do it to satisfy our sexual fantasies, and we do it to achieve a level of sensation and intensity in our lovemaking that magically, even spiritually, transforms us.

In order to realize divine projection we are slithering along the razor's edge of safety. So, to minimize our risks, we offer the following canons of consideration:

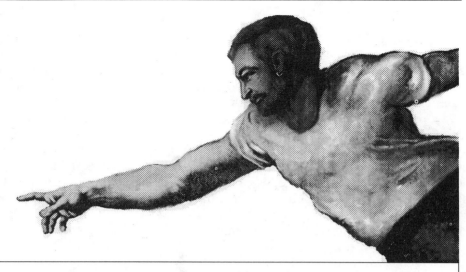

PHILIP'S TEN COMMANDMENTS OF FLAGELLATION

I   THOU SHALT NOT STRIKE IN ANGER.

II   THOU SHALT NOT DAMAGE THINE SUB.

III   THOU SHALT NEGOTIATE THOROUGHLY AND RESPECTETH ALL LIMITS.

IV   LEARNETH WELL THE ANATOMY OF THINE TARGETS.

V   THOU SHALT ABIDE BY SM SAFETY RULES.

VI   KNOWETH WELL THE EFFECT OF THINE WHIPS AND TASTE THYSELF OF THEIR NECTOR.

VII   THOU SHALT DEVELOP PROPER STANCE AND TECHNIQUE.

VIII   SEEKETH EXPERT TRAINING FOR THE WEAPONS THOU WOULDST MASTER.

IX   THOU SHALT PRACTICE! PRACTICE! PRACTICE!

X   NEVER STOP WATCHING! FOCUS IS NEXT TO GODLINESS.

I. Thou shalt never strike thine submissive in anger.

If you get mad at your partner, stop the scene. You cannot control someone else when you are not in control of yourself. You have no business whipping somebody unless your every move is designed to add to your mutual pleasure. Every emotion you feel during a corporal scene will be transmitted through your whip. Sending a message of anger is counter-productive. Likewise, if you find that your whippee is getting pissed off, she isn't going to be any happier with another ten strokes. Stop the scene. Discuss the problem, hug each other, then decide whether to try again or call it a night.

As a somewhat-related issue, dominants frequently have to discipline a willful slave. Hey, you don't enjoy dishing it out, but the wench served your guests cold coffee! Your honor is at stake, man, and the harlot belongs over your knee!

While many enjoy the fantasy of punishment, the real thing is a no-no. Some find punishment useful as a way of expiating guilt. If this works for you fine, but, we don't buy it. We don't think it is a healthy way to play. Fantasy guilt and real guilt are very different animals. The former is playful and silly and fun, and when you get punished for it, it is hot and sexy and when it is over, everybody is happy. The latter is much trickier; real guilt is an unresolved psychological dilemma. Punishing someone for it in the context of sexual play can compound the problem immeasurably. The dom should be performing for the good and enjoyment of both.

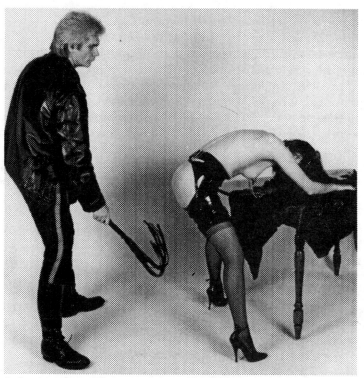

A dom performs for enjoyment of both partners. (photo: Jerry)

II. Thou shalt not damage thine sub. Knoweth the difference between hurt and harm.

Ms. Marie Constance (considered by many as the first lady of the English cane) is fond of telling her submissives, "Darling, I would never harm you, but there is a world of difference between hurt and harm, you know." We want to give hurt that stimulates and satisfies our submissives. Hurt is pain, a sensation capable of imparting delight. Harm is a result of uncaring treatment, physical or emotional, that yields nothing more than unhappiness for both dominant and submissive.

Amazing amounts of pain, if that is your goal, can be administered without leaving permanent damage to the skin or underlying tissues. In fact, it isn't necessary to leave a mark at all. As you flog your honey, her skin becomes more resistant to damage. Distribute the strokes evenly, slowly increasing their force and you are less likely to leave any evidence beyond a warm, rosy glow that will fade quickly.

Most people do not want or cannot afford the visible evidence of what is still socially unacceptable behavior. Wives prone to wearing teeny bikinis, girlfriends who live with their mothers, boyfriends who work out and would rather avoid embarrassing questions in the locker room, all have legitimate reasons not to be marked. In fact, any reason a bottom gives for not wanting marks is legit in my book. Find out your whackee's preference in advance.

Even if your sub fancies some souvenir marks, it's your responsibility as dominant to know when to stop and how deeply you are bruising.

Marking

Bruises left by whipping are called marks. A lot of bottoms who fancy corporal like to be marked. They see marks as gratifying souvenirs of a memorable session; red, black, and blue badges of courage, if you will.

Whips mark by breaking the tiny blood vessels that feed the cells in the skin. If you want to mark, bruise the skin, not the tissue and muscle beneath it. This means you must be very, very competent with your whip and you must know how your submissive's skin reacts to beating. Some people bruise very easily (or should we say "badly") and a great deal of damage can be done with the same force that would barely color the skin of another person. Generally, fat bruises more easily than lean, but this is only one of many factors. Deep bruising (bruising below the skin) is to be avoided. It can cause clotting and/or coagulation of blood in muscle tissues which can cause all sorts of problems. It can also result in adhesions between the skin, fascia, and muscle tissue, causing other problems. Deep bruises can take days to become evident on the surface of the skin.

To the experienced eye, the marks left on a tush can be read as easily as *The Cat In The Hat*. Each implement leaves a unique signature. Your mistakes will show, as well.

Canes, riding crops, cats, floggers, paddles and single-lash whips mark differently. A stroke with the cracker of a single-lash whip leaves a thin, red line, unless you hit too hard in which case it will leave a cut, which is something we try to avoid. Rattan canes leave double tracks with a bruise between them. Crops can leave a wide, deep bruise because the shaft of a crop is quite dense. (Crops can be used in such a way as to leave very little damage, or none, as well; it depends on the techniques and parts of the crop employed.) Whips with multiple, braided thongs are generally considered "cats." Floggers generally have flat, unbraided thongs, though there are floggers with round rubber thongs, as well. Both leave marks mimicking the width and shape of the thongs.

The popular image of a "criss-cross" of welts left by a whip or a cane is great for fiction, but lousy for your lover's skin. Where the strokes cross you are doubling (at least) the damage you are doing to one spot. This can easily result in breaking the skin. Parallel strokes will avert this kind of damage. It takes a lot skill and control, but, after all, if you are about to mark up your honey, you'd better be skilled enough not to disfigure her.

The above are merely guidelines to help you understand some of the dangers of whipping, offered with the hope that you will better respect the "toys" with which we "play." Marking is an expert's sport requiring training and experience.

I'd like to say a word here about paddling. Paddling has its uses and some people adore the feel, but too much paddling is a bad idea. A paddle whack compresses the skin. With a lot of paddling, the skin will lose its resilience and a lot of nerves will die. This results in a condition we commonly call leatherbutt. Use a paddle as an accent, occasionally, and find less-damaging toys for the majority of your corporal play.

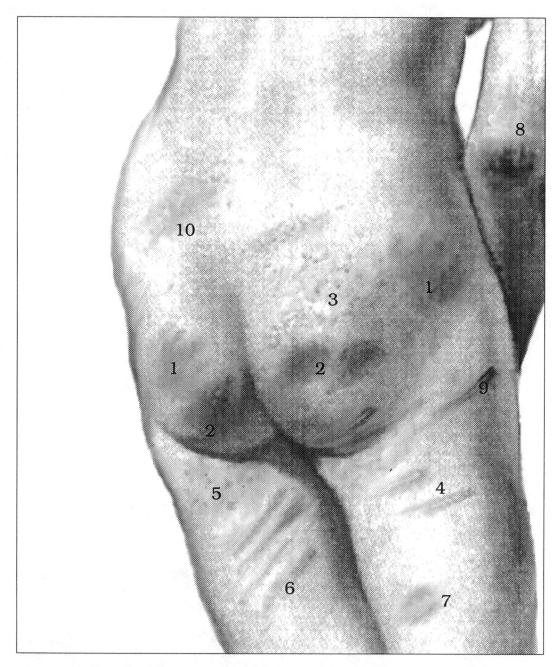

Reading the Submissive's Butt After A Scene

1) Spanking, it appears the top was right-handed
2) Paddle
3) Knotted whip, notice the bee-sting like marks
4) Cane tips
5) Whip
6) Riding crop
7) Bite mark (a fun night)
8) Sub fell while running after bus in four inch heels. Cute but uncoordinated lady.
9) Ooops, cane wrapped
10) Ooops again, whip got a bit too high

III. Thine sub and thee shalt negotiate thoroughly and each shall respecteth the limits of the other.

In case you've skipped the chapter on it, negotiation is scenespeak for discussing fantasies, limits, preferences, existing medical conditions, and selecting and practicing safewords before beginning a session. Negotiating is a cute ice-breaker and way of finding out about your partner. This is the perfect time to admit that you have a fascination with straight jackets and applying Tabasco sauce to the nether regions. Negotiation also serves to find out if there are pre-existing medical conditions before you add your damage. We are not kidding about this.

Ask your lady if she has had any broken bones, surgery, weak joints, or internal problems. Then, you both decide how comfortable you are about subjecting those areas to a whacking. Find out about your sub's physical and emotional limitations. Find out what she likes; people's tastes vary tremendously. (See our chapter on Negotiation.)

IV. Learneth well the anatomy of thine targets.

Areas well-padded with fat can withstand heavier treatment. The face, neck, kidneys, and areas with bones close to the surface of the skin (backs of hands, tops of feet, knees, shins, etc.) are a no-no. Delicate tissues (genitals, bellies, breasts, etc.), should be treated gently. Hit the library for an afternoon. If the librarian asks about the nature of your research, tell her, you may have found a friend! One librarian we know would adore helping you along.

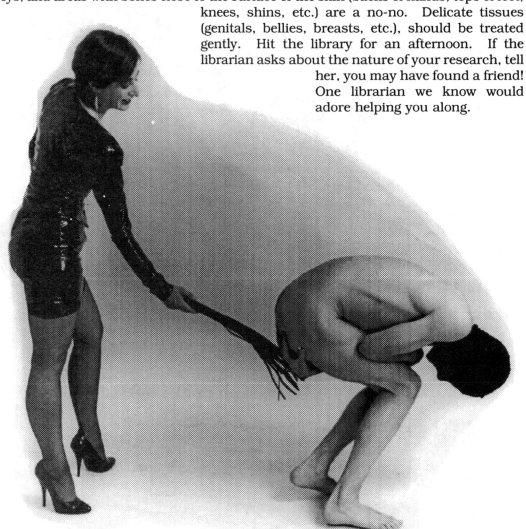

Careful of delicate parts: Mistress Sabrina has the sub cover his balls. (photo: Jerry)

V. Thou shalt abide by SM safety rules and practices.

Do you know what to do if the unexpected occurs or if you make a mistake? Keep a first-aid kit on hand for treating minor cuts or abrasions. Laying in a supply of vitamin E capsules is a good idea, too. Vitamin E is great for healing skin and keeping it supple. The capsules are better than the vitamin E skin cream because the content of the vitamin is much higher than it is in the cream. (There is a nifty side-benefit to the jell inside vitamin E caps. When you squeeze it onto your hands and rub your palms together, it generates a terrific heat that feels great on a submissive's breasts, belly or whatever.)

Heavier wounds, suspected bone fractures, significant bleeding, internal pain, etc., are to be treated by doctors. DO NOT HESITATE TO SEE A DOCTOR FOR SERIOUS INJURIES! The staff in your hospital's emergency room have already seen it all, from the bloody whipstrokes to the golf ball stuck up the anus. Waiting too long can cause permanent damage; swallow your pride for the sake of your loved one.

Learn CPR! Isn't it logical for anyone whose hobby includes stressing and traumatizing bodies, while instilling goodly doses of fear, anxiety, and surprise to be fully trained in cardio-pulmonary resuscitation (CPR)? We think so, too, even though we have never experienced a need for it. In fact, we have never heard of an actual case where it was needed in the practice of SM (outside a couple of movies and TV shows). Still, we figure it's better to be safe than to take up residence with the worms.

VI. Knoweth intimately the feel, range, and effect of each of thine implements of destruction. It is better for all to receive before one gives.

There is no substitute for experience. You had better know the effect of each implement you plan to use on your partner before you start walloping away on that trusting bum. This is Philip's golden rule. When you bought that gorgeous cat with the red, snakeskin handle did you give yourself a few whacks first? Try it now. Give yourself a few good shots across your inner thigh. Of all the landing zones around your legs and ass (the sadist's Mecca), that's about the most sensitive spot. Not so bad, was it? Now take your leather pants off and try it again. That smarts a bit more, doesn't it? It is impractical to wield many toys on yourself. To understand their range of sensation and the messages they impart, get a fellow sadist to give you a taste. Philip gets to play with bunches of pretty dominas this way.

How does it feel?

In scenespeak, heavy and light refer to the amount of pain and/or damage an implement will do to the someone with a solid stroke. Whips are often said to be heavy or light. One of the scene's best whipmakers is Adam, of Adam's Sensual Whips and Gillian's Toys. He classifies his whips with more descriptive terminology: gentle, moderate, severe, and savage.

The materials used as the tresses of a whip make for different feels. Usually deerskin, lamb and suede are soft and make gentle, sensual whips. These are the whips to learn on; you can make all your beginner's mistakes with them and not be concerned about the results. Cowhide comes in a variety of finishes from suede to latigo. Whip tresses of cowhide range greatly between moderate and severe. Rope whips also have a wide range of feel. Rubber is usually very severe.

Whip construction makes a big difference, too. Braided tresses vary from moderate to severe depending on the thickness, length, density, and finish of the materials used. Knotted and looped tresses start entering the realm of savage. Knots tend to make little dots of bruises with a gentle to medium stroke and can tear flesh with a good, solid swing.

Looped tresses are commonly leather woven over a core of tightly bunched leather or flexible nylon rod and will bruise the skin easily.

We consider whips with pieces of lead or other hard substances woven into the thongs too damaging to be used safely. Being pansies, we shy from scenes that involve death or dismemberment.

Stingy or thuddy

Some whips sting and others thud. Sting is a sharp, biting, or slap-like feel. Whips with slender thongs tend to be stingy. A deeper, duller feeling than stingy, thuddy is more like a whack than a slap. Whips with thick, heavy thongs tend to deliver a thuddy whack. A simple rule of thumb is, the thicker the thong, the thuddier the feel. A larger number of thongs will add to heaviness of the thuddy variety; a smaller number tends more toward sting. "Cat-o-nine" and "flogger" style whips made for the scene typically have more than nine thongs, though some have fewer. We have seen cats with as few as three and as many as fifty thongs.

Cutting

Cutting generally mean breaking the skin, but a whip can also have a cutting feel which is a very sharp pain that does not break the skin, but damned if it doesn't feel as though it had. Whip thongs made of stiff leather or rubber have a cutting feel, as do canes and crops.

Ummmmmmm

The sound made by a sub when it feels just right.

Orchestrating your percussion

People vary in their preference for stingy, thuddy and cutting. What's heavenly to some will just piss others off. Also, don't make the mistake of thinking that stingy whips are gentle whips. Try a thin-thonged rubber whip on your thigh sometime. It's very special!

By really understanding the feel of a whip you can compose the music you want your submissive to hear. You have set the stage with demonic scenery and lit it all with the skill of Rembrandt. You've written a splendid script and costumed the players with spirit and panache. Are you going to hand the orchestra a score written only for a banjo?

Hell no! You're going to conduct a symphony! You're going to tease her flesh with strokes of softest deerskin, *sotto voce*, amoroso. You'll patter her fanny with a suede cat, meting out a muted staccato, building, ever building. You'll move up to a heavy, harness-leather flogger, weaving a mosaic of syncopation across her cheeks; seeking, searching, probing for the pulse of the ancient drummer at her very core. A single searing swipe and rest a full measure. Is it there? No. Up an octave, switch to a stinging round braided cat. Ah, closer. Up another octave, a sting to her thighs, closer still. Trill up and down the scale, yes! At last, you find it, rejoicing in a flourish of sound and sensation, sending her soaring. Your whip splits the heavens -- thongs whistling like a chorus of angels! Bravo! Bravo!

Well, maybe you'll do the banjo bit if you are doing the rape scene from *Deliverance* ("Squeal like a pig, slut!"), but you get our drift. Learn your instrument well. Feel its range from soft to hard. Absorb its texture, appreciate its weight. Listen to the sound it makes, fast and slow. Sing the lady a sweet song.

VII. Thou shalt develop proper stance and technique.

Mom was right, posture is important. A comfortable, steady stance is critical for control. Stand up straight, but relaxed. Erect posture throughout each stroke helps insure that the tips of the whip will land in the same place every time. (See next chapter)

VIII. Seeketh an expert's advise, training, and counsel for the weapons you wouldst master.

One of the great advantages of being part of an SM community is the range of experience among its members. Most people consider it a compliment to be asked to demonstrate their technique. Don't waste the opportunity to learn what you can. Everyone has a pet skill that they've spent months, if not years, developing and some people have become internationally recognized for their talents. No one knows it all, and a few of our little toys can be lethal in the hands of a novice.

IX. Thou shalt Practice! Practice! Practice! and use upon a fanny only those toys with which thou art an expert.

Practice on a pillow or other inanimate object (see the whipping tutorial in the next chapter for more details). A sleeping submissive, however tempting, should not be considered an inanimate object. You should practice until you know exactly where the body of the lashes and the tips of your whips will fall. Pain in a scene should always be deliberate.

X. Never stop watching! Focus is next to godliness.

The first rule of whipping is to keep a constant watch on what you're whacking. If you're going to watch what you're whipping it might be a good idea to leave the lights on, huh? Room lighting does not have to wreck a romantic setting. A couple dozen candles afford plenty of light to see your target clearly. (Hint: Though lighting is seldom distracting, if she's asking for something to read, you should be hitting your girl a little harder.) If you want your lady's mood to be accentuated by darkness, blindfold her, but you'll need enough light to examine the damage you're inflicting.

You must maintain focus on both your victim's mood and the specific patch of skin you are currently engaged in mistreating. I mentioned earlier that anger is transmitted through your whip. So is inattention which can be every bit as hurtful as anger and more demeaning. When you are whipping a submissive, she deserves your full concentration. Even if there are other people watching you do your whipping, do not play the showman. People will be much more impressed by your intense concern for giving your lady a good scene and your skill and accuracy will come across undiluted.

10 When the Inner Child Deserves a Spanking
Philip's (and Phriend's) Phurther Pheelings on Phlogging

ield testing a new design of a whip is always great fun. Of course, I invite my master to try it on me first, before I use it on my submissives or loan it out for evaluation.

After I made my first few whips, of which I was quite proud, a friend and I went to a local leather bar to show them around. All the guys thought they were beautifully crafted, and they even admired the color and texture combinations. However, they were unanimous in wanting heavier equipment and showed me some of their favorites.

A ruggedly handsome man introduced himself, and with a broad smile, invited, "Come over to my place next Saturday night; I'll show you how we play!" I was thrilled. Next day I rushed up to Los Angeles and searched to find just the hide I wanted. Back home I worked hour after hour to create just the right whip.

That weekend my heart was racing as I descended the stairs to my host's dungeon. What an education to watch him and his slave as they played! Their sweat poured, their flesh quivered, and their whips cracked as they hit the target. It was most powerful; it was erotic; I got hot just watching.

Stopping to take a rest my host spotted the heavy flogger I had made. "Now, that's some whip, little woman," he said, "can I try it out?"

"By all means," I beamed, handing over the big whip with the handle braided in checkerboard black patent.

And did he make those tails fly! I could tell he loved the whip; he and his slave played with it until they were both spent. Thus, my heavy floggers were born.

by Janette Heartwood, reprinted by permission
Janette is one of the most esteemed creator's of whips in the SM community. Her company, Heartwood Whips of Passion, in Laguna Beach, CA, made the whips for the movie, *Exit to Eden*.

Learning the sensual use of whips is a journey combining emotional, intellectual, and physical disciplines. There is no substitute for hands-on training and experience and we urge you to find a skillful teacher to set your feet in a positive direction. The best we can hope for here is to escort you to the beginning of the joyous path along which our teachers have so lovingly guided us. Whichever stretch of the road you choose travel and your eventual destination are up to you. We wish you godspeed and offer these maps and journals of our own passage through the rocky highlands of corporal bliss.

Preparing the skin for a beating

We stated above that you should avoid contact with vital organs during a beating. Yet there is no organ more vital than our skin. Skin performs the functions of filtration, diffusion, secretion, and absorption and it is a major diagnostic indicator for the condition of internal bodily systems. Skin regulates our heat and protects us from the radiation of the sun. It is our first line of defense against infection, plays a great part in what physically attracts us to a person, and affords us a tremendous range in experiencing sensation. Skin is a complex organ made up of delicate and fragile cells specializing in many capacities critical to our health and well-being. But we're going to beat on it, aren't we?

When we beat on skin, we are going to do damage. We are going to hammer oil and dirt into the pores. We are going to scrape away some of the outer protective cells, burst a few blood vessels, destroy some nerve receptors, wreck some connective tissue, damage hair follicles, and generally wreak havoc on our living wrappers.

So, it's probably a good idea to know how to minimize the damage, or not do any beating at all. If you prepare the skin properly, and perform your whippings prudently, the damage will be minimal and the skin will repair itself.

Skin is a self-regenerating organ. We'll be discussing fanny skin, since that's the stuff we are suggesting is most whackable. Skin is generally considered to be of two types: thin and hairy skin, or thick and hairless (or glabrous). The latter type refers to the skin on the palms and bottoms of the feet. Both types vary considerable in thickness in differing areas of the body.

Covering the surface of a muscle beneath the skin is a protective layer of tissue called fascia. Working toward the surface of the skin from the fascia, we have a subcutaneous layer consisting of fat and connective tissue, then the dermis, housing the sweat and sebaceous (oil) glands, blood and lymph vessels, nerves, the beds of hair follicles, and arrector pili muscles (which are the muscles that give you goose bumps and raise the hair when you're cold or frightened). The dermis is sometimes referred to as the "real skin".

The top layer of skin is called the epidermis. This is where cells are manufactured to form a tough protective layer of dead and dying cells that degenerate to a fibrous protein and are completely replaced every forty-five to seventy-five days. This is also where our skin color lives. As they die, these cells begin to separate and are washed away in bathing, rubbed off by clothing, computer keyboards, and a good friend's body parts, or, they are smacked right the hell off by a whip.

The anatomy lesson is to illustrate the complexity of functions that the skin performs and to build respect for it. I actually perform a little ritual celebrating the wonder of the skin and shapeliness of the fanny before I proceed in beating the hell out of it.

Touch can distinguish temperature, pressure, sharp, and dull. Through interpreting patterns of movement, touch can communicate mood, as well. If one is sensitive to the energy of the body, s/he can apply sensation without actual contact with the skin.

My ritual ceremony is my way of focusing my mind and intent on the lady and on the task before me. I believe it also forges an intimate connection between me my submissive on a purely physical plane. On approaching a fanny, I look for the fine hairs and appreciate the appearance of the surface of the skin. I try to see everything about it that my eyes are capable of seeing, then try to imagine the structure beneath the surface. I try to focus my body's energy through my hands and direct that energy to my submissive's skin, spreading my fingers and holding my hands an inch or two above the surface. Sometimes the fine hair will stand up as if reaching out to me. Sometimes I have to move my hands close enough to graze the hairs.

This first contact stimulates the nerves attached to the hair follicle and causes the muscle attached to it to contract. I try to imagine this process occurring. Slowly, then, I'll make contact with the surface of the skin, imagining the nerve endings in the dermis acknowledging my touch, awakening to my presence. Next, I might lightly caress the skin, I might give my lady a quick, sharp spank, or I might simply take my hands away. It all depends on my mood and intent.

OK, this sounds like hocus-pocus, and maybe it is, yet it works for me in the same way a golfer addresses the ball before making his swing ("Hello, ball!"). We are both focusing our attention on an object before hitting it (and I'll bet I have a lot more fun hitting my object than he does hitting his).

Aside from gaining focus, I've also begun to wake up the nerves in my honey's fanny and have made the tiny muscles flex and become active. Now I can begin to warm up the area for a whipping.

Where to hit

In general, safe places to beat are places with a lot of fat or a lot of muscle. Steer clear of areas where bones are close to the surface or where major veins, arteries, nerves, or organs can be bruised or damaged by flogging.

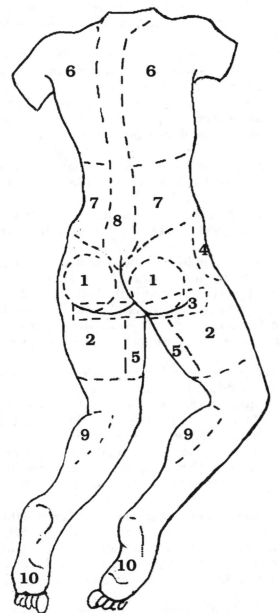

(1 & 2) The ass and thighs are well-padded with fat. They can weather more abuse than other parts of the body, and this is where you'll spend most of your time. Only hit the round parts of the fanny, avoiding the sides of the hips. Your target area is a four- to six-inch, circle right on the top of each cheek. Visualize twin, imaginary yalmulkas capping each cheek and make sure the tips of your whip fall within them.

(3) The place were the thighs join the tush, while able to withstand great punishment, is quite sensitive and thus is often referred to as the "sweet spot." These are great places to vent your sadism.

(4) Avoid hitting the sides of the hips. Lots of important nerves run through these areas and the bones are rather close to the surface.

(5) The insides of the thighs are very sensitive. They are safe to hit, but be aware that the pain potential is quite high here.

(6) The upper back on either side of the spine is protected by a thick layer of muscle. The shoulder blades are there, too, and relatively close to the surface. You can flog these areas with flexible whips of leather and perhaps even rubber, but you will want to avoid using paddles, canes, and the shafts of crops so that you don't bruise the bones. A lot of people really enjoy being beaten on their upper backs. It frequently feels like a vigorous massage.

(7) Avoid hitting the lower back. The kidneys are attached directly to the muscle wall there and can be easily bruised or damaged.

(8) Always take care to avoid whipping the spine and tailbone! At the bottom of the lower back is the tailbone, or sacrum. This is a wide, almost heart-shaped group of bones that become fused together in adults. At the bottom of the "heart" is the coccyx. This small bone is actually a fused section of bones, too. The coccyx can easily snap off which is excruciatingly painful. Be careful to avoid both the coccyx and the sacrum. Likewise, do not beat the spine. There, individual vertebrae have bony protuberances that point toward the surface of the skin and could be bruised or damaged.

(9) Calves can be whipped with moderation, but why would you want to bother?

(10) Some people like the bottoms of their feet beaten and others will rip your eyes out for touching them with anything but the tenderest kiss.   There are a lot of bones close to the surface of the feet, so what ever you decide to do, be cautious.

(11) The vulva, penis and scrotum are very sensitive areas. (Big surprise, huh?) They can be whipped with great care. Use only very soft whips made of deerskin or lambskin at first; experiment carefully with heavier toys later.   Besides the obvious clustering of nerves on and around the vulva, there are sensitive glands that can form cysts when irritated. Obviously, cocks and balls don't like very heavy treatment.   Some women enjoy moderately heavy spanking or whipping of their vulva, but there is also some discussion that the area can become desensitized with a lot of heavy punishment.   Discuss your lady's preference for this and proceed cautiously.

(12)   Breasts are mostly fat. There are quite a few nerves at the nipples and surrounding aureole. Women differ greatly in sensitivity and enjoyment in having their breasts beaten.   Some people say that beating breasts can cause growths, others say that breasts are OK to beat. It should come as no surprise that the AMA has not done a study of SM breast beating, so the decision on breast beating should be made during negotiation.   Even if you do decide to whack her breasts, flog with care.

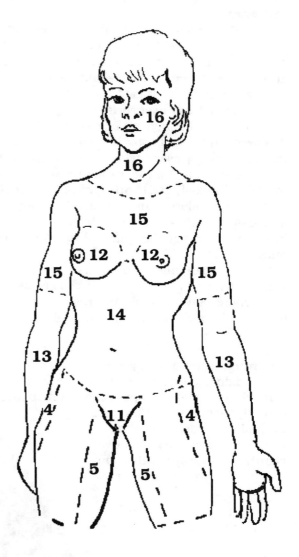

(13) Forearms are relatively free of dangerous areas, but they are also relatively free of erotic areas. There are a whole bunch of bones in the wrists. Don't beat them, but they are very nice to lovingly stroke and nibble upon. Some of my playmates really like wrist caresses and I don't mind doing it at all. Palms are another one of those "either they like it or they'll shove your whip handle way up your colon for touching them there" kinds of places. A few people have "schoolgirl or boy fantasies about being slapped on the palms with a ruler in a teacher/student thing, but I haven't noticed a mad rush in that particular direction.

(14, 15 & 16) So much is going on in the way of delicate organs and bones in these areas that I think they are better left out of a proper beating. Slapping the cheeks may have some interest as discussed above. The upper arms are the safest to beat among these areas, but I've never heard of anyone who cared very much to have them hit. Though it isn't pictured, the back of the head and neck are not safe places to whack and again, why would you want to?

The warm-up

Many make the mistake of delivering a hard shot or two with a crop when they begin a whipping without any preparation at all. Doing this invites massive bruising and can induce adhesions between the subcutaneous tissues and the fascia covering the muscle or between the fascia and the muscle. Without getting too technical, this makes too many boo-boos. It isn't necessary, either.

If you want to surprise your submissive with a sharp sting, slap her bottom with the flat of your hand, don't use a crop. The shaft of a crop is very dense and concentrates its energy in a small spot; the flat of your hand can deliver a hell of a sting and spreads the same energy over a wide area, thereby doing far less damage.

Generally, I like to warm up a sub slowly and evenly around the whole area I intend to whip. I usually start with light, stingy, surface spanking, bringing the blood up to the surface of the skin. While I'm spanking her, I'll occasionally massage her ass, and fondle and kiss m'lady's sex, breasts, belly, even her arms and legs. I want to get all of her skin into the act and get her juices flowing from her vagina, to her mouth, to her dirty little mind.

My spanking will allow us to establish a rhythm between us, it will toughen the skin for what is to follow, and it will get us both sexually stimulated. When her skin is somewhere between pink and rosy, and the color is evenly distributed over the area I intend to harass, she is ready for whipping or for heavier spanking.

Warming up for a heavy scene

I do not advocate using a cane, single-lash whip, or the shaft of a crop before being trained by a competent person and practicing with each implement until one becomes expertly accurate. However, I wanted to mention that the warm-up for these activities requires significantly more attention than described above.

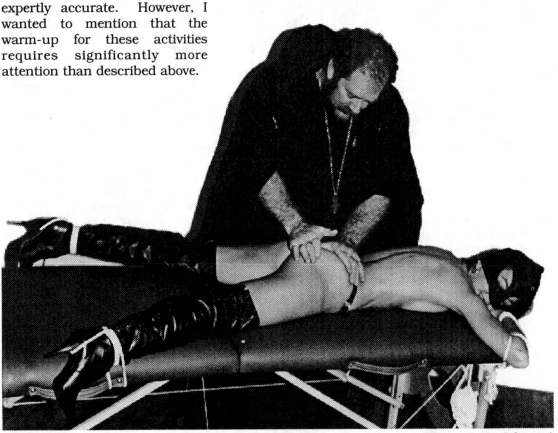

(photo: Kevin Johnson)

There are two roads to take, here.

The first is sufficient for those who don't mind bearing a few bruises from cane strokes. The difference between the warm up above and the one I'd recommend before caning is simply to step up the spanking slowly from light, to medium, to heavy spanking. Apply the cane only after achieving a bright, cherry-red color which should come along after fifteen to twenty minutes of effort, though some might cherry-up sooner than that. One's palm can be exchanged for a light or medium whip after the initial warm-up.

The second method will help to reduce or eliminate the amount of bruising for those who do not want to take home any souvenirs of their adventure. This second method, however, is more prone to doing lasting damage and one should not partake in a regular diet of it. As with the first method, the light spanking should be continued and the force increased until that bright, cherry-red is accomplished. Instead of using only the hand to accomplish this, mix some of the beating with strokes of a wooden paddle, such as a ping-pong paddle, a paddle-ball paddle, or one of the fraternity house specials.

The effect of paddling is to compress the skin, giving it a leathery feel. When this is achieved, a cane will not leave its trademark, railroad bruise. Use this method only with great care and sparingly. The leathery feel can last from several hours to a few days. Too frequent a use of this method will result in the permanent nerve and skin damage that we call leatherbutt. If severe scarring of capillaries and other tissues results from misuse of this method, far more serious conditions can arise.

Spanking

Spanking is the area of corporal where most people begin. After all, one's hand is readily available and, compared to a costly collection of whips, the price is right. Even after you learn to use the showier toys you will almost certainly continue to spank. Besides being very basic, spanking is useful for preparing the skin before using implements with a tendency to welt such as canes, crops, and whips.

To most doms, there is no prettier a sight than buttocks bouncing and reddening under repeated slaps. Using a hand does not require the same level of training as using a whip or cane. After all, MOST of us are coordinated enough to find someone's ass with our hand. You may be surprised, however, to find that the hand remains one of the heavier implements of destruction.

A certain dom we know, who is only slightly smaller than Paul Bunyon, has to yell "fore" before giving a full swing. He doesn't often let go with a full shot in a motel room as people in the next suite are likely to object to the sub's head smashing through the wall. As decorative at it may sound to have a pretty trophy emerging through the wall from the room next door, it is unnervingly obtrusive when it happens while you are shaving.

As simple and natural as spanking seems, you can easily deliver blows that will bruise too deeply. Whether you favor a flat palm with fingers together or slightly apart, or a slightly cupped hand, or even the backs of the fingertips, try to sting the surface of the skin only. Do not use "follow-through" in your strokes to avoid damaging the muscle beneath the skin.

The over-the-knee position is a classic for spanking because it keeps your honey's fanny in the most accessible place. Have her stand between your legs facing left if you are right-handed, right if you are left-handed. Bend her over your thigh, locking your other leg around both of her legs to neutralize her kicks and so that she can't squirm off your lap. Placing your non-spanking hand over her tailbone with your thumb right at the top of the crease between her cheeks both protects the tailbone and helps you hold her down when she starts to jump and wriggle. Then, just have at it!

Hands are the most expressive tools at the sadist's command. Sharp, stinging spanks, heavy spanks that end with the hand remaining on the fanny, and a quick series of light spanks all convey different messages. Caresses between the swats will reassure your partner that you love her. You can hold a whole conversation between palm and fanny. Strive to expand your vocabulary.

Steed's hand "conversing" with Tori's fanny. (Photo: Jerry)

Paddling

Paddling is similar to spanking as paddles are for close-order discipline and do not require a lot of training to use. Thick sole-leather strips, ping-pong and paddle-ball paddles, classic fraternity and schoolmaster paddles, slappers, and straps all fall into this category of weaponry.

Paddles are for fannies and, if you're feeling really nasty, for thighs. Leave the rest of the body to other happy toys like whips. They sting and burn as if you had backed up into a red-hot pot-belly stove. Apply paddles sparingly; there are many other ways to keep from spoiling the slave.

You don't really need any more instruction for using a paddle than you did for spanking, do you? Most of the same rules and opportunities apply. A word of caution, though: paddles create a condition of what we call leatherbutt rather quickly (see and heed the warnings in the warm-up section, above). That is, the skin compresses under a paddle and can thicken and lose sensitivity.

Face slapping

It is safe to give light, open-handed slaps to the cheeks of the face. I mention this separately from spanking, because the effect is different from that of whacking the body. It is largely mental rather than physical. There is an element of humiliation here. The effect (for those who like it, not everyone does) is a feeling of submission. Use face slapping with discretion, as a sort of punctuation within a scene, a condition of carrying face slapping "too far" arrives very quickly.

Caning and cropping

Canes are heavy toys. They can split a fanny like a water-balloon, so you'd best be damned good with them before you begin to welt a pair of cheeks. Most people never want this kind or degree of pain, but canes deliver such a unique brand of hurt that some masochists fall in love with them. There is no weapon in our arsenal that more effectively summons the attention of our beloveds; English schoolmasters knew whereof they whacked.

Canes are usually made from rattan and are generally from one-quarter to three-eighths inches in diameter and from two to three feet long. Bamboo tends to split makes this a dangerous choice. The bamboo sticks used to stake out plants are a definite no-no. Some of the newer canes are made from fiberglass rods or other stiff, but flexible synthetics. Synthetic canes carry richly deserved names like White Lightning and Fire Finger. These canes are undiluted hell.

Cane strokes compress the skin leaving two welts with a U-shaped trough between them. There are two sensations to the cane, as well. When you strike there is an initial sting, then, a few seconds later, the nerves that were compressed with the skin begin to return to their original size and a new, searing pain fires up radiating outwardly from the twin welts.

I was taught to cane by Marie Constance, the grand dame of the English cane who is mentioned above. She teaches that each cane stroke should be appreciated in its full glory. Too many strokes delivered in quick succession is overdoing it and defeats the elegance and depth of feeling inherent in each stroke. I wait for the pain of a stroke to die down almost completely before delivering another. This can take as long as a full minute.

Crops are similar to canes regarding the use of their shafts. The shafts were traditionally made of hickory as it was a dense, but flexible, switchy, wood. Now, the shafts are almost all made of fiberglass or some other synthetic that resembles the action of hickory, is more durable, and cheaper. The shaft of a crop is more dense than a rattan cane and is usually covered by a sheath of braided nylon threads. "Crop" is the nickname for "riding crop," meaning, these are designed for hitting horses. Since horse hide is a bit more durable than human hide, get an expert to teach you how to use the shaft.

On their tips, however, crops have a lovely flap, usually made of leather. When you buy a crop, this flap will be stiff and straight. After some use, it will soften and become more whippy. With practice, you can learn to whip the crop up and down (or left to right) using very little wrist action and the natural whippiness of the shaft. Once you develop some precision, you can place a nipple, the head of a penis, or even an inner thigh in the path of the flying flap to administer a hell of lesson.

Photo courtesy of Dressing For Pleasure of Upper Montclair, NJ.

We're not even going to attempt to teach you how to use canes or the shafts of crops in this book. They're just too deadly in the unskilled hand. Find a competent sadist to teach you how to use them. Still, canes and crops are lovely, amusing toys and should not be ignored. Perhaps we'll publish a caning and cropping primer when we're rich enough to move to a country without extradition.

Flogging

Of all the hitting toys at your disposal, the cat is perhaps the most dramatic and easy to learn.

Whipping or flogging with a multi-thonged whip, while relatively easy to learn, is a skill best learned from an experienced dominant. Proper technique not only makes the use of whips more enjoyable for participants on both ends, it prevents the need for frequent replacement of submissives.

Here, then, is a lesson on flogging with a cat-o-nine (or more) tails:

Cat-anatomy

Anyone who writes about whips or whipping is required by law to explain where the cat-o-nine tails got its name. We have heard a few differing stories though all agree that it began with the British Navy. The following account sounds likely so here goes:

Originally, the cat-o-nine tails was a few foot-long hunks of hemp rope used by British Royal Navy officers to punish seamen. The naughty seaman had to make his own flogger. The "cable-laid" rope they used was made of three main strands of rope "laid" (twisted) together. These strands were also made of three stands of thinner rope. The seaman unraveled the three main strands, leaving enough untwisted for a handle, then unraveled the each of those three strands. The result was a nine-stranded rope-whip that hurt like the devil's fork and was cheap enough to be tossed overboard after the whipping.

There, now I'm in the clear. The cats we use in SM have little resemblance to the original. But, I suppose if you find yourself falling in love on an old schooner and you forgot to bring your toys along, you could chop off a few feet of the halyard (whatever that is) and smack your newfound honey into oblivion. The crew will likely throw you overboard with your homemade cat when you're done, though.

The cats we use have stiff handles, commonly made of wooden dowels, drilled hollow and filled with lead shot for greater weight and balancing. At the butt end of the handle there is often a knob or "button" and many have a loop attached here, as well. The lashes, also called the fall, thongs, or tresses are attached to the other end of the handle which is called the whip's neck. The length of the lashes are referred to as the body, and the ends of the lashes are called the tips or points. Sometimes the tips are knotted. We call them blood-knots. Guess why.

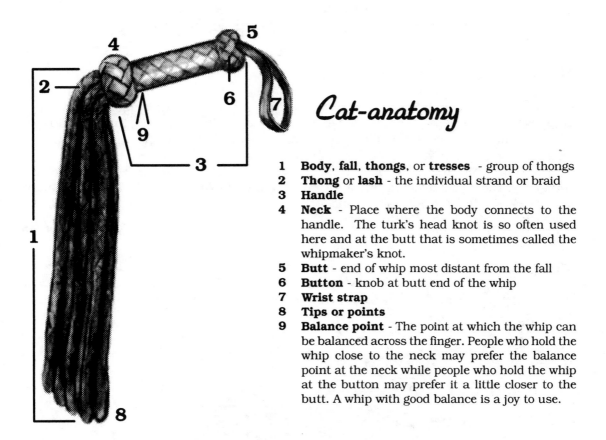

Cat-anatomy

1 **Body, fall, thongs**, or **tresses** - group of thongs
2 **Thong** or **lash** - the individual strand or braid
3 **Handle**
4 **Neck** - Place where the body connects to the handle. The turk's head knot is so often used here and at the butt that is sometimes called the whipmaker's knot.
5 **Butt** - end of whip most distant from the fall
6 **Button** - knob at butt end of the whip
7 **Wrist strap**
8 **Tips or points**
9 **Balance point** - The point at which the whip can be balanced across the finger. People who hold the whip close to the neck may prefer the balance point at the neck while people who hold the whip at the button may prefer it a little closer to the butt. A whip with good balance is a joy to use.

Flogger or cat?

As with everything else in the underground SM dialogue, there is a debate over terminology with regard to cats and floggers. Some insist that a flogger's tails are flat strips of leather (or rubber) and a cat's are always flat or round braided. The other camp maintains that both kinds of whips are subdivisions of the greater family of cats.

The people owning the asses that I whip don't seem to care what they are called and I don't lose much sleep worrying about it, either. Janette Heartwood, who generously contributed to the text and graphics of our book, is of the first camp, so I'll side with her. Hey, I can be bought.

How to practice whipping

Your first target is going to be a pillow (preferably down or feather). Pillows leave a dent where you hit so you can measure the accuracy of your strokes. Concentrate on the target and develop a clean, consistent, smooth stroke. The most important thing to develop is a stroke that lands the body and the tips of the whip exactly where you want them every time. Hitting in the general area of your target is not good enough.

While you are practicing, imagine that your pillow is a real submissive. It may sound silly, but it really does help your concentration. Most of the time you will be working over a back or a fanny. Several other areas are safe and fun to whack, too, but you must be very careful to avoid bones that are close to the surface and organs that are not well-protected. Never whip above the shoulders; heads and necks are just too delicate.

Let this be a lesson to ya:
A tutorial on using the cat-style whip, or flogger

Stance

Accuracy depends, more than any other single factor, on a solid, steady, comfortable stance. Stand squarely facing your target and place your feet apart about the width of your shoulders. Keep your posture erect, but relaxed. You will be swinging the whip with your arm pivoting at the shoulder. Do not turn your body into the stroke, keep your shoulders squared to the target.

Your whip and your arm are of a fixed length. If your back is straight and unmoving, and if your arm is straight the moment the whip makes contact with the target, your strokes will not over- or undershoot the mark. Always hold your whip with a loose, comfortable grip. If you tighten up, you'll become tired quickly and lose accuracy.

The strokes

I am going to teach you to whip a submissive who is lying down on her stomach in front of you. To practice, put your target pillow at waist height. It's best to use a pillow

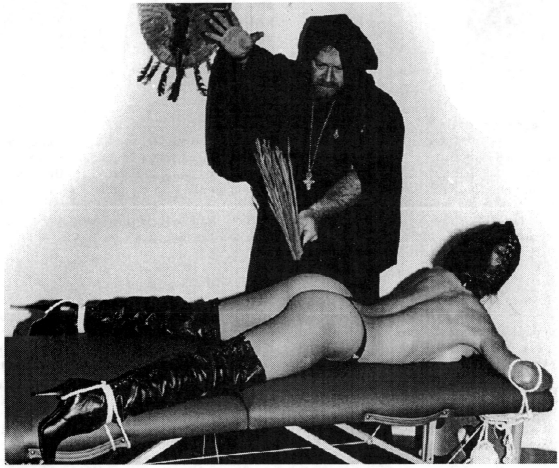

Photo:Kevin Johnson

cover with a pattern or your Congressman's picture on it to better aim the tips at a specific point. If you can spare an old pillowcase, use a wide-tipped felt marker to draw a picture of a fanny with outlines of the hips, the tailbone, the spine and the butt-cheeks. While you're at it, you might as well draw bull's-eyes on the tops of the cheeks and four inch circles for the centers of the cheeks. Remember that imagining the pillow as an actual fanny will improve your focus. Considering the integrity of our Congressional members, a substitution is perfectly acceptable and will seem quite natural.

Forehand overhead stroke

Grip the handle of your whip with an easy, comfortably grip and let your arm hang down naturally along your side. Notice that your palm is facing your leg. If you place your free hand comfortably at the base of your spine, palm out, it will help you keep your posture straight.

Try an easy practice stroke, turning your palm outward as you swing your arm behind you and up, over your head, toward the target in a smooth even stroke. If you have to lean into the stroke to reach the target, you are too far away and you will not be accurate. The solution is simple. Move closer to where you can have good access with out straining or bending. Regain a proper stance.

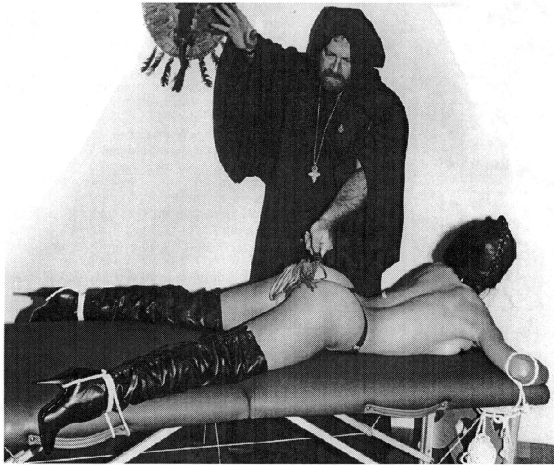

Photo:Kevin Johnson

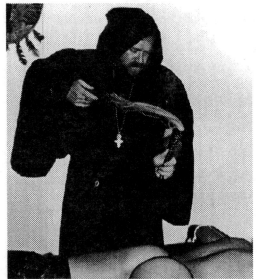

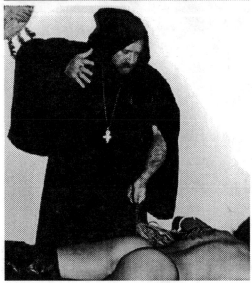

Photo series by Kevin Johnson

When you get into an actual scene, the first stroke is for checking your accuracy, making sure the tips will land where you want them. For whipping a fanny, you want the tips to land within an imaginary, four-inch diameter circle at the top of one butt cheek or the other. If you cannot consistently keep your strokes within those four inch circles, you need more practice.

Right now we are just trying to develop a smooth stroke and are not overly concerned with hitting the mark each time. However, if you are way off the mark, step toward or away from the pillow to adjust your aim.

Now do a series of easy strokes, slowly picking up the speed every five or six strokes. Focus your eyes on the target; do not watch the whip or your arm. At the end of each stroke, your arm should be almost straight and the handle of the whip should be pointing directly at the target. Be careful not to snap your elbow into a locked position. You will develop a nasty case of whip-elbow (archaically referred to as tennis-elbow) this way. Your arm should move naturally, straightening as you bring it back into an overhead circle, bending as it comes over your head, and straightening again as it approaches the target.

Notice that the whip does not strike the target at a ninety-degree angle to your shoulders. It lands about ten to twenty degrees to the left or right depending on which arm you are using. If you are whipping the butt-cheek furthest from you, make sure that the body of the lashes is not crossing the bottom of the tailbone.

Continue until you have done about thirty to forty strokes. Relax as you whip, focusing on the target and feeling the strokes becoming smooth and consistent. Notice where the whip tips are landing. Notice where the body of the lashes is landing.

The lashes may tangle and/or become twisted during repetitive strokes. Let the whip untwist or shake it until it untangles between strokes. Light, broad thonged floggers frequently have this problem.

Now try to make your strokes more accurate and consistent. Be aware of how your body is moving as you whip. If your shoulders are turning into the stroke, make sure they remain square to the target. If your torso is leaning forward or backward to make the tips land where they should, move your stance back or forward to correct your aim.

Practice hitting both cheeks and moving slightly so that the tips land at different points within the four-inch circles. Also, aim for the creases between the thighs and the cheeks. Those are very sensitive spots. During a scene, you will want to cover all of the safe areas of the fanny, though hitting one spot exactly the same way, stroke after stroke after stroke, will create a very intense, very specially painful, very frustrating few moments for your lady.

Do not snap the whip to hit the target. Your strokes should be smooth and constant in speed. The speed and weight of the lashes determines the strength of the stroke. Experiment with different speeds. Develop an accurate stroke at each speed to vary the effect.

You will want to have several differing levels of ouch for your submissive's pleasure. In the beginning of the scene you will be using light strokes for a while, so that she can get used to the whip. Then you will use heavier strokes, level off at a certain speed, then slowly taper off.

Always keep your eyes on your work, not the tool. In a scene, you should be watching what is happening to the bum you are whacking, and occasionally, you will stop to feel the skin's heat and texture (and to fiddle around with the lady's genitals if you are so inclined).

Practice until your arm becomes tired, then rest for a half hour or so. You are using your arm muscles in a new way; it is likely that you will have some soreness until you get those muscles in shape. As you practice each day, your aim, steadiness of stance, and evenness of stroke will improve dramatically.

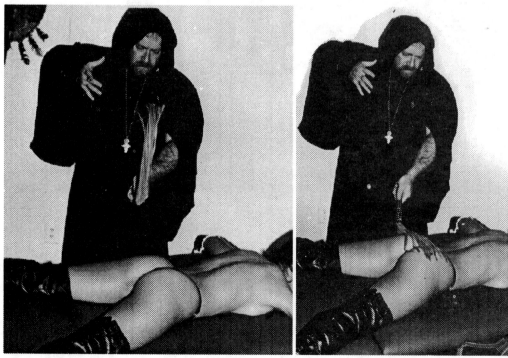

Photo series by Kevin Johnson

Backhand overhead stroke

My instructions for stance, posture, and speed apply to the backhand overhead stroke just as they do for the forehand overhead stroke. The difference is that you will pass your whip-arm in front of your body, palm inward as you bring the whip back and over your head. The whip lands with the same ten to twenty-degree angle as does the forehand stroke.

You can use your free hand to smooth, untwist, and untangle the lashes between strokes. I often catch the lashes between my free hand and my side as I raise the whip for a stroke. I also begin a backhand stroke over my head, the lashes in my free hand and my whip-hand poised to bring the whip down (as illustrated below).

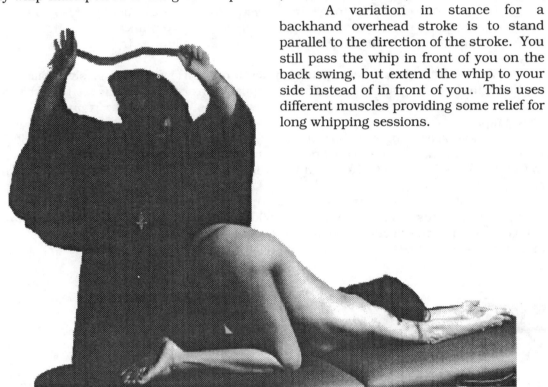

A variation in stance for a backhand overhead stroke is to stand parallel to the direction of the stroke. You still pass the whip in front of you on the back swing, but extend the whip to your side instead of in front of you. This uses different muscles providing some relief for long whipping sessions.

photo: Kevin Johnson

Figure-eight stroke

After you practice the forehand and backhand overhead strokes for a while, practice alternating the two. You may have a little trouble coordinating them at first, but stick at it, you'll get the hang of it in no time. This is called the figure-eight stroke.

You can use this stroke in the normal way or to graze the tips over the target, creating an abrasive feel.

Tips and traps

Overshooting the mark and striking the far side of the hip is a typical mistake beginners make. We call this "wrapping." There is much less padding on the outside of the hips than there is on the backside and you can do some real damage. Remember that the tips are the fastest-moving part of the lashes. You can actually cut with them. If you find that you wrap often, you need to improve your accuracy.

Develop a wide range of strokes with each whip you have and learn to vary the pace in creative patterns. The same stroke with no variation will bore your sub to tears.

Along the lines of variation, you may want to change your submissive's position from time to time. If you have her standing or kneeling, you will have to have different strokes developed to handle the new angle of her ass and/or back. Learn to use sidearm strokes, both forehand and backhand. Pinwheeling is another useful stroke. This is simply a continuous circular motion, most useful in grazing the tips across the flesh.

You may find that the tips of your whip spread out too much as they make contact with the target. Some whips are more prone to this than others, or you may not be picking up enough speed with your stroke. Put a little more speed into the stroke at the end of your swing. This should solve the problem.

Don't keep up a steady barrage of strokes for very long. Pause from time to time to let your lady catch her breath. As your strokes become heavier, your pace should slow down to allow the pain to sink in and not overwhelm your victim.

Remember that, ultimately, you have nothing to prove. If you are pushing limits, either hers or yours, proceed with caution and sensitivity.

Practice with the same music you intend to use in your scene. Becoming familiar with the peaks and valleys of sound can help you develop a sort of plot to your whipping.

Again, be especially aware of where the tips of the whip fall. Whips with longer lashes hit harder. A blow nicely aimed at a well-padded ass can be extremely painful if the tips land on the more delicate tissues between the cheeks. Anuses, pussy lips, balls, and cocks live there; you want to be a lot gentler with these than your average tush. Be expert and accurate!

When you are a beginner, or you are with a new partner, it is wise to leave the subject ungagged so you can get feedback. No matter how skilled you think you are, there should be a safe word or (if gagged) a safe signal as we discussed in the bondage chapter. As we stated there, you have been entrusted with your lady's care and safety; this is YOUR responsibility.

Lastly, have somebody whip you, from light to hard. Make sure you have some practice under your belt so you can appreciate what he or she is doing.

OK, you have memorized all the safety rules we can think of and you have mastered all your whips and all their strokes. You're ready to toss that sweet, bound girl on the bed and give her a religious experience. School is out.

****** IT'S SHOW TIME! ******

These "Whips of Passion" are made by famed whipmaker Janette Heartwood. (photo courtesy of Janette Heartwood)

The single-lash whip

Single-lash whips come in a variety of styles and lengths, from the four-foot black-snake to Australian stock- and western bullwhips as long as twenty feet. These whips are made for show or managing livestock, but there are experts who are good enough to use them in SM scenes. A single-lash whip can open you up like a can of ravioli and their use is way beyond the scope of this book. The tip of a single-lash has to move at Mach 1 in order to crack. Most people use them in scenes to frighten with the crack, then wrap the lash around the submissive after most of the energy has dissipated from the throw. A few people know how to give a safe beating with them, too. Do you feel like dangling on this edge? Find a bona fide expert with years of practice and busloads of references before you do.

Bullwhips are not only at home on the range

As beneficiary of the percussive arts, rather than bestower, I (Molly) have enjoyed sitting back and leaving it to Philip to explain all about whackin' and smackin'. (Yeah, I know, the doms do all the work.) Since my bad aim is legendary in three states I wouldn't dream of entering the discussion except for my delight in introducing our guest writer and bullwhip expert, Robert Dante.

The bullwhip is a fascinating toy that until recently, I knew nothing about that I couldn't glean from TV, rumor, and myth. Shows like "Gunsmoke", "Rawhide", and "The Rifleman" all paid homage to the bullwhip as a formidable and somewhat romantic weapon and, of course, everyone in the Western Hemisphere has seen Indiana Jones ply the whip with surgical precision. Way back in the sixties, there was Lash Larue, a TV cowboy who carried a whip rather than a gun and, though Zorro was more known for his lightning-fast rapier, he also wielded the occasional whip. (Both Lash and Zorro always dressed in black. You don't suppose they were into...naw.)

Using a bullwhip as a scene implement had been shrouded in mystery for me. Though it seems like a bullwhip would be a natural toy for SM play, it was only recently that I saw one used for more than a prop or for its dramatic crack. They require a tremendous amount of skill. It can take several months to develop the accuracy necessary to use them safely. Though, if safety isn't a big issue for you, there's nothing like a bullwhip to prepare meat strips for a chef's salad.

The only single-tail whip for which I could claim a passing familiarity with was the four-foot snake whip owned by Philip. The potential of this diminutive whip is scary enough. It leaves a searing red line of pain radiating a heat that metamorphoses into burning sexual desire. Philip shredded pillow cases for weeks learning to deliver its special sting without slicing me to ribbons. It is a pain I have learned to love. The sound of its crack inspires feelings of anticipation both terrifying and intensely sexual.

Philip and I first witnessed the expert use of a bullwhip at a 1993 Dressing For Pleasure seminar. We were sitting in the front row to get a good view. Robert Dante was demonstrating the proper handling of single-tail whips. In his hand was an eight-foot long whip. At the end of it was his lovely wife and object of his demonstration.

When he cracked the whip I made an involuntarily sound, something between a moan, a gasp, and a sigh. Robert Dante looked at me and said with a smile, "someone is having a Pavlovian response to the sound of the whip."

Red-faced for the rest of the demo, I watched with rapt interest as the whip was masterfully wielded. I saw the whip snap its terrifying crack a mere eight inches from the pretty girl's body, then wrap sensually around her waist. I HAD to know what that felt like. After the public lecture, Robert Dante kindly humored me. I was not disappointed.

Since then, we have had the pleasure of getting to know Robert better. Aside from being an all-round nice guy, he is a gifted writer, a journalist, and publisher of a delightful, enlightening scene magazine, **Boudoir Noir** *(see our appendix for subscription information). Because of his special expertise, we asked him to contribute the following article. Thank you, Robert Dante.*

The proper use of single-lash whips is Demonstrated by Robert Dante with the assistance of his wife Mary. (photo courtesy of Robert Dante.

The crack of a whip is the epitome of SM.

It explodes like lightning from the hand of a god or goddess, it snakes through the air like a dragon's claw. It's evil, languid, precise, supremely savage, and sensuous. In short, it is as sexy as it is dangerous.

It can create a range of sensations from delicate to cruel. It can be as subtle as a lover's tongue or as frightening as a chain saw.

Such is the fantasy, such is the reality.

In the hand of an expert whip handler, a well-made whip becomes a living thing, much the same way a samurai warrior's sword vibrates with the life force given to it by a master swordmaker. With any performing art, dramatic or athletic, the moment of truth is authentic and unique. It cannot be programmed or choreographed to be precisely the same every time.

I have presented seminars and workshops on bullwhip use. I've also given private tutoring sessions. Dressing For Pleasure arranged for one of my workshops to be videotaped (warts and all).

I do emphasize "safety first". Although I can show someone how to use a bullwhip, it's up to that person to invest the hours of practice required to get the basics down. Be prepared for calluses and blisters. From what I've seen, each person develops his or her individual style and relationship with a whip, but the basics are usually in place. I try to communicate those basics clearly and, fortunately, the single-tail whip experience has a sharp learning curve. If you've got patience and persistence, you can get there from here.

One nice thing about the bullwhip is that the wielder does not have to be a burley linebacker - some of the best whip crackers I've seen have been smaller men and women. Even a gentle stroke with a beautiful form carries more power and grace than a sloppy, strong swing.

Let's get down to it:

Basically, there are three different types of single-tailed whips: black snake, bullwhip and stock whip. The difference is in the handle and the flexibility of the whip. The black snake (and in this category I put signal whips, dog sled whips, and other shot-loaded, flexible--handled, short whips) is a faster, shorter, meaner mother than the other whips. On the plus side, it is better for use in confined areas and does not require as much expertise to master. On the negative side, it has a narrower range of SM play potential.

The bullwhip has a short rigid handle and a flexible thong or lash which can come in various lengths. On the plus side, it is a highly versatile instrument. On the negative side, it demands that its user knows what he or he is doing or it will hurt someone (including the handler). It looks easier than it is and the potential to do damage is significant. This is a good place to tell you SAFETY RULE NO. 1: Protect your eyes. You were born with only two - you don't grow new ones if you damage the ones you have, so wear glasses, goggles, or a hat with a brim.

The stock whip has a longer, rigid handle with the thongs attached. In this category I will put buggy whips, horse whips, dray whips, lunge whips, and the whole class of wrist action whips. They are easier to master than bullwhips, but again, the range of play is narrower. They do require less effort to crate satisfying cracks, relying more on a fishing rod cast action than a whole-body, Tai-chi-like, bullwhip throw.

The different whips require slightly different throws to effect cracks, but they all crack for the same reason: the cracker or popper at the end of the lash breaks the sound barrier and makes a small sonic boom. A good whip acts like a magnifying glass, taking the motion, momentum, and energy you place into the whip's handle focusing that energy more tightly into the whip's tip (Newton's Law of the Conservation of Energy). A well-made whip will conserve most of the energy put into it until it reaches its explosive release in the cracker. A shabbily made whip will dissipate its energy, requiring more effort to be put into it in order to create a halfway decent crack.

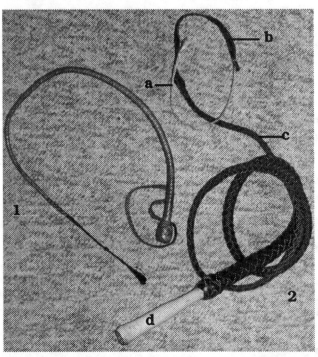

Using the bullwhip as our model, here is the basic anatomy of a whip: the handle attaches to the lash or thong, which attaches to the fall (a round length of leather or a flat, slapper-type length of leather), which attaches to the cracker or popper, the piece of string at the end. Most crackers are replaceable; some falls are replaceable. The idea is that if you bang the whip on the ground or into a wall, let the cracker or fall take the beating, not the thong of the whip. The cracker or fall are easier to replace; the thong will need to be rebraided, or replaced.

A good whip will have a good core, almost like a secondary whip inside the outer covering. That second whip will have a bolster around it, around which the outer covering is braided.

1) signal whip (a black snake type whip)   2) bullwhip
a) cracker or popper b) fall c) lash or thong d) handle

164

I recommend people start off with a shorter whip, usually a 4-foot bullwhip. It is faster, much less forgiving of mistakes and requires a stricter form. The advantage is that it is less expensive to buy than a longer whip, can be used in a smaller space and it will not tire out the user as quickly as a longer whip will. And once you have the basics down with a 4-footer, it is a relatively easy matter to take that knowledge and experience up into a 6-footer or an 8-footer.

The longer the whip, the less accurate it will be. Up to eight feet is about as long as you can go and still play fairly spontaneously with any precision. Beyond this length, the whip should be used primarily as a psychological toy -- a "bullwhip ride" can be exhilarating and emotionally draining -- even under a thick leather jacket (it will mitigate cuts but severe bruises are still possible).

A new whip will be particularly stiff; I tend to prefer a more flexible thong, but some others prefer their whips to have more body, density. A whip needs to be conditioned and cared for. It is an instrument, a tool. It is leather: it will dry out, so it will need to have its oils replaced to maintain its health (I use Dr. Jackson's Hide Rejuvenator, available from Tandy - but others use tallow, lard, beeswax, even Neutragena soap). Don't get it wet. Most whips are made of either cowhide or kangaroo. Cowhide is much less expensive and easier to find, but kangaroo is lighter and stronger, allowing a tighter braid without sacrificing strength.

You don't have to play with the cracker attached. Texas bullwhips have flat falls which can slap; Australian-style whips have single thongs. For the versatility, I like the Texas bullwhip because you can detach the cracker easily and use the whip like a flexible rider's crop. Still, don't underestimate the potential for damage here. Go easy, even on a slow, wide and flat, slapping-type swing.

Safety: once again, protect your eyes. You can identify a new whip user by the welts on the arms and the nicks on the ears. Treat the whip as if you are learning to play with a chain-saw. The analogy is not exaggerated. Do not snap the whip down so it flies back at your face - unless you desire to sport a welt or scar on your cheek or lip. Wear long sleeves. Wear a hat with a brim. Before you start swinging the whip, make sure there is no one behind you and nothing loose on the ground around you - if you strike just right with the whip, you can send an object flying like a bullet.

Before we begin, spin the whip in a circle around you, like a propeller, using your wrist. Visualize the whip's arc creating a disc in the air beside you, with the handle at the center. If you spin it on your other side, you have moved the disk. If you spin it over your head, the disk is now above your head. You are always at the center of the disc. If your body is not at the center of the imaginary disk...you will hit yourself. If you send the whip out and jerk it back at yourself, the whip will hit you. The whip will do exactly what you tell it to do. If you give a whip two different instructions, it will try to obey both of those instructions and will probably end up hitting you in the face. There is nothing as single-minded as a whip, so be unambiguous in the messages you give it.

After the whip cracks, it is ready to crack again, so continue the motion. Tell the whip with your hand where you want it to go. Always keep the whip moving away from your face. If you need to, drive it into the ground beside you.

There are three basic shots, all building from each other: The overhand throw (including backhand, side-arm "flick" and upward shot), the circus crack (or S-shot, "serpentine" shot) and the reverse snap.

With the overhand throw, lay the whip out on the ground behind you. Pull the whip handle-first, so you can pull the lash over your shoulder. Keep your wrist passive. Use your whole forearm as an extension of the whip, aiming the handle at the point where you want the whip to crack. You want to create a hairpin, a wave rolling along the length of the whip as it unwinds before you. Do not go for speed - if your form is correct and the hairpin is tight, the whip will crack all by itself. Listen to the quality of the crack; a sharp report means you've hit the sweet spot. A dull thud means the fall is cracking, but there is not enough energy to make the cracker pop.

Keep your elbow and forearm on the same plane. If your elbow is aimed outward and your hand tries to compensate by twisting the whip back, you are sending two different messages into the whip. Make every component of your throw a single thought, a single action, a single follow-through. Be single-minded.

Keep the whip moving over your shoulder, close to your face (but away from it, forward). If you minimize the parallax (the discrepancy between your eyes and your aim), you become more accurate, more likely to hit what you are looking at and aiming at.

Be flat-footed (at least, at first). Get grounded. Flex your knees, relax your ass muscles, commit yourself to the throw with your whole body, from the soles of your feet, up through your back, into your shoulder, right through your hand, into the whip, all the way to the cracker. Make it a whole-body experience. Go slow. Don't worry about trying to make the whip crack. If your form is clean, the whip will crack, all by itself.

The second stroke is the circus crack. With this, you make a chopping motion as if you are holding a meat cleaver. Pull the whip forward and up, forming an S shape over your shoulder. Have it double back on itself so your hand now travels down. This is a single stroke, not two strokes. If it is done as a single stroke, by doing this you double the distance the whip travels, placing more momentum and potential energy into the lash, resulting in a louder crack. This is the cutting stroke.

The third stroke is the reverse snap. Make a circle over your head. Now cut the handle back along the same plane, sending a hairpin wave into the thong. Whip will crack, fairly close to you (half the length of the whip or less). This is the easiest stroke for the longer whips, but it is also the least accurate. Powerful stroke. Basically the same as the circus crack, but on a different plane. It helps to line the whip up by swinging it twice in one direction, then cutting back on the third swing.

Tip: use both hands, first one, then the other. It will keep you from getting overdeveloped on one side. Also, the practice you get using your off hand will make you a better whip handler with your preferred hand. And when you have burned out the muscles in one arm, you can continue to practice by using your other arm until your tired arm has rested. All this switching hands will continue to educate your eye and the rest of your body, increasing your instinctive understanding of the rhythm of the whip and teaching your brain better whip handling protocol.

For the rest of it, practice, practice, practice. That's the one thing someone else cannot do for you. Every stroke you invest in practice goes into your bank of experience. And it pays great interest, once that learning curve kicks in.

Playing with someone else: in a word, DON'T - at least, not until you are good enough to take leaves off a tree a quarter-inch at a time. Play with plush toys and teddy bears (their fur will show you where you are hitting). Once again, safety first. Keep the whip moving away from your partner's face. Expect to mess up; expect to miss a stroke. If you expect to screw up, you will make an effort to minimize the possibility for damage or injury. You will be glad you did. Have your partner wear glasses, goggles, hat. Even more, have him or her wear gloves, jacket, jeans, chaps.

Wrapping can be particular fun. Have your partner put a hand out (in a glove). Send the whip out so it cracks a bit above and behind the other's arm. After the whip's energy is expended in the crack, the thong will wrap around the arm harmlessly. If you get really good, you can minimize the time between the crack and the wrap so they sound almost simultaneous. It's a head trip, a scary ride, but no damage will be done. If, however, the crack occurs at the surface of the skin, you may wind up taking your partner to an emergency room to have a deep cut stitched up. At the least, your partner will have a welt, or an abrasion, which may or may not be permanent. Proceed with great caution.

Don't wrap the neck. The cracker may inadvertently stroke an eye or the thong may abrade the neck or the fall may cut.

I have read a whip user write that a bullwhip does not cut -- it "burns." Well, in my own rodeo-style public stage performances I cut paper and playing cards and slice bananas, stroke by stroke. A crack from a bullwhip can burn, and it can raise a welt -- and it can cut. Just ask my favorite bottom."

I will not get into the intricacies of heavier play here. Some things are better (more safely) shown than described.

There is no substitute for having a friendly relationship with a good whip handler. If you can find someone who knows what he or she is doing, introduce yourself. Most of the good whip people I've met are happy to share their passion with other experts and neophytes alike. There's always something new to learn and there is always someone out there who can do something you can't.

Tricks are great fun and can sharpen one's ability with a whip. Cutting newspaper sheets down smaller and smaller is a good one. Putting out candle flames is always dramatic. Popping balloons is fun, but harder than it appears. Hanky snatching is pleasurable, but is more easily done with a blunter cracker.

Resources are more easily available than they used to be. The Wild West Arts Club (3750 S. Valley View, #14, Las Vegas, NV 89103) has regional gatherings where people of a like mind get together to share their fascination with whip cracking, knife throwing, and rope twirling. It is also a stunt man's association with a membership of about 500 people worldwide. Founded by Mark Allen, its catalog features decent bullwhips and videos by such experts as Alex Green. Anthony De Longis, the coach who trained Michelle Pfeiffer to wield a whip as Catwoman, also has a homemade video out there.

My own foray into video whip teaching, "Whip It Up," was recently released by Invision Productions." For information, contact me through The BOUDOIR NOIR (see appendix).

The Boudoir Noir, a magazine published by the author of this article, also sells good working Texas bullwhips and straightforward, cowhide stock whips through its catalog (Box 5, Stn. F Toronto, ONT M4Y 2L4). The Dressing For Pleasure Boutique in Upper Montclair, NJ, has "The Spirit of the Whip", a videotape of a workshop I presented in 1993.

The Australian Stock Saddle Co. at P. O. Box 987, Malibu, CA 90265 has stock whips from Australia available. Roger Patterson of Arizona makes a unique spiral-wrapped whip from Australia available from some select stores in the U. S. and Canada. David Morgan, author of the comprehensive *Whips and Whip Making* is a first-class whip maker and importer in Washington (phone 206-485-2132), but if you indicate you are part of the Leather/SM scene, he will hang up on you. Tandy's Leather has a small booklet by Dennis Rush called *Whipmaking, a Beginner's Guide* which is clear, concise, and informative.

Remember there are two dimensions to whip play -- the psychological and the physical. Blend them responsibly.

There you have it - enough information to make you a danger to yourself and others, so please remember, Safety First. I've tried to make sure the training wheels are on and you're wearing a helmet, but there always comes a time when you have to go out on your own and find out what it's all about for yourself. Practice, practice, practice. Consider this a push in the right direction. Just like a motorcycle -- all that power, right there in your hands. Have fun -- that's what it's supposed to be about.

11 It's only Pain, Dear, and It's Only Yours

Why Take a Long Road To Enlightenment, When You Can Haul Ass On a Super Highway?

How singular is the thing called pleasure, and how curiously related to pain, which might be thought to be the opposite of it; for they never come to a man together, and yet he who pursues either of them is generally compelled to take the other. They are two, and yet they grow together out of one head or stem; and I cannot help thinking that if Aesop had noticed them, he would have made a fable about God trying to reconcile their strife, and when he could not, he fastened their heads together; and this is the reason why when one comes the other follows, as I find in my own case pleasure comes following after the pain...
Plato

A sexy body-building type plumber answered my service call the other day. I conducted him into my private bathroom and waited while he contorted those great muscles in his efforts to restore my big tub to full health.

"What's this for, Ma'am?" he asked, fingering my glove-soft, lightweight flogger hanging on the wall.

"Strictly pleasure," I replied with a glint in my eye and the trace of a smile on my lips.

"Really, Ma'am; how is it used?" he questioned further, with just a hint of flush on his cheeks.

"Whips of passion look so stunning against naked flesh," I mused, and then I commanded, "Strip off your clothes!" and grasped my sensuous purple and black flogger with the soft deerskin tails.

"Yes, Ma'am."

He hastily obeyed and presented me with a luscious pair of firm young buns. As you can imagine, dear reader, we both got pretty hot; working with a virgin has its own special charms. I massaged his body with those short tails, and when I thought he was enjoying it rather too much, I switched to my heavy flogger with the red diamond braid handle and long, sweet-mean tails. With this grand whip, it didn't take me long to give him a lasting impression.

The afternoon was a fair trade; the plumber went home tender, but hungry for more, and I filled my tub with warm bubbling water in anticipation of my lover's arrival.
Janette Heartwood
(reprinted with permission)

Liberty consists in doing what one desires.
John Stuart Mill

lack and white. Good and bad. Pleasure and pain. To children these are distinct entities, opposing ideas. As we grow older we learn that the real world is filled with gray areas and paradoxes. Still, it's tough to swallow the concept that pleasure and pain can be one and the same. Nothing is more incomprehensible to SM-outsiders than the idea that pain can be enjoyable. Yet, many, perhaps most people have already had some experience with erotic pain.

Have you ever had a session of hot and heavy lovemaking only to notice some soreness the next day? Or have you discovered bruises, bites, or scratch marks that surprised you as you didn't remember anything that hurt enough to have left such marks? This is not unusual; nips and pinches can be very pleasant sensations while making love. Perceiving pain as pleasure doesn't sound so strange put in this way, does it?

If this sounds familiar, you have experienced erotic pain. Does this mean you are a masochist? Possibly, but not necessarily. (However, ladies, if you think you might be, Philip still has openings on Tuesdays and Fridays.) A large part of corporal practices within SM are based on our natural ability to convert pain into erotic stimuli.

We call practices based on pain "corporal" from the term corporal punishment. Some people take to corporal very readily. In the scene, they are usually referred to as masochists (as opposed to those outside the scene who think that all submissives fall in this category, as well as being totally nuts). Others experience the conversion of pain into pleasure as a learned response.

Knowing that people can be conditioned to respond sexually to things that are not generally considered erotic, such as touching, commands, etc., why bother using pain? It isn't that we just like to hurt our sweeties. You can tap into the body's own mechanism for dealing with pain to produce dramatic and intense events. There are both psychological and physiological components to this.

Pain is an emotional sensation. It is a cognitive interpretation of a stimulation that is, or might be, damaging the tissues of our body. A slap on the fanny stimulates specialized sensors in the skin called nociceptors. Nerve fibers transmit the occurrence of a spank to other nerve fibers in the spinal cord which relay the message to the brain. The brain locates the source of the spank, evaluates it, and determines an appropriate response to it.

If the spanking is severe enough to warrant it, the brain signals the body to manufacture powerful, opium-like substances called endorphins which enable people to endure high levels of pain. An endorphin rush feels great! Have you ever heard of "runner's high?" Heavy exercise is painful, but people actually learn to enjoy exercise for the endorphin rush they achieve through heavy exertion. Pain, it would seem, is a step toward bliss.

Part of the brain's interpretation of a spanking has a psychological effect, as well. Studies have shown that anticipation of pain can intensify the experience by producing anxiety. Does our helplessly bound submissive expect another swat after the first one? You bet she does, that's rather the point of the exercise. But when the next one comes, how hard it will be, and how long she'll have to endure the pain are matters she cannot control unless she wants to stop the scene by using her safe word. Anticipation and anxiety may also add adrenaline or other substances to the body's chemical stew. Who knows? Neither of us advanced further than a "B" in high school biology, so we admit these are unscientific, but educated guesses based upon "experiments" that have yielded rather spectacular results.

Add to our submissive's dilemma the fact that her dominant is caressing her body amid the spanks, urging her ever closer to orgasm, or perhaps, inducing orgasm after orgasm. Now, the conundrum of mixed messages and responses taking place in her mind and body enormously amplify the experience. The skill, inclination, and instincts of the dominant, the nature of the emotional connection the submissive feels for him, and the degree to which the scene fulfills each lover's fantasies determines the outcome of the scene.

The anxiety produced by being helplessly bound, thereby relinquishing control of your fate to the will of another may be enough to send you soaring. Having someone over you wielding whips and paddles might be just what Dr. Delight ordered or it may be too intense. For this reason, we advise you to progress slowly, carefully observe your reactions, and communicate clearly with your dominant.

Whipping or sexual torment in addition to the standard libidinous heat and desire can produce feelings ranging from exhilaration to intoxication. Pain caused by injury or accidental pain does not have the same effect because it is not a part of a sensual or sexual experience. Random pain of this type is nasty stuff, bad pain. Erotic pain is good pain, it is deliberate, given with love, and executed skillfully.

Flying
"Ground Control to Master Tom"

There is a phenomenon within the practice of SM that renders an ecstasy beyond orgasm. It is an altered state of consciousness that we unblushingly call transcendent. (Navels are nice to contemplate, but we find a spankable fanny a much more intriguing alternative.) Though it may sound far-fetched, it has been described by too many people to doubt its existence or its connection to SM. SMers call it flying, at least most of us do. Some people call it melting away or an "out-of-body" experience. Some may even call it Bob, how the hell would we know?

Altered states of consciousness produced by sexual or erotic means are noted throughout history. The sexual practices and meditations of Tantric Hinduism and Vajrayana Buddhism are said to be paths toward enlightenment. Similarly, some adepts of Taoism pursue *fang-chung shu* (arts of the inner chamber), employing a sexual breathing technique called *ho-ch'i* (unification of breaths) during sexual union as a "gateway" to spirituality and immortality.

Mind-bending sexual technique is not solely the turf of easterners. The West also has its fair share of explorers. Aleister Crowley's gang achieved altered states with their brand of "Sexual Magick." Crowley gave us a mouth-stuffing, but enlightening expression; his initiates were ritually pushed to sexual exhaustion inducing a consciousness that he called erotocomatose lucidity. If Crowley meant what we think he did, that a person can be erotically stimulated into a temporary, coma-like stupor while experiencing lucid visions and sensations as though they are experiencing a separate reality, then erotocomatose lucidity is what we call flying.

Not everyone who is into SM has the experience of flying. In fact, it seems to be a phenomenon experienced by the few who get into heavier corporal (whipping and spanking) scenes than those into other practices, but it is not exclusively within the corporal domain. During flying, the dominant is the pilot and the submissive is the space shuttle. There are several different ignition buttons and lots of techniques for pushing someone past that final shove into orbit which we'll cover later. Some say they take off when they sink into deep feelings of submission and their independent will goes out the window. Others maintain that feeling vulnerable and exposed is enough to make them fly. Still, the ever-popular "high state of sexual excitement" when mixed with the pain of a whipping seems to do it for most of us.

People who fall into this latter category begin to soar one of two ways. They can be kept for a prolonged time on the edge of orgasm, or they can be made to orgasm repeatedly. Women can be pushed over the edge either way. Continuous sexual teasing and denial of orgasm increases tension to the point of take-off. Multiple orgasms push them higher and higher and the orgasms start to blend together. Before long, they are in orbit. A man's sexual energy diminishes quickly after orgasm, so teasing is the best route for them.

The flight experience varies widely as one would expect from a journey that begins and ends within the confines of one's skull. But commonalities do exist. First of all, there is an incredible sensation of freedom. The flying submissive feels like she is actually flying or floating, disengaged from her body. She becomes vaguely aware of what is going on around her and her sole connection to the real world is through her dominant. She also senses that her brain is shutting down, that reason and ordinary perspective have gone on vacation. In this state, there are few inhibitions. Speaking feels sluggish, as though one is talking through water. Flying subs rarely say anything unless prompted by their doms.

Most flyers we know report similar visual perceptions, too. They see themselves enveloped in darkness, yet there is light just beyond their immediate surroundings. Often they can see images with brilliant clarity, visions of mountains, clouds and skies, even the darkness of outer space as they drift among the stars. Sometimes they see nothing; sounds, words, or music in these cases are their predominant impressions. We cannot define exactly what these altered states of consciousness are, or what causes them. Everyone has their own pet theories; cosmic connections, chemical reactions, emotional overload, mystical or spiritual states, and out-of-body experiences are the primary conjectures. Does this mean doms are rocket scientists and subs are space cadets? (Sorry, we can rarely pass up a pun).

All we know is that flying works, it's wonderful, and we can reproduce the results using the same techniques. Philip has experienced flying with several women and Molly has flown with other men. Don't you think we should be given a government grant to continue our research? What we do is a hell of a lot cheaper than launching a space mission, it is undeniably more fun, and everyone can do it.

Sensations of pure experience without any apparent meaning and seeing totally unrecognizable images are common. Below is one such account:

> I know you've been waiting to see this. It still does not describe the actual experience as well as I would like it to, but much of it is so difficult to translate into words. I have no idea where I was. I saw things and places that I have never seen before. Honest!
>
> I am naked. My hands are bound over my head, my legs, spread-eagled and bound. I close my eyes under the blindfold. There are light caresses all over my skin. I hear voices off in the distance, soft and alluring. My body is shivering, but I am not cold. I feel my mind going blank and I feel myself drifting. I am aware that violent tremors are running through my body, but I no longer feel them.
>
> The sky is a mystical blue above me with a soft scattering of clouds, though darkness directly surrounds me. I am still aware of the voices in the room but they are detached, not a part of my inner surroundings. I want to say what I see, but I no longer have control over those muscles which would allow me to speak.
>
> I'm floating higher and the dark skies around me are a soft blue. I extend my arm into the clouds and my guide tells me I can go no further. He tells me, "Come back." I turn to look below me. I see the mountains thickly surrounded by silver laced clouds. I want to reach for them, but he tells me no, that I must go with him. His voice is becoming distant as I drift further into the clouds below me. I feel my hands clench together as I am reaching.
>
> In an instant he surrounds me, pulling me back with a force that I can no longer resist. I am returning to the room where I still lie bound upon the bed. I feel my body shuddering as I become more aware of the voices around me. They seem to be bringing me together again.
>
> I am now aware that my hands are no longer bound, yet they are still clenched as if to hold onto the clouds that once surrounded me. I feel the trembling, and as it becomes stronger I know that all of me is now together. I feel a tear fall from each eye and I am once again completely earthbound.

Philip was piloting this lady, who shall be dubbed Mary to conceal her identity. Also present for the scene were Molly, another submissive lady, and another dominant. Mary had received a light whipping and caressing which brought her to a mild state of arousal. She was then stripped sensuously, bound, spread-eagled to a bed, and blindfolded. Philip and the other two submissives began to caress her and fondle her while Philip guided her into submitting and relaxing into their ministrations. We can only speculate, but we believe, on subsequent discussion, that Mary flew because of her intense sexual arousal, her desire to give Philip control over her, and high level of trust in the people involved.

Philip felt a strong mental connection to Mary just as she began her take-off. Philip felt as though his consciousness was surrounding Mary like a protective envelope. She began to drift off very quickly. It started with heavy shivering which lasted a only few minutes, then she settled down. It seemed that she was mildly startled or that she felt off balance at times as her body flinched briefly a few times.

Though her account might seem to indicate that her flight lasted only a short time, Mary was sailing around for about twenty minutes. Then Philip began to hold her close and speak very gently to Mary, coaxing her to come in for a landing. He removed her blindfold and let her come down very slowly, holding her for a long time after she was back among us. It was a beautiful and mysterious encounter for all of us.

"Flying" may not be considered the most appropriate term for this phenomenon as the sensation is not one of being airborne for everyone.

> I have a landscape, but I do not 'fly'. I am on the land.
> [My] experience starts out with me in a green pasture or field. I am looking up at the sky and it is almost an unreal hue of blue! I start looking around the landscape and I feel an immense pleasure, not knowing why or what, but I know I am happy and content.
> Slave Kitiara

Another submissive comments:

> This past weekend my Mistress was using a combination of whip, flogger and pinwheel on me that was unbelievable! I have no idea how long I was 'gone' but I was definitely up in the ozone!
> It didn't take long to get me there, and when she brought me back down, I could feel her gently stroking my skin and calling me back, telling me to 'come back down' and join her. [Tonight] is Wednesday night and friends of mine at work have commented that I've been glowing since Monday and they all wanted to know what my secret was.
> The way flying feels to me is like being on the top of a mountain during a storm, feeling the winds lashing at my skin and leaving my nerve endings tingling. My skin will literally tingle for hours afterwards.
> Hmmmmm... I wonder if the Mistress [X] airport will be open this weekend?
> Coquette

A dominant we know disagrees that flying is a phenomenon apart from what we call sub space. He views flying as part of a continuum of submissive emotionality. Each facet of the multidimensional "sub space" he refers to, is controllable as a separate entity:

> Most folks think of sub space (and top space) as being two dimensional, and I feel that this is an error, we spent most of the last year playing in exploring just how many dimensions exist.
> Two dimensions would be like an elevator, a 'I am really close to the top, please make me less verbal' kind of thing; up being close to coming out of sub space and down being a place where the sub is deep into [her] space.
> I define 'flying' as a very precise location in an individual's sub space, and not the same location for every individual. It is where her needs are being met in an environment that allows her to maintain her point in space with minimum or zero effort.
> We played with more than three dimensions, and were never able to identify all of the major ones, let alone the minor ones, but I will use three to try to explain where I am coming from, and what we were doing.
> If you consider volition, mentation, and verbosity as different elements of sub space, let us agree that each can be controlled separately. The sub can range from the normal ability to communicate all the way to being totally non-verbal, the

will of the sub can range from being perfectly capable of making decisions and acting on them, to being totally docile, from having the full capability of thinking things through to being totally incapable of thought. The common point of origin for each of these qualities is at the deep end, and if you bring your sub all the way down there you have your basic vegetable, unable to think, communicate, or react.

Now we can construct a three-dimensional space, each of these qualities having an axis in a different dimension...if you visualize it as a cube, you can see that it is fairly easy to describe exactly where subs are in their space, and by working on one element at a time, move them around in their space.

We were using this as a tool to explore sub space, and we were getting a grip on how to use sub space, as a tool to explore our relationship."

...I see the dom's role as one of assisting the sub into [her] space, rather than, as I sometimes see around me, the Dom being totally concerned with meeting [his] own needs, and leaving the sub to struggle along to enter space without guidance.

       Cosmo

Perhaps this is the best time to suggest that you shouldn't resort to drastic measures trying to make someone fly. You are liable to do more damage than good by trying to force it. Heavy whipping will not necessarily result in flying, in fact it can have the opposite effect. Endorphin highs, caused by heavy pain or exhaustion are not flying. One submissive friend of ours related a scene where a bad dominant was whipping her ever more frenetically. He even ignored her when she used her safe word, over and over again. She said that she was able to put herself into a mental state where she no longer resisted this jerk's abuse, she simply blanked out. This is not flying either, it is one of the mind's methods of defending itself against abuse, extreme fear, or trauma. This "dominant" should be drawn and quartered. Flying just cannot be forced.

As with any other natural phenomenon, flying will happen easily when all the elements are in place. Since people vary so greatly, the same elements that make one person soar may not work for another.

We cannot say exactly what these elements are, but we suggest that trust, confidence, sexual attraction, and a strong connection between the players are prerequisites. Other elements may include: being open to what might happen during a scene rather than expectant; intense, prolonged sexual tension; and concentration or focus. All of these take time, patience, and caring to develop. Relax, proceed with your scenes in a way that you both enjoy, gently and slowly pushing some of the boundaries of your scenes. You might experience flight, and you might not. If you are bound and determined to have the experience, find someone you can trust implicitly, who has flown submissives before and ask if he might help you.

Flying is similar to being stoned, but much better. (Or so we have been told. We wouldn't know, as we have always been good and proper citizens who never dreamt of abusing controlled substances.) Some drugs that cause brain shut-down also numb your feelings, while SM does not. As far as we're concerned, flying is a high far better than drugs. We don't recommend using drugs while playing SM. Drugs can cut off the very sensations you are striving for. They also slow your responses during potentially dangerous situations. We don't think drugs are an intelligent choice while doing scenes.

Watch her closely while she's out there. You are very likely to find that you feel some unexplainable connection with her; that you feel you are controlling her flight. The funny thing here is that when you feel that connection, odds are that she is feeling the same thing. We have felt that connection between us and it is felt in the same way; either as though Philip was holding some invisible strings tethering Molly to him, or that his consciousness was surrounding her, protecting and directing her. These two distinctly different sensations have occurred during the same sessions to each of us at the same time and have happened the same way in scenes with other people.

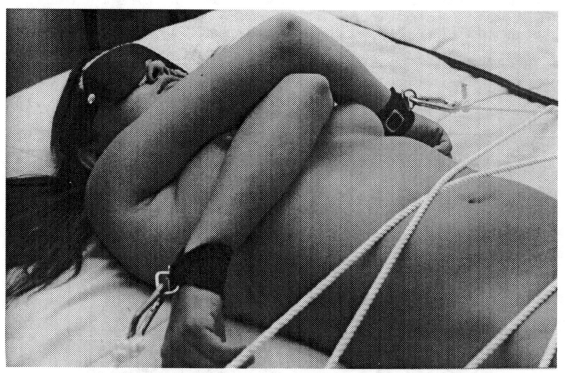

Be Careful! Subs who are flying are unable to make decisions, to determine damaging levels of pain, and would never think of using a safe word.

There are several things a dominant must be aware of when confronted with a flying sub. SUBS WHO ARE FLYING ARE UNABLE TO MAKE DECISIONS! If you told her you were going to cut off her arm, she would sweetly and casually reply, "Yes, Master." She will also be unable to determine damaging levels of pain. If you are using whips or spanking to launch your submissive BE CAREFUL! Once she's "on the fly" she's not going to use a safe word; it will never occur to her.

You, the dominant, as her link with reality, must not break contact or leave her. Stay with her also for the twenty or thirty minutes it takes for her to drift back to earth. Yes, it can easily take twenty to thirty minutes, and don't be surprised if she remains fuzzy for hours. It isn't unheard of for her to feel the exhilaration from flying for days. While your lady is in orbit, make her comfortable. You don't want her to experience any strain or anything else that will defuse the free feeling of flying. Untie her or not as you see fit, but make sure that she is comfy, warm, and feels safe. Check her hands and feet if she's bound to make sure her circulation is good. Never take your attention from her, her sense of well-being relies largely on that mysterious mental connection to you. Lie beside her and let her feel your presence, but don't interfere with her voyage by asking her if she's OK. She's fine. In fact, she's as fine as she'll ever be!

People act different ways when they fly. They might tremble violently (as Mary did) or drift off as peacefully as lambs. Some appear as unresponsive as a doorknob. Don't panic, your lady is just dandy. She's just ping-ponging around the galaxy feeling all kinds of swell stuff. This is a time for you to be brave and patient; she will be back with you soon, better than new.

Let the dear girl sail around for a while, then stroke her gently and speak softly to her. Kiss her lightly, she will slowly begin to come around. The key here is to bring her down very gently, a fast free-fall back to earth can be a terrifying experience. Assure her that she has been wonderful and that you will not leave her alone. Cuddle with her.

As she begins to regain herself, she will be remarkably happy and appreciative. This is an opportunity to enjoy some of the most gratifying snuggles and nuzzles you will ever experience. Don't rush off to take a pee or to get a bottle of wine to celebrate. Take your time, just hold one another and sop up all that love.

photo of Steed and Tori by Jerry

The maiden voyage of rocket Molly

If you are still skeptical, we don't blame you. Rest assured we were equally skeptical once upon a time. Molly was a champion skeptic, distrusting anything mystical or lacking in empirical evidence. The following is an account of Molly's conversion:

I was eager enough, but totally novice to the scene. My sizzling fantasies about dominance and submission only lacked a compatible partner to fulfill them. I was in awe of the spectacle of players on my third visit to The Vault, one of the best known SM clubs in New York City. Late in the evening, a girlfriend introduced me to Master Rick, a dominant visiting from a Southern city.

Rick explained the action as we watched a few scenes together. He was a hot-looking guy with a quiet drawl and an old-fashioned chivalry that could have charmed the robe off Sandra Day O'Connor.

Clearly, the attraction was mutual as he invited me to visit him for a chance to experience rather than just watch. Being the paradigm of gentlemen, he requested that I consider his invitation to give me an opportunity to ask my friends what they knew of him. I learned that he had been active in the public SM scene for years and enjoyed an impeccable reputation as a good and careful dominant. I was delighted. I accepted. I was very, very nervous.

In preparation for the impending weekend, Rick and I held long telephone conversations in which he coaxed information from me, learning my worries, concerns, and most intimate fantasies.

"What implement do you fear most?" he asked during one such discussion.

"The cane," I replied after thinking a moment.

"Then," he replied, "I will reserve that for punishment."

My urgent gulp of air must have been heard because he immediately responded softening my anxiety by saying that timely, sincere apologies for mistakes might earn me a pardon. This, I later realized, was yet another ruse Rick used to learn more about me.

During one of our chats Rick said he intended to make me fly. I assumed this was merely male hyperbole. "Yeah sure," I thought. It seemed unwise to vocalize these doubts to a man who would shortly have me bound and helpless.

Before my visit, I was given instructions and little tasks to do. He knew I did leather-work and he bade me make a collar and cuffs that I would be comfortable wearing all night. I was told to sit bare-bottomed on leather each night for fifteen minutes and write down my thoughts. Rick instructed me not to wear panties on the flight down. "No one has to know," he said, "it will be our secret." When I arrived I was to walk by his side or behind him, never ahead of him. These conversations and assignments kept me in a submissive frame of mind with just the right mixture of anxiety and anticipation.

My scene-wise friends alternated between fanning my fears and allaying them. First, they would remind me I was soon to spend the weekend with a guy who planned to tie me up and beat me, and my anxiety would rise. When I appeared to be getting too nervous they would remind me how safe and experienced Rick was, calming me somewhat. Keeping novice Molly on an emotional roller coaster had become community sport. What fun!

Finally the day came for my escapade to begin. During an uneventful flight, the mundane felt tinged with unreality. I felt like a little kid with a secret, bursting, but not daring to share my thoughts with the passenger in the next seat. He was a soldier returning from a tour of duty in Germany. What would he think if I told him that I was flying five hundred miles from home to surrender myself for sexual torture to a man I barely knew? What should I be thinking of myself? Was I crazy or would this turn out to be a wonderful adventure? My imagination was going berserk.

The seemingly innocent information, suggestions and instructions Rick so subtly planted in my mind during our conversations were hammering away at all my sexual buttons. Every time I shifted in my seat I was reminded of my nakedness beneath my skirt. Luckily, the plane didn't crash; I'm sure my seat was far too saturated to function effectively as a flotation device.

Rick was waiting for me at the airport. I wasn't sure how to behave and carefully watched him for clues. He carried my bag for me. The reason I was told not to walk in front of him became clear as he opened doors for me. He was a gentleman, how charming! We made small talk during the ride to his apartment and he showed me his city. I was beginning to relax, he seemed like such a nice, normal guy.

The tour of Rick's apartment set my nerves back on edge. I was ill-prepared to see evidence of his proclivities displayed so openly. The den could have been filled with priceless antiques, but my mind only logged a padded sawhorse with eyebolts near the bottoms of the legs. It was identical to the whipping bench used at The Vault. Finding eyebolts in the ceiling of his bedroom and a massive chain running beneath the waterbed wrenched my nerves several notches tighter. By the time he showed me a closet lined with hooks dripping with whips, paddles, and the dreaded canes, I was ready to rabbit out of there. But, in retrospect, I don't think tear gas would have induced me to leave. My dream was coming true.

Rick casually ordered me to take off my clothes and to put on my collar, as if it was the most ordinary thing in the world. It did not feel so ordinary to me. My pulse raced. He sat me on his bed and we talked.

Rick said he was tempted to begin playing with me in the car, but had checked himself, deciding it was better to give me his final instructions when I was "properly dressed" in private. He gave me two safe words. Uttering my full name would stop a session and "umbrella" would slow things down. He ordered me not to allow myself to orgasm without permission. He told me to say, "thank you Master," if something felt good and, "edge," if I felt close to having an orgasm. When we were alone I could speak freely about things I did or didn't want to do try. In public I should respond to an instruction by saying, "If it pleases you, Master," for things that sounded fun to me. If I was uncomfortable with a command I should say, "Only if it pleases you, Master."

Finished with his instructions, Rick blindfolded me and placed suspension cuffs on my wrists. He attached the cuffs to chains that ran through the eyebolts in the ceiling and pulled them until my arms were over my head with my feet still flat on the floor. I was comfortable, but securely fastened and quite vulnerable. Every bondage that Master Rick put me in that weekend was secure, but comfortable.

He rubbed oil on my back, bottom, and thighs. It was sensual and arousing. He begin whipping with a very light deerskin whip. It felt like an odd massage; there was no pain at all. At some point he put something tight on my nipples. The left one felt good, but the right one must have been tighter because it hurt and I made a face (though I said nothing). Rick noticed my discomfort immediately and he loosened it. I don't remember when he took them off. I almost wished he hadn't, but I had said nothing to let him know I liked them.

The strokes of his whip slowly became harder. He changed to a heavier whip. It felt wonderful, nothing like anything I had imagined whipping would feel. Rick made a funny noise with something which startled me. It sounded like a knife being sharpened, a scary sound considering my helplessness. Rick knew the effect the of sound and after pausing to enjoy my reaction, he assured me that it was not what I thought it was.

I felt something less stingy and bouncier than a whip. Later I learned that these were fiber glass rods and the sound came when he rubbed them together. Next, I was gently paddled. All this attention was really turning me on, everything felt so good. He moved from one thing to another very smoothly.

Finally, Rick unfastened me from the ceiling and bent me over the bed-frame for more whipping. When he slithered a silky whip gently down my back, past the cleft of my bottom, and over my thighs, I was done in.

"Edge," I barely managed to whisper.

Rick quietly asked me if I wanted to come as a refined host might offer tea to a guest. I heard myself respond, "Yes, thank you Master," matching his tone, as though I were saying, "Oh, tea sounds like such a splendid idea." No one had ever asked me if I wanted to come before. It was like being part of a surrealist play, requesting an orgasm with such dignified, detached decorum. Without another word, Rick caressed my labia and clit, pushing me into the first orgasm of the night.

When I recovered, my cuffs were changed and I was told to lie in the middle of the bed. My wrists and ankles were stretched wide and chained. The excess links were draped over my arms, feeling cool against my now very warm skin. He used various whips on me for a little while. Finally, he freed my legs and took me. He said I belonged to him now that he had taken me. These words, and the whole scene Master Rick was unfolding for me, fit my fantasies like a pair of fine, kidskin gloves. I wanted nothing more at that moment than to be owned by this incredible man.

As the evening progressed, I was repeatedly brought to the edge of orgasm. Master Rick kept me on that verge for long periods of time before permitting me several very intense multiple orgasms. And when I came...wow! It seemed unbelievable that he was able to keep them going so long. I felt past the point of being coherent. Things were foggy. I was totally disoriented and making sobbing noises.

Somewhere in all this, while chained to the bed, after numerous multiple orgasms, I took off. I saw myself high atop a mountain, and the thought occurred to me that it was like a scene with Mickey Mouse in *The Sorcerer's Apprentice*, watching the stars, comets, and planets zoom past me. Then I felt as if I was rocketing through the galaxy. In my ecstatic journey I became only dimly aware of my surroundings and the things happening to my body. Always though, I could feel the presence of my dominant surrounding and protecting me. I came down slowly, aware that I was no longer chained and I fell asleep, held snugly in my master's arms.

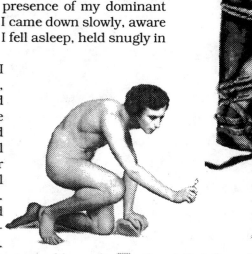

Over the next two days I experienced whips, paddles, crops, hot wax, ice, clips and vibrators. I received not a single bruise and rarely experienced anything that I could really call pain. I went off into flight four more times, sometimes a gradual rise, other times like a rocket. Even had I not flown, it would have been the best and most intense sex I had ever experienced.

It was several days after I returned home before the smile left my face and my feet touched *terra firma*. I am now a believer. Thank you Master Rick, and please accept my apologies for having doubted you.

Endorphin highs and other vacation spots

Another altered state sensation experienced by bottoms we call the "endorphin high." We use the term "bottoms" here instead of submissives because achieving an endorphin high is a physical process with an emotional result and does not rely upon dominance and submission. Unlike flying, an endorphin high is a sensation of intoxication. There is no sense of being "out-of-body" or of transcendence. A person experiencing an endorphin high experiences pain as a subjective reality, even as he or she are able to endure more of it. Endorphin highs are more common in SM than flying. While we conjecture that the journey into bliss we call flying is tied to endorphins and similar pain-reducing chemicals manufactured by the body, clearly, there are other factors at work, as well.

We'd like to make an important observation here. We have found that starting with heavy pain instead of a gradual, erotic build-up forces the endophins, a body defense mechanism, to kick in too early. Flying cannot happen. Sexual response is often also diminished (if not demolished) by the early endorphin high, making orgasm more difficult or impossible to achieve.

Many submissives are content with this, but an endorphin high that cuts off orgasm is a bummer. Rather than the chemical rush induced by one's own body, many people enjoy the whacking, smacking, and torture because of the intensity of the orgasms produced. (Yes, Virginia, people do have orgasms just from being flogged.)

Probably the most common use of pain is by the folks who use the mild spanking or whipping as foreplay. Here, pain is simply used to initiate and enhance sexual tension. These whipping scenes are followed by sex. (An orchid, dinner, and a movie just aren't enough for some people.)

The two relatively minor highs described in the last two paragraphs are modalities of using pain for its intrinsic erotic properties. Before we launch into a discussion of painful loving and loving pain, let us revisit a segment of the players in the game.

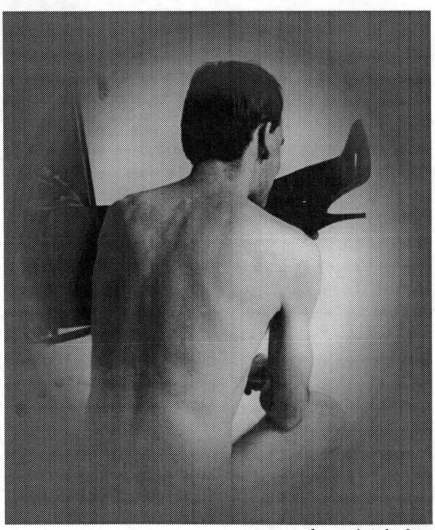

from a photo by Jerry

Reprise; tops, bottoms, and switches

Democracy means simply the bludgeoning of the people by the people for the people.
Oscar Wilde

Using pain for only sensual or sexual purposes does not rely on dominance and submission. The purely physical stuff, the whipping, smacking, pinching, slapping, etc., has an attraction all its own.

The scene term for the receiver is "bottom" and the one who dishes out the delights is the "top." You might hear dominant and submissive being used interchangeably with top and bottom, but the former terms imply something more about the relationship than whipper and whippee. Tops and bottoms frequently swap roles because they enjoy both sides. People who do this are called switches, but a switch can also refer to person who enjoys both dominant and submissive roles.

"Ouch... Mmmmmmmmmmmm!"

There are four modalities for experiencing pain as pleasure.

"Total conversion" or the "ouchless ouch" is a technique wherein there is no subjective experience of pain. A scene employing total conversion might begin with soft caresses, erotic touching, and sexual teasing, moving up to soft strokes with a light, deer- or lambskin whip. The bottom experiences the light whip as an erotic massage. Heavier strokes and harsher implements are incorporated very gradually as sexual arousal increases.

The top maintains the level of the pain stimulation in sync with and slightly below the level of sexual stimulation, so that the bottom never becomes aware of feeling pain. Frequently, the top pauses to fondle and caress the bottom to fuel her arousal. The strokes become a tease as the bottom wants more, so that she is always hungering for greater stimulation than her top allows her, building the fire steadily toward orgasm. The experience is one of total pleasure and eroticism.

"Contrapolar stimulation" is mixed pleasure and pain that also uses a gradual buildup, but starts at a slightly harsher level. Molly likes to think of it as, "Hurts so good!" The bottom experiences some pain, but only enough to enhance the rise of sexual tension. Pain and the pleasure meld as the session intensifies. The balance here is tenuous, with some stimulation feeling like pleasure and other stimulation more like hurt. This works as long as the overall feeling is sexual. This is also partially dependent on conditioning and expectation.

"Derivative pleasure" is a love it/hate it kind of thing. A deliberately painful beating can end up feeling wonderful. This is a sport for experienced players. There are two categories of derivative pleasure: contiguously derived pleasure and delayed derived pleasure.

Contiguously derived pleasure is a warmth that radiates as the body seems to absorb the shock after a lick from a whip, paddle, slapper, cane, riding crop, etc. The stroke itself is experienced as pain (but pain that is easily endurable). The pain subsides rather quickly and the warmth radiates away from the area of the skin that was hit.

Tops carefully avoid inflicting too much pain as that would cut off any sexual response at all. Bottoms endure the pain because it is followed by warm, sensual feelings. You develop a rhythm of ouch...ahhhhh, ouch...ahhhhh, ouch...ahhhhh. This is an acquired taste, it isn't advisable for novices. We were going to use the old joke, "Don't try this at home..." but where the hell else are you going to try it without getting busted?

Delayed derivative pleasure is hardly sensual at all during the actual beating. Delayed derived pleasure is much more difficult to achieve. It relies heavily upon a well-developed connection between the players and the bottom's conditioning to pain. Most commonly, the players are involved in a dom/sub relationship that tends to strengthen their bond. The sexual heat from delayed derived pleasure comes sometime after the beating, from five to thirty minutes or so. The pain administered accumulates and metamorphasizes into an explosion of sexual heat and desire. After administering a beating, the dominant can relax, have a drink, and wait to be sexually assaulted by his partner.

Corporal scenes often incorporate all three types of pain. Some people are content to stick to total conversion and some find they enjoy a bit more stimulation. Blending modalities is a common practice. Typically, scenes mix contrapolar and derivative pain building to a state of total conversion. In a state of total conversion, a bottom can be given a full force cane stroke and be unaware that it ever occurred.

"Punitive pain" is the fourth modality of pain experience in SM. We are hesitant to mention this because it is so easily abused. Some submissives receive emotional satisfaction from enduring pain that is never intended to provide physical pleasure.

"Naughty girl!" Play punishment is an excuse for a scene that both people enjoy.

This is not to be confused with play punishment. Play punishment scenes use punishment for an excuse for a sensual encounter. This can be an enjoyable game and part of the fantasy. Punitive pain is meant to hurt with no erotic purpose. We believe that most of the goals stated for this type of pain giving are accomplished better by other means. There are destructive elements in the practice itself.

Some bottoms justify their desire for punitive pain as a need for catharsis or expiation of guilt. Frequently, the tops in these situations say that they are merely giving what is desired. True help for this person would be to encourage self-love and self-forgiveness, allowing catharsis to occur naturally as a result of increasing self-esteem.

Macho submissives may wish to endure heavy pain as proof of their devotion and submissiveness. Since we can think of hundreds of ways to show devotion better than the accepting of gratuitous violence, we are sure any dom could suggest a few to his sweety.

Another reason given for administering punitive pain is that obedience requires punishment. This rationale belies a misunderstanding of the nature of consensual submission. Submissives have an intense desire to please their dominants. The harshest penalty for not obeying is disapproval. Here again, dominance can quickly turn to abuse.

"If both parties want it, where is the harm?" is the final argument. Harm is possible. If punitive pain is frequent, it can undermine the consensual element of the relationship by inducing fear of the dominant. This can erode trust. The fear can inhibit the conditioning process where pain converts to pleasure. Lastly, it places on the dominant the responsibility to be the finally arbitrator of good and bad. The submissive has been reduced to a child rather than an equal adult partner.

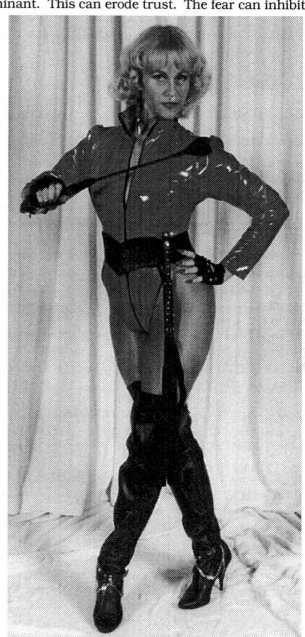

Though harm is possible by frequent use of punitive pain, it is far from being the rule. It isn't the way we like to play, but many have told us something like, "Yes, I understand the difference between abuse and role playing, but I really like being punished for misbehaving, for being a naughty girl, for neglecting my duties, or for behaving in a manner unseemly for a slave (or wife, husband, butler, maid, prisoner, pet, etc.)."

A lot of people really enjoy these fantasies. The humiliation of an over-the-knee, bare-bottomed, being-reminded-of-one's-place spanking is a real turn-on for them. It is very Victorian, which is a wonderful treasure-house of fantasy. To these folks we bow humbly and recant all of the above arguments. We really don't want to tell you what to do, we just want to help keep relationships off the rocks and brains from being dashed on them.

As long as there is some space provided for stepping out of role, you'll be fine. If the submissive gives herself permission to grow and does not lose sight of herself as a valuable, independent person, role play isn't going to be damaging. Honest communication is the key to staying out of trouble.

Photo from Dressing For Pleasure Fashion Show, courtesy of Dressing For Pleasure of Upper Montclair, NJ

12 Making the Upper Cheeks Red

Embarrassment, Humiliation, and the Mindfuck

olly's Diary: Being given away.

A desire submissives often express is being "given away" or lent to another dominant for his sexual pleasure. It is a fantasy about ownership, giving up control, surprise, and adventure. It is a fantasy I had expressed as a request to Philip, my master.

Acting out a fantasy seldom ends up quite like the daydream. We think we know ourselves, especially those of us with a bent for introspection, but SM has a way of revealing feelings within us which we have long denied. Psychological buttons can be pushed before we even know they exist.

When the evening began, I was both nervous and excited. Six of us were gathered in Philip's apartment that night: Philip; Vicky, Philip's other more experienced submissive; Master David, a very experienced dominant and a friend; and Elizabeth and Steve, a young couple beginning to explore SM.

Several days before, we did a scene with Elizabeth and Steve that pushed me pretty far. Philip had instructed me to kneel in front of Steve, and though I barely knew him, to play with Steve's cock. I found myself more anxious than I had anticipated.

No one else was engaged in sexual play and I was the center of attention. It was embarrassing. It was humiliation of the type I find exciting. I wanted to go further, to be even more sexual, but it also frightened me. If just touching a penis in public made me so nervous, what would more do? It was like touching a sore tooth with your tongue: it hurts, but you can't keep yourself from doing it.

Philip knew that Elizabeth and Steve wanted a scene where I, as slave, was ordered to serve Steve sexually and he knew this would dovetail beautifully with some of my fantasies, too. These were the kind of fantasies that used to make me giggle when Philip verbalized them.

I had been requesting a publicly sexual scene since the beginning of my relationship with Philip. The scene where I was ordered to play with Steve's cock was Philip's way of testing the waters.

Master David's presence made this evening more difficult for me. He was someone I knew, liked, and respected; someone with whom I would continue to have contact. I didn't know his feelings on this type of behavior. If he saw me act like a slut, would that change his opinion of me? I didn't worry as much about Steve and Elizabeth. They would be moving out of state and I might never see them again.

Nonetheless, I complied with Philip's order to undress while five fully clothed people watched me. I was at center stage once again. I was put into bondage on a large sofa cushion. The bondage device used was a small cross I had constructed from PVC pipe. Chains running through the pipes were attached to my wrist and ankle cuffs and a short chain near the center of the cross was clipped to my collar. The bondage forced me to my hands and knees with my legs spread wide and my tail raised like a pro-montory point. In this utterly vulnerable position, my genitalia were shockingly exposed.

Philip and Steve dragged the cushion I was perched on into the center of the room while they casually discussed my position. It was all very humiliating and I could feel myself falling into a deeply submissive state of mind.

184

Philip announced that he had a new butt plug, small and of soft vinyl that he would use on me. This was a shock. Sexual things are embarrassing to me, but anything anal feels ten times more private and intimate. It wasn't long before that I thought anal sex was disgusting and perverted. Part of me still thinks so, even though I love the way it feels. The idea of have an object inserted in my nether regions, in front of all these people, was horrifying. God, was I wet.

I had been publicly whipped in the nude a dozen times, but this was an entirely new level of intimidation. I was incredibly disturbed by the thought of David sitting behind me. Embarrassed as I was, the scene was becoming intense.

It became almost too much when Vicky said, "relax your muscles for my master, dear." (So that the plug could enter.) Humiliation from master was fun, but coming from another woman, it felt degrading. I tried to block her voice. It was a discordant note in an otherwise sweet symphony. Philip slipped the well-lubricated plug inside me and tied it in place with ropes going around my waist and through my crotch. The ropes were a further advertisement of my shame.

Master David could not stay. Upon offering his apologies and bidding the others farewell, he tossed me the standard, bound submissive joke, "Goodbye Molly, don't bother to get up." As he walked by me to reach the door, I didn't raise my eyes. I wasn't sure if I could ever look him in the face again.

Philip and Steve began whipping me in unison. The flogging fell like a gentle rain of leather on my back and rear. Emotions so overwhelmed me that I had little body awareness. Events around me became distant. Only the connection to my master seemed to strengthen as his will became my sole significant reality.

Philip unbound me and helped me to stand. My legs were made of rubber and hard to control. In a soft, but firm voice he told me to go upstairs and serve Master Steve. At this instant, I was hit with a psychological shock. I wasn't nervous, I was absolutely terrified. I was cold, dizzy, and I felt a wave of nausea sweep over me. I was frightened to go from him and break the bond.

While I was upstairs, Philip would not be there. He would not be close at hand, directing others to do things to me. During our other public scenes it felt as if other people were merely his instruments, while all that happened to me still came from him. This time, I was actually being given away, delivered into the hands of a relative stranger.

A curious thing happened, something unforeseen in all the hours I spent in reverie with this fantasy. I became aware of a conflict within me. Thoughts, almost like voices, reminded me of serious relationships ending because I had been unfaithful.

It is said that your life flashes before your eyes while dying. In this instant I had a taste of this. Many years before, a man who had been my friend, confidant, and finally my beau, had stopped just short of bedding me. He became as cold as ice to me when I took a lover, even though he had suggested it. Another man, who took my virginity and left me pregnant, broke off with me when I saw someone else, though he agreed to it in advance. My last serious, passionate relationship (until my late thirties) had ended the same way.

Two voices were warring in my head. The older one said that to go upstairs with Steve would be acting the slut and would change my relationship with Philip forever. Another voice, a stronger one, said to trust and obey.

I felt so deeply submissive I could barely talk. It was impossible to look at Philip's face, it felt like attempting to look directly into a desert sun. I knew Philip's faith in me was as deep as my confidence in him. If I said, "I can't," he would accept that.

Philip was, and is, secure enough in his dominance to demand knowing surrender rather than accept blind obedience. His priorities are never confused by the needs of his ego. He is vigilant and would not hesitate to end a scene if he saw any risk of damage, physical or mental. He trusts his subs to tell him if there is a problem he does not see.

This master of my heart, my lover, and my best friend accepts only acts consented to in a positive spirit. There were no petty penalties for disobedience and no punishments to fear. That made the choice to obey a difficult order more profound. Obedience had to be totally motivated out of a desire to yield to his will.

"Do you really want me to do this?" I managed to get out the question in a soft, squeaky and almost trembling voice.

Philip hesitated for a moment, then answered, "Yes, I do." He took me in his arms, hugged me tightly and said softly, "I love you."

That affirmation was all I needed. I went upstairs, out of his sight, resigned to whatever would be. I couldn't think anymore. The sex upstairs with Steve was strangely non-sexual, though I did orgasm. My mind set was so submissive, it was as if my body belonged to another person. I felt like a puppet, without a will.

My mind is almost blank on what happened after the scene, except that nothing changed and I still had Philip's love. Later that night, or early the next morning, he made love to me, which I wanted very badly. It erased any lingering questions and made me feel totally his again.

A few days later we discussed the session. We habitually did that when significant conflicts or emotions were involved. The intensity of my reaction that had followed the order to go with Steve had surprised him. My face had gone so ashen that he had prepared himself to catch me should I faint. He admitted that having me go out of his sight was difficult for him as well. It was an emotional push for us both.

Outsiders cloak SM within a shroud of mystique and horror. It feels impossible to explain to them why we love it so. Whips and chains are downright scary to look at! When we say, "Hey, it isn't what it looks like, folks," we get nothing but blank stares. So, we tell them, "Look, bondage allows the bondee to set herself free inside her head and whipping acts as a sexual stimulus when done with love and intense concentration to the submissive's responses."

"Uh, yeah, sure."

"It does, honest!"

"Right, um, I gotta go. Bye! Nice welts, thanks for sharing."

As difficult as the physical dimensions of SM are to understand, the emotional elements are a lot more confusing. Here, that the paradoxical nature of SM blooms full. By now, you should have a rather good idea of how bondage, corporal punishment, and kinky sex act as a turn-on. It takes a greater cognitive leap to understand how verbal abuse, embarrassment, humiliation, or being owned can become vehicles for advanced sexuality, even promoting emotional growth.

In the story above, the dominant takes a fantasy requested by the submissive and uses it to push her into a very deep state of submission. "I felt so deeply submissive I could barely talk. It was impossible to look at Philip's face..." This trance-like state carries various names; "sinking into submission," "entering sub space," and "entering bottom space" are the most common.

Molly requests a fantasy that she thinks will emphasize the elements in SM she enjoys the most. "It is a fantasy about ownership, giving up control, surprise, and adventure." While her dominant is in the business of fantasy realization and is happy to grant her this, Philip is not one to follow a script. He uses her desires as an opportunity to give her a deeper push than she expects.

She feels the ownership she craves when he treats her as if she were property, loaning her for use to another man. Loss of control is complete. Philip has always controlled the action, but he is the partner she has selected to be involved with in a relationship. Now, even the choice of partner is removed. She is taken on an adventure, a journey whose destination is only partly revealed to her.

Still, her dom controls the situation. This is more complicated in a scenario that involves several others. He has made sure that the other people involved in the scene have complementary goals. When others are involved in your scenes, it is important to realize that they will have a significant effect on your scene. You will be affecting them as well. A dom in charge of a group scene is responsible for and to everyone involved.

Intensity of emotion is the primary goal for the scene. Sex plays a subordinate role in what might seem to an outsider a basically sexual situation. Actually it is the submissive's conflicts about her sexuality that are explored. Humiliation is used as a vehicle to achieve this. Molly has residual negative feelings about her sexuality that Philip wants to help her overcome. He is giving her a safe situation in which to resolve, or at least confront, these conflicts. Molly's fantasy is, in her terms, "acting the slut." She revels in the fantasy and is afraid of it at the same time.

Each of the humiliations Molly endures centers around this basic conflict with her sexuality. Never does the humiliation Philip puts her through attack her worth as a person. Philip leads Molly, step by step, into more and more emotionally compromising positions.

First, she is made the only nude person in the room. She becomes a sex object as she is bound in a provocative position and dragged into the center of the room. She is being discussed as if she were a toy. Philip knows her well and proceeds to employ her disquiet about anal activities which propels Molly's humiliation to a much higher level.

Humiliation, like beauty, is in the mind of the beholder. Being treated as an object, a pet, a toy (as in the story) or a piece of furniture (as in the photo by Jerry on the right) may feel like either a degrading experience or a hot and sexy giving of control depending on the people involved.

This is a critical moment in their scene. Molly is already entering a submissive state of mind. Philip watches very carefully. Using the anal plug is the push that will either sink Molly deep into her sub space or become too much for her to bear. Until this point, the acts of humiliation have been things Molly was familiar with. Being nude in front of friends was no big deal, but being the only unclothed person in the group was a little unnerving. A small push. Being put in such a revealing position was another gentle nudge, again, nothing entirely unfamiliar to her. These things were embarrassing, but only mildly so. Philip was fairly certain how she would react to being publicly "plugged", but they had never tried it before.

By announcing the purchase of a new anal plug Philip gives Molly the opportunity to opt out of the scene and use her safe word. Molly's shock was half of what Philip was hoping for. Her eyes flew open and her head came off the floor to look for Philip. He met her eyes and held them. She knew well that Philip didn't make empty threats. His announcement was proof that he was willing to go through with the plugging. It was time for Molly to decide her fate. She closed her eyes and let her head lower to the cushions.

It is this submissive response that Philip was looking for before allowing the scene to proceed. "Only the connection to my master seemed to strengthen as his will became my sole significant reality." As he gently inserted the anal plug Philip knew Molly was falling deeply into submission.

Her conflicts about how others might view her was another issue being confronted. She still worried about what Master David would think of her. If she were in a clearer frame of mind she would have realized that Philip had taken care to allow the presence of those who would understand and accept the actions taking place. Unknown to Molly, Philip was checking the reactions of everyone in the room. Had the plugging been too much for anyone in the group, Philip would have abandoned it and proceeded in a lighter vein.

"It became almost too much when Vicky said, 'Relax your [sphincter] muscles for my master, dear.' Humiliation from master was fun, but coming from another woman it felt degrading." Even with scrupulous planning, the unexpected often happens in a scene. Philip was not aware of Molly's discomfort at Vicky's remark. Molly said nothing, nor made any outward sign. Yet, this is just the sort of thing that can interfere with the submissive's enjoyment of the scene. Scenes can turn sour in an instant. Dominants must constantly be aware of their subs' reactions.

Philip also didn't realize the impact of Master David's participation on Molly until they discussed the scene afterward. A grimace, trembling, and crying are all signs that something may be going badly. It is not a sign of weakness to check with a submissive if these, or other signs of distress are presented by a submissive. Rubbing her shoulder and quietly asking if she is okay will not spoil the scene. Reassurance that her dominant is watching out for her may be all that she needs to hear.

If the warning signs persist, it is best to stop the scene, release the submissive, and hold her to give her time to recover in a loving atmosphere. If others in the group object, it is the dominant's responsibility to stop them in their tracks and insist that they either assume a supportive attitude, or leave. Scenes rarely get out of hand, but it only takes one to do a great deal of harm.

Molly was only vaguely aware of the subsequent whipping, but it was not insignificant. Steve was being instructed by Philip and he was handling the whip beautifully. The whipping slowly increased to a very heavy level. Molly came several times during her beating. But the heaviest blow was yet to fall and it would not be a leather lash that found its mark.

Everyone has sexual fantasies that we really do not want to come true. We may fantasize about being raped or committing rape, thought the reality is a horrible act of violence in which we'd never take part. Many fantasies are best left to the imagination. Yet, sometimes, one of them just gnaws at us.

It might be something that is dangerous, like being kidnaped and sexually abused by a group of strangers. This is something that can actually being arranged for by a partner without serious physical risk, but the emotional risk is an unknown factor. Scenes that are designed to push us up to and/or beyond our known limits are called "edge play".

For Molly, being given to someone as a sex-slave was edge play. The limit she wanted pushed by the scene was her inhibitions about being a slut. The fact that Molly and Philip discussed and agreed to pursue the fantasy made it no less devastating. As it turned out, she learned more about her limits than either she or Philip had anticipated.

Edge play scenes do not always pan out as well as Molly and Philip's. Before attempting such a scene discuss forgiveness. Agree that you are attempting the scene as an experiment without a known outcome. Then, after the scene, when you have had a chance to cool down, agree that you will talk about what happened and how it made each of you feel. You can save a lot of heartache with this simple understanding.

Politically incorrect but emotionally valid

Take one very large pot. Toss into this vessel feelings of inferiority, missed opportunities, memories of failure, and unresolved struggles with sexuality. Add to the mix conflicts about body, gender, authority, and religion. Season well with rejection, doubt, hurt, shame, guilt, and fear. Is there anyone who has not tasted at least a little of this bitter witch's brew?

Reality inevitably clashes with society's ideals resulting in emotional, even occasional physical scars, but most often the damage is barely perceptible. We didn't invent society's attitudes, but we do reflect them. All the emotional baggage that we carry with us from our youth isn't safely tucked away in some neat little mental corner. Nope, it is lying all over the brain waiting to trip-up the unaware.

Sadomasochists turn this negative energy upside-down and transform it into a cosmic implosion of sexual energy, shielding ourselves with trust and love. Most people survive their emotional turmoil by resolving what they can and repressing or denying the rest. We SMers are made of sturdier stuff. We give our demons free rein in the dungeon, play with them there. We expose our demons for what they are and get to know them as pieces of who we have become. In time, some of them go poof and are gone forever. Some of them we just learn to accept with a new understanding.

Playing with emotions, especially negative ones, is every bit as dangerous as cracking a bullwhip and the safe spots to hit aren't as well mapped out. This is territory to venture into slowly.

For example, anxiety can be debilitating. Pharmaceutical companies make a fortune helping people cope with it. But, anxiety can also be delicious. The anxiety one experiences when riding a roller coaster or when seeing a horror movie is fun, because in the back of the brain remains an awareness that the danger is illusion. Think of the anxiety-turned-to-thrill that is experienced while climbing, repelling, or bungee jumping when one is pushing himself to meet new challenges.

Consider the situation a submissive puts herself into, imploring an admitted sadist to bind and use her as he will. It is certainly something to make the adrenaline flow fairly freely. This anxiety is sought. Trust keeps the anxiety fun, and the mind-numbing fear at bay. Master will control, challenge, tease, and torture, but never harm. Ultimately, the rewards of the trust will likely be intense levels of pleasure.

Still, bondage is a basically a physical situation with an emotional component. There are other forms of submission with little or no physical helplessness. Bondage rather enforces the issue of submission.

Interesting levels of anxiety can be reached when a Dom requires a sub to do something embarrassing or that challenges her inhibitions. The emotional desire of a submissive to obey impels compliance.

Some dominants know how to throw a submissive into a state of mental confusion by demanding an answer to an embarrassing, paradoxical, or confusing question, so that the sub doesn't know what to say. This is an unique style of teasing.

Often submissives experience a phenomenon known as "brain-fade," characterized by a progression from blushing, to nervous giggles, to stuttering. Submissives who enjoy this are looking for a type of control that makes them feel helpless and childlike. Taking a sub's own words and twisting them so it sounds as if the sub has been inappropriately critical is a favorite technique for achieving this. Another is requiring a sub who is embarrassed to ask for sexual acts, bondage, or what have you, to beg for it. A skilled dominant can achieve a situation where the sub is so confused that she will be begging without remembering the object of her request.

Most mind play in SM falls into the category of teasing and embarrassment. Much of it involves identifying, then dredging up or reintroducing a submissive to her own internal conflicts. We didn't invent the conflicts, but we can seldom pass up an opportunity for creative mischief. Surprisingly often, the conflicts are resolved as the victim grows.

Verbal abuse

Verbal abuse during sexual play is so common that people are often stunned to learn it is really a type of humiliation. People called "punkin'," "sweety," or "honeybunch" in less intimate moments are now "bitch," "slut," or "whore" or some similarly sexually derogative term when the sexual steam is turned up. This is the child in us. Sex is naughty and naughty is fun. If we had grown up unconfused about sex being good, right, and healthy, these words might be meaningless sounds.

As usual, SMers take this to extremes. We demand a sub to spell out in great detail exactly how naughty she is. Forcing an otherwise demure lass to list in exceptional detail each of the horribly disgusting kinks she enjoys can create a monologue that would do a marine proud. This verbal sewerage makes some ladies hotter than leather car seats in Death Valley. In others, it barely evokes a yawn.

Words can hurt. The sting of the cane is nothing to the pain that can be felt if words are taken the wrong way. A few women have enough real discomfort with sexual innuendo that rather than a turn-on, it will be a decided turn-off. Your partner may bulk at being called a slut, but be thrilled to be "my slut." The possessive can make a world of difference. Most of all it may be injurious if your utterances make her feel put-down or degraded. Once again, know thine submissive!

Aside from the immediate heat generated by nasty, naughty, name-calling, there is a desensitizing aspect. We in the scene tend to bandy these words about rather freely. It is partly a childish joy in the perverse. Consider for a moment the implications of these words. Most are words that imply that a women who enjoys sex is bad. Therein lies their power to hurt.

Lenny Bruce used to have a routine in his act. He'd say, "nigger, nigger, nigger," repeating it over and over again to the stunned look of his audience. As he'd repeat the word he would explain that he intended to repeat this word until it became a meaningless sound. He intended to repeat the word until it would "lose the power to hurt a little black child."

"Slut," "bitch," "whore," "nympho," and "tramp;" wouldn't it be nice to use them so often that they lose the power to hurt? Better yet, shouldn't we redefine the words in such a way that they become praise? Women should have pride in the enjoyment of their bodies. Can women stand up and say, "Hell, yes. I'm a sensual woman, a sexual being and I'm proud of it?" (Molly, a bit abashed at the stridency of her tone, climbs down off her soapbox.)

We declare, from this day forward, these words to be compliments. We will define "slut" as a person who enjoys his or her sexuality. A "bitch" shall be a woman who takes control of her own destiny. A "whore" shall be a woman so desired that men will give much to be with her. Call m'lady "nympho" if she demonstrates a healthy sexual appetite, and a "tramp" is merely a very giving person, one who know how to share. It does kind of diminish the naughty fun, though.

Humiliation

Humiliation is typically is no more than embarrassment. The paradox of humiliation in SM is that it builds the individual up rather than tearing him or her down. It frequently involves taking inhibitions and turning them topsy-turvy.

191

There is a subtle element of humiliation throughout the practice of SM. You are compelling a girl to partake in ridiculous, but naughty ceremonies that make her feel belittled by her own compliance, yet, oddly, she'll feel stimulated by it. It is the compliance that does it.

Your lass may feel silly standing still to let you tie her up. She might feel like it is a childish game. She'll feel embarrassed being naked in front of you while you're dressed. It is a very one-sided issue. You're in command, she's the willing servant.

When you redress your lady for misbehavior it is from a position of authority. It may be like a parent to a child, like a teacher to a pupil, like a jailer to an inmate, or a kidnaper to hostage, the possibilities of authority figure to subject are endless. Within this structure your partner defers to your sovereignty.

Together they create a legend that elevates a dominant to a position of nobility. (Photo courtesy of Dressing For Pleasure of Upper Montclair, NJ)

When the dom accepts the surrender of the submissive they together create a legend that elevates a dominant to a position of nobility. Honoring this conferred rank by kneeling, wearing a leash, foot-kissing or other seemingly abasing acts may actually engender pride in the sub. The dom becomes lord by his submissive's empowerment and she takes reflected glory in the exercise of his dominion over her.

Humiliation is assertion of power. She has offered you control over her in some way, and you have accepted the responsibility for making that work. She finds yielding of control to be erotic or she would not do it. Can you humiliate her and compliment her at the same time? Can you make her feel humble without degrading her? You want to bolster, not demean, her femininity.

Humble her for her desires or embarrass her by making her reveal herself to you without your reciprocating. Suggest that this is important to you, but that she need not comply. If she often chooses not to comply, it may mean the end of the games between you. She will comply because she wants to be vulnerable and because within the desire to surrender is the need to please you.

As in all SM, humiliation is dictated by the needs of the individual. The pretty young beauty who is trying to be taken seriously may feel threatened by being called a slut. While the average-appearing women in her forties may take the recognition of her sexuality as a compliment. "Slut" may seem an improvement over "mom", "wife", or similar titles as it recognizes a woman as an erotic being rather than as an auxiliary to another person.

Mindfuck, not mental rape

There are many who dominate quite successfully without ever touching a chain, a whip, or a paddle. For most of us the mental control is integrated with the physical. When a submissive suspends disbelief and allows the dominant to assert control over her perception of reality this is called the mindfuck.

We gave several examples of this in chapter six in the "Smoke and Mirrors" section. We cited the example of making a submissive believe she was being branded and mentioned the possibility of a fake piercing. Even when the activity occurs totally between the ears of the sub, safety and informed consent are paramount.

There is a big difference between coercion and seduction. It is fine to set up music, lighting, and atmosphere calculated to assist while you convince a lady to play a round of hide the salami. It never right to make her feel that she must give in to your attentions or be forever labeled a frigid bitch. The same is true of stretching limits. You seduce a submissive to new limits, but never coerce.

In many submissives this is remarkably easy with a process we call seeding. A dom says he would like particular thing if the sub would agree to it. Initially, the idea repulses the submissive. "Oh my, I couldn't do that," is her first response.

Time goes by while she runs the idea through her head, testing it in fantasy. Soon it is a little less awful to contemplate. "Maybe I could try it," she thinks. Before too long she is obsessing about the activity and really must try it.

Simple mindfuck can be a type of play similar to teasing. While she is playing a submissive role, you can ask your sub a question in such a manner as to ensure her discomfort no matter how she answers. For instance, "Do you think I'm handsome or macho?" Marine drill sergeants are masters of this. No response is considered satisfactory; always force a dilemma. Whatever her response, twist the words back on her until she has dug herself a pit the size of the Grand Canyon. Soon she is hemming, hawing, and stuttering. If she is also giggling, wet and enjoying losing control over her own words, you achieved your goal. The point of your efforts is to break down her resistance. The reason she lets it happen is that she wants you to succeed. Play drill sergeant, but don't yell, you might disturb the romance.

Exhibitionism

Dominants often put their submissives on display. Within this display are the kernels of humiliation and control. The sub is rendered an item to be viewed. She is a sexual object if the display includes nudity or provocatively sexual attire. She may be subject to lewd remarks and lascivious suggestions by casual observers. In many submissives, the blushes and the embarrassment create an amorous thrill and a strange kind of pride.

People display that in which they take value. Within the exposure there is a compliment. The person exhibited possesses a beauty worth sharing. It isn't only the woman with confidence and a great body who enjoys being put on display. The body is the temple of sensuality and sexuality. Every body deserves to be adored.

The exhibitionist in SM may be a basically shy person who has always envied the outgoing. The Dom is "forcing" the sub into behavior that she has admired, but been unable to express. We have seen introverts gradually overcome their inhibitions and learn to enjoy being the focus of attention. SM can help people grow; changing people's manner of social interaction works only if the desire for change already exists.

Play parties and SM clubs are excellent places to put your submissive on display. Here, people will appreciate and contribute to the fantasy of exhibitionism. Here, people will enjoy watching you bind your lady's hands behind her, perching her on your lap and undressing her slowly, fondling her as each garment falls away.

Some exhibitionist submissives like to be blindfolded while being publicly displayed, never sure who is watching, never sure whose hands are caressing her breasts. The blindfold protects her from her shame and, secure in her bondage she cannot do more than submit to a hundred anonymous hands and mouths pawing, teasing, and nibbling her flesh.

Photo of Queen Guillotine by Jerry

Imagine the spectacle of a party where each attender is dressed to his and her fantasy nines in corsetry, collars, lingerie, leather, and period dress. A dozen bound men and women are strewn about the room in various states of torment and arousal, masters and mistresses applying their craft from scene to scene, clotting around one moaning submissive after another. Yes, play parties can be big fun.

Public play

Play parties and SM clubs usually have a clear set of house rules regarding acceptable play. Clubs almost always have staff on hand to ensure that scenes are safe and within the house rules of play. Many of the larger parties also select people to make sure things go smoothly. Commonly, limits are set to exclude blood sports and exchange of body fluids during the party to avoid the spread of STDs. Standard play party etiquette also precludes touching any submissive without her permission or her implied permission through her dominant. It is considered grossly impolite to interfere or participate with any ongoing scene without being invited to do so by the dominant in charge. This includes loud conversation, speaking to the players, and even standing too close. Expect all these standard rules at any play party you attend. They are designed to enhance the concentration of the players which makes for better scenes.

Playing in public is a type of "theater." The players have two audiences. The primary audience is always your partner. If you lose sight of that and become too aware of the secondary audience it will ruin your performance. Concentrate on what you are doing rather than the reactions and judgments of the people viewing. All too often the dominant who forgets this makes some horrible mistake and ends up looking like a sap.

Remember that submissive people are not necessarily submissive to everyone. A submissive always maintains the right to submit to whom she chooses. Dominants can save themselves from embarrassment by treating everyone with respect. Haughty, strutting dominants seldom evoke a submissive response and most often come off as assholes. As a submissive, you may find yourself submissive to some people and dominant to others; the roles are not always clear. Many subs detest scene situations where all subs are expected to defer to all doms. This is natural and valid and must be respected.

You may find that you like to be bottom to people you are not feeling submissive to, as well. A submissive response is a very intimate response. Some people feel extremely uncomfortable showing their submissive side publicly, while others revel in it. Bottoming to someone you do not feel submissive to can be a good time, too. In this case, the experience is sharing sensuality with a friend with less sharply defined roles. Switching from top to bottom roles is also common.

One of the problems of public play is that subs are hesitant to make the doms look foolish in public. So, saying no or using a safe word is even harder than it is in a private setting. Dominants should always sharpen their focus on their submissive for public play. It is also best to try out new techniques and toys privately to be more aware of a submissive's reaction to them.

If your fantasies include rigid rules of behavior, you may want to make contingencies for public scening. To let things flow smoother, formulate signals for public play that can be used without breaking role. Whereas a submissive might respond to an order by saying, "If it pleases you, master," to let her dominant know that all is peachy, codes phrases like "ONLY if you wish it, master", will let the dom know, "Uh, uh, I don't want to do that." This is a face-saving way of allowing him to appear to have changed his mind, while the submissive still appears obedient.

Scening in a public scene place ensures an audience that has an attitude of acceptance. When you engage in play in a vanilla arena, you run the risk of offending someone's sensibilities. The general public has not been asked to consent to your activities. So, besides the risk of arrest there are ethics to consider. Be very, very careful. And never, ever do any sexually provocative activity if there is a chance for a minor to see it.

We have found many people who enjoyed being involved in a mild scene like the following: Late at night in a near-empty diner we engaged our waitress in a conversation about piercing. She seemed open-minded and amused, so she was asked if she wanted to see the sub's pierced nipples. She said that she was very interested and the sub was ordered to show her breasts to the girl. Note that the waitress showed interest and was asked for her consent. In the same situation, however, the waitress might have felt coerced into agreeing without emoting her difficulty. Most people don't understand what we are about at all and can freak out at what we might consider the mildest situation. If you are even the slightest bit uncertain as to how a vanilla person might react, err on the side of safety and discretion.

Dressing

NOTE: We must apologize to those hoping read something about cross dressing under this heading. Cross dressing, and transvestitism has a rich involvement in the SM scene, but neither of us has any expertise in this area. Though we know and admire many people who are into these fantasies, we feel we simply cannot do justice to the topic. Some of the principles we will address do apply to cross dressing, but will hardly satisfy your appetite. Our bibliography does, however, suggest some materials for you.

From childlike and innocent to sultry and revealing, attire is the accouterment of whimsy. Clothing can be no more than props to support your shared saga or it can be an extension of control, calculated to create the heat of embarrassment.

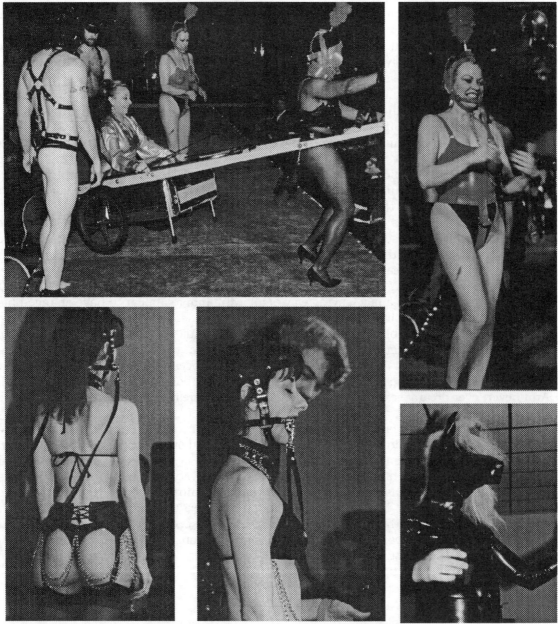

Ms. Marie Constance rides in a pony cart drawn and surrounded by ponygirls and ponyboys at the Dressing For Pleasure Fetish Weekend. Turning a submissive into a pony by dress and training is a common SM fantasy. (Photos courtesy of Dressing For Pleasure of Upper Montclair, NJ)

Dressing is related to exhibitionism. The sub is often compelled to wear clothes emphasizing her sensuality. A woman who is not particularly proud of her body may take special pleasure in being forced to wear clothes exposing her wanton desires. Stiletto heels, stockings and garter belt, a short, tight skirt, and a shaved pubis are so commonly required by doms that we refer to it as the submissive uniform.

This submissive slut costume is an expression of lascivious yearnings and availability. Having sexual access to the sub at any time is part of the concept of erotic control. Mimicking the instructions given to the sex slaves in *The Story of O* some doms may forbid the sub from sitting on her skirt. This adds to the erotic effect. The message to the submissive is that she is desirable, and, while in costume, she is a sexual being.

Some of the clothing that emphasizes femininity may require gradual training. Walking in very high heels is not learned overnight and the SM scene is renowned for encouraging five- to seven-inch high heels. Awareness and sensitivity is required by the dom who puts his sub into very high heels. If your lady is striding with difficulty in three- or four-inch heels remember to assist her when walking.

There are even safety factors to consider with clothing. Standing for a long time in heels may create problems for the foot, legs, and back. Constant wearing of high heels can cause shortening of calf tendons, making the wearing of normal flat-heeled shoes uncomfortable or impossible. Molly had two numb toes for months after stubbornly wearing poorly fitting heels. Hopefully you will demonstrate better sense.

The weather, neighborhood, and potential viewers must be considered when ordering a person to brave the out of doors scantily garbed. Sounds silly, but we know a submissive who broke off the relationship when ordered to go out in January wearing stockings and a very short skirt. She felt her Dom's fantasy life was more important to him than her physical welfare. We think she had a good point.

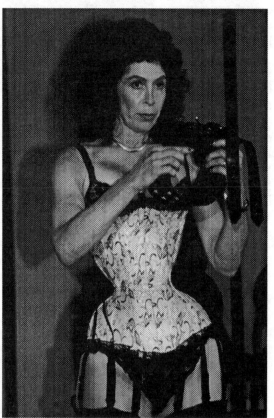

Photo of corset trained lass with amazingly tiny waist courtesy of Dressing For Pleasure.

Corseting is another area to consider thoughtfully. Many subs find in restrictive clothing an element similar to bondage. The corset emphasizes the feminine shape. Corset training can actually cause changes in the body. As the waist is reduced in size internal organs move to accommodate the changes.

Sexual denial, the ultimate weapon

A dom must be willing to meet a challenge from his submissive. If she says, "You'd never do that, you wouldn't have the guts," he must be willing to do it without hesitation. This does not mean he has to meet every challenge she makes, in fact, the more selective he is about meeting them, the better it works. B.F. Skinner observed that the Pavlovian response works better to condition a subject if the responses to the desired behavior are not always rewarded.

It may appear, at times, that a submissive is in control of an SM relationship. After all, she is encouraged to set limits, she can stop a scene instantly with her safe word, and the whipping and torture are done in a manner calculated to give her sexual pleasure. If it seems like the balance of power is overly tipped in the submissive's direction, this technique may serve to rehabilitate the relationship.

In a sexual denial scene, a submissive is deliberately aroused and left needy. Deliberately is the operative word here. This doesn't include the times where the sub wants sex and the dom has a headache. Arousal can include such things as commanding the sub to read, watch a movie, or read erotic texts ("Tell me how this affects you"), or doing' experimental' scenes ("I just want to test out this new equipment/whip"). A more direct example is a bondage and/or torture scene that is ended just as the submissive becomes aroused.

Denial can be done for a multitude of reasons: to enhance the pleasure the submissive feels in a subsequent scene, as a play punishment; or to reassert the control of a dominant by lowering expectations of the submissive. As in all torture and pain in SM, denial works best when deliberately inflicted.

If you are wondering why it might become necessary to lower a bottom's expectations, consider the following. A dominant busts his buns during the course of a typical scene, to give his submissive intense sexual pleasure. A submissive can easily become addicted to these scenes and want them so much that a dominant can begin to feel pressured to perform. This is a situation to avoid and one area where submissives can demonstrate their sensitivity and appreciation for everything their dominants do for them.

> "...bottoming is quite relaxing, and a good antidote to stress (or at least I find it so). Topping, when I'm feeling stressed and pressured, just feels like one more damned thing to do. Since I can't really cut loose and cathart in top-space without losing control and doing harm, trying to top when I've got all that negative energy running feels a lot like driving with one foot on the brake and the other on the accelerator.
>
> "Thus, of course, it behooves my bottoms to make sure my life is as relaxed and stress-free as possible."
>
> Lady Green (author of *The Sexually Dominant Woman: A Workbook for Nervous Beginners*)

Many subs feel a need for sex as completion following a whipping or torture scene even if they have an orgasm during the course of the scene. A period of sexual denial, where the sub is given scenes that arouse without completion and is sent home needy, may help the dom feel more in control as the sub becomes grateful for whatever she gets.

The dom may or may not allow other outlets for the submissive's sexuality. Masturbation can be forbidden or not, as can involvement with other people. Though, understanding the difference in the ways men and women deal with sexuality this may be less help than one would suppose. Many women experience lust in a more person-specific manner than males. Sex from another source or masturbation may merely take the edge off of need to only a slight degree. This rather forces the sub to develop some internal discipline in coping with sexual need.

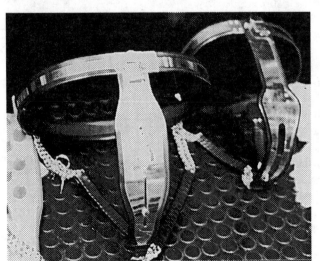

Many subs consider sexual denial in itself to be a form of sex and enjoy it. We have met submissives who spend years wearing chastity belts. Denial is their major form of sexual turn on. Paradoxical? Sure, but by now you should expect that in SM. It is the submission and the loss of control in denial that gives them the ultimate pleasure.

These chastity belts are from Dressing For Pleasure.

Emotional growth through SM

You've seen a sample of the way SM uses emotions as a medium of sexual expressions. We employ inhibitions and emotional buttons, turning the mind into an erotic playground. We expose fears and buried insecurities, and in the revelation, change occurs. Below, is a true story of how SM helped to heal and to raise self-esteem.

HAS ANYONE SEEN MY SELF ESTEEM?
A search for myself.

"Recently, I was initiated into both sides of SM. It was an experience I will not soon forget. I experienced things which I find extremely confusing and I cannot even begin to explain their emotional and physical impact on me.

"A little background might lessen any confusion, and may serve to explain the river of emotions that came out in this scene. I have been working to change a self-esteem problem that I have felt most of my life. This is something that I am sure many struggle with. Feelings of never being good enough to be around people, of not fitting in, and of not looking good enough made me feel alone most of the time, even in the company of others.

"My ex-wife (while we were married) wrote in her journal that if she and I could choose whether to do it over again, she would never have married me, while I would probably do it again. She mentioned in the same writing that as soon as she found someone else she was getting out of our relationship.

"I could never do enough to satisfy her. She lived to destroy my ego and self-esteem. She once said to me, "I wish this marriage were strictly PLATONIC."

"She had written how bad a lover I was and that I was insensitive. After reading those entries in her journal, I made two decisions: 1) I was going to start evaluating my life and making the much-needed attitude changes to see myself in a better light, and, 2) I was going to see if I really was as bad a person as my wife kept saying I was.

"I started BBSing in February, calling adult BBSs. I was looking for feedback and advice on rebuilding my life. I caught my wife cheating on me a year earlier and knew it was only a matter of time before she and I would split.

"In May I met a married female on a California-based BBS. She and I were the only East Coasters on this BBS. We had a lot in common. We both were in unhappy marriages to people who were fourteen years older than we were. There were several other coincidences, as well, one more bizarre than the next. Not to belabor the point, we became obsessed with meeting, and after meeting we fell in love. Making love to her showed me that I could, in fact, make a woman feel good.

"I dated another BBS friend from New York. She, too, felt that I was able to satisfy her physically and mentally. This is not meant as an ego trip, but to make a point about self-esteem. Finally I decided that I was not living, I was stagnant.

"I decided that since my wife would eventually leave me, I might as well do the honors of ending it. She told me later that she had thought that I could never shock her because she knew me so well. This was totally unexpected for her.

"After ending the six-year marriage, I dated another woman from New York. She had a desire to be "taken." I had always been a very gentle person, but decided to give a it a go. Deep down inside, I had always wanted to try this.

I fulfilled her request and found it very intriguing. She guided me to the English Palace BBS.

"The English Palace was a great tool for meeting people and for learning the "ropes." I became a regular at E.P. and found myself sharing more and more everyone's fascination with SM. I read the forums, chatted with some experienced players, and saw my first live scene as an observer. I decided I needed to experience the lifestyle in order to understand what was going on inside of me. After several weeks of talking to BBS members and meeting several, I made a move to learn more. I set up a day to learn about some of the toys and was taught to use them both as dom and sub.

"Experiencing my first scene, I found myself in a trancelike state focused on the "reality" of the moment. Emotions which had been locked away like old "toys" in the attic started to surface. The dom was really great with me. She started slow and we built our way from hand spanking, to whips, to the cane. She took plenty of time saying supportive, good things to me. She made me feel things I had never felt before. I can't begin to put in words the strange sensations I felt. Twice during the first session, I felt like I could not go on as my emotions were reaching volcanic proportions.

"At the end of this scene she held me tightly with my head in her lap and said something like, 'Don't ever let anyone tell you that you are not a good person, because you are.'

"Just as she said this, the volcano erupted. For no reason I can explain, I started crying uncontrollably. It really confused me. My tears weren't tears of sadness, but, somehow, tears of relief. When the tears subsided I felt as if my whole body had climaxed. I don't mean like an orgasm as you would have in sex, because there was no orgasm or sexual intercourse involved at all. There was, however, affection from my dom.

"After my emotional eruption, I stood up and could barely stay upright. My knees were wobbly and unstable, again, as if I had climaxed. I am sure this feeling is not unique for those who have played the scene. For those who have never done so, it is an experience never to be forgotten.

"I do not crave corporal punishment as a sub, will give it as a dom, but, with the right party, I might endure it as a sub. I hate pain, but am still curious about the feelings that I experienced. I will continue to research the SM world.

"For those of you in the scene, this may be boring. Those of you wanting to experience new things, but who are afraid to try, there's only one way... JUST DO IT!!"

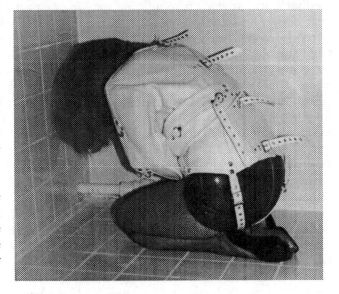

13 Furnishing Your Dungeon

laborately wrought iron gates were the only visible opening in the tall, ivy-covered rock walls. The limo driver stretched a thick arm to reach a button on the dash. Susan, William's latest conquest, felt a rush of anxiety as this portal swung open silently. (She was certain it had been meant to creak, some overzealous slave must have oiled it.) One expected to see a brass plaque hovering over the gate emblazoned with Dante's admonition: "Abandon all hope you who enter."

Beyond the gate, only untended woods were visible. Shafts of sunlight shot through the deep forest green as gentle breezes parted the dense canopy of ancient oak and mountain laurel. The first time one visits a place, the drive seems much longer than it really is. Yet, surely they had driven more than a mile down the estate's secluded dirt lane before the woods opened on the expansive lawn. Susan realized that if she were to scream, no one would hear her. Shivers sailed up the spine of William's guest knowing that her welfare was totally dependent upon her host's sense of honor.

The car stopped in front of massive, medieval double doors with ornately cast iron hingework. It was an imposing mansion. From the tracery around the leaded glass of the windows to the stark strength of the granite walls, this was a dwelling designed to reflect the personality of a man who was truly a king in his castle. She hadn't expected a simple home, but this was indeed, an edifice complex.

The double doors of the manor house yielded inward, answered by a collared, leather-clad woman. Susan pondered the woman's amused smile as she was ushered inside. William was just coming down the stairs to the foyer. With a brief, but affectionate greeting the slave announced Susan's arrival and disappeared.

William granted Susan a tour of his opulent digs displaying a variety of elegantly appointed rooms, each fraught with ominous possibility. In the Victorian drawing room a riding crop lay on the straight-backed chair by the fireplace. Heavy, nickel-plated rings hung from thick bolts, inset in the granite walls of the great room. Silk scarves decorated the massive four-poster in the master's bedroom.

Only William's warm baritone and supporting arm kept panic at bay when at last their footsteps echoed on the stone floor of the dungeon. The walls, ceiling, and floor were festooned with chains and rings. Whips, paddles, and crops hung black and shiny in contrast with the rough gray stone. A rack, a pillory, and a whipping block kept company with complex machines she had no name for, but whose functions were, no doubt, portentous.

Where to play while the castle is being repainted

Few of us have a baronial estate like William's, far removed from neighbors with a well-stocked dungeon in which to torture securely. For the average person, the bedroom of your house or apartment will be the scene of your loving crimes. Of course, other rooms, other buildings, and the great out-of-doors hold marvelous potential, too. Your first thought, as always, must be safety. Discretion and security must be considerations, as well. You don't want neighbors to think you are beating your wife (especially if you are beating your wife).

In cultures where people live closely together, a tradition of creating mentally imposed privacy often develops. They learn not to see that which does not concern them. Americans, on the other hand, coming from a pioneer tradition of open spaces and neighborly helpfulness, often feel it is their right and obligation to observe and judge their compatriots' behavior.

This can be an admirable quality when real help is required, though, barn raisings are now fairly uncommon, these days, and few worry about an Indian attack. It is important to remember that consensual play seldom appears consensual to the vanilla world and that you can get "helped" to a visit by the local authorities if your kink is discovered.

In an ideal world where differences are accepted and understood, everyone could be open and honest about SM. As things stand, one must be discreet. Be prepared for impromptu visitors. When your mother-in-law drops by to check the house for dust, you don't want her stumbling upon a spreader bar, particularly if the cuffs are still attached. But, if you enjoy the rare good fortune to have open-minded friends and family, you can set up your restraints without restraint.

Sound can be your biggest problem, especially for those living in an apartment. Women who moan softly and demurely during vanilla sex may hit glass-shattering notes during SM sex. They moan, they sob, and they shriek while their bodies are being wracked by multiple orgasms. Gags can be useful to muffle these happy noises, but they are not always desirable.

Furnish your bedroom/playroom to minimize noise. There are several easy ways to do this. Carpets on floors and tapestries on walls are excellent sound absorbers. Thick cork panels work well, too. If possible, put your bed against an outside wall and keep your windows closed during play. A running air conditioner masks a lot of noise. Of course, every playroom requires a stereo system to provide mood music which will also disguise your loving noises.

Visual evidence is often easier to cover than auditory clues. You can camouflage hooks in the ceiling with hanging plants and swagged lamps. A hanging wicker chair may be an apt addition to your living room.

Toys should be stored in an out-of-the-way closet, one that locks. It is fairly easy to change a doorset to a locking one. Another solution may be a trunk that locks, or several, as your toy collection grows. An armoire or wardrobe can easily be fitted with a lock and is a convenient place to hang your whips and such with the addition of inexpensive cup hooks. While basements and attics are excellent for storage, remember that dry heat and mildew damage leather.

We may seem overly cautious here with all the security, but especially for families, we believe that toys should be stored under lock and key. Consider the following.

Life with children

A close friend of ours (we'll call him Dudley) became involved in a messy divorce. Though they were both very much a part of the scene (she was a professional mistress when they met), Dudley's wife told the state's child welfare agency that our friend wasn't a fit father because he practiced SM.

Naturally, the state sent investigators to Dudley's home. They probably fought with each other for the opportunity. The couple's son was living with Dudley and Dudley had always been careful to shield his bedroom antics from his son's eyes and ears. The investigators, a man and a woman, inspected the house, interviewed Dudley, and, finding nothing untoward, insisted upon seeing Dudley's toy collection. All his toys were neatly stored in a locked trunk stored in the back of the bedroom closet.

Because he was frank with the investigators, because he never discussed SM with his son, and because he displayed the wisdom to keep his goodies stashed carefully away from immature eyes, the state filed a report that cleared Dudley of misconduct.

Anyone, a teacher, a neighbor, even a passerby, can file an abused child report with the authorities and it will be investigated. Do right, like Dudley did. Keep those goodies hidden where you're sure that they will not be found and be careful not to use them when the kiddies are around.

If you are living with children, we extend to you sincere condolences. Not that we dislike kids; they are fine when marinated overnight, char-broiled and served with a tossed green salad. Live children, however, can be a problem. Their inborn urge to ferret out a mystery rivals the tenacity of an ace reporter and they report everything to everyone. If they glimpse a whip carelessly left out or notice that only their mommy's high heels lock at the ankles, disquieting questions will be asked.

On the topic of sex, we believe in parents being as honest as the child's ability to understand allows while not overwhelming him or her with adult sexual concerns. Honest communication has benefits you come to appreciate when they reach their teens. But, parents also have a right to personal privacy.

Reconciling ideals of openness and privacy, we answer general questions honestly and openly, skipping details about our personal preferences and proclivities. We are comfortable telling young children that some grownups like to play fantasy games ("play pretend" in kidspeak) and that sometimes props or dress-up are part of this grownup game. This is, in fact, the truth. Children understand better than anyone the fun in fantasy. It is wise to explain that while Mommy and Daddy are not ashamed of anything they do, sex is Mommy and Daddy's private business and it should not be discussed outside the family.

Hanging slaves and other decorative touches

There may be places where hooks in the ceiling would be unnoticed that have not occurred to you. In Philip's kitchen is a heavy cast-iron rack for pots and pans. The heavy duty steel hooks holding it look perfectly appropriate for the task.

If you have the good fortune to have a room with exposed beams, you still may not like large steel rings as a focus of decor. Brass woodworker's inserts allow you to screw in an eye bolt in when needed, yet are very discreet. They will not, however, support the weight of full body suspension. Be aware that many exposed beams are not true beams at all, just hollow mockups, which are not made to bear any true weight. What you are looking for, in this case, are solid two-by-ten-inch support members or something even more substantial.

Installing eyebolts for bondage requires some attention to safety. Full suspension means that the entire weight of the bound body is totally supported by the bondage. In partial suspension, on the other hand, the submissive's feet still contact the floor and support most of her weight. In either case, hooks intended to support a ten pound potted petunia will shear. Only heavy steel or brass eyes or hooks securely screwed into wood should be used.

Never depend on plaster or wallboard to support any weight at all. Aside from the potential injuries, bringing the ceiling down on your sub's head will definitely disturb the mood of the scene. Always bolt or screw eyes securely into the ceiling joists or into the double headers of two-by-fours above archways or doorways. This means screwing all the way through the decorative trim and way into the two-by-fours.

If you own a home with a basement you are in luck. Basement "playrooms" are ideal. Basements are naturally sound-absorbing. Also, they frequently have exposed beams. But even without exposed beams, the floor joists for the first floor are plenty strong enough to support the hardware for full suspension. The current passion for home workout equipment provides a great cover. Create an exercise room. Pulleys and wenches in the ceiling are for "storing equipment and freeing floor space for a workout"... right?

How to recycle Aunt Sophie's ottoman, or, why buy a rack when there's a perfectly good workbench in the basement?

Having located your space in which to play, it's time to consider the furnishings. If you have an unlimited budget there are plenty of retailers and hobbyists who sell dungeon furniture. Besides being pricey, the items are unmistakable as to function. Minor modifications to existing furniture are, however, cheaper and more discreet. Many pieces of equipment are simple to construct even by the not-so-handyman.

A rack is really just a table where a victim can be stretched for torture. Unlike the Middle Ages, though, our spine stretching stops where discomfort begins. So, with the addition of eye hooks a table becomes a rack. If you must have the hand winch for effect, your local boating store sells them at a moderate price. (Oddly, stamped into each winch we've seen is the warning: "Not for movement of humans." What, do you suppose, they mean by that?) Table legs should be cut so the victim is at a height comfortable for you to work on your "experiments." You also may want to consider padding the table or making a removable padding by upholstering a piece of plywood to fit your table. You can modify a table to be dual function and remain in plain view. If the table is framed under the top, you can put eyehooks just inside the frame, if not, woodworker's inserts on the underside of the table lie flush and are virtually unnoticeable. Your removable pad can be augmented by putting a velcro strips on the underside of the table, though this is gilding the lily a bit.

Beds with wooden frames can be modified with eye hooks the same way and, of course, the bed legs, posts, head and foot boards make handy tie-off points. Bear in mind possible damage to finish by chain or rope rubbing and use padding, soft scarves, or leather to protect the wood. If your bed is of the platform type, you can create bondage bars (see section on building toys) or simply put eyebolts beneath the platform.

A dungeon tour

Before we return to suggestions for your dungeon we pause for inspiration. Fantastic adult playgrounds do exist. Mistress Eva Bathory is our guide for a tour of Pandora's Box, Mistress Raven's house of domination. The next few pages will show you play spaces ingeniously created as settings for a variety of fantasies. (For information about Pandora's Box write to: Pandora's Box, Suite 256, 177 Main Street, Fort Lee, NJ 07024).

The picture at right shows our lovely hostess, Mistress Eva Bathory.

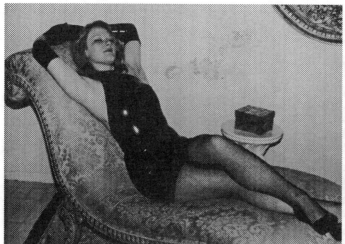

Brocade, marble and gilt highlight the first elegant fantasy rooms. An hourglass (top right) times the sessions. Ornate furniture (middle photos) highlight a space for crossdressing. A throne (bottom right) sits on a marble dais near an wall with a fountain that hides a entrance to the dungeon. Whips on the wall provide a twist to the gracious decor (lower left).

A place for the child within us to come out (top right).

Ravenswood Academy is where naughty boys may learn an interesting lesson (top left).

For more adult tastes, a mock-up of a street corner where naughty ladies ply their trade (bottom). A unique device "on the corner," locks one's head into a box.

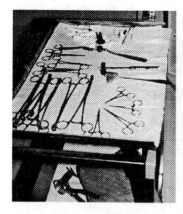

This simulated medical facility boasts a mirrored ceiling and a white leather examining table.

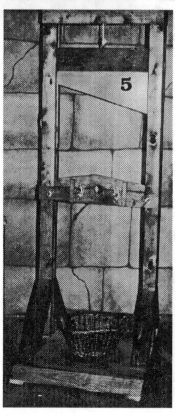

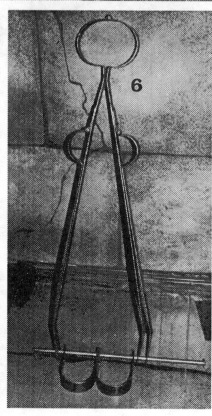

Last, but certainly not least, on this page and the facing page we see the dungeon complete with faux stone walls and guarding gargoyles.

The following are a few of the fiendish devices:

1. katherine wheel

2. cages

3. pillory

4. bondage chair

5. modified guillotine (for the small head)

6. traditional steel restraints

Just for the Dungeon

After modifying your existing furniture, you may want to collect a few of the larger play pieces. Okay, let's be honest, even if you don't have the money or space you'll want stuff. Lots of stuff. Good stuff. Neat stuff. Stuff to make one cream with anticipation. Is the term "toy whore" familiar to you? Philip and most of the scene people we hang out with are toys whores. We thought about summing this up as the philosophy of "he who dies with the most toys wins." This was too profound so we shortened it to the more accurate, childish phrase, "Gimme!"

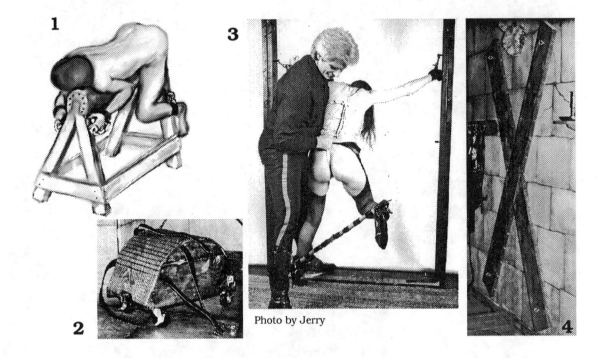

Photo by Jerry

1. Spanking horse - One of the most common pieces of furniture made expressly for dungeon use. Essentially, this is a modified saw horse. Cross-pieces are added for stability across the legs, the top is padded and eye hooks are added. Women, especially those of Rubenesque proportions, often find a narrow top uncomfortable for long sessions. This situation is relieved by screwing a wider piece of wood to the top (a two-by-six will usually do) and padding it.

2. Spanking block - these are both comfortable and easy to build. They support the weight of the spankee while keeping them in a good position for corporal and sexual activities.

3. Whipping posts - Whipping posts when free standing, allow access to the submissive from all sides.

4. The **St. Andrew's Cross** is basically an "X" shaped crucifixion device. There are also upright crosses of the traditional style. Submissives are chained to these crosses for whipping, teasing, and whatever. In spite of the shape, using nails to fasten your submissive is considered cheating and in bad form. Attach a few eyebolts and tie your ladies to the cross; save yourself some legal bills.

5. Slings make a submissive feel particularly vulnerable and, if you blindfold her as well, she loses some sense of where she is and which direction she is facing. Lack of spatial reference is a powerful type of sensory deprivation, especially when combined with a blindfold. This is the safest type of total suspension (See our plan for constructing this simple but effect device.) Slings are also incredible "fucking machines." To quote a submissive leatherman we know, "You've never had sex done right until you've been screwed in a sling."

6. A **rack** is a horizontal surface for binding the submissive in a stretched position.

7. Stocks - our puritan ancestors had a few ideas worth emulating. Better yet, mount the stocks on whipping posts and you have a **pillory** (see page 209).

8. A **katherine wheel** is a vertically mounted bondage device used when the dominant feels like taking the sub for a spin (see page 208).

9. X-frame - A cross for mounting your little lady in a horizontal position. Pad it well and stretch a piece of leather across the arms of the "X" to support the head and neck (not illustrated).

SMers like to play with "toys." We like to think of SM as having four basic toy groups. Just as you would select a variety of foods for a well-balanced diet, select carefully from these groups to keep your pet slave happy, healthy, and well-unbalanced.

The torture group

Clothespins, nipple clips, breast bars, rubber clothing and sheets, cinnamon oil, wintergreen oil, itching powder, Ben-gay, electric shock devices, ice, hot wax, chastity belts, cock and ball harnesses, feathers, speculae, Epilady, power tools, and small furry animals. Wonderfully sick and creative minds are constantly working to invent new and elaborate torture devices. (No, we are only kidding about the small furry animals. Rest easy, ASPCA fans.)

The bondage group

Collars, cuffs, chains, straight jackets, scarves, ties (Ah ha, there actually is a use for those "well-intentioned" Father's Day presents!), body bags of cloth, leather, or spandex, bits and harnesses, rope, gags, blindfolds, hoods, corsets, spreader bars, corsets, stocks, bonds, government securities, and mutual funds.

The sex-toy group

Dildos, vibrators, cock rings, benwa balls, anal beads, butt plugs, coconut oil and various "emotion" lotions, mink mittens, suction devices, inflatable dolls, and Madonna.

The hitting group

Paddles, riding crops, slappers, canes, and whips. Many ordinary household objects, such as wooden spoons, spatulas, rulers, belts, and ropes, can be good for this purpose, too. Of course, it is hard to beat that spanking staple of SM, the open hand. This group can also be referred to as percussion instruments.

The torture group

A few of the devices used to tease, torture and torment. (Their use and safety issues were explained in chapter six. You did read chapter six, didn't you?)

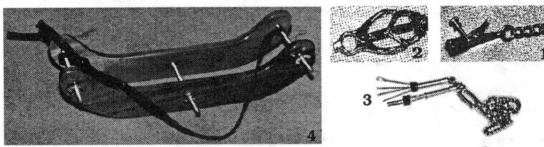

The clover and alligator clamps are from the Leather Master's catalog. The breast bars and the clinging claws were photographed at Dressing For Pleasure.

1. A standard type of **nipple clip**, the adjustable **alligator** style clips shown above, are found everywhere. Timing is important with nipple clamps, read about proper usage.

2. The **butterfly** or **clover clip** is another common nipple clamping device that we prefer to the aforementioned alligator style.

3. The **"clinging claws"** are placed delicately on the tip of the nipple.

4. Breast bars are placed above and below the breast and tightened.

5. The **gates of hell** are a linked series of consecutively smaller rings to fit around the penis with a leather strap that buckles around the balls. Typical of cock cages in general, as the male becomes aroused, the device becomes tighter and more uncomfortable; an intriguing dilemma for the male masochist.

212

6. **Chastity belts**, as in ancient times, are for people who prefer not to share their toys. Versions of this device are made for both men and women. They come in leather and metal, lined with rubber and usually lock securely. They do not allow sex or masturbation. Submissives request these to bolster their feelings of being wanted and owned (see page 198).

7. The **speculum** is used to open, expose and embarrass the submissive. It is a common prop for playing doctor. For true authenticity of a gynecologist's exam, store this device in your refrigerator (not illustrated).

The bondage group

So many things can be used for bondage. Most are illustrated elsewhere in the book. Here, a few devoted to special use.

1. **Collars** and **leashes**, while nominally for bondage, are symbolic of the submissive state. People in the scene regard the collar in much the way a new bride feels about her wedding ring. It is an icon of the covenant between dominant and submissive, a tangible manifestation of the love, trust and caring in the relationship. For many, simply snapping closed the lock of a collar induces a submissive mind set. This is reinforced through conditioning (see chapter two) (photos page 123).

2. **Leather 'bracelets'** are the type of wrist cuff most commonly used. They are comfortable for long wear. If you are real good, your dom might buy a pretty pair to match your collar. Similar cuffs are worn on the ankles, as well (photo page 122).

3. **Suspension cuffs** are made to reduce any strain on the wrist. Full suspension, even with these devices, by the wrists alone is a bad idea; the joints of the arms and shoulders are not strong enough to support full body weight for long periods (photo page 122).

4. Metal **handcuffs** and police-type shackles are quite uncomfortable for any bondage where the submissive pulls against her bonds. They are also illegal to own in many places. Uncomfortable, illegal, impractical, but secure and scary appearing, most people feel they must have them. Philip owns a lovely pair of Smith and Wesson handcuffs that he never uses (photo page 122).

5. **Spreader bars** keep legs apart and arms away from the body to allow access to vital areas. These are necessary items for every toy kit, yet very simple to make. Don't even consider buying one unless you have money to burn.

6. A **Suspension harness** for full body suspension must be a body harness designed for this purpose. Properly made harnesses of leather and steel rings are modeled after parachutist's or climber's harnesses, but cost several times as much. Proper distribution of stress, fit and comfort are a must. Less expensive, but less attractive body harnesses can be found for about $170 from climbing gear retailers and vendors catering to police departments and emergency rescue squads. (The Gall's, Inc. catalog is one reliable source, see our appendixes for details.)

7. **Gags** come in all sorts of shapes. The classic ball gag shown here and favored by many dominants not only muffles noise, but also makes the submissive drool in a most embarrassing fashion. Endless variations include gags shaped like penises (extending out from and/or inserted into the mouth), gags that force the mouth open for oral sex, gags attached to head harnesses, and even gags that have a built-in ashtrays for a dominant's use as his slave kneels by his feet. Of course, common dish towels and scarves make perfectly suitable gags, too (photo page 125).

8. **Blindfolds** obstruct vision. Almost any piece of cloth can restrict vision, but as you may have figured out by now, scene people will seldom pass up a chance to spend money or recreate an item in black leather. Frequently, leather blindfolds are padded inside with lamb's wool or the synthetic substitute.

9. **Hoods** create a sense of isolation. Many hoods restrict hearing and vision, thus, they are used for sensory deprivation. They also have the advantage of being creepy to look at (photos page 128).

10. **Corsets** are another dual function device. The stated purpose is enhancement of the submissive's already beautiful form, but an additional benefit is the feeling of constriction they give when worn. What shopaholic can pass up the temptation to buy a garment that is expensive, usually custom-made, and sexy as all get out? A slender person who undergoes strict corset training can realize waist reductions of four to eight inches. The movement of vital organs and changes in bone structure resulting from strict corset training deter many. Locking high heeled shoes are similar in being both attractive and restrictive (photo page 197).

11. There are several types of **Body bags**. The spandex ones stretch tight over the whole body, altering skin sensation and restricting movement. The leather bags lace tight and allow almost no mobility and a sense of total constriction. Take your choice. Take 'em both!

The sex-toy group

While these sex toys are not exclusively used for SM or scene activities, they represent an important role. A large number of dominants favor a form of torment that never involves hitting or pain of any kind. They merely force their poor subs to orgasm again, and again, and again until this ultimate pleasure becomes the torture. Many of these devices are used to force a submissive to endure covert sexual stimulation in a public situation where she can not show her feelings without extreme embarrassment.

1. **Dildos** and **strap-ons** - Dildos are, as everyone knows, artificial cocks. Add a harness and voila, "le strap-on", as the French might say. The better harnesses are made of leather and adjust for a good snug fit. Two headed dildos are for shared pleasure.

2. **Vibrators** - This standard variable speed vibrator runs on two "C" batteries. Molly wouldn't call herself an expert on vibrators. She does, however, get a Christmas card every year from the Eveready bunny. Vibrators come in all shapes and sizes to be placed in and on various orifices and organs. There are vibrators that vibrate, rotate, squirm, and some with a piston-like action. Vibrators come shaped like cocks, animals, and hands. Some are even bent to reach the G-spot. There are battery powered vibrators, rechargeable vibrators, and industrial strength vibrators that plug into the wall. There are probably even vibrators that mow the lawn and hum Beethoven's Fifth.

3. The **butterfly** is a vibrator shaped like a butterfly, body and all. The "body" fits against the clitoris and straps on the "wings" fit around the wearer's legs. It is remote-controlled and favored for wearing under a skirt in a public place.

4. The **vibrating egg** is another remote-controlled vibrator used for discreet public play. A small plastic egg containing the vibrating motor fits inside either the vagina or rectum.

5. **Cock rings** are used to increase a man's sexual staying power by allowing blood flow to his member while restricting the outflow. Vibrating cock rings are similar in name and location only; they do not restrict blood flow, they just buzz. Both enhance intercourse in their own way.

6. **Benwa** balls look like oversized ball bearings and are meant to be placed inside the vagina. With normal movement they roll around doing their nasty little job by clicking against each other. Some modern versions have balls within the balls to increase the amount of play and vibration.

7. **Anal beads** are well-lubricated and positioned in the rear passage. The trick is to pull them out at just the right moment.

8. **Butt plugs** are exactly what they sound like. They come in a variety of sizes and shapes from "oh gee" to "my god, I couldn't possibly!" Gradually, a person can acquire the ability to wear larger sizes, but the cardinal rule of anal play is never force anything.

9. **Condoms** - Aside from properly packaging you pecker for porking, condoms should be also used for sex toys. Any toy that is used internally or comes into contact with body secretions should be used exclusively on one person or covered with a condom. Aside from preventing the spread of disease, condoms make after-party cleanup much easier. If things get really dull, or if you are in a very silly mood, condoms make great water balloons. Not that we would ever stoop to such boorish behavior.

The hitting group

This is just a small sampling of the typical hitting toys in a dominant's arsenal. One of the reasons that bills go unpaid, the kids are without shoes, and the dom is in hock up to the third button of his leather vest is the cost of collecting these wonderfully fearsome toys. It is often said that a dominant's only reason for keeping a submissive is to have an excuse for buying another little goodie.

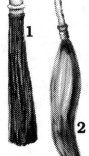

1. A **Fringe whip** is designed for pure pleasure. The fringe whip has no sting and just a bit of thud. The fall is made of soft, braided nylon threads that tease and delight. Novices find it an excellent introduction to the pleasures of the lash. These and other very gentle whips are frequently referred to as "pussy whips" as they are fine for beating pussies. Cocks and balls like them, too!

2. The **Horsehair whip** might more properly be named "The Submissive's Revenge." Sold as a fly-whisk in equestrian shops, this whip should only be used for soft, sensual whipping. For some unknown reason everyone ignores this advice and wails away with abandon. This causes the ends of the hairs to break off and stick in your beloved's fanny. Every dom who has encountered the horsehair whip (including Philip) groans about his hour's labor over his sub's caboose with a tweezer and magnifying glass.

215

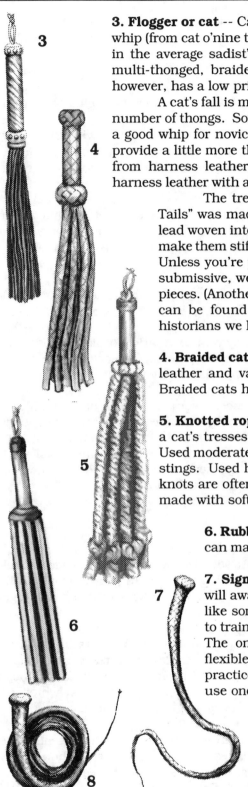

3. Flogger or cat -- Cat is the term generally used for a multi-thonged whip (from cat o'nine tails). Cats are the largest category of hitting toys in the average sadist's weapons cache. Purists insist that cats are multi-thonged, braided whips and the others are floggers. Purity, however, has a low priority with us so we'll continue to call them cats.

A cat's fall is made from a variety of materials and can have any number of thongs. Soft deer- or lamb-skin cats are sweet and sensual; a good whip for novices or to start a scene. Suede and soft cowhide provide a little more thud for moderate beating. Heavy falls are made from harness leather, rubber, and rope. We've even seen cats of harness leather with a few chain tresses embedded in the fall for spice.

The tresses of the traditional British Navy "Cat O'Nine Tails" was made of cotton cord or cod line with bits of iron or lead woven into them. Each tress was then dipped in hot tar to make them stiff and durable. Some whip-makers still sell them. Unless you're planning to make tacos from what's left of your submissive, we recommend owning these only as conversation pieces. (Another conflicting version of the origin of the cat o'nine can be found in chapter ten, being better politicians than historians we have included both versions in our book.)

4. Braided cat -- The braided thongs of these whips are usually leather and vary from soft suede to brutal harness leather. Braided cats have more thud than flat-tressed whips.

5. Knotted rope cat -- Knots in the ends or along the length of a cat's tresses will bruise more deeply than non-knotted falls. Used moderately, the knots leave marks that look like little bee stings. Used heavily, they can do a lot more than bruise. The knots are often called blood-knots; can you guess why? Even made with soft nylon rope, rope cats are rather hellish.

6. Rubber whips have a stingy, cutting feel like fire, they can make even rope whips seem like a stroll in the park.

7. Signal whip -- The crack of these single lash terrors will awaken the sleepiest submissive and the sting feels like something akin to napalm. Signal whips are used to train dogs and are usually three to four feet in length. The one pictured is a snake whip, or black snake, flexible all the way to the butt. It takes skill and a lot of practice to control one of these beauties. Don't you dare use one without training.

8. A bullwhip of the Simon Legree type is good for show, to evoke fear, and for its sound. Honestly though, how many people have the free space required to swing a 12 foot whip or a real desire to reduce a sub to strip steaks? A few very proficient players do, however, know how to use bull-whip in a scene.

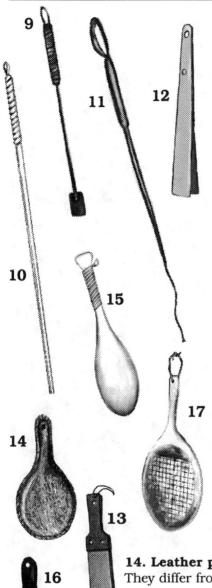

9. Riding crops, usually just called crops, are traditional SM toys. Dominants strike with the shaft and the leather flap at the end. They are relatively easy to use, but require practice for accuracy. Both thuddy and stingy under a full stroke, crops can be deadlier than they look.

10. Canes were a traditional fixture in European classrooms of old. Canes are usually made of rattan. Nylon and other synthetics are beginning to be used, as well. The synthetics are far denser than rattan, therefore, they do deeper bruising. Canes require careful training and extensive practice. Used incorrectly, they can severely cut a bottom, but used well they can provide addictively exquisite pain. Ummmmmm!

11. A **buggy whip**, or dressage whip can inflict significant pain or simply be used to tease by tickling with the fuzzy tip or whistling through the air for fear value. It is constructed like a crop, though rather longer, with a string or woven cracker on the end.

12. The term **slapper** usually refers to a semi-flexible leather paddle. They are frequently two pieces of thick, stiff leather attached at the top to form a handle. They vary in feel from moderate to heavy, depending upon their construction. Slappers and paddles are much easier to control than whips.

13. The original Scottish **tawse** was used to discipline naughty schoolboys. It is a thick leather strap with one or more slits cut into the business end.

14. Leather paddles are generally inexpensive and a good basic toy. They differ from slappers in that they are not at all flexible. Some are simply a piece of shoe-sole leather. Others are made from thinner hides glued or sewn around a wooden or metal core.

15. That **miniature oar** that you picked up as a souvenir from Jellystone National Park makes a terrific paddle. It might be wise to sand off the picture of Yogi and varnish it again, unless you don't mind a few giggles mixed in with the moans.

16. The **studded paddle** looks fearsome, but closer inspection reveals that the studs are rounded with no edges that can cut. Still, it is intense enough to inspire a good, healthy respect.

17. Finally, there is a decent use for that nasty piece of sports equipment, the **wooden game paddle**. Really now, doesn't it sound like a lot more fun to work up a sweat over a helplessly bound lass, than to chase a stupid rubber ball? Not that we have anything against rubber balls; they make lovely gags.

Dressing For Pleasure Boutique in Upper Montclair, NJ carries a huge array of fetish fashions in leather and rubber, bondage toys, SM gear, books and videos. It even has a room devoted to fetish-related fine art. More than a store, DFP sponsors fashion shows and scene events. (Photo of Ms. Marie Constance, proprietor, at a DFP gala weekend courtesy of Dressing For Pleasure)

Where to get your goodies

SM retailers and boutiques catering to the fetish community are rarer than vanilla sex shops, but have toys, clothes, and books that are hard to obtain elsewhere. Many of them also do a brisk mail order business, so, the most esoteric of sadomasochistic gear is obtainable even in Bumblefuck, Nebraska. For variety and one-stop shopping it's hard to beat these bizarre bazaars. You also get the benefit of their expertise and advice. Some of these same items can be purchased elsewhere at a lower cost, but this requires some research. (Check out our source lists.)

The typical sex shop carries sexy lingerie, a variety of dildos and vibrators but few SM items. The whips and crops, if any, that are carried are usually poorly made and more for show than real use. However, often items such as alligator or butterfly nipple clips are cheaper in vanilla sex shops than where SM is the specialty of the house.

The tide seems to be turning, though! Famed vibrator magnate, Doc Johnson has begun to foray into the dark, dungeon lair. We just saw some of his latest offerings which include leather head harnesses, ball gags, and a couple of rather pathetic cat o'nines all decked out in slick bubble packaging with "Made in China" stickers on them. K-Mart is, no doubt, eying the market with a lusty leer.

Whipmakers, leather craftsman, and furniture makers sell their art to individuals directly or through the mail, as well as to stores. The most famous and skilled of these, while not cheap, are less expensively ordered from directly than through resale at the SM store. To be fair to the retailer, though, less well known, but highly competent artisans are everywhere. Word of mouth and association with reliable retailers are often their only source of distribution and advertisement. Craftspeople tend to leave the market sporadically or move away without a trace. Finding these people can be a chore. Even the list we provide in our appendix may be out of date by the time you read it. Still, the all-time greats; Adam and Gillian, Janette Heartwood, J. Marston, Northbound Leather, and several others seem to have the staying power to provide some stability to the marketplace.

Tandy Leather outlets are found in every state and several countries. While there are cheaper places to buy leather, for most people this is the easiest source for leather, leather crafting tools, and supplies, as well as buckles, rings, and whatnot.

Hardware stores and lumber yards are two of our favorite places for browsing. These are the places to buy rope, chain, rings, and hooks. Not to mention dowels, PVC pipe, and other materials for fabricating spreader bars and other devices. We frequently just walk up and down the aisles seeking new objects to pervert to our uses.

Equestrian, tack, and harness shops are best places to buy riding crops, buggy whips, and horse-hair fly-whisks. While they can be purchased at adult and SM stores they are significantly cheaper here. If you can find a place run by an old fashioned harness-maker, you can sometimes convince him to make you custom devices at a very reasonable price.

When you want a winch to winch your wench go to a marine supply store. Here you can find pulleys, tie downs, and weight-bearing equipment. Fishing rod blanks make good excellent fiber glass canes. (A fishing rod blank is the shaft of a rod before the line keepers are tied on.) Gun shops sell locking cases for their weaponry that are inexpensive and terrific for carrying toys discreetly. Isn't it odd that we would disguise pleasure items as assault weapons to garner social acceptability?

Sporting goods, camping stores, and the aforementioned vendors catering to the rescue squads sell nylon webbing, rope, and mountain climbing gear, all of which are great for bondage. A climber's harness for suspension makes sense if you do not require the look of leather and steel. You can be assured that these items are properly made to support and distribute human weight. Weight-lifter's lumbar support belts with the addition of D-rings are more than passable bondage belts.

For decorative chain that will bear no weight try the pet department of your local discount store. Collars can be found here also. Pets stores carry basically the same thing at a higher price. Do not overlook toy departments as a source. Flea markets, garage sales, and renaissance fairs can provide some interesting items, too. Creative toy shopping is all just a matter of reevaluating what you see.

Found objects

Before you put your sister up for sale so you can afford to equip your dungeon, consider alternatives found around the house. While we admit that we don't know how horrible your sister is, we figure you might prefer to spend your savings on a vacation in the Bahamas, instead. As the artist learns to look at everyday objects with a fresh viewpoint, so does the sadomasochist. Let's see what every household has to offer.

Scarves, dishtowels, and cloth diapers are fine as blindfolds, gags, and cuffs. Clothesline, belts, sashes, plastic wrap, and duct tape are dandy for bondage. Rubber bands around a breast are quite wonderfully evil.

Hairdryers and candles can add a bit of heat to your ardor. Ice is nice dripped or rubbed on various organs, and popsicles are just flavored ice in a convenient shape with a handle. (Use popsicles carefully, please. Pieces can break off inside someone and may damage mucous membranes before melting. Also, only use the sugarless kind vaginally or yeast infections may result.) Belts and rope can take the place of whips. Wooden spoons, ping-pong rackets, wooden rulers, plastic spatulas and breadboards make quite acceptable paddles.

The clothespin is a reasonable substitute for the nipple clip. It is cheap, readily available, and easy to use almost anywhere on the submissive's body. A simple toothpick to a blindfolded victim feels like a needle. Plucking a body hair with tweezers also gives the illusion of being pricked with needles. Broom straws are great for tickling and teasing. Feather dusters and silk scarves are excellent for sensual massage.

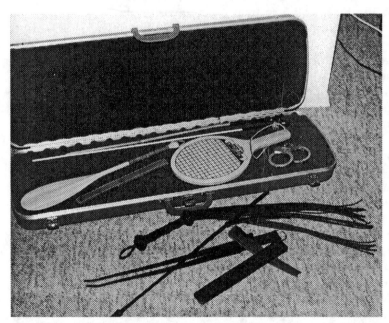

Traveling with toys

If you get into the public scene, you will want to take your toys to parties. Gun cases, fishing rods cases, and sports bags are all typically used to schlep stuff. You can turn a garment bag into a nifty case for whips by adding hooks to the wooden hanger.

While you may consider these implements merely tools for making your honey cream with delight, the powers that be oft view these items as less than benign. In most states metal handcuffs and shackles are considered weapons and illegal for private individuals to own. Considering that, it is amusing how easy they are to obtain.

While driving, always lock your stuff in the trunk of your car. If stopped for a violation, any item sitting on a car seat that seems curious to a police officer can be opened and examined. To open a locked trunk requires a warrant. While owning these toys may not be illegal, they may illicit some questions that are a nuisance.

When forced to explain the ownership of whips, collars and such, we have heard the following excuses used to varying degrees of success: That you are a theater person, member of a rock band, or a costume maker and these are props. Claim membership of the Society for Creative Anachronism (SCA) or participation in a renaissance fair.

Whatever you say, try to say it with a straight face. Most people merely respond when questioned about their gear with a blush, a wink, or both.

Airports are of particular concern to many. Molly went to visit a friend in a distant city; her air carry-on was heavy with chains, collars, cuffs, and whips. Her mind was filled with images of setting off the airport security system. Her fertile imagination saw her having to open her bag, being subjected to questioning, even being subjected to a body cavity search. Molly was both relieved and mildly disappointed that nothing happened, but at least she drew a knowing smile from the attendant as her stuff passed x-ray.

Be especially careful if going overseas to check on the legality of bringing these items into another country. Canada has laws regulating the importation of sexually related articles as do several other countries. If you violate these laws confiscation may be the least of your concerns.

Making your own toys

Leather tips
Following are some designs for simple devices you can make yourself. Here are a few general tips on working leather.

1) Cut leather from the finished side using a very sharp tool and a metal ruler. Cutting wheels are nice, but leather dulls blades quickly. Your best bet is a utility knife with changeable blades. These are cheap and you can get the blades in packs of a hundred.

2) Don't expect glue or pressure-closed rivets to bear weight or withstand much stress. Tandy sells keyposts that, when screwed together with a drop of glue hold very securely.

3) Never sew any leather, except very light, soft garment leathers or suede on a home sewing machine. Besides breaking a zillion needles that are supposed to work for leather, you may burn out the motor.

Spreader bars
The most common spreader bar is made by simply adding screweyes to a wooden dowel. You can give the spreader bar a more finished appearance by painting the dowel and using decorative washers at the ends. An equally simple short spreader bar is made by using a belt inside a length of PVC pipe. For a longer spreader bar use two belts running in opposite directions inside PVC pipe.

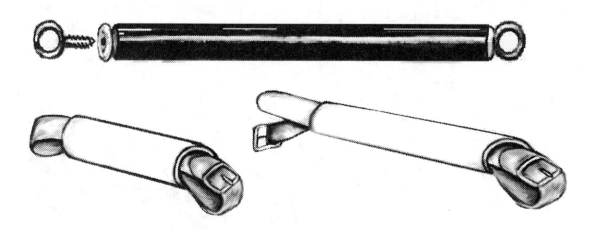

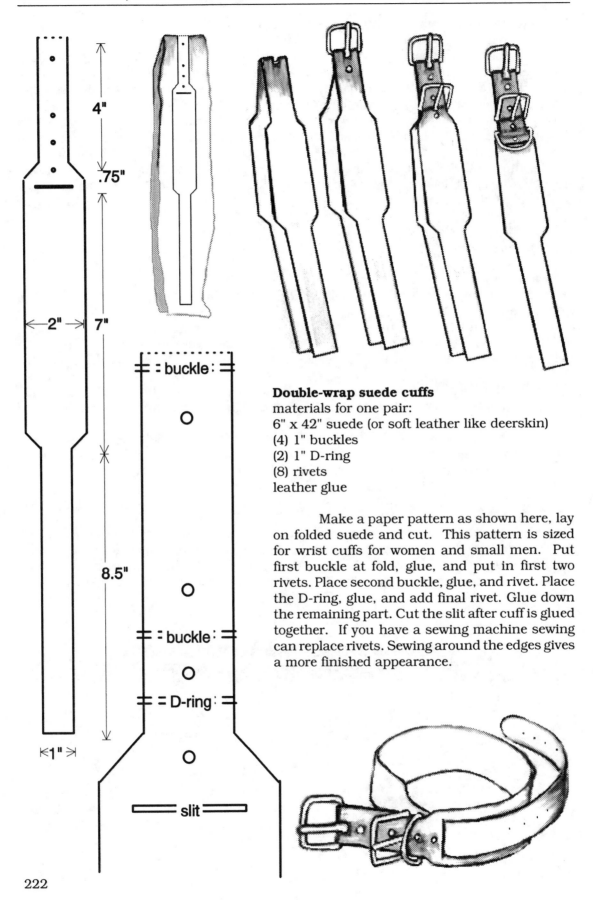

4"

.75"

←2"→ 7"

8.5"

⊢1"⊣

:= buckle :=

○

○

:= buckle :=

○

:= D-ring :=

○

= slit =

Double-wrap suede cuffs
materials for one pair:
6" x 42" suede (or soft leather like deerskin)
(4) 1" buckles
(2) 1" D-ring
(8) rivets
leather glue

Make a paper pattern as shown here, lay on folded suede and cut. This pattern is sized for wrist cuffs for women and small men. Put first buckle at fold, glue, and put in first two rivets. Place second buckle, glue, and rivet. Place the D-ring, glue, and add final rivet. Glue down the remaining part. Cut the slit after cuff is glued together. If you have a sewing machine sewing can replace rivets. Sewing around the edges gives a more finished appearance.

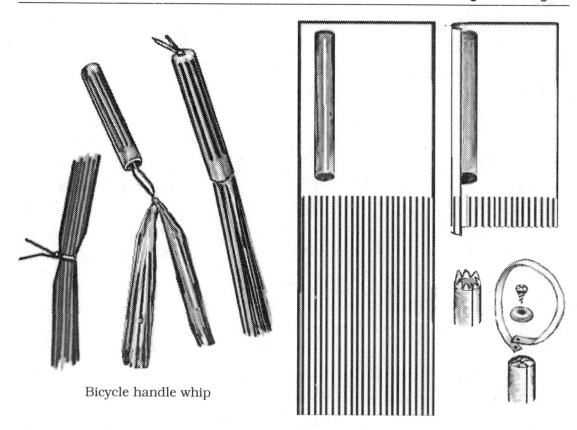

Bicycle handle whip

Basic wooden dowel whip

Simple whips

To make a bicycle handle whip simply gather a group of thongs. For thongs use strips of deerskin or suede, rawhide shoe laces (a nasty stingy whip), or soft nylon drapery cord. If you use nylon cord do not melt the ends as this will create hard tips. Instead, whip the ends (page 108) with embroidery floss, or for a really sensual toy allow the cord to unravel. Tie the group of thongs tightly in the middle with a cord. Pull the cord through the hole in the top of the handle and make a knot.

The next whip uses a wooden dowel one-half to three-quarters inch in diameter and eight to ten inches long. Cut a rectangle of leather twentyfor to thirtytwo inches long and six to ten inches wide. Cut the bottom portion of the rectangle into even strips about a quarter-inch wide. The top and uncut portion should be one inch longer than your dowel.

Wrap and glue (Tandy leather glue) the leather around the dowel leaving one half inch at the top. The wrap should be as tight and even as you can make it. Use decorative upholstery tacks around the top and bottom of the dowel. Finish the top by cutting triangles in the left over leather, fold and glue down. At the top add a quarter-inch strip of leather, a decorative washer and a wood screw (you may want to cover the wood screw with a dot of leather).

There are variations you can make to improve this basic whip. You can weight the whip by drilling out the dowel and filling with a mixture of lead shot and glue, then capping with a wood peg. You can add decorative knots and fancier handle treatments.

If you continue to experiment with whipmaking you will eventually want to handle the fall portion of leather separately from the handle portion. You may wish to try making braided whips. There are basically two types of braids. The flat braid is made from three thongs and can be created from one piece of leather (sometimes called a "magic braid"). The round braid is woven from four thongs.

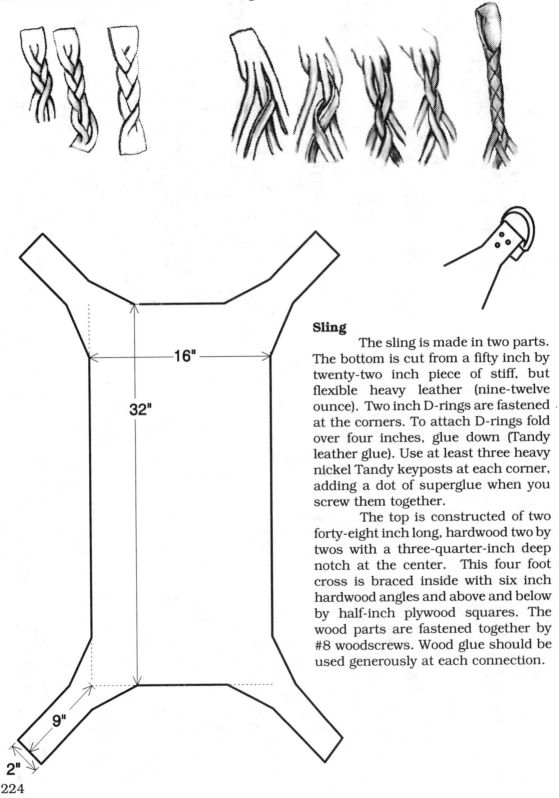

Sling

The sling is made in two parts. The bottom is cut from a fifty inch by twenty-two inch piece of stiff, but flexible heavy leather (nine-twelve ounce). Two inch D-rings are fastened at the corners. To attach D-rings fold over four inches, glue down (Tandy leather glue). Use at least three heavy nickel Tandy keyposts at each corner, adding a dot of superglue when you screw them together.

The top is constructed of two forty-eight inch long, hardwood two by twos with a three-quarter-inch deep notch at the center. This four foot cross is braced inside with six inch hardwood angles and above and below by half-inch plywood squares. The wood parts are fastened together by #8 woodscrews. Wood glue should be used generously at each connection.

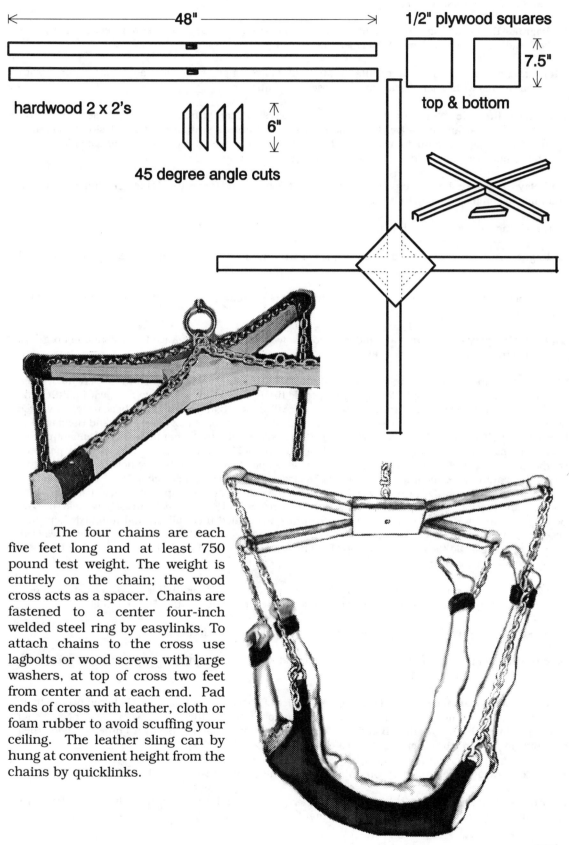

|←———————————————— 48" ————————————————→|

hardwood 2 x 2's

45 degree angle cuts ↕ 6"

1/2" plywood squares ↕ 7.5"

top & bottom

The four chains are each five feet long and at least 750 pound test weight. The weight is entirely on the chain; the wood cross acts as a spacer. Chains are fastened to a center four-inch welded steel ring by easylinks. To attach chains to the cross use lagbolts or wood screws with large washers, at top of cross two feet from center and at each end. Pad ends of cross with leather, cloth or foam rubber to avoid scuffing your ceiling. The leather sling can by hung at convenient height from the chains by quicklinks.

GLOSSARY

Age play - A type of role play to gratify a fetish surrounding age; typically daddy/child or mommy/child fantasies [see also: Infantilism]

Algolagnia - The act of transforming pain into sexual pleasure. A synonym for sadomasochism (SM). [see Sadism, sadist; Sadomasochism; Masochism, masochist]

Alternative sexuality - A sexual orientation that differs from a preference for vaginal intercourse (with minor variations) within a monogamous heterosexual relationship.

Alternative lifestyle - Having a sexuality that differs significantly from the "norm" (see Alternative sexuality) may make an alternative lifestyle necessary or desirable. A sexual orientation less common than the norm may stigmatize the individual pushing the person to seek a more accepting subculture. An example is homosexuality and the formation of the gay community.

Anal play - Any sexual or fetish practice concerning the anus and/or rectum, chiefly includes: anal sex, rimming, enema play, and anal fisting.

Anal training - Preparation of the anus for anal play.

Anilingus - Anal-oral sex. Dental dam or plastic wrap is helpful for preventing exchange of harmful organisms.

Animal play - Role playing wherein one or both partners assumes the role of an animal, chiefly: puppy, dog, and pony.

Asphyxiation play - Restricting air (and/or blood) flow by choking to enhance the sensation of orgasm. Very dangerous play, we don't recommend it.

BDSM - Once upon a time this was all called Sadomasochism (SM, S/M or S&M) and we were all deemed very bad, sick, perverted people. We were just people though, as horny as everyone is, with a little kink to make us special. But some of us didn't want to be called sick, bad perverts and these people invented names like Dominance and Submission (D&S, DS or D/s), Love Bondage (Love Bondage) and Bondage and Discipline (B&D) to make themselves and the pleasure police think that what they did was different from what those sad, twisted, nasty old sadomasochists did, no no! Then we all got online with our personal computers (well, a lot of us did) and began doing what people do best when they're not having sex: argue. For months arguments about labels for our kinks clogged up the computer networks.

Finally, the term BDSM was born. This made many kinky people happy because it incorporated Bondage and Discipline (BD), Dominance and Submission (DS) and Sadomasochism (SM). We told the Love Bondage set that we loved them very much. To prove it, we tied them all up and dumped them in a deserted warehouse in East L.A. where we kept them bound in a circle whining Barry Manilow tunes from behind their gags. Did the arguments stop? Fat chance. Most of us, though, have found other things to argue about between sexual encounters.

Black lightning - A common nickname for a black fiber glass or resin rod that is used as a cane. Denser than rattan, it can inflict deeper damage and the feel is described as "cutting." [see Cane]

Black snake - A type of single-lash whip that is flexible all the way to the knob.

Bloodsport - SM practices that result in drawing blood. Can include whipping or caning that breaks the skin, branding, cutting, and piercing.

Body fluid monogamy, body fluid bonding - A practice of sharing body fluids only between two partners in order to observe safer-sex recommendations. Commonly, the partners have been tested negative for HIV, sometimes also for hepatitis B and C. The partners may or may not play with others outside their relationship, but only by observing strict safer-sex rules. [see Safer Sex]

Bondage - Any practice involving restraints placed on the body to restrict freedom of movement.

Bondage and discipline, B&D - A classic term referring to several sexual practices including: bondage, slave training, corporal punishment, and dominant/submissive role play.

Bondage belt - A belt, usually leather with metal rings attached, to assist in performing bondage. Bondage frame - Any stationary device used to assist in performing bondage.

Bondage harness - A configuration of straps, usually leather or nylon designed to: 1) ornament the body, and 2) aid in bondage and suspension bondage.

Bottom - An SM practitioner who submits to bondage, training, role play, corporal punishment, etc., but who is not necessarily emotionally committed to his/her dominant partner (top).

Bottoming from the top - Originally a derogatory term for a top who allows his bottom to run the scene, "bottoming from the top" has become a valid style of play. Most tops experience some scenes where they prefer to take at least some direction from their bottoms. Some even prefer this style of play and may call themselves submissive sadists. [see also, Topping from the bottom]

Bottom-space or **sub-space** - A type of erotically altered consciousness (EAC) identified with feelings of falling into a state of submission. Generally, bottom- or sub-space may be characterized by, diminished ego awareness, less active cognitive behavior, surrendering of will, and/or inability to verbalize. Frequently these functions are assumed by the dominant partner who becomes the submissive's center of focus.

Brat - A bottom who enjoys struggling against control or challenging the top. Brattiness has a wide spectrum from the playful "uppity bottom" to the smart-ass masochist (which see). Some brats are "testing" their dominant, others have a desire to be "conquered and tamed", while some simply do not wish to be controlled. [see Smart-ass masochist]

Brain fade - A state of confusion and/or inability to reason experienced by the submissive. This effect usually results from psychological domination, the mind-fuck, or a deepening submissive state. [see Bottom-space, Sub-space]

Breast bondage - Tying the female breasts with cord, string, rope, rubber bands, scarves, etc. as a part of SM or erotic play. May include nipple bondage or clamping.

Breath control - Control of breathing by the dominant through use of a gas mask or similar apparatus, by choking, or by covering the mouth and nose.

Body modification - The general term for practices that reshape or ornament the body for ritual, erotic, decorative, or fetish purposes. The practices commonly include tattooing, piercing, branding, cutting, and corsetry.

Boundaries - Usually refers to limits (which see) negotiated prior to SM play.

Branding - Burning the skin, usually with heated metal, to produce scarification. Branding can be a part of a scene, ritual, or body modification. The design often consists of several unconnected lines and curves, each requiring a separate strike with heated metal, bent to form its part of the design. The reason for the unconnected lines is to assure that elements of the design do not scar into a shapeless mass; human skin heals differently than the hides of livestock.

Buggywhip - A single thong whip with a rigid core and a flexible cracker at the end.

Cage, bondage cage - Yup, a cage is a cage. These are big enough to hold the whole submissive.

Cane - Traditional canes are flexible rattan or bamboo optionally having a leather wrapped handle. Modern canes may be plastic or fiber glass.

Caning - The art of using a cane on a bottom.

Cat or **cat o' nine tails** - The term originally referred to a whip used by British navy. Now, cat usually to refers to all multi-thonged whips.

Catharsis - Purgation of emotions and or stress through an SM scene may or may not be intentional.

CHDW or **Chudwa** - Acronym for a Clueless, Horny (or Het), Dominant Wannabe (pronounced chudwa). Term of derision used on alt.sex.bondage Internet newsgroup. [see Wannabe]

Checking-in - Asking the submissive how they are doing, feeling, etc. during a scene. Specific questions get more useful answers. An affirmative response to "Are you ok?" may merely indicate that death is not impending, but there still may be problems, particularly with a macho sub. "Would you enjoy heavier (or lighter) sensations?" is a better question. In SM play "is this good for you?" is asked during a scene rather than the typical "was it good for you?" afterwards. Checking-in should not replace a dominant's own observation and focus, it is another part of the safety net.

Cinching - 1) Wearing of a cincher, a garment similar to, but less encompassing than a corset. 2) A bondage technique, for example, to tighten coils of rope holding the wrists together by wrapping the coils between the wrists by one or more "cinch loops" of rope. (See the bondage chapter for further details.)

Clamp, clamping - Nipple clamps, clothespins, and binder clips are used to pinch or squeeze a small bit of flesh. The target areas for clamping are nipples, cocks, vulvas, and other erotically sensitive areas such as the sides of the torso and inner thighs. Weights can be added to increase the rigor.

Clip - [see Clamp, Clamping]

Clean - A code word used to describe a condition of being disease free. [see Code word]

Clueless - Being without understanding of a given topic. Also, a person without this understanding. [see True Master]

Cock and ball torture or **CBT** - Tortures are inflicted on these body parts using clothespins, clamps, cock cages, weight, and various kinds of bindings.

Code word(s) - Word(s) used in personal ads to disguise sexual proclivities that may be unacceptable to mainstream society, eg: English culture, French culture, Greek, clean, discipline, strict, leather, etc.

Collar, collared - 1) A symbol of surrender worn by a submissive. A collar is given in a relationship as a profound symbol of a commitment and bond. A "collared" submissive is considered to be owned (which see) or partnered with a dominant player. 2) A piece of bondage equipment worn around the throat.

Conditional compliance - The SM one-nighter, a limited exchange of power negotiated by a dom and sub for a single scene or brief period of play, such as overnight, one day, or one weekend. [see Power exchange levels]

Conditioning - The term used in psychology for the deliberate process of creating a psychological link between a desired response and an unrelated stimulus. Much of what people in the SM community refer to as training or slave training uses classic conditioning techniques. Psych 101 would have a huge enrollment if university professors realized that training a sub to orgasm on command is a lot more interesting than training pigeons to play ping-pong.

Condom - A latex sheath used on a penis or toy as a barrier to prevent the transmission of disease or pregnancy. Natural lambskin condoms are also available, but don't function effectively to prevent the spread of viral illness. [see Safer Sex]

Consensual - Behavior or activities agreed to by all parties involved. True consent is informed consent and requires a reasonably accurate knowledge of possible risks.

Contrapolar stimulation "Hurts so good!" - A type of physical stimulation that incorporates feeling of both pleasure and pain.

Corporal - Activities that involve the striking of one individual by another are called corporal from the term corporal punishment. Typically corporal activities include spanking, flogging, paddling, and caning.

Counting - The ritualized counting of strokes received. The sub may be required to thank the dominant with each count. Example: "One, thank you Sir. Two, thank you Sir, etc." A typically diabolic practice is to start the count over again each time a mistake is made. Some masochists never seem to get the count correct, even with their shoes off.

Covenant of dominance and submission - A deeply committed symbiotic relationship between a dominant and a submissive. [see Levels of power exchange]

Crossdressing - Dressing in clothes of the opposite gender.

Crucifixion - Bondage incorporating a stationary cross. The submissive's arms and legs are tied, not nailed. Care must be taken to ensure that the torso is properly supported, otherwise, strangulation may occur.

Cuff, cuffing - 1) Placing handcuffs, manacles, or similar restraints on the wrists and/or ankles. 2) Also refers to the restraints in the noun form. For example: "That is a nice cuff you're wearing," or "This cuffing is very comfy."

Cutting - 1) Slicing the skin as a part of body modification, ritual, or scene. Most frequently, designs are transferred to the skin as they would be for the creation of a tattoo. Then either scalpels, razor blades, art knives, or other cutting tool incise the skin at a depth of 1/16" to 3/16." Cuttings can include color by means of tattoo inks or cigar (not cigarette) ash rubbed into the fresh wounds. Care should always be taken to insure sterile conditions. 2) The breaking of skin by use of a corporal instrument. Single lash whips, canes, crops and others can cut if used improperly. 3) The deep stingy feel of some toys.

Dental dam - A latex barrier used for cunnilingus or anilingus to prevent disease transmission. Plastic food wrap is an inexpensive, but satisfactory, substitute.

Derivative pleasure, immediate/delayed - Corporal strokes that are painful at impact, but pleasurable following initial execution. An immediately derived pleasure stroke feels good right after the impact. Delayed derivative pleasure is an accumulation of painful strokes that explodes into sexual heat some time later.

Discipline - The "D" in B&D that can mean; 1) punishment 2) structured training of a submissive.

Do-me queen/king - A bottom that takes passive delight from the physical activities of scening without a desire to give submission or pleasure in return.

Dominance, dominance & submission, D/S, D&S - The consensual empowerment of one partner by the other for erotic enhancement. Dominance and submission are the psychological and emotional underpinnings of SM. [see Power exchange]

Dominant, Dom, Domme, Domina, Dominatrix - The person who is given control in a consensual exchange of power. Domme, Domina, and Dominatrix refers to women. Dominant, or Dom can refer to either gender.

Dressing for Pleasure, DFP - 1) An annual, international fetish community event featuring a weekend of socializing, workshops, boutiques, a fashion show and a ball. This convention of the strange and wonderful is sponsored by a SM boutique in Upper Montclair, NJ by the same name. The proprietress of the DFP is the world renowned dominant, Marie Constance.

Edge play - Erotic role play near or at the edge of a submissive's or dominant's limits. The term also refers to activities that carry a higher than usual element of risk.

Electro-torture - The use of electrical stimulation to create a desired physical sensation.

Emotional buttons, emotional triggers - Associations with words, behaviors, or activities that provoke a strong emotional reaction. Dominants will do well to become familiar with the unique triggers of his submissive. It is important to know, as much as possible, which buttons evoke positive and negative responses.

Endorphins, endorphin high - Endorphins are substances created by the body to help endure pain or stress. Entirely natural, but theoretically similar in feel to opiates. The body's release of endorphins may create a feeling of well-being, even intoxication, which is called an endorphin high. People differ dramatically in their ability to release endorphins. The possibility of addiction to endorphins has been conjectured.

Enema - The instrument used for, or the act of injecting fluid into the anus to flush the lower intestines. Some people include enemas in SM scenes for humiliation, for preparation for other activities (such as fisting or anal sex), and/or simply because they may enjoy the sensation.

English - An code word for spanking or corporal punishment sometimes used in ads. We will have achieved social acceptance when ads in mainstream papers can say, "Romantic sadist seeks masochist lover," instead of nonsense like, "devotee of English culture seeks receptive partner."

Erotic power - Erotic power is like potential energy, becoming significant only when it is exchanged or used to empower a dominant by the transfer of control. [see Power exchange]

Erotic pain - Stimuli that are painful under normal circumstances, but are pleasurable or arousing in a sexual context.

Erotic restraint - Restricting movement for erotic play. Also, refers to the devices used for said purpose.

Erotic surrender - The sexually motivated gift of control of one's self (within negotiated limits) to one's partner. A more accurately descriptive phrase for submission.

Erotically altered consciousness, EAC - Any one of several altered states of consciousness achieved by erotic stimulation. [see: Bottom-space, Sub-space; Endorphin high, Flying, Top-space]

Erotocomatose lucidity - Term coined by Aleister Crowley to describe the state of mind resulting from sexual practices used by his followers of Sexual Magik. We believe it to be the erotically altered consciousness (EAC) that we call flying (which see).

Fang-chung shu (arts of the inner chamber) - The collective term for Taoist (Chinese) sexual techniques practiced to achieve unity with the Tao and/or immortality. They are said to have induced altered states of consciousness. Ho-ch'i (unification of breaths) is a technique of fang-chung shu. The goals and techniques of the fang-chung shu are similar to some employed in SM.

Fetish - A sexual fixation on an activity or object.

Fetish community - The name given to that group of people having an alternate sexual or gender orientation, but excluding the (vanilla) gay and lesbian communities.

Fire & ice - The use of hot and cold for sexual stimulation, especially hot wax dripped from a candle and ice applied to the skin.

Fisting - Insertion of the entire hand into the vagina (vaginal fisting) or the anus (anal fisting).

Flagellation - The act of whipping a human being.

Flogger, flogging - An unbraided multi-thonged whip is a flogger. To whip using a flogger or other corporal instruments.

Flying - A transcendent state of consciousness sometimes achieved during an SM scene. This rapturous state has been so often described in a similar manner by independent sources that we have no doubt of the validity of the experience. Feelings described by the submissive seem similar to that of out of body experiences and often include a psychic link to the dom. Most commonly, this link is felt as either a tether to the dominant or as a feeling of being surrounded and protected by the dom's presence or consciousness. Elation and spaciness experienced after flying may be felt for hours, even days after the session has ended.

French - A common code word for kissing involving the tongue, cunnilingus, and fellatio.

Foot fetish, foot worship - A sexual obsession directed toward the feet and/or shoes.

Forced oral, forced sex - Sexual role play where the dom pretends to force an activity that the sub pretends they are under duress to perform. It involves a shared suspension of reality. (A dom only "forces" the sub to perform activities he or she has requested.)

Gag, gaggage - devices that are inserted in or cover the mouth to muffle sound.

Gear - Toys, props, clothes and what-have-you used for scene purposes.

Gender community - People with cross-gender fantasies or cross-gender identification. Cross-dressers, transvestites, and transsexuals make up the gender community.

Gender orientation - Gender orientation is an issue apart from sexual orientation. It is self-identification and feelings of maleness or femaleness, rather than issues of sexual attraction. A person with an alternate gender orientation may or may not have an alternate sexual orientation. For example; a transvestite or a transsexual may be either heterosexual or gay.

Gender play - To dress up or take the role of the opposite sex during a scene. [see Sissification]

German - A code word for Sadomasochistic desires.

Golden shower - Urination on or in another person.

Gorean - The term comes from a series of books written by John Norman about an imaginary planet called Gor. The slave culture described in these novels has acquired a cult following and Gorean elements are used in some SM fantasy role play.

Greek - The code word for anal sexual activities.

Handcuffs - These metal shackles are used to bind wrists by law enforcement personal, legally, and by sadomasochists, covertly. Handcuffs are considered weapons and illegal to own in most states, but are easy to buy and commonly used.

Head games - 1) Domination where the focus is primarily mental, such as humiliation, rather than physical, such as bondage or whipping. 2) Non-consensual psychological manipulation to make a person respond in a particular way for one's own purposes.

Heavy - 1) Intense SM play or whipping. 2) A term describing an SM toy such as a flogger or cane that is capable of delivering intense sensations.

Hedonic engineering - A phrase coined by Timothy ("turn on, tune in, drop out") Leary and Robert Anton Wilson to describe techniques of sexual reimprinting to overcome negative sexual imprinting by societal and/or parental influences. Some people use Leary's and Wilson's techniques in their scenes.

Hood - A covering for the head. Hoods used in SM are made of various materials, especially; leather, spandex, and rubber. Some hoods are constructed as ornamentation, others are used as a part of bondage to control or restrict sight, sound, speech (by incorporating a gag), and/or breathing.

Humiliation - Playful embarrassment or humbling a person by teasing them about their sexual desires can be part of erotic control. Humiliation in SM can paradoxically build a person's self-esteem rather than tearing it down by reinforcing their sexuality. Real attacks on a person's self-worth or sexuality, or manipulations designed to break their spirit are abuse not within the appropriate practice of SM.

Infantilism - Role play involving infant-like behavior such as diaper wearing, nursing, etc.

In-role - Assuming the persona of a sexual archetype or fantasy character.

Isolation - 1) A fear of interrelating with others. People are often; a) afraid to "come out" about their attraction to SM out of fear of societal repercussions, or b) they may think that no one shares their attraction to a particular SM (or other sexual) practice. In both cases, this can lead to feelings of inadequacy, self-doubt, depression, and/or loneliness. 2) A technique of sensory deprivation, bondage, and trickery to make a submissive feel as though he or she is being left alone.

Japanese bondage - [see Oriental bondage, rope dress]

Kajira - A term taken from John Norman's Gore series to refer to a Gorean female pleasure slave.

Katherine wheel - A piece of dungeon equipment that looks like a large, vertically mounted wheel to which a submissive is bound, allowing her to be turned or spun. Warning: not for use with the sub that is inclined toward motion sickness.

Knifeplay - Play that includes the use of a knife (does not necessarily imply cutting). Knives are more often used as props for psychological effect, to scrap wax from a body after a fire and ice scene, to remove clothing, and endless other devious purposes.

Latex - Latex and rubber are used to make clothing, sheets and other fetish items.

Leather, Leather sex, Leather lifestyle - We dress conspicuously in leather, bind each other with straps of it, and whack each other with leather toys. This might be why leather has become synonymous with SM. Duh.

Leather butt - 1) A term that describes a person who has been beaten so often that only intense whipping has any effect. 2) The condition of the buttocks after heavy paddling. The skin compresses and becomes stiff or "leathery" to the touch. The compression effect is most pronounced with paddles, so leather butt can be avoided by using a mixture of implements.

Lifestyler - A person who lives a lifestyle that supports rather than conflicts with his SM fantasy archetype. Some lifestylers object to the characterization of their SM identities as fantasy role play, feeling that it is integral to their personalities rather than a sexual game. It is easy, and often attractive, to confuse reality and fantasy. [see Alternate sexuality; Alternate lifestyle; In-role]

Limit - The boundaries of SM activities set by both dominant and submissive during negotiation defining what each is willing and unwilling to do within a scene. Limits must be respected and never intentionally breached by either partner. Limits apply to roles, levels of dominance and submission, and duration of time, as well as physical activities such as whipping, paddling, etc.

Live-in slave - A lifestyle submissive in a committed relationship who lives within the context of a slave/master (or mistress) fantasy.

Living In Leather (LIL) - A leather-SM-fetish convention held annually in the fall. This huge pansexual SM gathering includes seminars, workshops, events and parties. It is held in a different location every year. For details contact your local NLA chapter or look for advertisements in the major scene magazines.

Macho sub - A submissive with a reluctance to show distress, use a safe word, or who feels a need to stoically endure what is not pleasurable. The macho sub may be motivated by a desire to prove her mettle, show devotion, or reflect her internal fantasy. The macho sub must make sure the dom is aware of her inclinations during negotiation. The dom of a macho submissive should rely more on a checking-in technique and less on spontaneous feedback. The macho sub's saving grace is a strong desire to obey. Ordering her to communicate clearly about stress, as it occurs can override some of her reluctance to "be a wimp."

Masochism, masochist - The erotic enjoyment of pain, humiliation, and/or of being dominated. One who enjoys pain, etc. Sometimes the terms are used to describe one who enjoys heavier pain.

Master - A male that takes the dominant role in SM role play. The title may be bestowed upon the male dominant in appreciation of his skill. It may be a term of endearment or a loving tribute to a dom by a submissive in a relationship. Equally often, the term is self-aggrandizement by a male with dominant fantasies, not infrequently with "true" or "real" tacked in front.

Mental bondage - Ropeless bondage by command. A submissive instructed by her dominant to remain in position will feel bound to obey.

Mind - The predominant human sex organ.

Mistress - A female dominant. [see Dominant, Dom, Domme, Domina, Dominatrix]

My kink is okay, yours is not - A self-limiting and community-destructive attitude amongst intolerant SM practitioners. It is always best, and polite, to reserve judgment about someone's sexuality and interests. Every kink, no matter how mild or far-out, will offend some and delight others.

Mummification - A bondage technique of completely or almost completely wrapping a submissive in restrictive material, such as; plastic wrap, spandex, elastic or gauze bandages, etc.

Negotiation - The process of determining the practices and boundaries of sexual and SM activities between a top and a bottom. It may apply to the whole relationship or just a specific scene. Negotiating is an ongoing process that is repeated as the players' needs change.

"9 1/2 Weeks" - A book about an erotic, but abusive SM relationship and a movie made from the book. There is some debate whether the story is based on reality or is pure fiction, but the kind of events depicted can and do happen to real people.

Nipple clamps, nipple clips - [see Clamp, Clamping]

Nipple play/torture - Stimulation of the nipples for corporal or erotic purposes. Often includes; sucking, pinching, clamping, fire and ice, or piercing.

Nonconsensual - SM play that is not sanctioned by either player.

Nostril strap - A device, usually of bent wire, with a string attached for hooking into the nostrils for humiliation and torment. Commonly used in Japanese SM.

Novice - A person with an interest in SM, but lacking in experience.

"O" fantasy - The Story of 'O by Pauline Reage telling of a young women's descent into submission and her slave training remains one of the classics of SM. Elements from this fictional piece find their way into many a fantasy. "O" is also used as a code word for SM.

Oriental bondage, rope dress - Any of a number of styles of rope bondage stemming from styles used in the Far East. Typically, the bondages are highly decorative, uniform, and symmetrical.

Over the knee, OTK - A classic spanking position. Also a code word for same.

Ownership, absolute ownership - 1) Within master/slave role play ownership means having control of the submissive. 2) Loosely used in the SM community to mean an ongoing dominant/submissive relationship. 3) Absolute ownership is a lost-in-fantasy relationship based on sadomasomythology and fictional lore.

Paddle, paddling - A rigid flat-surfaced implement usually of leather or wood used for spanking a fanny. Paddling is the act of using a paddle. A paddle is also the implement that a wise-ass masochist often finds herself up the creek without.

Pain slut - A masochist who derives pleasure from physical pain.

Pansexual - Nongender specific sexual orientation. A group that encompasses all sexual and gender orientations is said to be pansexual.

Paradise Electro Stimulation, PES - A device that electrically stimulates muscle contraction, made by a company of the same name. The base control unit regulates attachments for vaginal, rectal, penal, and clitoral stimulation. After all the years of being screwed over by technology, finally a machine that delivers a intensely pleasurable fuck.

Pervert - One who deviates from the sexual norm. Yeah, we're perverts, and proud of it, too!

Philip - [see Toy Whore]

Piercing - Piercing the skin with a needle in an SM scene, as ritual, or as body modification. Most frequently, piercings are accompanied by the installation of jewelry. An exception to this is play piercing. In play piercing, the needle is inserted into, or through, the skin as a part of a scene, but the wound(s) are often allowed to heal without jewelry being introduced.

In play piercings, many parts of the skin may be pierced at the same time. Sometimes, the needles are left in the skin throughout the scene, tied together by string, thread, or rope, then removed at the close of the scene.

Piercings that are intended to be permanent usually are placed in sites common among people of the Near East for ornamental and erotic value. These sites are, typically; nostril and septum of the nose, ears (in the lobes, tragus, and helix), lips, nipples, along the shaft and head of the penis, the scrotum, inner and outer labia, and the hood of the clitoris. Some newer fashions of piercings include the webs between the fingers, the eyebrows, and the bridge of the nose.

Erotic piercings are said to enhance sensation to the body parts that are pierced. Raelyn Gallina, body modification expert (she performs piercings, cuttings, and brandings) and jeweler from Oakland, CA, invented a piercing called the "Triangle", which penetrates the clitoral hood on both sides, and underneath the clitoris. Thus, the ring installed contacts the clitoris in a place totally beneath the skin.

People seeking piercings are warned not to use piercing "guns", sewing needles, or safety pins. It is best to seek professional assistance which is available in most parts of the United States, Canada, and Europe. Very often, tattoo shops will be associated with professional piercers. These people have the equipment to provide sterile piercings and the knowledge to recommend proper after care.

Pillory - Handed down from the reign of the Puritans, a pillory is usually wooden-framed, free-standing stocks that imprisons the head and wrists for immobilizing a person. For use with the humiliation of your choice.

Pizzle - The dried and stretched penis of a bull, or other large animal, formed into a whip. These are actually deadly toys.

Plastic wrap - Regular, old plastic food wrap can be used for encasing the body for bondage. Unlike food, it will not keep your submissive fresh. [see Mummification]

Play - Participating in an SM scene or SM scene activity.

Playroom, Play space - Any area you designate in which to perform an SM scene. Hotel rooms, secluded woods, and delivery vans qualify as well as a permanently furnished basement or dungeon. Also referred to as dungeon space.

Play punishment - The use of punishment as an excuse for an erotic encounter. She burnt the toast that morning, forgot to say, "Sir," or some other trivial misdeed and, alas, must be corrected. Somehow, both end up getting what they crave. As a game, this beats the heck out of strip monopoly. Punishment is an erotic game that should never be used to address serious problems.

Ponygirl, Ponyboy - A classic SM fantasy immortalized in the drawings of John Willie and used in the Sleeping Beauty Trilogy by Ann Rice. Typical pony garb includes a horsehair tail attached to a buttplug, a bit gag and/or bridle headharness, and reins. Often very high heels, a corset, and feather plumes in the hair are added. The arms are typically bound behind the back. Pony activities range from being displayed and directed by rein to being ridden or pulling a cart.

Pony training - The fanciful transformation of a girl (or boy) into "pony" to be ridden, to pull a carriage, or to perform as a well-trained horse in obedience and deportment.

Position training - The training of a submissive to assume a given position upon command or under certain circumstances.

Post-scene plunge - Feelings of let-down, depression, fear, disgust, remorse, etc. after participating in SM play. Can be experienced by either dominant or submissive.Jay Wiseman, author of SM101, uses the term "Top Drop" to describe these feelings on the part of the dominant.

Power exchange - The empowerment of the dominant by the submissive's surrender to his/her control. Power exchange is consensual and should be well negotiated. The depth of the power yielded by the submissive is equal to level of responsibility assumed by the dominant.

Power exchange levels - A system for linking emotional involvement and depth of feeling with degree of power exchange. The Five Levels are: one - Conditional compliance, two - Restricted ongoing acquiescence, three - Provisional submission, four - the Covenant of dominance and submission, and five - Absolute ownership. The first four levels are based in reality.

Provisional submission - An ongoing relationship negotiated between a dom and a sub characterized by power exchange and emotional involvement, but lacking serious commitment. [see Power exchange levels]

Psychosexual - Emotionality, attitudes, orientations, or mind sets associated with erotic behavior or sexual fantasy life.

Punitive pain - Pain that by intention is designed to hurt for nonerotic purposes, usually for punishment. This is abusive and often motivated by a misunderstanding of appropriate control mechanisms.

Pushing limits - 1) A careful process of gradual expansion of limits. 2) Intense play that comes close to the unbearable. [see Edge play]

PVC - poly-vinyl-chloride - 1) A type of plastic used for fetish clothing. 2) The PVC pipes made for plumbing that can be constructed into bondage devices.

Quirt - A corporal toy that looks something like a crop with a flexible, whip-like cracker at the end.

Restricted Ongoing Acquiescence - An agreement, negotiated by a dom and sub, to play casually for an extended period of time without serious emotional involvement. [see Power exchange levels]

Rimming - Common term for anilingus (anal-oral sex).

Roissy - An imaginary place from The Story of O, by Pauline Reage, where young women were brought to be trained as slaves. Also used as a code word for SM.

Role play - 1) Elaboration of one's sexual inclinations by creating a fantasy framework for them. 2) People with compatible sexual fantasies taking on complimentary persona to interact with each other.

Rope dress - [see Oriental bondage, rope dress]

Rubber - [see Latex]

S.A.M. - [see Smart Ass Masochist]

Sadism, Sadist - Deriving sexual pleasure from the giving of pain, humiliation, and/or domination. The honorable sadist only gives pain or humiliation to those desiring it, respects limits, is caring and careful.

Sadomasochism, SM - Advanced sexual practices incorporating the consensual use of pain, humiliation, and power exchange for erotic enjoyment. SM includes dominance and submission, bondage and discipline, love bondage, and erotic spanking. The term is frequently misused to indicate heavier or more extreme practices.

Sadomasomythology - The misconceptions of society in regard to what sadomasochism actually entails. Also, an ill-informed idea about a particular practice within SM.

Safe, sane, and consensual - Characterizes the acceptable play within the SM community; players adhere to safety precautions within their activities, do not participate in practices that will injure their partners (mentally or physically), and obtain consent by negotiating scenes and scene related activities before carrying them out.

Safe sex, Safer sex - Practicing sex wherein no body fluids are exchanged; includes the use of condoms on insertion toys as well as penises, dental dams, or plastic wrap for cunnilingus, cleanliness with regard to corporal toys, abstention from penetration, etc.

Safe word, Safe signal - A word, a phrase, or an action (like dropping a ball by a gagged submissive) used by the submissive as a signal to stop the scene or reduce the intensity.

St. Andrew's cross - An upright cross in the shape of the letter "X" to which people are bound for flogging or torture.

Scat - Feces, also, play with feces.

Scene - 1) The SM or fetish community; or things associated with it. 2) An occurrence or session of SM play.

Scene friendly - Familiarity with, and acceptance of the SM scene and SM players, usually refers to a professional's attitude (-therapist, -lawyer, etc.)

Scene gear - The SM (and often vanilla) toys we play with. [see Gear]

Sensory deprivation - Restricting or diluting a submissive's ability to use one or more of his/her senses of touch, hearing, sight, taste, or smell as a part of an SM scene.

Sensory relocation - Transferring the feeling of a stimuli to a different body location than it is received.

Sensual play - SM play that focuses on stimulating the senses without the use of pain.

Service - Acts, chores, or labor, sexual or otherwise, performed by a sub for the benefit of a dom.

Session - A scene. [see Scene]

Serpent's Tongue - A type of slapper made of a thick strap of leather, two or three inches wide, with a deep "V" cut into most of the length of the piece. Commonly, the handle will have a double thickness with a ring stitched at the end. This is a very nasty toy.

Sexual imprinting, reimprinting - There is a school of thought stating that sexual responses result from imprinting based on past associations, experiences, background, and environment, often dating back to early childhood. Altering sexual behavior by changing responses and creating new associations is a technique called reimprinting.

Sexual magic, sensual magic - Positive descriptive terms for sadomasochism.

Sexual Magick - Neo-pagan practices and rites related to the writings of Aleister Crowley involving sexuality in altering states of consciousness.

Silent alarm - A safety precaution used by players who are new to one another. For example; a submissive, playing with a dominant for the first time, might arrange for a friend to be near a telephone at a pre-arranged time. If the submissive does not call at that time, the friend will be alerted that something has gone wrong and will take steps to see that the submissive is safe.

Sissification, feminization - A practice desired by a male sub of "forced" cross-dressing and/or gender reassignment.

Slapper - A flexible semi-rigid strap used like a paddle.

Slave - 1) In the scene community sometimes used loosely as another word for submissive. 2) A submissive involved in a committed relationship incorporating a shared slave/master fantasy.

Slave contract - A written agreement elaborating the terms, goals, and limits of an SM relationship.

Slave training - The processes of; instructing a submissive in a dominant's preferences, and, conditioning the submissive's behavior.

Sling - A cross between a swing and a hammock in which a bottom may be comfortably suspended.

SM positive - An sympathetic or accepting attitude toward sadomasochism and/or SM play and players. [see Scene friendly]

SM virgin - An person with little or no experience in SM practices.

Smart Ass Masochist, SAM - A bottom, who rather than submitting, challenges or annoys to entice a dom to punish her. [see Brat]

Spandex - A very stretchable synthetic cloth used for fetish clothing and bondage gear.

Spanking - Striking a submissive, usually with an open hand, on her fanny. Some use this term to include paddling, as well.

Spanking bench - A piece of stationary equipment with attachment points to designed to secure a submissive in preparation for a spanking. Properly bound or positioned on a spanking bench, the submissive's arse is in an accessible, convenient angle for a spanking or whipping.

Spanking skirt - A skirt or dress with cut-outs over each fanny cheek, designed to allow bare-skinned spanking. The spanking skirt is a classic piece of scene-wear that enhances humiliation/exhibitionism aside from its practical application.

Spreader bar - A strong bar, usually wooden, bamboo, or metal, with rings or holes on each end, used as a bondage tool to keep a submissive's arms or legs apart.

Sting - A sharp biting feel to the surface of the skin.

Stocks - A device (usually wooden) with holes designed to imprison a submissive's wrists and head, or wrists and ankles. [see Pillory]

Stoplight safe words - A commonly used system of safe words wherein red means stop the scene immediately and release the sub, yellow warns the dominant that the current practice is pushing the submissive's endurance, and green lets the dominant know that what is happening is awfully nice and should be continued.

Straight - 1) Code word for heterosexual. 2) Adjective for someone or something that is not SM oriented. In this sense, a synonym for vanilla.

Strap - 1) As a noun, this is either a bondage restraint (usually leather with a buckle) or an instrument of corporal punishment (also, usually leather sans the buckle). 2) As a verb, it is the act of binding or beating a submissive with a strap.

Submissive, Sub - One who surrenders control of her body and behavior (within pre-defined limitations) to another for erotic play.

Sub-space - [see: Bottom-space]

Submissive uniform - A common mode of dress worn by submissives emphasizing their sexuality, usually very short shirts, revealing tops, high heels, and stockings supported by a garter belt or bustier.

Suspension - A bondage technique wherein the submissive's weight, totally or partially, is borne by the restraints used in the bondage. Great care must be exercised in this practice; usually, bondage harnesses and suspension cuffs are used in suspension.

Suspension cuffs - Wrist and/or ankle restraints designed specifically for safe suspension. [see Cuff, Cuffing; Suspension]

Switch - 1) A person who enjoys taking either side in SM role or physical play; i.e. top or bottom, dom or sub. 2) A slender flexible branch from a tree or bush used for corporal punishment.

Sybian - This amazing variation on the vibrator is ridden rather than handheld. The vaginal insert is mounted on a saddlelike box that houses the twin motors that make the insert rotate and vibrate. (For more information contact Abco Research Associates in the Illinois Section of our store appendix).

Tampon training - Rectal insertion of tampons by male submissives to empathize with the female menstrual cycle.

Tantric Yoga, Vajrayana Buddhism - Indian means for achieving a transcendent spiritual state that incorporates sexual and meditative techniques. There are many paths to enlightenment and erotic exploration is one.

Tawes, taws - Thick rigid leather with a lengthwise slit (or slits) in it used in a paddle-like fashion.

TENS unit - The Transcutaneous Electrical Nerve Stimulation unit is used by chiropractors to cause involuntary muscle contraction. Sadomasochists use it for fun rather than therapy.

Thud - A blow that is felt at a deeper level than sting. Thud is usually easier to tolerate, but may actually be more damaging as it can cause deeper bruising.

Tit torture - Erotic play involving the breasts.

Tolleyboy - A locking chastity belt made in England of rubber-lined stainless steel. A similar device made in Chicago by Bob Jones is often referred to by the same name.

Top - One who takes the active role in physical scene, but not necessarily emotional/mental control.

Top's disease - A state of self-delusion wherein the top believes his own fantasy of dominant superiority. This dementia is characterized by the fallacy that his feces lacks the usual malodorous quality.

Topping from the bottom - Maintaining the fiction that the top is in charge, where the real control and direction of a scene rests with the bottom. [see also, Bottoming from the top]

Top-space - An state of erotically altered consciousness (EAC) achieved during a scene by the dominant or top. It is characterized by feelings of intense focus, clarity of thought, a sense of extreme power or high energy, and/or exhilaration. Feelings of distance and objectivity, as if one where commanding from a mountain top, may paradoxically accompany feelings of connection to the submissive, as if there were a psychic link. A dispassionate perspective may combine with erotic ardor. Top space may be followed by either a continued sense of well-being or by feelings of fatigue, depression, or lethargy. [see Post-scene plunge]

Torture - Actions that would be painful outside of their erotic context used to enhance sexual pleasure for a bottom.

Total conversion or the "ouchless ouch" - Whips strokes or corporal stimuli delivered during an erotic scene that begins light and rise gradually. The level of sexual arousal is always kept at a high enough level so that the blows are never experienced subjectively as pain.

Toy whore - One who adores collecting SM toys. Toy whores have been known to trade away their own children for a finely made cat o' nine. It has been suggested that a Toy Whores Anonymous support group be established for people who ruin their lives trying to support their toy habit. The idea has been shelved because the toy whores see no problem with this. [see Philip]

Training - Any of many disciplines wherein the dom and sub act together to modify the sub's behavior, condition, and/or attitude. Includes, but is not restricted to; pony training, anal training, position training, voice command response, and so on.

TS, Transsexual - A person who born in a physical gender that does not match his or her personal psychology. These people are commonly going through "gender reassignment" by means of counseling, hormone treatments, and surgery to correct their situation. A TS is called a "pre-op" before surgical modification and a "post-op" afterwards.

TV, Transvestite - A man or woman dressing in the clothing of the opposite gender.

True Master/True submissive - A term of self-description usually used by incompetent newcomers or lost-in-fantasy others to entice a people to play with them. The "True Submissive" (or more typically "True slave") is one who buys into the nonsense that the "True Master" is selling. "True sadomasochism" is also used to allude to a non-existent, "genuine" standard of SM excellence. Fooey. [see CHDW, or Chudwa; Wannabe] We would like to see a moratorium on the use of the words "true" and "real" because they imply that other concepts are false or invalid.

Vampire glove - Vampire gloves are most often thin leather driving gloves that have sharp, metal tines or tacks lining the palms. The tines are typically snap, or rhinestone settings that are poked through the leather from the inside and glued in place, though some very mean gloves utilize thumb or carpet tacks. Fur mitts can be embellished with tines in the same manner, yielding textures from very nice to yowee!

Vanilla - Describes things, activities and people who are not part of the SM scene, for example; "We had vanilla sex last night," meaning, "We had sex without including any SM scene elements." The term is no longer derogatory except as used by immature, cliquish, snobby, poopieheads who don't think the way we do.

Verbal humiliation/abuse - The use of sexual epithets and similar verbalizations to excite or humble one's partner. Verbal humiliation is good when it is used to support the value of the submissive. It becomes abuse when it is used to tear down the self-esteem of the sub. The line between the two is not always clear and may vary within one person's psyche depending upon mood. Use with caution and sensitivity.

Virgin rapture - Period of time (often years long) wherein newcomers are so overwhelmed by SM that they think the world revolves around it and can never imagine returning to any other form of sexuality. When the infatuation ends feelings of disappointment and loss are common. It may be reassuring to know that this is a normal process as SM is integrated into a person's sexuality.

Vinyl - A material used for fetish fashions. [see PVC]

Violet wand - A static electricity generator, frequently with multiple glass attachments including: globes, thin tubes, fork-shaped tubes, etc., used to send virtually harmless, violet-colored static "lightning" to a submissive's skin.

Visualization - The use of story-telling and verbal fantasy sharing to achieve a mood or desired mind set prior to, or during a scene.

Wannabe - A poseur pretending to be a skilled dominant without the requisite knowledge. The wannabe confuses masturbatory fantasy with real life experience, often with injurious results. [see CHDW, or Chudwa]

Wartenburg pinwheel - A neural response tester consisting of a metal handle with a free-spinning, metal pinwheel attached to one end. The "pins" are very sharp. Wartenburg pinwheels are used to test neural responses of spinal chord injury patients and to make submissives jump over the moon.

Water sports - Sexual play involving urine or enemas. [see Golden Showers and Enema]

Weights - Lead fishing weights or other weights hung from clamps that are attached to the body to increase torment. [see Clamps, Clamping]

Whip - A whip is an object used to beat on a submissive. Many people in the scene use the term whip to include canes, crops, paddles, slappers, etc., as well as single- and multiple-lash whips.

Whipping - 1) The act of beating a submissive or bottom. 2) Finishing a rope-end to prevent fraying by wrapping it with thread or string.

White lightning - A common nickname for a white fiber glass or resin rod often with a leather or rubber handle that is used as a cane. Being much more dense than rattan, it can inflict deeper damage and the feel is described as "cutting." [see Cane]

Worship - 1) To lavish attentions upon a part of the body, usually feet, pussy or cock. 2) A role playing attitude toward a dominant, typically of a male sub toward his goddess/mistress.

Wrapping - Allowing the tips of a whip or cane to strike parts of the body other than the intended target. For example, aiming for the fanny and hitting it, but the tips of the whip wrap around the fanny and strike the hip. Bruising on the hips is often a sign of a careless or incompetent top who is frequently unaware of the damage that is occurring.

Wrist cuffs - Restraints designed to fit the wrists. [see Cuff, Cuffing]

X-frame - A stationary bondage frame in the shape of an "X", usually mounted in a horizontal position. [see St. Andrew's cross]

The following pages are included for use as a resource. Appendix A: Support Groups and Organizations contains group lists and some public leather and SM clubs. Appendix B: Computer Bulletin Boards contains our list of fetish oriented bulletin boards and some information about network and internet modem resources. Appendix C: Stores, Suppliers and Artisans is intended to help you find the toy, book, video, or clothing of your dreams. Appendix D: SM and Fetish Magazines lists periodicals with an SM or fetish theme. Appendix E: Recommended Reading is included to share the books we have read and loved.

Every reasonable effort was made to verify the information as accurate and current. Limited resources kept Molly from visiting every store and Philip every support group, as unfair as that sounds. So, we cannot vouch for the quality of any stores we have not seen, nor the integrity of support groups we have not attended. Also, stores, groups, BBSs, even books and magazines come and go without getting our written permission. If we've missed something on a list that you were looking for, we're sorry. There were very few entries we omitted intentionally.

Appendix A: SM Support Groups and Organizations

UNITED STATES

ALABAMA
PEP: Alabama
(205) 384-1840

ARIZONA
Arizona Power Exchange (APEX)
5821 N. 67th Avenue
Suite 103-276
Glendale, AZ 85301
(602) 848-8737

CALIFORNIA
Avatar
7869 Santa Monica Blvd. #316
Los Angeles CA 90046
(213) 669-3302
men only

Black Leather Wings/Leather
Faeries
c/o Rivendell on the Hayes
843 G Hayes
San Francisco CA 94117
men only

Cogent Warriors
2261 Market #250
San Francisco CA 94114
women's group

Defenders: San Francisco
c/o Dignity San Francisco
1329 7th Ave
San Francisco, CA 94122
(415) 487-7669
gay & lesbian Catholic group

Diaper Pail Fraternity
38 Miller Avenue, Suite 127
Mill Valley, CA 94941

Disciples of de Sade
3121 Hamilton Way
Los Angeles CA 90026

men only

Fifteen Association, The
P.O. Box 421302
San Francisco CA 94142
men's group

Knights of the Second Liberty
12226 Victory Blvd. #137
North Hollywood CA 91606
men only

Leathermasters
4470-107 Sunset Blvd #293
Los Angeles CA 90027
(213) 664-6422
men only

Links
P.O. Box 420989
San Francisco CA 94142
(415) 695-7955

M.A.S.T. (Masters and Slaves Together)
7985 Santa Monica Blvd.
Suite 482
West Hollywood CA 90046
men

MP Bands
P.O. Box 2843
Canoga Park, CA 91306

NLA: Los Angeles
7985 Santa Monica Blvd #109-217
West Hollywood, CA 90046
(213) 856-5643

Orange Coast Leather Assembly
Gay & Les Community Center
12832 Garden Grove Blvd, Ste A
Garden Grove CA
714-534-0862

The "O" Ring
P.O. Box 291
Hayward, CA 94543
(510) 538-8490
men only

Original Leathermasters Club
P.O. Box 93643
Los Angeles CA 90093
men only

Outcasts
P.O. Box 31266
San Francisco CA 94131
women only

Pervert Scouts
3288 21st Street, #19
San Franscisco, CA 94110
(415) 285-7985
PervScout@aol.com
women only

San Diego Power Exchange
Network
P.O. Box 87564
San Diego CA 92134-7564
(619) 467-1745

Service of Mankind Church
P.O. Box 1335
El Cerrito CA 94530
(510) 232-1369

Service of Mankind Church
Box 1407
San Francisco CA 94101

Society of Janus
P.O. Box 426794
San Francisco CA 94142
(415) 985-7117
http://www.blackiris.com/SFLe
atherMC/Janus/janus.html

Threshold
2554 Lincoln Blvd. Suite 1004
Marina del Rey CA 90291
(310) 452-0616

Trident
11750 Kittredge St. #33
No. Hollywood CA 91606.
818-508-5412
men, uniforms & leather

Womanlink
2124 Kitteredge #257
Berkley CA 94704
women only

COLORADO
C.O.P.E.
1015 S Gaylord St. #200
Denver, CO 80209

Defenders: Denver
P O Box 3072
Denver, CO 80202
(303) 322-8485
gay & lesbian Catholic group

NLA: Denver
P.O. Box 18568
Denver, CO 80218
(303) 860-8344

PEP: Denver
(303) 727-9744

CONNECTICUT
United Leatherfolk of CT
P.O. Box 281172
East Hartford CT 06128-1172
Email: ulofct@aol.com
pansexual, SASE for info

FLORIDA
Defenders: Tampa Bay
P O Box 201
Lutz, FL 33549
(813) 996-4738
gay & lesbian Catholic group

NLA:Florida
P.O. Box 4911
Ft. Lauterdale FL 33338-4911
(305) 742-6923

P.M. Club
P.O.Box 151604
Tampa, FL 33614
spanking club

GEORGIA
Atlanta Corporal Punishment
Club
P.O. Box 11863
Atlanta, GA 30355

male

Atlanta S/M Solidarity (ASS)
P.O. Box 8361
Atlanta, GA 30306-0361
(404) 521-3829 (Voice mail)
gay, holds pansexual classes

NLA: Atlanta
P.O. Box 78131
Atlanta, GA 30357-8131
404-624-1676
Pansexual

PEP:Atlanta
P.O. Box 921291
Norcross, GA 30092
(404) 621-7961 voice mail

Southern Kinks (W)
P.O. Box 36718
Decatur, GA 30032-0718
women only

ILLINIOS
Chicago Hellfire Club
(Windy City Hellfire Club, Inc.)
P.O. Box 5426
Chicago, IL 60680
men's group

Dedicated & Safe, Inc.
Meets at The Golden Flame
(Ruby Room)
6417 W.Higgens Rd.
Chicago, IL
(312) 463-2178.

Leather United-Chicago
P.O. Box 138-058
Chicago, IL 60613

E.N.I.G.M.A.
(genital modification)
2329 N. Leavitt
Chicago, IL 60647
men only

INDIANA
NLA: Indianapolis
P.O. Box 1632
Indianapolis, IN 46206-1632
317-638-8109

Sweet Misery
P.O. Box 11690
Indianapolis, IN 46201-0690
women's group

KANSAS
NLA: Kansas City
P.O. Box 414545
Kansas City, MO 64141

KENTUCKY
Louisville Area Trust Exchange
(Latex)
P.O. Box 647
Louisville, KY 40118

MAINE
Harbor Masters, Inc.
Box 4044 Station "A"
Portland, ME 04101
men's group

MARYLAND
F.I.S.T. (Females Investigating
Sexual Terrain)
P O Box 41032
Baltimore MD 21203-6032

The Phoenix Society
1131 S. Clinton Street
Baltimore MD
410-385-3331
email: cane@ix.netcom.com or
Hunter@palace.com

Women's Rap Group
P.O. Box 76
College Park, MD 20740
women only

MASSACHUSETTS
Black Eagle M.C.
381 Adams Street
Dorchester, MA 02122
motorcycle

Bound & Determined
P.O. Box 602
Hadley, MA 01035
women only

Boston's Unified Leather Legion
Mike's Men
P.O. Box 287
Charlestown, MA 02129

Common Bond
P.O. Box 390313
Cambridge, MA 02139
women's group

Defenders of Boston
55 E. Springfield St.
Boston, MA 02118
(617) 437-0998
gay & lesbian Catholic group

Dignity's Defenders
95 Berkeley St., Suite 610
Boston, MA 02114
men's group

Dreizehn
P.O. Box 1486

Boston, MA 02117
men only

East Coast FTM Group
P.O. Box 60585
Florence Station
Northampton, MA 01060

The Esoterica Society
P.O. Box 37
Randolph, MA 02368

Leather Knights
P.O. Box 1969
Boston, MA 02149
men's group

MOB (Mass. Orgasmic Bitches)
SASE c/o Kim
Grand Opening
318 Harvard St., Suite 32
Brookline MA 02146
Kim at G.O. (617) 731-2626
email: malmros@id.wing.net

Moving Violations
P.O. Box 2356
Cambridge, MA 02238-2356
women's group

NLA: New England
831 Beacon Street #9100-164
Newton Centre, MA 02159
pansexual leather/SM

Riders M.C.
P.O. Box 519
Boston, MA 02258
men's group

Shelix
P.O. Box 416
Florence Sta
Northampton, MA 01060-0416
women's group

T-Bears
72 Van Kleek Street
Millis, MA 02054
women's group

Urania
P.O. Box 499 Astor Sta.
Boston, MA 02130 499
women only

Vikings M.C.
101 Glenwood St.
Malden, MA 02148
men's group

MICHIGAN
L & L Society
P.O. Box 2145

Bay City MI 48707
(517) 892-8054

NLA:Detroit
P.O. Box 2844
Southfield, MI 48037-2844
(810) 354-5841

The Recruits
P.O. Box 725121
Berkley, MI 48072
women only

Stocks and Bonds
Detroit, MI
Mist Lisa@AOL.com

MINNESOTA
Knights of Leather
P.O. Box 10601
Minneapolis, MN 55440
women's group

Minnesota Links
Irish Well
Twins Motor Inn
1975 University Avenue West
(612) 645-0311
meets monthly 7:30, 1st tuesdays

MISSOURI
Gynecrocrat Alliance
P.O. Box 13034
St Louis, MO 63144

NLA: Kansas City
P.O. Box 414545
Kansas City MO 64141

PEP: St. Louis
c/o TFN
10028 Manchester Road, Ste 214
St. Louis, MO 63122
(314) 995-9599

NEBRASKA
The Club
P.O. Box 1292
Omaha, NE 68101-1292
men only

Omaha Players' Club
P.O. Box 34463
Omaha, NE 68134-0463

Two Wheelers Auxiliary Troop
P.O. Box 3216
Omaha NE 69103
women only

NEW MEXICO
AEL
P.O. Box 80676
Albuquerque, NM 87198

(505) 345-6484

PEP: Albuquerque
1113 Delemar NW
Albuquerque, NM 87107
(505)764-5748
(908)284-8040

NEW YORK
Black Fire
P.O. Box 354 University Sta.
Syracuse NY 13210
men only

Conversio Virium-Columbia Univ.
New York NY
email:conversio@columbia.edu
http://www.cc.columbia.edu/cu
/cv/
Columbia U. students & staff only

Defenders: New York
P.O. Box 1146
Old Chelsea Station
New York NY 10011
(908) 324-6475
gay & lesbian Catholic group

GMSMA
332 Bleeker St. #D23
New York NY 10014
(212) 727-9878
men's group

Iron Guard
P.O. Box 291
Village Station
New York NY 10014

Lotus Foot Love Club
Drawer G
Coram NY 11727

LSM (Lesbian Sex Mafia)
P.O. Box 993
Murray Hill Station
New York NY 10156
L.Cub@aol.com
women

New York Bondage Club
P.O Box 7280
New York NY 10116
(212) 315-0040
men's group

NLA: Tri-State
332 Bleaker St., Suite F-4
New York NY 10014
(718) 597-0019
A pansexual SM & Fetish support
and educational group

NYSPA (New York Strap & Paddle

Association)
332 Bleecker Street, Suite F4,
New York, NY 10014
men only, meets 2nd and 4th
mondays at Cellblock 28

Renegades
P.O. Box 1457
Canal Street Station
New York NY 10013.
Men's Leather S/M club
meets at Cellblock 28

S.M.A.C.E.S.(Sexual Minorities
Aligned for Community,
Education and Support)
Bard College
Annandale NY 12504
Email: LiamTu@aol.com
Bard students, pansexual

Sirens MC
530 W 46th St #3E
New York NY 10036
women only

The Eulenspiegel Society (TES)
24 Bond Street
New York City, NY
(212) 388-7022

NEVADA
Escape - West
330S. Decatur #106
Las Vegas, NV 89107
(702) 226-5441

The Orb and Scepter
c/o The New Visionary Press
252 Convention Center Drive
Suite 483
Las Vegas, NV 89109
(702) 251-7201

NORTH CAROLINA
Tarheel Leather Club
P.O. Box 16457
Greensboro NC 27416-0457
(910) 288-4709

Tradesman, Inc.
P.O. Box 36712
Charlotte, NC 28204

Triangle Area Power Exchange
P O Box 98708
Raleigh, NC 27624
men's group

OHIO
Briar Rose
P.O. Box 16235
Columbus, OH 43216
women's group

Leather & Lace Society
P.O. Box 26731
Akron, OH 44319
cz@universe.digex.net

NLA: Columbus
P.O. Box 2763
Columbus OH 43216
(614) 899-4406

OKLAHOMA
Prometheus
P.O. Box 57213
Oklahoma City, OK 73157
men only

OREGON
NLA: Portland
P.O. Box 5161
Portland, OR 97208
503-727-3148

Oregon Guild Activists of S/M
(ORGASM)
P.O. Box 5702
Portland OR 97208
(503) 688-0669

Portland Power and Trust
P O Box 3781
Portland, OR 97208
women's group

RCDC (Rose City Discussion Club)
P.O. Box 1370
Clackamas, OR 97015
(503) 650-7052

Northwest Gender Alliance
(INWGA)
Box 4928
Portland OR 97208.
(503) 646-2802

PENNSYLVANIA
Female Trouble
P.O. Box 2284
Philadelphia PA 19103-0284
women's group

GMSMA (Gay Male SM Activists)
P.O. Box 58694
Philadelphia PA 19102
men's group

L.B.W. (Leather, Bondage &
Whips) Attn: Lisa
3140-B West Tilghman #139
Allentown, PA 18104
couples into female domination

NLA: Pittsburgh
P.O.Box 81245
Pittsburgh PA 15217

PEP: Philadelphia
P.O. Box 812
Morrisville PA 19067
(215) 552-8155

Pocono Warriors
P.O. Box 54138
Philadelphia PA 19105
men's group

Tri-State Couples Club
P.O. Box 99626
Pittsburgh PA 15233
Newsletter, parties

TENNESEE
PEP: Tennesee
P.O. Box 767
St. Bethlehem TN 37155
(615) 255-6970

Women of Leather
181 N. Willett
Memphis, TN 38104
women only

TEXAS
Bound by Desire
PO Box 1322
Austin, TX 78767-1322
(512) 764-9900
(512) 345-6989
Women

Brotherhood of Pain
P.O. Box 66183
Houston TX 77266-6183
men only

Disciples of de Sade
3920 Cedar Springs
Dallas TX 75219
men only

Flying W's
P.O. Box 345485
Dallas TX 75234-5485
women's group

Group With No Name (or GWNN)
P.O. Box 18301
Austin TX 78760-9998
gwnn@io.com

Leather Rose Society,
The POB 223971
Dallas TX 75222
(214) 289-0619 or (214) 375-1994
Email: rabbit@metronet.com
Open monthly meeting at TGIF

NLA: Austin
P.O. Box 684013
Austin TX 78768-4013

(512) 370-4713

NLA: Dallas
P O Box 7597
Dallas TX 75209-7597
(214) 521-5342 ext.820

NLA: Houston P.O. Box 66553
Houston TX 77266-6553
(713) 434-2417

PEP: Dallas c/o Neal
1102 Enterprise #216
Grand Prairie TX 75051

PEP: Gulf Coast
P O Box 1682
Pasadena TX 77501
(713) 947-8993

WIL Power (Women in Leather)
P.O. Box 811702
Dallas TX 75381
women only

UTAH
Wasatch Leathermen
P.O. Box 1311
Salt Lake City, UT 84110
men's group

VIRGINIA
The Black Rose
P.O. Box 11161
Arlington, VA 22210-1161
(301) 369-7667

PEP: Tidewater
(804) 488-5724

WASHINGTON DC
Black Rose
P.O. Box 11161
Arlington, VA 22210-1161
(301) 369-7667

Defenders: Washington, D.C.
P O Box 33098
Washington, DC 20033
(202) 387-4516
gay & lesbian Catholic group

SigMa
P.O. Box 11050
Washington, DC 20008
gay men mostly, but open

S&Mazons
P.O. Box 53394
Washington, DC 20009
(202)722-0056
msdaddy@aol.com
women's group

WASHINGTON STATE
Cascade Handballers
112 Broadway E
Seattle WA 98102
(206)329-8287

The Evangelical Perv Association
Corvallis, Oregon
hackbod@cs.orst.edu   or
garyr@peak.org
BDSM Student Organization at
Oregon State University

Kinky Couples
65 Southcenter Mall
Seattle WA 98188

NLA: Seattle
P.O. Box 20674
Seattle WA 98102

Northwest Bears
1202 E Pike, #802
Seattle WA 98122
(206)223-1003
men only

Northwest Bondage Club
1202 E Pike, #1212,
Seattle WA 98122
(206) 824-1226

Northwest Leather Goddeses
(206) 938-2449
dominant & switchable women

Northwest Rainmakers Network
A watersports contact group
10115 Greenwood Ave N, #150
Seattle, WA 98133
(206)298-1830

Outer Limits
1202 E Pike, #819
Seattle WA 98122
Women

Seattle Men in Leather
1202 E Pike, #1199
Seattle WA 98122
(206)233-8141

SM/Leather/Fetish   12   Step
Recovery Meetings
402 15th Ave
Seattle WA
(206) 323-7483
(enter from back of building)

Tacoma Pride in Leather
24th Street Tavern
Tacoma, WA
Monthly meeting, 2nd Tuesday

WISCONSIN
Crucible, The
P.O. Box 951
Stevens Point, WI 54481-0951
Wicca, Pagan SM group

Dames
P O Box 1272
Milwaukee WI 98122
women's group

AUSTRALIA
The Dungeon Club
meets at: New Pharaohs
121 Sussex St.
Sydney 200
(010 612) 299-3777

BELGIUM
Doornroosje
St. Hubertusstrat 115
B-2600
Berchem, Antwerp
(0 3) 239-3961

CANADA
Association des Adeptes SM
Montreal (ADSM)
P.O: Box 278 N.D.G. Stn.
Montreal QC H4A 3P6
men only

Club Winnipeg
P.O. Box 1697
Winnipeg, Manitoba R3C 2Z6

Durham Alliance Association
Social Club
7-717 Wilson Road South
Oshawa, Ontario
Canada L1H 6E9
(905) 434-4297
lesbian and gay

Megalesia
4399 Notre Dame West
P.O. Box 61043
Montreal, Canada PQ H4C 3N9
couples of all kinds

Monarch Social Club
Mississauga "A"
P.O. Box 386
Mississauga, Ontario
Canada L5A 3A1
(416) 949-6602
crossdressing/transgender

NLA: British Columbia c/o GLC
1170 Bute St.
Vancouver, BC
Canada V6E 1Z5
(604) 451-7402

NLA: Toronto Box 98
268 Parliment St.
Toronto, Ont.
Canada M5A 3A4
(416) 925-9872 ext:2089
Monthly meetings at: 519 Church
Street, Toronto

Ottawa Knights
P.O. Box 9174
Ottawa, Ont.
Canada K1G 3T9

SAAFE (Southern Alberta Assn for
Fetish-Fantasy-Education-
Exploration)
Box 42014
Acadia Postal Outlet
Calgary, Alberta
Canada T2J 7A6

Tight Ropes
P.O. Box 33067
Halifax, NS
Canada B3L 4T6

Vancouver Leather Alliance
P O Box 2253
Vancouver, BC
Canada V6B 3W2

VASM (Vancouver Activists in
S&M)
P.O. Box 4579
Vancouver, BC
Canada V6B 4A1
men only

Winnipeg Leather & Levi Club
P.O. Box 3079
Winnipeg, MB R3C 4E5

X-Corrigia
109 Vaughan Road
Toronto, ON
M6C 2C9 Canada
pansexual

DENMARK
SMil Denmark
Box 188
DK-8100 Aarhus C.
8619 5335

ENGLAND
De Sade
SASE: Steve
P.O. Box 4
Weston-Super-Mare
Avon BS24 9BB

Lady O Society
BCM/3406
London WCIN 3XX
submissive women

Motivation
P.O. Box 19
Pangbourne, Reading RG8
8LW
England

Submission
SASE: BCM
Box 4542
London WCIN 3XX
(0171) 284-2180

SM Bisexuals
Central Station
37 Wharfdale Road
London N1 9SE UK
listserv@andelain.demon.co.uk
smbi@andelain.demon.co.uk

SM Gays
BM SM Gays
London WC1N 3XX
men only

Unlimited (was NAFF)
PO Box HP50
Leeds, England LS6 1TR
http://www.ccs.neu.edu/USER/
pallando/BDSM/

FINLAND
S/M Group
c/o SETA ry
Toinen Linja 10
00550 Helsinki 55

Kinky Club
SMF Finland
PL296
FI-00151, Helsinki
+358-(0)400-795895

GERMANY
AG S/MOFF
Holstenstrasse 5
D-24534

NETHERLANDS
Schlechte Meiden
Postbus 201
NL 11 10 AE Diemen
Netherlands
women only

SM Studio Phoenix
P.O. Box 9702
4801 LV Breda
Netherlands
16 505-6789

VSSM
att. Werkgroep Vrouwen en SM
Postbus 3570
NL 1001 AJ Amsterdam
Netherlands

SWEDEN
BWW (Black Widow's Web)
Box 11489
404 30
Gothenburg, Sweden

NORWAY
SMil Norway
Box 3456
Bjelsen
N 0406 Oslo 4 Norway

Places to Meet - Public SM/leather/fetish Clubs

CALIFORNIA
Adashi Ranch
Tracy, CA
(209) 836-0169
Pony girl/boy races, parties.

The BackDrop Club
P.O. Box 390486
Mountain View, CA 94039-0486
Office: 415-965-4499
BBS: 415-964-3100

Bondage A Go-Go
520 4th Street
San Francisco CA
(415) 995-4600

The Chateau
7407 Fulton Ave.
North Hollywood CA 91605-4116
(818) 503-3034
http://www.thechateau.com

The Crypt
1712 E. Broadway
Long Beach
(310) 983-6560)

The Faultline
4216 Melrose Ave
Hollywood, CA

Floyd's
2913 E. Anaheim
Long Beach, CA
(310-433-9251)

Los Angeles Gotham Club
2817 W. Beverly Boulevard
Los Angeles, CA
(213) 651-1005 ext.2

Sin-A-Matic,
7969 Santa Monica Blvd.
West Hollywood, CA

Vice Club
5657 Melrose Ave.
Hollywood, CA
213-463-7868

GEORGIA
The Eagle
308 Ponce De Leon Ave. NE
Atlanta, GA
(404) 874-4732
gay men's leather bar

Mon Cherie's Club Fetish (two locations):
The Masquerade
695 North Avenue
Atlanta, GA
(404) 577-8178
also:
The Chamber
2115 Faulkenr Road
Atlanta, GA
(404) 248-1612

MASSACHUSETTS
Boston Ramrod
1254 Boylston St.
Boston, MA 02215
(617) 266-2986
mostly men but open to women

Club Manray
Brookline St near Central Square
Cambridge, MA

Club 119
119 Merrimac Street
Boston, MA
367-0713
male leather bar

Quest
1270 Boylston St.
Boston, MA
gay, but dungeon is pansexual
Saturday nights

The Sling Sporters
228 Cambridge Street
Boston, MA

(617) 742-4084
gay & gay leather bar

MICHIGAN
Club Hell
info:Noir Leather
(810) 541-3979

OHIO
Columbus Eagle
232 N. 3rd Street
Columbus, OH
gay leather club

Eagle In Exile
893 N. 4th Street
Columbus, OH

NEW YORK
Eagle's Nest
21st Street at 11th Avenue
New York, NY
leather bar

Hellfire Club
(also as The Manhole Club, gay)
28 9th Ave.
(between 13th & 14th Streets)
New York, NY
(212) 647-0063

Jackie 60
432 West 14th Street
New York, NY
(212) 677-6060
fetish nights on Tuesdays

Lure
409 W 13th Street
New York NY
Men, Fetish Dress Code

Paddles
(also as Zone DK - gay)
540 West 21 Street
New York, NY
(212) 463-8599

Spike
20th Street at 11th Avenue
New York, NY
Leather Bar

The Vault
(also as Cellblock 28 - gay)
28 10th Avenue
NYC, NY
(212) 255-6758

BELGIUM
Moda Moda
343, Chausee de Waterloo
B-1600 Bruxelles
Belgium

(32) 02 537-6919

CANADA
Betty Page Social Club
Fetish Night at Boots
Hotel Selby
592 Shelbourne Street
Toronto, Ont
(416) 921-0665
1st & 3rd Thursdays

Betty Page Social Club
Fetish Night
P.O. Box 28
199 W. Hastings St.
Vancouver BC V6B 1H4

The Crypt
22 Albert Stret
Winnipeg
(204) 774-1076

The Kinky Kabaret Fetish Night at
Savage Garden
550 Queen Street West at
Bathurst
Toronto, Ontario
(416) 504-2178
last Friday of month

Madame X's Fetish Night
Limelight Club
250 Adelaide Street West
Toronto, Ontario
Madame X: (416) 537-2896
last Tuesday of month

Montreal Fetish Night
info: Johnny at Il Bolero
6842 St. Hubert St.
Montreal, Quebec
(514) 270-6065

ENGLAND
Fantastic
info:
Skin Two
(0891) 445-5911

Marquis Masquerade
info: 25 Monks Way
Silverdale, Nottingham
NG11 7FG
(0115) 981-9113

Torture Garden
Info: BM The Torture Garden
London WC1N 3XX

Whiplash
SASE: P.O. Box 2610
London W14 0TP
(0171) 603-9654

FRANCE
Avi - tickets:Demonia Shop
(1 4) 785-2225
Cuir et Dentelles
Tickets through Phylea
Info: (1 4) 427-6080

GERMANY
Atomage
Monchengaldbach fetish parties
info:Kleinenbroicherstrasse 3
41238 Monchengaldbach-
Giesenkirchen
(2166) 87530

Sin-A-Matic
Nurnberg club nights info:
Gluckstr. 13
90763 Furth
(091) 170-9017

Ex Kreuz Club Berlin
info: Michael & Manfred at
Hautnah, Uhland Str 170
10719 Berlin
(030) 882-3434

NETHERLANDS
Doma
SASE: Asterstraat 107
2565 TT Den Haag
(070) 360-1822

'Europerve' -Demask
info: Demask
Zeedijk 64
1012 BA
Amsterdam
(20) 620-5603

G-Force
Oudezijds
Armsteeg 7
(020) 420-1664

SBIC
48 Marnixstraat
(020) 624-2988

SPAIN
Rouge et Noir
19 Inglaterra St.
Madrid, Spain
info:Apdo. 2052-39080
Santander
(908) 829821

SWEDEN
Fetish Family
Ovre Majorsg. 4a
413 08 Gothenberg
(031) 775-9623

National/International Headquarters & Community Outreach

The Defenders - gay & lesbian Catholic Leather/Levi support group. For information:
Defenders: New York
P.O. Box 1146
Old Chelsea Station
NY, NY 10011
(908)324-6475

Education Tranvestite Channel (ETVC) Information Hotline
415-335-3439

Femina Society & School
Mother Chapter
P.O. Box 1873
Haverhill, MA 01831
female dominance

Houston Council of Clubs
2400 Brazos St.
Houston, TX 77006

National Association Of
Crossdressers
P.O. Box 497
Flint, MI 48501
male crossdressers

NLA: International
3439 N.E. Sandy Blvd.#155
Portland, Oregon 97232
NLA:I Membership
C/O NLA:Austin
PO Box 49801
Austin, Texas 78765-9801

NLA: Deaf International

P.O. Box 30286
Columbus, OH 43230

People Exchanging Power (PEP)
(National) Information Literature
(908) 284-8028
(412) 284 5028

Womanlink (National)
2124 Kittredge #257
Berkeley, CA 94704
women's group

FFE/USA (Feminists For Free Expression/USA)
Contact: Catherine Siemann
FFE/USA
2525 Times Square Station
New York NY 10108-2525

"KAP"
c/o Race Bannon
584 Castro St., #518
San Francisco, CA 94114.
Kink Aware Professional - Listing of professionals in psychological and medical practice who are aware and accepting of kinky sexuality. Send a SASE (two .29 stamps in USA) for current list.

SM/Leather/Fetish Community
Outreach Project
P.O. Box 1617
New York, NY 101-11617
gopher:unix.tpe.com   or
vector.casti.com

http://www.tpe.com
listing of SM-fetish resources

Leather Pride Project
P.O. Box 23326
Seattle WA 98102,
(206)325-4275
Lthrpyde@shadowplay.com

SOC-PAC
P.O. Box 40625
Portland OR 97240
503-222-6151
political action committee

University of Washington
Society for Human Sexuality
SAO 141, Box 352238
Seattle, WA 98195
E-Mail:sfpse@u.washington.edu
http://weber.u.washington.edu/
~sfpse/

Appendix B: Computer Bulletin Boards

Eastern Time Zone

Adult Fun Castle (through Fidonet: 1:3613/9.0)	404-685-1455 (GA)
Adult Hotline	914-361-1102 (NY)
Afternoon Delight BBS	407-957-0231 (FL)
Atlanta Connection	404-929-1291 (GA)
Blanche's Place	202-547-9270 (DC)
Boudoir Online	416-622-7198 (ON)
Bound For Pleasure (Telnet bfp.com)	617-374-9255 (MA)
Boston Dungeon Society (Telnet bdsbbs.com)	617-397-8844 (MA)
The Cat House	904-778-4236 (FL)
Connecticut Adult Connections	203-889-0735 (CT)
Con-X-tion BBS	803-772-4624 (SC)
The Covenant BBS	717-394-2819 (PA)
Cyber-eroticom	212-233-4328 (NY)
The Digital Obsession BBS	215-678-4214 (PA)
The English Palace (through Telnet/FTP/WWW: palace.com) The oldest (we think) and largest BDSM and Fetish BBS in the world	908-739-1755 (NJ)
The Fetish Network BBS (through Telnet/FTP/WWW: fetish.wisenet.com)	305-370-7007 (FL)
Final Frontier	312-334-8638 (IL)
Forum BBS	215-722-1482 (PA)
Fountains of Pleasure	313-348-7854 (MI)
Harbor Bytes	410-235-6753 (MD)
Heartland BBS	614-772-7669 (OH)
Images At Twilight	519-649-2672 (ON)
Inferno	609-886-6818 (NJ)

Lifestyles	516-698-5390 (NY)
The Love Connection	317-236-6740 (IN)
LuvCat's Lair	215-467-7407 (PA)
Montreal's Electronic Dungeon	514-522-3866 (PQ)
Night Life	614-876-2116 (OH)
Pain & Pleasure	518-785-6643 (NY)
The Pig Pen	613-723-3143 (ON)
Pleasure Dome	804-490-5878 (VA)
Pleasure Net (great windows graphic software)	203-831-0547 (CT)
Plumber's Helper	601-832-5132 (MS)
The Power Exchange (through Telnet/FTP/WWW: tpe.ncm.com OR tpe.ds.ncm.com)	703-749-9150 (VA)
Titan	904-476-1270 (FL)

Central Time Zone or Mountain Time Zone

Denver Exchange	303-623-4965 (CO)
The Farmer's Daughter	414-728-4058 (WI)
Garbage Dump BBS	505-294-5675 (NM)
Intimate Mansion	708-934-3045 (IL)
Laura's Lair	417-683-5534 (MO)
Mirrored Dragon's Dream	402-734-2073 (NE)
OmniVersity Online (through Telnet: Omnikc.com)	816-753-8700 (MO)
Pizazz	816-468-6900 (MO)
Specific Solutions	713-568-8482 (TX)
T&B	414-253-0454 (WI)
Throbnet	314-327-5878 (MO)
2/3 Board	217-877-1138 (IL)

Pacific Time Zone

Angel's Heart	714-434-7948 (CA)	Hedonism	310-631-7697 (CA)
Backdoor	415-756-6238 (CA)	North Keep	503-289-4872 (OR)
Boothill	213-962-7436 (CA)	PBW Annex	619-294-5888 (CA)
Chemin De Guerre	619-528-8842 (CA)	Plain Brown Wrapper	619-294-6592 (CA)
The Chateau	714-455-2790 (CA)	Rapture	707-573-9438 (CA)
Common Bonds	415-234-3518 (CA)	Scheherazade	206-650-1469 (WA)
D&S Liaison	415-485-1384 (CA)	Shadowplay	206-706-8764 (WA)
Der Baron's Schloss	206-324-2121 (WA)	(through Telnet/FTP/WWW: shadowplay.com)	
Enigma Variation	714-751-5309 (CA)	Sir Dep's Dungeon	714-740-1130 (CA)
The Great Escape	310-676-3534 (CA)	SM Board	818-508-6796 (CA)
Heels of Domination	714-832-1566 (CA)	The Wee Cabin	619-552-0449 (CA)

In addition to the private BBSs mentioned above, the large BBS systems like America On Line, Compuserve, Delphi, and GEnie all have BDSM sections.

Internet

The Internet IRC, Internet Relay Chat, has a standing SM conference that you access by entering #bdsm when selecting a chat area, Bdsm is always open. Also on the Internet are several newsgroups (message bases) related to SM. The biggest one is alt.sex.bondage (asb), which boasts about 400,000 readers. Asb people all over the country (even abroad) hold informal meetings regularly and several local asb groups host parties, as well. Alt.sex.bondage is not the only SM oriented newsgroup,though, you might want to check out these others, too: alt.personals.bondage, alt.fetish, alt.sex.spanking, alt.personals.spanking, alt.sex.femdom, alt.sex.fetish.tickling, alt.sex.services, alt.sex.fetish.fashion, and alt.fetish.feet.

BBS echos

Some groups offer message bases welcoming participation from the public or from BBSs with similar BBS software. These message bases are called "echos". BBSs can subscribe to these echos by writing to the group and requesting access.

CatNet offers various echos about sexuality. Their SM echo is called CT_SM_BD. You can obtain information pertaining to access to CatNet by writing to:

AUSTRALIA OPAL HOUSE INC.
FAKES INC.
Bianca Thomas, Pres.
6246-H2 S.Congress Ave.
Lantana, FL 33462

There are many adult echos designed to be accessed by BBSs using The Major BBS software. One of the echos is an an SM echo called ML@ADULTS.EXTREMES. To access these echos from a Major BBS your BBS needs a $150 piece of software called Mail Link from Sirius Software. For information write to:

Sirius Software
1049 Cardiff
Casper, WY 82609
307-237-0065

Appendix C: Stores, Suppliers, and Artisans

UNITED STATES
Tandy Leather
(stores nationwide)
(817) 551-9600
Catalog of leather, tools and books on leathercraft

ARIZONA
JK Perfect Personal Products
P.O. Box 13384
Scottsdale AZ 85267-3384
Rubber sheeting sold in bulk

Master Leathers
PO Box 36091
Tucson AZ 85740 (602) 744-4131
Mail order: Custom/classic leather designs for women. $7.00 for catalog

CALIFORNIA
Anonymous Leather & Mfg., Ltd.
519 Castro St. #38
San Francosco, CA 94114
415-431-4555
anon@best.com
http://www.anonlthr.com
custom leather, excellent whips, chain maille

A Taste of Leather
336 6th St.
San Francisco CA 94103
Catalog - Leather, SM toys, magazines, custom work

Adashi
1878 W. 11th St. #122
Tracy CA 95376
(800) 832-2744
Fax: (209) 836-0169
Dungeon equipment in stainless steel, custom fabrication, lubricant-safe nylon slings and suspension devices, chastity belts, wholesale/retail

Astral Ocean Cinema
Box 931753
Hollywood CA 90093
Fax: (818) 886-0017
Large catalog of videos, also toys, novelties, books, posters, comics, photo sets, fashions, fetish wear and more

B. R. Creations
P.O. Box 4201
Mountain View CA 94040 (415) 961-5354
Catalog - Custom fitted corsets, perhaps the best name in the business

Backdrop Club
PO Box 426170
San Francisco CA 94142-6170
(415) 552-6000
(415) 431-8167
B/D club, educational/social events, publishes, sells bondage equipment and lingerie, photo developing & custom photo, art.

Black On Black Leathers
P.O. Box 1485
El Cajon CA 92022
(619) 442-6614

Blowfish
2261 Market Street, #264
San Francisco CA 94114
(415) 864-0880
Fax: (415) 864-1858
Very extensive line of audios, books, magazines, CD's, fetish fashions & equipment, jewelry, laser discs, and videos. Catalog available.

Bon-Vue Enterprises
901 W. Victoria, Unit G
Compton CA 90220 (800) 827-3787
Fax: (213) 631-0415
Excellent collection of BDSM and spanking videos, also; bondage art portfolios,
books, photo sets, and magazines.

Bullock Leather and Accessories
7985 Santa Monica Blvd.
West Hollywood CA 90046
(213) 665-5343
"Leather for Leathermen" 'nuff said!

Butler's Uniforms
345 9th Street
San Francisco CA 94103
(415) 863-8119
police uniforms and gear

California Stan's
7505 Foothill
Tujunga CA 91042
(818) 352-8735
Leather, lingerie, SM toys, adult toys, novelties, videos, CD ROMs

Catherine Coatney
P.O. Box 194492
180 Steuart Street
San Francisco CA 94119-4492
Catalog - Plastic scene wear

Centurian/Spartacus
13331 Garden Grove
Garden Grove CA 92643
(714) 971-1113

"The largest fetish dealer in the world" has catalogs of "over 10,000 items" for all fetishes.

Crypto Technologies Corp.
3132 Jefferson Street
San Diego CA 92110
(800) 331-0442
Mfg. and retailers (The Crypt) of SM gear, toys, books, magazines and leather, owns 8 stores

The Crypt on Washington
1515 Washington
San Diego CA 92103
(619) 692-9499

The Crypt
North Park Adult Video
4094 30th Street
San Diago, CA 92104

The Crypt
1712 E. Broadway
Long Beach CA 90802
(310) 983-6560

The Crypt at Wolf's S.D.
3404 30th Street
San Diago, CA 92102
(619) 574-1579

The Crypt at Wolf's, L.B.
2020 E. Artesia
Long Beach CA 90805
(310) 984-9474

Dark Garden
2215-R Market St.
Box 242N
San Francisco CA 94114
(415) 522-9651
Catalog - period corsets, in satin, brocade, leather, patent, silk

Draconian Leather by Metz
2325 Chester Lane #A
Bakersfield CA 93304
(805) 631-8760
Free Brochure - Some of the finest handcrafted whips available.

Eastern Currents
3040 Childer Lane
Santa Cruz CA 95062 (800) 946-9264
Needles & accupuncture supplies

Erotec
6928 Shadygrove St.
Tujunga CA 91042
(818) 352-4344
Specialty toys including violet wands, erotic sculpture, SM toys

Especially For Me
113 N. First Ave.
Upland CA 91786
(800) 946-4204
Fax: (909)946-5500
Mail order: caters to crossdressers
and adult baby fetishist

Fantasy Lingerie
16112 Harbor Blvd.
Fountain Valley CA 92708
(714) 775-8356
SM toys, large bondage selection,
lingerie, leather, latex,boots and
shoes, a Centurian store.

Fashion World International
P.O. Box 277506
Sacramento CA 95827
(916) 631-8777
(916) 631-9339 Fax
Bob   Holt   Internet:
bobh@fashion.win.net, bbs:(916)
985-3307 - Corsets, lingerie, latex,
boots, PVC, sissy maid clothes

Fit To Be Tied
222 Main Street
Suite D
Seal Beach CA 90740
(310) 597-1234
Latex clothing

Flash Productions
Box 410052
San Francisco CA 94141
Fetish videos and photos.

Frederick's of Hollywood
Box 229
Hollywood CA 90C99-0164
(818) 993-3988
Lingerie, slutwear

Gauntlet
8720 Santa Monica Blvd.
Los Angeles CA 94101
Piercing and piercing supplies,
body modification magazines,
videos, instructional materials

Gauntlet
2377 Market St.
San Francisco CA 94114
(415) 431-3133
Body piercing jewelry and services

Gravity Plus
P.O. Box 2182
LaJolla CA 92038
(800) 383-8056
Gravity boots and inversion tables

Heartwood Whips of Passion
412 N. Coast Hwy. #210
Laguna Beach CA 92651
(714) 376-9558
One of the finest crafters of

floggers and cats in the business -
sell your family heirlooms, if you
must, to buy these, you'll not
regret it!

Heartwood Corsets of Desire
412 N. Coast Hwy. #210
Laguna Beach CA 92651
(714) 376-9558
Full torso corsets, custom made to
client specifications. We haven't
seen these, but if her whips are
any indication, the quality is
bound (no pun intended) to be
superb.

Image Leather
2199 Market St.
San Francisco CA 94114
(415) 621-7551
Custom leather and adult toys

Iron Line
4001 San Leandro St, #30
Oakland, CA 94601
510-436-0662
Blacksmithing, collars, manacles

JT Toys
4649 1/2 Russell Ave.
Los Angeles CA 90027
(800) 755-8697
(213) 666-2121
(213) 913-5976 fax
tucker@oxy.edu internet
Catalog - Leather, sex toys, videos
and SM gear

Lashes by Sarah
415-621-6048
Excellent whips and floggers

Leather   for   Lovers   (Voyages
catalog)
PO Box 77101
San Francisco CA 94107
(415) 495-4932
(415) 495-5109
Mail order: leather and chain wear,
devices and restraints, catalogs
available.

Leather Masters
969 Park Ave.
San Jose CA 95126
(408) 293-7660
(408) 293-7685
All kinds of fetish toys, novelties
and fashions, catalog available

Leather, Etc.
1201 Folsom St.
San Francisco CA 94103
(415) 864-7558
(415) 864-7559
Manufacturers of leather, clothes,
lingerie, and latex fetish wear.

Leda Productions
PO Box 632
San marcos CA 92079
(909) 763-4556
Mfg. & dist. specializing in
Fem-Dom and spanking videos

Ledermeisters, Inc.
4470-107 Sunset Blvd.
Los Angeles CA 90027
(213) 664-6422
Mail order: Male oriented bondage
gear, books

The Love Table
1023 University Ave.
San Diego CA 92103
(619) 465-5566
Mfg. of "The best fuckin' table ever"

Lyndon Distributors Limited
15756 Arminta Street
Van   Nuys   CA   91406   (818)
988-0228

Mark I. Chester
P.O. Box 422501
San Francisco CA 94142
(415) 621-6294

Mind Candy Emporium
P. O. Box 931437
Cherokee Ave.
Hollywood CA 90093
Catalog - rubber, PVC and leather
clothing

Monique of Hollywood
P.O. Box 85151
Los Angeles CA 90072
Lingerie, heels, boots, books,
magazines, videos

Mr S Leather Co. & Fetters USA
310 7th St.
San Francisco CA 94103
also:
Mr S-2
4202 18th Street
San Fransisco CA
(415) 863-7764 (voice)
(800) 746-7677 (orders)
(415) 863-7798 (fax)
Catalog - SM toys and bondage
gear, incredible variety and a great
reputation

New Twist, Inc.
520 Washington Blvd.
Marina Del Rey CA 90292
(310) 645-1069
(310) 645-3949
Mfg. & dist. of women only
bondage videos

Noelle Nielson Software
P.O. Box 69826
Los Angeles CA 90069

Spandex bondage clothes, body suits, sleep sacks, hoods, and other stretchy innovations

Nu-West Productions
PO Box 1239
San Marcos CA 92079
(619) 630-9979
Mfg. & dist. of female submissive & spanking videos

Passion Flower
4 Yosemite Ave.
Oakland CA 94611
(510) 601-7750
(510) 658-9645 Fax
SM & other sex toys, leather, ligerie, books, magazines, videos, jewelry, music, etc. Female oriented store and mail order.

Platinum Video
4501 Van Nuys Blvd.
Sherman Oaks CA 91403
(818) 503-0280
Mfg. of fetish videos & magazines, 150 titles, also sells equipment

Playmates
6438 Hollywood Blvd.
Hollywood CA 90028
(213) 464-7636
Lingerie, erotic fashions, PVC, latex, some SM toys

QSM (Quality SM)
PO Box 880154
San Francisco CA 94188
(800) 537-5815
qsm@crl.com
One of the largest SM and alternate sexuality literature sellers, also holds SM classes.

Raelyn Gallina
P.O. Box 20034
Oakland CA 94620
(510) 655-2855
Piercer and makes piercing jewelry.

Redboard Video
PO Box 2069
San Francisco CA 94126
(415) 296-8712
(415) 362-1141 Fax
Spanking, Bondage, Fem-Dom & shaving videos, catalog available

Rob of San Francisco
22 Shotwell
San Francisco CA 94103
(415) 252-1198
Catalog - SM toys and leathers

Romantasy
199 Moulton St.
San Francisco CA 94123
(800) 922-2281

(415) 673-3137
Sensual art and accessories for romantics, art, books, PVC, lingerie, Victorian corsets, jewelry, toys, soft-core videos, catalog.

SAM Co.
C/O Bill & Debby Majors Enterprises
P.O. Box 92889
Long Beach CA 90809-9988
Custom leather work

Sarah's Bare Necessities
1909 Salvio St.
Concord CA 94103
(510) 680-8445
Leather, SM toys, lingerie, swim wear, sexy outerwear for men and women, books, mags, hosiery, etc.

Sarodz
P.O. Box 10692
Oakland CA 94610
Catalog - SM toys, whips, synthetic canes, and bondage gear

Seraglio
273 Milton Ave. (mail only)
San Bruno, CA USA 94066
Phone: (415) 952-6235
Email: wander@hooked.net
High-end custom made leather restraints and fetish clothing, specializing in unique corsets.

Sportsheets
PO Box 7800
Huntington Beach CA 92646
(714) 962-8946
Mfg. of the popular velcro bondage sheets. Complete versatility in positioning and secure, but easily escapable. Fun!

Stormy Leather
1158 Howard St.
San Francisco CA 94103
(415) 626-6783 - office
(415) 626-1672 - store
Excellent leather and SM toy boutique, leather latex, shoes & boots, bondage & SM toys, books and mags

Syren
7225 Beverley Boulevard
Los Angeles CA 90036
(213) 936-6693
Rubber designs by Andy Wilkes (made Catwoman's outfit)

The Leather Maker
5720 Melrose Ave.
Los Angles CA 90038 (213) 461-1095

The Pleasure Chest

7733 Santa Monica
Santa Monica CA
(213) 650-1022
(800) 75-DILDO
Catalog - One of the world's largest collections of adult sex toys

The Source Leather Shop
P.O. Box 1069
Forestville CA 95436

Versatile Fashions
PO Box 1051
Tustin CA 92681
(714) 538-6498
(714) 538-7950
Mfg. of B&D & fetish equipment, fashions & accessories. Also sells videos, 14 catalogs available.

Voyages
Post Office Box 78550
Department 903
San Francisco CA 94107-8550
(415) 495-4937 (service)
(415) 896-0706 (orders)
(415) 896-0933 (fax)
Hot fashions in spandex and satin

Wayne's LeatheRack
4216 Melrose Ave.
Hollywood CA
(818) 891-4228
Leathers, SM toys and custom clothing (located in Griff's leather bar)

Xandria Leather Collection
PO Box 31039
San Francisco CA 94131
(415) 468-3812
(415) 468-3805 Fax
Mail order: Fetish fashions and accessories

COLORADO
The Crypt
131 Broadway
Denver, CO 80203
(303) 733-3112
Large selection of SM toys, leather, books, and videos

The Crypt Entertainment Center
139 Broadway
Denver CO 80203
(303) 778-6584
SM toys, books, magazines, videos and leather

Dreams and Desires
1956 Wabash St.
Denver CO 80220
(303) 329-0778
Lingerie, leather, lotions and adult toys

Imi jimi

609 East 13th Ave.
Denver CO 80203
(303) 832-1823
Sensual leather

Kitty's East
735 East Colfax Ave.
Denver CO 80203 (303) 832-5155
SM toys, leather, adult toys

Leather and Lace
2028 E. Colfax Ave.
Denver CO 80206
(303) 333-4870
(800) 441-4695
Fax: (303) 333-8141
Lingerie, leather, PVC & shoes.
catalogs

UZI
508 Colfax
Denver CO 80203
Fetish rubber clothing and
bondage gear

Zip-Up Leathers
19 East Bayaud Ave.
Denver CO 80209
(303) 733-7442
(303) 863-9233
Creates erotic leather apparel.
Custom work available at the
Denver retail store, catalog

CONNECTICUT
Beth Tyler Labs
Box 2551
Hartford CT 06146-2551
Fax: (203) 871-0293
Interests are enemas, spanking
and bondage. Videos and
equipment, also will shoot custom
videos and photo sets.

Fantasy Isle
2 Mill Ridge Road
Danbury CT 06811 (203) 743-1792
Adult & SM books, mags, adult
toys, SM toys and furniture

Jim Young - Leather Creations
P.O. Box 2212
Hartford CT 06145, E-mail:
75730,3031@compuserve.com
Catalog - Leather gear and custom
designs

Lacy Lady
530 Kings Highway Cutoff
Fairfield CT 06430
(203) 259-7399
Lingerie, leather, SM and adult
toys, books

The Leather Harvest
1165 Main Streeet
East Hartford, CT 06108
(860) 290-8981

SM toys, books and leather.
Male-order Leather
P. O. Box 787
Danbury CT 06813
Bondage gear by Laura Goodwin
(founder of CT Leatherfolk)

Posey Company Northeast
Thomas S. Haley Assoc. Inc.
P.O. Box 8097
Berlin CT 06037
(800) 243-0627
(203) 828-0547
Medical restraints

Rena's Ultra Boutique
76 Bank Street
Seymore CT
(800) 828-7362
Specialists in TV fashions and
accessories, but have a wide
selection of lingerie, bondage,
leather, SM and adult toys also.

Silk Stockings
68 Sugar Hollow Rd.
Danbury CT 06810
(203) 778-5511
Lingerie, leather, SM & adult toys,
videos

Strangeblades & More
286 Broad St.
P. O. Box 154
Manchester CT 06040
(203) 645-9394
E-mail: Sblades@aol.com
Chainmail, custom leather and
metalwork, knives, and jewelry

The Water Hole
982 Main Street
East Hartford, CT 06108-2220
800-390-6674/860-528-6195
fax:860-528-3025
brandrog@netcom.com
Custom leather & SM gear

FLORIDA
Lady C. Leather at
Christine's Lingerie
11124 N. 30th St.
Tampa FL 33612 (813) 979-0154
Leather and lace lingerie, SM toys,
magazines, videos. lingerie catalog

Eurotique
3109 45th Street
West Palm Beach FL 33407
(561) 684-2302
(561) 684-2877
SM toys; lather, rubber & PVC
clothes; and books.

Exotique
Northwest Plaza
4023 W. Waters Avenue
Tampa FL 33614

(813) 889-9447
Catalog - Leather, rubber, toys,
and SM gear

Fallen Angel
3045 N. Federal Hwy
Store 98 Coral Center
Fort Lauderdale FL 33301
(305) 563-5230
10-5 Monday, Catalog - SM toys,
leather, and gear

Fantasy Island Innovations, Inc.
1304 SW 160th Ave.
Sunrise FL 33326
(800) 785-9955
Mail order: Leatherwear, SM toys,
books, novelties

French Addiction
819 West University Ave.
Gainsville FL 32601
Lingerie

Leather Master
418-A Appelrouth Lane
Key West FL 33040
(305) 292-5051
Mostly leather toys w/onsite
leather workshop, but also sells
rubber toys, erotic cards,
magazines & SM books.

Outrageous Creations
PO Box 1608
Orlando FL 32802
(407) 898-5897
Leather and rubber floggers, straps
and paddles, hoods, harnesses,
restraints and bondage equipment,
and custom leather, lovely work!

Shadowfax Leathercraft
P.O. Box 10451
Sarasota FL 34278-0451
E-mail: mshadowfax@aol.com
SM & bondage gear. Master
Shadowfax does custom work

Silk & Lace
8466 N. Lockwood Ridge
Sarasota FL 34327
Lingerie, SM & fetish toys, adult
toys, erotic fashions, private
modeling services, also sells
through BBS. 10 stores in Florida

Silk & Lace
1910, Suite A1, Courtney
Fort Meyers FL 33903
(813) 275-6066 (se above)

Silver Anchor Enterprises, Inc.
PO Box 760
Crystal Springs FL 33524-0760
(800) 848-7464
(813) 788-0147
Fax: (813) 782-0180

Body jewelry (pierced) catalog

Tender Moments
4635-3 Coronado Pkwy.
Cape Coral, FL 33904
(941) 945-1448
SM toys and books

The Leather Closet
496 Orange Blossom Trail
Orlando FL (407) 649-2011
Leathers, toys and SM gear

GEORGIA
Blast Off Video
1133 Euclid Avenue NE
Atlanta GA
(404) 681-0650
Kinky and cult videos

Brushstrokes
1510 Piedmont Avenue NE
Atlanta GA
(404) 876-6567
Gay bookstore with a small
selection of SM books, and toys

Elegant Trash
3180 Roswell Road
Atlanta GA
(404) 233-3877
(404) 336-0358 for appointment
fetish clothing & custom toys

Lalapalooza
6624 Dawson Blvd.
Norcross GA (404) 378-6558
Fetish clothes and gear

LifeStyle Leather and Wood
156 Piedmont Avenue
Braselton GA 30517
(706) 654-2702
whips, collars, wood paddles, cuffs,
clamps

Midnight Blue
394-D Cleveland Avenue
Atlanta GA
(404) 766-6288
Lingerie and leather

Mohawk Leather
308 Ponce De Leon Ave. NE
Atlanta GA
(404) 874-4732
Leather goods and toys located in
The Eagle, a gay leather bar

Nine and a Half Weeks
1023 W. Peachtree Street NE
Atlanta, GA
Large selection of fetish gear

Pegasus Leatherworks
PO Box 670191
Marietta GA 30066
Mail order - creative whips

The Leather Post / Taz Men
842 N. Highland Ave. NE
Atlanta GA
(404) 873-5080
Leathers & SM toys, custom work

The Pleasure Zone
1329 Brocket Road
Clarkston GA
(404) 414-1137
XTC leather, toys, lingerie

Warlords
2165 Cheshire Bridge Rd.
Atlanta GA 30324
(404) 315-9000
Sensuous leather

HAWAII
Submission
1667 Kapiolani Blvd.
Honolulu HI 96814
(808) 942-0670
Rubber, leather, PVC, erotic
fashions, SM toys - Also houses a
piercing studio, "Paragon", Body
Piercing by Gus (808) 949-2800

IOWA
Amazon Drygoods
Dept. H-6
2218 East 11th St.
Davenport IA 52803
(319) 322-6800
Catalog - corsets, historical
reproduction clothing & patterns

ILLINOIS
Abco Research Associates
PO Box 354
Monticello, IL 61856-0354
(800) 253-6135
Makers of the sybian.

C.A.T.
P.O. Box 25842
Chicago, IL 60625-0842
Corsets and dungeon furniture

Cupid's Treasures
3519 North Halsted
Chicago, IL 60657
Adult & fetish boutique

Dressed to Kill
3635 North Broadway
Chicago IL 60613
(312) 248-1860
fetish fashions

Erotic Warehouse
1246 W. Randolph
Chicago IL 60607
(312) 226-5222
SM & adult toys, books, videos

Fantasy Fashions by Suzette
PO Box 910
Westmont IL 60559
Pierceless nipple jewelry, SM fetish
clothing

House Of Whacks
1800 West Cornelia
Chicago IL 60657
(312) 761-6969
Leather, lateex toyys & clothing

Joe Wheeler
858 West Armitage
P.O. Box 104
Chicago IL 60614
(312) 835-3468
Mr Wheeler was apprenticed to
David Morgan. He makes gorgeous
kangaroo skin single-lash signal
whips & other whips with amazing
quality at reasonable prices.

JuRonCo
P.O. BOX 5992
Peoria IL 61601
(309) 673-8724
cf542@cleveland.Freenet.Edu
Posey & Humane Restaints
cuffs, straight jackets, etc.

The Leather Rose Gallery
1800 West Cornelia St., Ste 111
Chicago IL 60657
(312) 665-2069
An all-in-one SM boutique, with a
lovely variety of SM toys, literature
and paraphernalia, also has The
Leather Rose BBS (312) 665-0111.

Male Hide Leathers
2816 N. Lincoln
Chicago IL 60657
Leather, rubber, boots, custom

Paul C. Leather
Post Office Box 285
Prospect Heights IL 60070 (312)
508-0848
Molly loves her Paul C corset.
Gorgeous leather corsets and fetish
clothing at good prices

Px3
P.O. Box 388361
Chicago, IL 60638
312-854-6172
Leather Equipment & Apparel

S&L Sales Company
2208 N. Clybourn Ave.
Chicago IL 60614
Fax: (708) 963-2268
Mail order: Resources, services &
products for alternative lifestylers,
publisher of Wild Times

Silver Smoke
156-A East Lake Street #101
Bloomingdale, IL 60108
SM toys, wood paddles

INDIANA
Naughty, But Nice
104 W. US Highway 30
Michigan City IN 46360
(219) 879-6363
Lingerie, fetish wear

KENTUCKY
D.A.B.
1501 S. 7th Street
Louisville, KY
Toys, books, videos, piercing
supplies, leather, and lingerie

Gall's Inc.
2680 Palumbo Drive
PO Box 54308
Lexington KY 40555-4658
(800) 477-7766
Catalog - Police and Public Safety
Equipment supplier; handcuffs,
climbing harnesses, bandages,
restraints; not SM-friendly.

The Leatherhead Shop
1601 Bardstown Rd.
Louisville, KY
Leathers

Sun, Leather and Lace
1501 1/2 S. 7th Street
Louisville KY
(502) 634-4705

LOUISIANA
All That Jazz
419 Bourbon St.
New Orleans LA 70130
(504) 522-5657
SM and adult toys, equipment,
fashions, books and mags.

Gay Mart
808 N. Rampart St.
New Orleans LA 70116
(504) 523-5876
An adult & SM shop with male
emphasis, dungeon facilities
available for private sessions

Panda Bear
415 Bourbon St.
New Orleans LA 70130
(504) 529-3953
SM and adult shop - good selection
of toys, equipment and fashions

Rings of Desire, Inc.
1128 Decatur St.
New Orleans LA 70116
(504) 524-6147
A beautifully appointed piercing
studio run by Master Piercer,

Elayne 'Angel' Binnie, peaceful
atmosphere, good people, wide
selection of jewelry

Second Skin Leather
521 Rue Saint Philip
New Orleans LA 70116
(504) 561-8167
Excellent SM store, mfgs. own
leather goods, very creative
designs, also wholesales products

MARYLAND
Firefly
3714 Eastern Ave.
Baltimore MD
(410) 732-1232
Leather and lingerie

Indecent Exposure
14631 Baltimore Avenue
Laurel MD 20707
(301) 725-5683
Lingerie, video, and SM toys

"Leather Bob"
Bob Grimes
P.O. Box 937
Rockville, MD 20848
(301) 816-3251
leather craftmen

The Leather Underground
136 West Reed St.
Baltimore MD
(301) 528 0991
Leather gear, clothes

Montague Custom Leather
8954 River Island
Savage MD 20763
(301) 498-3398

Naughty Victorian
2315-B Forest Drive #68
Annapolis MD 21401
(410) 626-1879
Mail order: Traditional Victorian
spanking implements, art and
literature. $5.00 for catalog

The Sandcrafter
PO Box 70013
Baltimore, MD 21237
410-574-2898
Leather crafts, knives

Stocks & Bonds
P.O.Box 3592
Baltimore MD 21214
(410) 426-8158
Dungeon furnishings

MASSACHUSETTS
Bound to Please
P.O. Box 353
Marston Mills, MA 02648

Restraints, whips, and bondage
furniture.

Diversified Services
Box 35737
Brighton MA 02135
Mail order: SM equipment and
related books, supplies and other
products. The owner authored the
book, The Loving Dominant.

Dragon's Design
P.O. Box 976
Byfield, MA 01922
Craftsmen of toys and furniture

Eros Boutique
581a Tremont Street
Boston, MA 02118
(617) 425-0345
Large selection of Sm toys, fetish
clothing, books

Grand Opening
318 Harvard St. Suite 32
Arcade Building, Coolidge Corner
Brookline MA
(617) 731-2626
A women's fetish and sex shop with
a great attitude, one of our
favorites! They have a dildo
collection in an array of colors and
styles that would make John
Holmes would hang his head in
shame.

Hideous Garb
(617) 338-4254
Craftsman, chain mail

Hubba Hubba
932 Mass Ave.
Cambridge MA 02139
(617) 492-9082
One of Philip's favorite SM stores,
leather, toys, clothes, shoes, etc.

Leather by Danny
Internet: LBD@tiac.net
Nicely designed suspension cuffs
and other leather toys.

LJ Productions
1212 Boylston Street #192
Chestnut Hill, MA 02167
(508) 655-0337
Videos, Paddles and SM art.

Marquis De Sade Emporium
73 Berkeley Street
Boston MA 02116
(617) 426-2120
Leather and SM toys

Subtle Signs by Suki
P.O. Box 441661
Boston, MA
Sterling silver and crystal jewelry

Toys of Eros
205 Commercial St.
Provincetown MA 02657
(508) 487-4434
(508 487-4435 Fax

Vernon's
386-BA Moody St.
Waltham MA
(617) 894-1744
Catalog - Lingerie and SM toys

MICHIGAN
Noir Leather
415 S. Main Street
Royal Oak MI 48067
(313) 541-3979
Excellent selection of SM toys and
leather fashions

NEVADA
Erotica Plus
4029 W. Sahara
Las Vegas NV 89102
(702) 362-0079
Lingerie, leather, lace, custom
outfits, dancers' costumes, body
jewelry

Paradise Electro Stimulations
3172 N. Rainbow Blvd. Suite 325
Las Vegas NV 89108
(707) 656-9641
The PES is a toy that is an amazing
substitute for vibrators, uses
electric stimulation of muscles and
wears your lover to a frazzle. Many
attachments available including
cock rings, dildoes and anal plugs.

Unique Creations
3868 Pennwood #13
Las Vegas NV 89102
(702) 365-1818
Leather and fetish wear, dungeon
equipment, hardware, restraints

NEW JERSEY
Aristoc
PO box 9133
Lyndhurst NJ 07071
(201) 933-5151
Imports footwear, hosiery, leather,
rubber, and PVC

Constance Enterprises
P.O. Box 43079
Upper Montclair NJ 07043
(201) 746-4200
Catalog - Wide range of SM &
Fetish books, magazines and toys

Dark Alley
P.O. Box 693
Franklin, NJ 07416
(201) 209-8206
Clothing, SM gear and videos

Dressing For Pleasure Showroom
590 Valley Road
Upper Montclair NJ 07043
(201) 746-5466
Retail store for Constance
Enterprises, has a wide selection of
the finest quality leathers, latex,
shoes, boots, SM toys, fantasy
accessories, and a fine art gallery.
The Nieman-Marcus of SM stores.

Leather and Lust
424 Roselle St.
Linden NJ 07036
(908) 925-7110
Fetish & erotic clothing, spandex,
leather, PVC, lingerie, whips and
chains, bridal gowns and high
fashion hosiery (including large
sizes), and more.

P.S. I Love You
264 Highway 35
Eatontown NJ 07724
(908) 935-9192
Lingerie, dancers' costumes, SM
toys & books

Maspien Armors
67 Prentice Ave.
South River, NJ 08882
(908) 257-4890
(908) 254-6362
Leather and chain armor, their
terrific "bearclaws" with workable
claws still permit handling of
whips.

Pleasurable Piercings
417 Lafayette Ave.
Hawthorne NJ 07506
(201) 238-0305
Piercing Studio and body jewelry
suppliers

Pleasure Productions
PO Box 458
Tennent NJ 07763
(800) 999-2483
(908) 308-1777
Dungeon Video International
videos, fetish & BDSM, and others,
catalog

Serious Sex
P.O. Box 1048
Maywood NJ 07607-7048
(201) 843-3941
Leather, PVC, SM Toys

Tim Swig Associates Group
Box 234
Stone Harbor NJ 08247
(609) 368-2482
Distributor for Posey and Humane
Restraints

X TEXT
PO Box 164
Monmouth Beach NJ 07750
(908) 870-0495
X TEXT@aol.com
Luxurious custom embroidered
silk velvet & silk blindfolds,
gags & restraints

NEW MEXICO
The Leather Shoppe
4217 Central, NE
Albuquerque NM 87107
(505) 266-6690
Leather, SM bondage gear, adult
toys & novelties

Original Sweater Bumpers by RC
PO Box 1854
Los Lunas NM 87031-1854
(505) 865-1488
Mfg. of fitted rings in stirling silver
and 14k gold that encircle the
nipples, sized to fit.

NEW YORK
Adams Sensual Whips and Gillian's
Toys
c/o The Utopian Network
P.O. Box 1146
New York NY 10156
(212) 686-5248 or
(516) 842-1711 (workshop)
Beautifully crafted whips and toys
in a startling array of designs from
very light to very, very heavy play.
Philip owns several pieces of
equipment by Adam and Gillian
and would happily sell his children
into slavery to buy more. A&G also
make some lovely & unique torture
toys including the popular Black
Suckerfish, call for their catalog.

Bizarre Video
20-40 Jay Street
Brooklyn NY 11201
(718) 626-8031
Fetish videos

Body Worship
112 East 7th Street
New York NY 10019
(212) 614-0124
Leather and fetish fashions

Come Again
353 East 53rd Street
New York NY 10022
(212) 308-9394
Catalog - Store is jammed with
leathers, lingerie, corsets, videos,
and the most complete book
collection we have ever seen

Enelra Lingerie
48 1/2 E. 7th. St.
New York NY 10003

Eve's Garden
119 West 57th St.
Suite 420
New York NY 10019
(800) 848-3837
A neat womens's store with bondage gear, sex toys, and books

Executive Imports, Int'l.
PO Box 1839
New York NY 10116-1839
SM toys, videos, fetish manuscripts, fetish fashions

Fantasy World Products
PO Box 608
Webster NY 14580
Mail order: Cathy's cuffs

Gauntlet
144 Fifth Ave.
New York NY
(212) 229-0180
Piercing studio and jewelry

Intimate Fashions Inc.
P.O. Box 599
East Islip NY 11730
(800) 477-8552
A Fetish fashion store on Long Island

Jeffrey's Toybox
521 Fifth Avenue
Suite 1740
New York NY 10175
(212) 989-3044

KW Enterprises
89 Fifth Ave.
New York NY 10003
(212) 727-2751
Mail order: Bondage equipment, books, toys, videos, male oriented

Leather Lady
248 Rt 25A
Suite 100-I
Setauket NY 11733
Catalog - Leather, chain, and PVC fashions; standard & plus sizes

Leatherman, The
111 Christopher Street
New York NY 10014
(212) 243-5339
Huge selection of leather and SM gear, helpful, friendly staff

Lucifer's Armory
874 Broadway
P.O. Box 808
New York NY 10003

Bondage items, Sports Sheets and vampire gloves

M'Lady's Panties
Vicki Jo DeRocker
Queens, NY
718-544-1726 by appt.
Renaissance/fantasy
custom clothier & corsets

Nero Emporium, The
218 Plymouth St.
Brooklyn, NY 11201-1124
718-596-6376
leather apparel & toys/medieval fantasy wear

Pink Pussycat Boutique
349 Sixth Ave.
New York NY 10014
Leather, SM toys, and sex toys

Purple Passion
242 West 16th Street
New York NY 10011
(212) 807-0486
SM toy store

Raven Distributors
25 Franklin St.
Rochester NY 14604
(800) 724-9670
(716) 262-2265
Mail order: Satin, leather, PVC, & rubber lingerie, huge selection of nylons to sizes XXL (including nylons with seams and heel, hard to find), also SM toys, clamps restraints, fetish magazines and videos. $3.00 for catalog

Regalia
1521 State St.
Schenectady NY 12304
(518) 374-1900
Catalog - Rubber, PVC, leather fetish fashions

Rochester Custom Leathers
274 N. Goodman St.
Rochester NY 14607
(716) 442-2323

SAMCo - Home of SceneWear Originals
9728 3rd Ave. Box 514
Brooklyn NY 11209
(718) 748-7593
SM dungeon equipment and scene clothing, custom and stock, private dungeon, call for app't & directions

Savage Leather
88 Central Ave.
Albany, NY 12210
(518) 434-2324
leather and toy store, catalog available

St. Michael's Emporium
156 East 2nd Street
Suite 1
New York NY 10009
Catalog - Unique leathers, masks, collars, corsets, clothes and wonderfully made, unique leather armor

Star Maker Video
PO Box 289 Canal St.
New York NY 10013
(212) 541-6877
(212) 541-4397
Full line of bondage and fetish videos. catalog

The Cane Man
c/o George Roman
PO Box 202
Burnt Hills NY 12027
Specializing in authentic (imported) English school canes

The Noose
261 W. 19th St.
New York NY
(212) 807-1789
Catalog - Quality SM toys, leather, and custom work

Triphammer
PO Box 356
Sparkill, NY 10976
914-359-1803
Innovative, heavy duty restraint devices

Unique Quality Products, Inc.
2170 Broadway
Suite 3307
New York NY 10024
Catalog - hoods and clothes

Venus Body Arts
199 E. 4th St.
New York, NY
Piercing studio and jewelry.

Veterans Leather
Brooklyn NY
(718) 768-0300
Catalog - Leather, tools, supplies and leathercraft books

NORTH CAROLINA
Queen City Video & News
2320 Wilkinson Blvd.
Charlotte NC 28208
(704) 344-9435
Books, CD ROMs, SM & fetish toys and fashions

OHIO
Acme Leather and Toy Co.
326 E. 8th St.
Cincinnati OH 45202-2217
(513) 621-4390

(513) 621-2668
Latex fashions for men, women, TVs, SM toys, videos.

Axion Transformation Studio
11829 Detroit Avenue
Lakewood, OH 44107
TV and SM supplies

Adult Toy & Gift
1410 Market St.
Toungstown OH 44507
(216) 743-2051
SM toys, adult toys

Bedroom Whips
P.O. Box 14126
Columbus, OH 43214
(614) 470-1227
Gorgeous whips & custom work

Body Language
3291 W. 115th St.
Cleveland OH 44111
(216) 251-3330
(216) 476-3825 Fax
Store for gay/les & SM, leather and rubber goods, books, mags, videos

Chain Link Addiction
13385 Madison Avenue
Lakewood OH 44107
(216) 221-0014
Leather goods, SM toys and equipment

Chain Link Addiction
11623 Euclid Ave.
Cleveland OH 44106
(216) 421-7181

Hide Park Leather
PO Box 79355
Lakewood OH 44107-0355
Leather

Laws Leather
3016 Chatham Ave.
Cleveland OH 44113
(216) 961-0939
Leather craftsman by appointment only

VIPPS
PO Box 81508
Cleveland OH 44181
(216) 899-1326
Portable erotic swing, self-supporting frame

OKLAHOMA
Christie's Toy Box
1176 N. MacArthur
Oklahoma City OK 73127
(405) 943-3118
Adult and SM toys

OREGAN
Barry Clune
PO Box 86686
Portland OR 97286
(503) 771-6136
(503) 777-2065
Custom made bondage furniture, all designs are rustic and heavy-duty, beds a spe cialty. $1.00 for information or call.

Blue Spot, All Adult Video, The
3232 NE 82nd
Portland OR 97232
(503) 251-8944
SM toys, large fetish & SM video selections, mags, preview rooms

Exclusively Adult
1166 South A St.
Springfield OR 97477
(503) 726-6969
Videos, SM toys, adult toys, lingerie

Fantasy Leathers
PO Box 173
Springfield OR 97477
Mail order: Leather lingerie

Fresh Life Forum
PO Box 42494
Portland OR 97242
(800) 669-3941
Manufacturers of "The Love Swing" Though we haven't tried this, we highly recommend a swing or sling when "flying united."

Leather and Lace Lingerie
8327 SE Division
Portland OR 97266
(503) 774-8292
Leather, lingerie

Spartacus Leather
1002 SE 8th Ave.
Portland OR 97214
(800) 666-2604 or
(503) 224-2604
(503) 239-4681 Fax
Adult toys and leather goods

The Leatherworks
2908 SE Belmont
Portland OR 97214
(503)232-3280
Leather and SM toys

PENNSYLVANIA
Alpha Factor
Valley View Road
Box 6246
York PA 17406-0246

Both Ways
203 S. 13th St.
Philadelphia PA 19107
(215) 985-2344 or
(800) 429-7529
(215) 985-2020
Excellent SM shop, wide range of SM toys and leather creations, fetish wear, books, mags & cards

Carter Stevens Presents
Lexington Ave. PO Box 727
Pocono Summit, PA 18346
717-839-2512 fax: 717-839-2632
films/videos/SM News

Condom Kingdom
South Street
Philadelphia PA
Condoms in every size, strength, color and hue, safer sex literature, adult and SM toys.

Danny's New Adam & Eve
133 S. 13th St.
Philadelphia PA 10107
(215) 925-5041
Adult and SM toys, leather, videos, books, magazines

Infinite Body Piercing, Inc.
626 South 4th St.
Philadelphia PA 19147
(215) 923-7335
An attractive piercing studio with a unique collection of jewelry, some from Asia and Africa, several competant piercers on staff

Le Chateau Exotique
5 West Bridge Street
New Hope, PA
(215) 862-3810
Http://WWW.lechatexotique.Com
Nice variety of SM toys, books etc.

Leather Luxuries by Wm. Iserman
PO Box 313
Drexel Hill, PA 19026
610-789-8571
Jewelry & leatherwork, custom/medieval

Lesbianage
by appt.
215-382-3135
custom leather by Shawna

Cindy Mohr & Liz 'Tailor'
c/o Both Ways
203 S. 13th St.
Philadelphia PA 19107
(215) 985-2344
Leather, corsetry, custom work. Onsite expert craftswomen for Both Ways

Supergraphics
PO Box 4489
Reading PA 19606-4489
(215) 370-0666
(215) 370-0867 Fax
Mail order division of Prevue: art, books, magazines, photo sets, videos, extensive BDSM collection, $20 for 64-page catalog

The Pleasure Chest
2039 Walnut St.
Philadelphia PA
(215) 561-7480
Adult & SM toys, novelties, leather

Zaks Designs
P.O. Box 212
Indiana PA 15701
(814) 446-5319
(814) 446-5755 Fax
Costumery, spandex bondage restraints, and stocks

Zipperhead
South St.
Philadelphia PA
(215)928-1123
Large head-shop with a lot of fetish fashions, some SM toys

RHODE ISLAND
Miko
45 Weybosset Street
Proidence, ZRI 02903
(401) 421-6646
www-miko45.com
Leather clothes, SM toys, videos, books- wholesale, retail and custom work.

Sunli Specialties
221 Waterman Street
Providence, RI 02906
(401) 861-9258
Leather and rubber SM gear

SOUTH CAROLINA
Big E X-citing Emporium
4333 Fort Jackson Blvd.
Columbia SC 29205
(803) 738-3703
Art, books, erotic and fetish fashions, SM toys, mags, videos

Chaser's Magazines 'n' Mixers
3128 Two Notch Road
Columbia SC 29204
(803) 754-6672
Adult bookstore with SM toys & videos

Kim Rushing
Preferred Lovers Collection
PO Box 1-1178
Nashville TN 37224-1178
(800) 798-7261
Mail order: Toys, novelties, videos,

& restraints. catalog

TEXAS
Apollo News
2376 Austin Hwy
San Antonio TX 78218
(210) 653-3538
(210) 590-8645
Books, videos, adult & SM toys

Chain Maille Fashions
1706 Norris Dr.
Austin TX 78704-2808
(800) 729-4094
Catalog - Metal fashions and custom work

Christie's Toy Box
2614 SW Parkway
Wichita Falls TX 76308
(817) 696-1851
Books, erotic and SM fashions, SM and adult toys, videos, mags

Christie's Toy Box
3012 Alte Mere
Fort Worth TX 76116
(817) 224-8008
Books, erotic and SM fashions, SM and adult toys, videos, mags

Forbidden Fruit
512 Neches
Austin TX 78701
(512) 478-8358
SM toys, leather, latex, lingerie, body jewelry, piercer on staff, adult toys & sex accessories, gifts

Leather By Boots
711 Fairview
Houston TX 77006
(713) 526-2668
Leather, PVC & SM gear

Leather By Boots
4038 Cedar Springs Road
Dallas TX 75219
(214) 528-3865
Leather, PVC & SM gear

Shades of Grey
3928 Cedar Springs Road
Dallas TX 75219
(214) 521-4739
SM equipment and toys, books, mags

Stainless Construction Company
P.O. Box 1594
Bryan TX 77806
Male and female stainless steel chastity devices (custom only)

UTAH
Stocks and Bonds, Ltd.
PO Box 800-115
Midvale UT 84047

Complete line of bondage handcrafted equipment, custom work available, $5.00 for brochure

VIRGINIA
Fashion Fantasy
9013-A Centerville Rd (Rt.28)
Manassas VA 22110
(Z03) 330-1900
Lingerie and leather toys

Giovanna & Silverwing Dungeon Designs (GSDD)
P.O. Box 2423
Fairfax VA 22031
(703) 515-HANG
Leather Apparel, Whips, Custom-built Dungeon Equipment

Night Dreams
8381 Leesburg Pike
Tysons Corner VA
Leather

The Toy Bag
P.O. Box 490
Herndon, VA 22070
(703) 834-0757

WASHINGTON
C.C. Sadist's Lashback Leather
901 Occidental
Suite 205-C
(206) 287-1642
email:ccsadist@cortland.com
Creative leathercraftsman, custom work with leather, rubber, patent leather, and "exotic materials."

The Cramp Leather
219 Broadway E.
Seattle WA 98102
(206) 323-9245
Leather and SM toys

The Crypt
1310 Union Street
Seattle WA
(206) 325-3882
SM toys, leather, and videos

David Morgan
11812 Northcreek Parkway, N.
Suite 103
Bothell WA 98011
(206) 485-2132
Famous single-lash whip maker, Mr. Morgan is anti-SM, if he finds out you're into SM he'll hang up. Buy from his scene-friendly ex-apprentice, Joe Wheele , Chicago.

Fantasy Unlimited
102 Pike St.
Seattle WA 98101
(206) 682-0167
Large adult store, includes fetish fashions and SM toys

Giovanni & Silverwing
PO Box 2423
Fairfax, VA 22031
703-515-4264
Leather apparel, whips, custom
dungeon equipment

Lover's Package
538 Rainier S.
Renton WA 98055
(206) 271-9393
Adult shop, carries SM toys &
fetish fashions. 12 stores owned by
PeeKay, Inc.

Lover's Package
2020 S. 320th
Federal Way WA 98003
(206) 946-1061
Adult shop, carries SM toys &
fetish fashions. 12 stores owned by
PeeKay, Inc.

Lover's Package
401 SW 148th, Payless
Seattle WA 98166
(206) 246-6047
(see previous listing)

Lover's Package
221 Auburn Way N.
Auburn WA 98002
(206) 939-9393
(see previous listing)

Lover's Package
3702 S. Fife St.
Tacoma WA 98409
(206) 472-2584
(see previous listing)

Peekay, Inc.
901 West Main A
Auburn WA 98001-5222
(206) 351-5001
(206) 351-0353 Fax
Own the 12 Lover's Package stores.
Handles & distributes all adult
items.

Shomer-Tec
P.O. Box 2039
Bellingham WA 98227
(206) 733-6214
Second Generation Israeli surplus
gas masks

Slimwear of America
P.O. Box 997
Eastsound WA 98245
(206) 376-5213 or
(800) 892-4030
(206) 376-5213 (voice/fax)
Catalog - PVC fetish fashion

Toys in Babeland
711 East Pike
Seattle WA 98122

Good selection of SM toys, books,
and equipment.

WASHINGTON D. C.
Dream Dresser
1042 Wisconsin Avenue
Georgetown
Washington DC 20007
(202) 625-0373
(800) 96DREAM
(202) 625-2764
Leather wear, latex, lingerie, toys
Catalog - Dream Dresser (mail
order), PO Box 3787, Washington,
DC 20007, (202) 625-0377 Fax:
(202) 625-2761

Felise Leather
2613 P Street, NW (2nd Floor)
Washington DC
(202) 342-7163
Custom leather clothing

The Leather Rack
DuPont Circle
1723 Connecticut Avenue, NW,
2nd Floor
Washington DC 20009
(202) 797-7401
Leather, rubber, and SM toys

The Pleasure Place
1063 Wisconsin Avenue, NW
Washington DC 20007
(202) 333-8570
Novelties, adult toys, SM gear,
lingerie, spandex, and vinyl

The Pleasure Place
1710 Connecticut Avenue, NW
Washington DC 20009
(202) 483-3297
Novelties, adult toys, SM gear,
lingerie, spandex, and vinyl

Tiger Designs
1420 N Street NW, #1011
Wasgington DC 20005
(202) 232-8355
Custom-made leather and rubber
restraints and harnesses

Wicked Ways
Washington D.C.
(703) 379-4735
wways@aol.com
Leather, toys, books, also sponsers
scene events at "The Edge"

WEST VIRGINIA
Market Street News
1437 Market Street
Wheeling WV 26003
(304) 232-2414
Adult store, carries fetish fashions,
adult toys, videos, etc.

WISCONSIN

Humane Restraint
PO Box 16
Madison WI 53701-0016
(800) 356-7472
Hospital restraints and equipment

Naughty, But Nice
I-90 at Shopiere Rd.
Beloit WI
(608) 362-9090
General Adult and SM boutiques

Naughty, But Nice
7070 South 27th St.
Oak Creek WI 53154
(414) 761-9272
General Adult and SM boutiques

Naughty, But Nice
2727 S. 108th St.
West Allis WI 63227
(414) 541-7788
General Adult and SM boutiques

Naughty, But Nice
W. 10521 Tritz Road
High 33 & 9094
Portage WI 53901
(608) 742-8060
General Adult and SM boutiques

Tie Me Down
1419 E. Brady St.
Milwaukee WI
(414) 272-3696

AUSTRIA

Blzarr-Mode
Inh Heinz berger, Schopenhauer
Strasse 8
A-1180 Wien
Austria
fetish clothing

AUSTRALIA

Hellfire Emporium
51 Bourke Street
Melbourne
Australia
(61) 613-654-2456
Rubber, shoes, boots, PVC, leather,
bondage equipment, body jewelry,
SM toys, books, & mags

Jayar Leather
P.O. Box 632
Marrickville, Australia 2204
(61) 612-331-7455

Kayser Novelties
P.O. Box 6
Australia NSW 2171
(62) 612-606-0002
Catalog - manufacturs leather and
wooden bondage equipment, props
and costumes

Studio Strak
Box 4838,
GPO Melbourne 3001
Australia
(61) 03-809-2632
Rubber fashions

BELGIUM

Les Folies de Sade
28b rue Fosse'-aux-Loups
1000 Bruxelles,
Belgium
(32) 02 219 7997
Fetish fashions

Glitter
82 Galerie Cathedral
4000 Liege
Belgium
(32) 041 220472
Fetish fashions

Jaybird
60, Rue Scailquin
B-1030 Bruxelles
Belgium
(02) 219-8007
Fetish & SM Magazines, Books,
Photos, Videos, Art

Minuit
60 Galerie du Centre
1000 Brussels
Belgium
(02) 223-0914
leather, plastic, rubber, high heels

CANADA

Big Lizard Leathers
1221 Thurlow St.
Vancouver, BC V6E 1X4
Canada
(604) 685-1753
Women's leathers and custom
work

Cuir Plus (Leather Plus)
1321 Ste Catherine St. East
Montreal, Quebec, H2L 2H4
Canada
(514) 521-7587
Leather, SM toys and clothes

Discreet Boutique
317 Ellice Avenue
Winnipeg, Manitoba, R3B 1X7
Canada
Leather and fetish gear

Fantasyland
274 8th St. E.
Box 682
Owen Sound, Ontario N4K 5R4
Canada
(519) 371-1215
Catalog - Fetish PVC clothing

Il Bolero
6842 St-Hubert,
Montreal, Quebec, H2S 2M6
Canada
(514) 270-6065
Latex, leather clothing and SM
gear

JG Leathers
5324 10A Avenue
Delta, BC
Canada
Catalog - Pony girl/boy equipment
and dress, discipline & suspension
harnesses

Leather Plus
1321 Ste Catherine East
Montreal, Quebec, H2L 2H4
Canada
(514) 521-7587
Leather clothing, custom work

Mack's Leathers
1234 Granville St.
Vancouver, BC, V6Z 1M4
Canada
(604) 688-6225

Northbound Leather
19 St. Nicholas Street
Toronto, Ontario
Canada
(416) 972-1037
Catalog - Leather, latex wear, and
SM toys of high quality and solid
design

Priape
1311 Ste Catherine St. East
Montreal, Quebec
Canada
(514) 521-8451
Catalog - Books, novelties, videos,
rubber, latex, leather and SM gear

Rubbertree Rainwear
PO Box 35135
Station E
Vancouver, BC V6M 4G1
(604) 885-7701
Catalog - rubber sheets, clothing,
lingerie

Sir Steve's Leather
P.O. Box 1282
Guelph Ont N1H6N6
Canada

DENMARK

Black Universe
Studiestraede 15
DK-1445, Copenhagen K
(45) 333-23113
Fetish clothes, SM literature and
art

Conflicto
Johnstrup Alle 1
DK-1923 Frederiksberg C
Denmark
(45) 3135 0380
SM and fetish clothing and toys

Latexa
Box 28
DK-4720 Praestoe
Denmark
Rubber, leather, clothing, and
corsets

Paradis
Gl. Kongevej 95
DK-1850 Frederiksberg C.
Denmark
(45) 3112 6017
Dealing in lingerie, PVC, spandex,
leather, latex, high heels and
corsets, SM toys, books, mags

Passion
P.O. Box 936
8600 Sikeborg
Denmark
(45) 86-813370
Handmade plastic/rubber clothes

Renate Buccone
Vesterbros Torv
Vesterbrogade 51
DK-1620 Copenhagen K.
Denmark
(45) 3122 1041
Lingerie, leather, PVC, rubber
corsets, SM toys, videos

SM-Shop
Studiestraede 12
DK-1455 K¢benhavn K
Denmark
(45) 3332 3303
Leather, latex, heels, S/M toys,
magazines, books

Subwave Design
Studiestraede 21
DK-1455 Copenhagen K
Denmark
(45) 3312 1452
PVC, leather, exotic shoes

ENGLAND

Roger and Sarah Adams
31 North Rd
Brighton BNl lYB
England
beautiful stiletto heels and boots

Atom Age Unit 3A
98 Victoria Road
London NW106NB
England
fetish fashions, toys

Axford's
82 Centurion Road
Brighton, Sussex BN1 3LN
England
Catalog - corsets

Banned
2 Cross Street
London N1 2BL
England
(44 71) 704-2766
Period costumry and fantasy
clothing

Belt Up & Buckle Off
BUBO P.O. Box 593
London SW4 0HT
England
(44 71) 737-6161
Catalog - Mail order leather, rubber
and SM gear

Black Magic
451 Roman Road,
London E3 5LX
England
(44 81) 980-1365
Leather fashions

Chez l'amour
25, The Triangle
Bournemouth BH2 5SE
England
Catalog - Leather wear

Chris Anderson
England
(44 81) 293-1947
Rubber masks, suits, etc.
custom work

Clone Zone
37/39 Bloom St.
Manchester M1 3LY
England
(44 61) 236-1398
Catalog - Leather, rubber, and SM
toys in four stores

Clothes For Practioners
140c Kenington Lane, London
SE11 4UZ
(44 71) 820-9393
Vicky Watson's PVC, Spandex and
Leather fashions made to
measure

Cocoon
1st Floor,
250 Kilburn High Rd.
London NW6
England
(44 71) 624-1074
Catalog- Rubber and plastic
restrictive wear
also:
Mackintosh House, Green Street
Kidderminster SY10 1JF

England
(44) 0562-829419

Craig Morrison
CMD PO Box 2975,
London N1 0RZ
(44 71) 278-5367
(44 71) 278-9928 fax
Spiky rubber fashions and
furniture

Doc Roc
59 Camden High Street
London NW1 7JL
England
(44 71) 916-9273
Rubber wetlook fashions

E-Garbs
9 Boyce St, Brighton BN1 1AN
(44) 0273-748887
Catalog - Unique leather clothing
designs plus rubber, jewelry and
corsets

East of Eden
519/523 Cambridge Heath Rd.
London E2 9EU
England
(44 71) 251 4960
Wetlook PVC, lycra clothing

Essex Intim
393 London Rd
Hadleigh, Essex 57 2BY
England
(44) 0702 555407
rubber, leather, PVC, magazines,
books, toys

Eagle Leathers
PO Box 57
Northholt, Middlesex
UB5 4SB
England
(44 81) 426-8047
Catalog - leather, rubber and toys

Ectomorph
Unit 1,
42-44 De Veauvoir Crescent
London N1 5SB
England
(44 71) 249-6311
Catalog - High quality fashion
fashions in rubber, PU and leather

Expectations
75 Great Eastern St.
London EC2A 3HU
England
(44 71) 739-0292
mail order: (see New York listing)
Catalog - Possibly the world's
largest and most complete fetish
and SM store

Fantasy Erotique
53A Romford Road
London E15RLY
England
Leather and lingerie

The Federation
33 Heathcote St.
Hockley, Nottingham
NG1 3AG, England
(44 60) 241-3435
Catalog - leather and wetlook

Femme Fatale
84 Berwick St.
London W1V 3RE
England
(44 71) 287-4766
Women's leather, rubber, PVC,
lingerie
also:1st floor, Kensington Market
London W8
England
(44 71) 937-0768

Fun Fashions
48 Windsor St
Uxbridge, Middlesex
England
(44) 0895-271668
Catalog - plastic clothes, corsets,
high heels, rubber

Fetish Fetish
4a Peter St.
London W1 3RR
(44 71) 734-8343
Catalog - SM gear and fashion

Fetters
Unit 2B, North Block
Westminster Business Square,
Durham Street
London SE11 5JH
England
(44 171) 820-7780 voice
(44 171) 820-7790 fax
Catalog - police and medical
restraints, straight jackets,
chastity belts, hoods, many other
goodies

G and M Fashions Ltd.
P.O. Box 42
Romford, Essex RM1 2ED
England
(44 40) 238-1861
catalogs, magazines, books, videos

Get Wet
BCM Box 3564
London WC1N 3XX
England
(44 71) 627-0290
Cataog - Leather rubber, books,
magazines, toys

Harmony Too
312 London Rd.
Westcliff on Sea, Essex
England
Rubber, leather, SM toys

Hidebound
76 Seel Road
Huyton L36 6DJ
England
Catalog - Custom leather, latex
clothes and toys

Invinceable
19a Tower Workshops
Riley Rd
London SE1
(44 71) 237-4017
Men's rubber fashions, bondage
suits, hoods and gasmasks

Honour
86 Lower Marsh
Waterloo, London SE1 7AB
England
(44 71) 401-8219
catalog - fetish clothing

Invinceable
19a Tower Workshops
Riley Road
London SE1
England
(44 71) 237-4017
Catalog - rubber clothes, hoods
gas mask conversions

Jack The Rubber
PO Box 2763
London E1 7LG
(44 71) 247-0799
Catalog - Spiky subversive rubber
fashions

Janus
Old Compton Street
London, England
canes, tawses, and straps

Jay Fashions
PO Box 606
Stanford Le Hope
Essex SS17 9BE
England
Women's PVC, shoes, boots

Julian Latorre
BCM Box 8827
London WC1N 3XX
England
(44 71) 613-0024
Catalog - Rubber fashions

Kastley Petherton,
Preston New Rd.
Mellor Brook, Nr Blackburn
Lancashire BB2 7QD
England

Catalog only- rubber bondage wear

Kim West
BCM Box 8875
London WC1N 3XX
England
(44 71) 729-6960
Catalog - Latex fashions and SM
gear

Klix Leather
PO Box 5
Bury BL8 2UQ Lancashire
England
Leather clothes, bondage wear
custom work

Libidex
BCM Libidex
London WC1N 3XX
England
(44 71) 613-3329
Catalog - Rubber fetish and
bondage fashions

Libido
83 Parkway
London NW1 7PP
England
(44 71) 485-0414
Fetish/Fantasy fashions

Lifestyle
PO Box 4,
Holsworthy, Devon EX22 7YL
England
Catalog - Leather, PVC, lingerie

Loco
shop:
32 D'Arblay St.
London W1
mailorder:
20a The Broadway
Stoneleigh, Surrey
KT19 0RP, England
(44 81) 786-7347
Catalog - rubber fetish fashions

Lush
Unit 310, Clerkenwell Workshop
31 Clerkenwell Close
London EC1
England
(44 71) 253-2975
Leather corsets, basques, jackets

Maxitosh
PO Box 1377, Long Ashton
Bristol BS18 9JW
England
Lingerie and outerwear in satin
and nylon with rubber lining,
custom work

Mediquip
Follygate
Okehampton, Devon

EX20 3AQ
(44) 837-3710
Catalog - Medical equipment and
restraints

Michelle Fashions
105 Epping New Rd,
Buckhurst Hill,
Essex IG9 5TQ
England
(44 81) 504-0418
Fetish fashions and rubber

Midnight Lady
20-24 Cardigan St.
Luton LU1 1RR
(44 5) 822-2180
Catalog - wetlook and leather

Modern Armour
Unit 82, Spirella Bldgs
Bridge Road
Letchworth Herts SG6 4HD
England
(44 46) 248-3458
fetish fashions in rubber

Murray & Vern
3rd Floor,
61/63 Whitworth St.
Manchester, M1 3MY
England
(44 61) 236-7440 voice
(44 61) 228-1776 fax
Wholesale fetish fashions in latex

Obsessions
1b Coleherne Rd
London SW10
England
(44 71) 224-8220
Fetish gifts and clothing

Pagan Metal
Unit 45a, Basement,
Trocadero, Piccadilly Circus
London W1
England
(44 81) 674-1076
Catalog - fetish fashions in leather
and metal

Pam Hogg
5 Newburgh St
London W1
England
(44 71) 287-2185
Leather, PVC, lycra

Paradiso
41 Old Compton Street
London W1
England
(44 71) 287-2487
Rubber, PVC, lingerie

Pentonville Rubber Company
50 Pentonville Rd.

N1 9FG.
England
(44 71) 837-0283.
Rubber sheeting

Pussycat
123 Hammersmith Rd.
London W14
Makers of rubberwear, latexacare
for rubber, Pussycat magazine

RAGE
6 Green Dragon Court
Bridge Arcade
London Bridge, London SE1
England
(44 71) 403-4337
Catalog - Rubber fashions

Rainshine
62 Poulton Rd.
Wallasey, Merseyside LL4 9DH
England
(44 51) 639-8602
Rubber lined satin raincoats,
latex fashions, rubber video

Regulation
9-17 St. Albans Place
Islington Green,
London N1 9QH, England
(44 71) 226-0665
Catalog - Military, medical,
industrial, bondage, leather
and rubber

Religion
The Clothes Shop,
50 Park Row,
Bristol BS1 5LH
(44 27) 229-3754
Catalog - Fetish clothing and gear

Remawear
Sherwood House,
Burnley Rd.
Todmorden,
Lancs OL14 7ET
Catalog - leather and rubber
bondage and SM gear

Rgl Designs
Glenfield Park, Lomeshaye Ind.
Estate
Nelson, Lancs BB9 7DR
England
(44 28) 269-7866
Catalog - SM equipment, custom
work

Ripplesmooth
117 Icknield St.
Birmingham, B18 6RZ
England
(44 21) 236-1743
Latex rubberwear, bondage & SM
gear

Rubber Fashions
Cambridge Industrial Estate,
Edward Stre
Salford M7 9SJ
England
Catalog - Rubber clothing

Sealwear
3rd Floor
Regent Chambers
15 Westover Rd.
Bournemouth, Dorset
BH1 2BY England
(44 20) 229-0675
Rubberwear, catsuits, etc.

The Sentry Box
PO Box, 722
London Se17 3NT
England
(44 71) 735-1116
Catalog - men's leather and rubber

She-An-Me
Hamersmith Rd.
Londom W14
(44 71) 603-2402
also at:
Fun Fashions 48 Windsor St.
Uxbridge, Middlesex
England
(44 89) 527-1668
Catalog - plastic clothes, corsets,
high heels, rubber

Showgrade
PO Box 10
Bramhall, Stockport, SK7 2QF
England
Wetlook clothing

Skin Two Retail, Ltd.
23 Grand Union Centre
Kensal Road
London W10 5AX
England
(44 71) 968-9692 voice
(44 71) 980-8404 fax
Catalog - Leather and rubber
clothing (Publishers of the famous
Skin Two Magazine)

Skint
P.O. Box 136
Norwich NR3-3LJ
England
SM and TV Leather, fantasy,
fashion wear

Studio 40
40 Berwick Street
London W1
England
437-0811
Catalog - leather and latex wear
and gear

Sunshine

Sherlock House, Wallasey
Merseyside LL45 4JB.
England
Latex lined raincoats

Tabby
PO Box 916
Westcliff on Sea, Essex SS0 8QD
England
Catalog - corsets, PVC, satin

Tagamah and Ieish
BCM Blindfold,
London WC1N 3XX
England
Fantasy outfits, custom work

Tentacle
P.O. Box 20
Grantham
Lincs NG33 5RB
Catalog - Rubber skin suits,
masks, fetish furniture

Tight Situation
P.O. Box 860
London SE12 0LL
(44 81) 857-7146
Catalog - Fetish clothing

Tollyboy Products
P.O. Box 27
Dronfield
Sheffield S18 6DN
England
(44 74) 289-0575
Male and female stainless steel
chastity devices custom only
wonderful work, but slow to deliver

Una Deva
PO Box 1426
Shepton Mallet
Sommerset BA4 6HH
England
(44 74) 983-1397
Catalog - Rubber, PVC gloves,
clothes

Victoria Regine
PO Box 192,
Wolverhampton WV4 5TS
England
(44 90) 233-6191
Rubber, leather, corsetry, custom
work

Voller's Mail Order Ltd.
112 Kingston Rd.
Portsmouth PO2 7BP Hants
England
Corset specialists, one of the big
names in corsetry
Westward Bound
27 Old Gloucester St.
London, WC1N 3XX
(44 56) 677-6907
Catalog - Famous (infamous?)

bed-and-breakfast-dungeon hostel, also sells SM clothes and gear

Wethervain
283 Sandycombe Rd,
Kew Gardens,
Richmond-upon-Thames
Surrey TW9 3LU
(44 81) 940-0156
rubberwear, magazines and videos

Zeitgeist
66 Holloway Road
London N7 8JE
England
(44 71) 607-2977
Catalog - high heels, rubber, leather, plastic clothes

Zipper
283 Camden High St
London Nw1 7BX
England
(44 71) 267-0021
Men's rubber and leather shop

FINLAND

Decadence
PO Box 245
SF-00181 Helsinki 18
Finland
O69 48 898
Fetish clothing and shoes

LL&SS
Taidekustannus, PL 361
65101 VAASA
Finland
(358) 962 42 123 (24 h)
Lingerie

FRANCE

Galactica
31 Blvd de Clichy
75009 Paris
France
(33 1) 4874-5671
Lingerie, rubber

Latex Seduction
c/o
Mme Guerif BP651
44018 Nantes
Cedex 01, France
Rubber fashions

Les Folies de Sade
28b rue Fosse'-aux-Loups
1000 Bruxelles, France
(33 1) 2219-7997
Fetish clothing and gear

Librarie des Artists
19 Blvd de Clichy
75009 Paris
France

(33 1) 4282-1190
Fetish fashions

MGL Sexy Lingerie
144 Rue St-Denis
75002 Paris, France
(33 1) 4221-3334
Fetish fashion and SM gear

Modern Style
Julicher Str 10
5000 Koln, France
(33 1) 2221-1080
Rubber, leather, and PVC clothes

Phylea
61 rue Quincampoix
75004 Paris, France
(33 1) 4276-0180
Fetish fashions

Planet Alice
4 rue Diodore Raoult
38000 Grenoble, France
(33 76) 42-7032
Fetish fashions

SCL <<O>> Fashion
5 rue des Vosges
68200, Didenheim
France
(33 89) 06-1040
SM, rubber, wetlook fashions

GERMANY

Annette K Fashion
Helmholzstr 28,
4000 Dusseldorf
(49) 021/137-4476
Rubber, PVC and heels

Boutique de Sade
Erichstrasse 41
D-20359 Hamburg
Germany
(49) 040/314-4119
PVC, latex, leather, shoes, SM toys

Boutique Highlights
Gabelsberger Str. 68
D-80333 Muenchen
Germany
(49) 089/527475
Leather, rubber, plastic clothing, shoes

Caprice
Erwin Balzstr 73
Stuttgart, Germany
(49) 071/176-9074 voice
(49) 071/176-1945 fax
leather and rubber

Dream & Fantasy Fashions
Postfach 410309
D-1000 Berlin 41
Germany
(49) 030/792-7760

Catalog - Rubber, leather, PVC, books, SM toys, custom work

Domination Mailorder Service
POSTFACH 81 02 43
Germany
(49) 089/930-6980
Leather, latex, shoes, SM toys

Fashion Cats
Vulkanstr 33
D-40227 Dusseldorf
Germany
(49) 021/178-7276
Rubber and PVC

Full Moon Fashions
Postfach 520430
2000 Hamburg 52
Catalog- women's rubber fashions

Hautnah
Uhlandst 170
D-10719 Berlin
Germany
(49) 030/882-3434
Rubber, plastic, leather, shoes

Karo Designs
Post Office Box 601303
D-22213, Hamburg
Germany
Catalog - Plastic bubble-wear

Kunzmann
Postfach 1047
7530 Pforzheim
Catalog - Rubber and fetish clothing manufacturer
shop: .
Lanhausstr 2
7536 Ispringen
Germany

Lampe
Postfach 500942
2000 Hamburg 50
Germany
Catalog - rubberwear

LGS
Bachumer Strasse 76
4650 Gelsenkirchen
Germany
(49) 0209/22214
Catalog - SM gear, furniture, books, videos

Love & Flash
Zentralstr. 13-17
D-31785 Hameln
Germany
(49) 05151/28769
Leather, rubber, high heels, corsets

Modern Style
Julicher Str. 10

D-50674 Koln
Germany
(49) 0221/211080
Rubber, leather, plastic, shoes

Moonlight Fashion
Postfach 18 01 28
D-33691 Bielefeld
Germany
Catalog - Leather and lingerie

MVS Erotik-Versand
Poststrasse 46
D-44269 Herne
Germany
(49) 02323/18028
(49) 02323/51471 (fax)
Catalog - High heels, boots,
corsets, rubber, leather, SM toys

Nima
Wolfstrasse 16
5000 Koln 1
Germany
(49) 02212/36328
Catalog - Leather

<<O>> Fashion Shop
TECHCOM GmbH
Kronprinzensstr. 30
D-42655 Solingen
Germany
(49) 0212/56626
(49) 0212/549094 (fax)
Fetish fashions

Opera
Zeughausgasse 20
3011 Berne
Germany
(49) 0312/28458
Rubber, leather, PVC, shoes, boots

Pourquoi Pas
BMBH, Mainzer Str 28,
D-6600 Saarbrucken
Germany
Catalog - fetish fasions

Schwarze Mode
Grunewaldstrasse 91,
1000 Berlin 62, Germany
(49) 784-5922
Fetish fashion in leather, rubber,
and plastic

Secrets
Marienplatz 1,
5000 Koln 1, Germany
(49) 0221/244100
Leather and rubber fashions

Schau Mode
Paul-Hindemith-Ring 18
D-63110 Rodgau
Germany
(49) 06106/18379
Catalog - Rubber, PVC, leather,

shoes custom work

Sin `A' Matic
Postfach 1561
D-91005 Erlangen
Germany
Catalog - Rubber, PVC, leather
shop:
Jakobinenstr. 1
D-90762 Fuerth
Germany

SW3
Herschelstr. 32
D-30159 Hannover
Germany
(49) 0511/1317229
Fetish fashions

Sexy Cats
Industriestrasse 10
D-40227 Duesseldorf
Germany
Rubber, PVC clothing

Walter's Leder Boutique
Martin-Luther-Str. 45
D-10779 Berlin 30
Germany
(49) 030/2111897
Leather, latex
also:
Reichenbachstr. 40a
D-8046900 Muenchen
Germany
(49) 089/2015062

Zweite Haut
Wllhemshoher Str 16,
D-12161 Berlin
Germany
(49) 030/8218603
Catalog - mail order rubber
custom work available

ISREAL

Air Transilvania
Sheinkin 58
Tel-Aviv, Israel
Latex & PVC wear

JAPAN

Azzlo
21 Sakamachi
Yotsuya, Shinjuku-ku
Tokyo 160, Japan
(813) 3356 9267
Fetish Fashions and gear

Dynasty
3-2-4, Shioji-cho,
Mizuho-ku, Nagoya,
Japan
(81) 052 853 1144
Wetlook, PVC, and rubber fashions

THE NETHERLANDS

Ben's Fashion
P.O. Box 3184
3101 ED Schiedam
Holland
(31 10) 435-0785
(31 10) 435-0811 Fax
catalog- rubber fetish clothing,
bondage and SM gear

Bizarre Design
P.O. Box 3184
Marnixstraat 394a
Amsterdam 1017 PL
Holland
(31 20) 627-6844
custom leathers, corsets, SM wear

CHRISTINE LE DUC
Schieweg 108
NL-3038 BC Rotterdam
Holland
(31 10) 467-9527
Chain of adult shops with wide
selection of rubber, leather, and
SM toys Catalog sales also (see
mail order address)
also:
Walstraat 55
NL-6811 BD Arnhem, Holland
also:
Ged. Zuiderdiep 88
NL-9711 HL Groningen, Holland
also:
Amsterdamsestraatweg 310
NL-3551 CT Utrecht, Holland
also:
Vughterstraat 62-64
NL-5211 GK s'Hertogenbosch,
Holland
also:
Willemstraat 33
NL-5611 HB Eindhoven, Holland
also:
Haagdijk 14
NL-4811 TT Breda, Holland
also:
Generaal Cronjistraat 77
NL-2021 JC Haarlem, Holland
also:
Piet Heinplein 1
NL-2518 CA den Haag, Holland
(31 20) 362-5295
also:
Reguliersdwarsstraat 107
NL-1017 BL Amsterdam, Holland
(31 20) 623-1321
also:
Leidsekruisstraat 33
NL-1017 RG Amsterdam, Holland
(31 20) 623-2646
also:
Dautzenbergstraat 5
NL-6411 LA Heerlen, Holland
also:
Bloemenstraat 78
NL-6511 EM Nijmegen, Holland
also:

Spui 6
NL-1012 WZ Amsterdam, Holland
(31 20) 624-8265
also:
Oudebrugsteeg 21
NL-1012 JN Amsterdam,
Holland
(31 20) 623-8732
also:
CHRISTINE LE DUC
(MAIL ORDER)
P.O.Box 170
NL-1130 AD Volendam,
Holland

Demask
Zeedijk 64
1012 BA,
Amsterdam, Holland
(31 20) 620-5603
Netherlands
catalog-rubber and leather clothes
SM & bondage toys

Ellen Schippers Design
1E Jan Steenstraat 112
Third Floor, 1072 NR
Amsterdam, Netherlands
(31 20) 662-3883
catalog- fantasy and fetish wear in
leather, plastic and rubber

Expectations
Warmoes Str 32
1012JE Amsterdam
(31 20) 624-5573
Catalog- Leather and rubber
fashions. SM and bondage toys.
Repair service

Funny Skin
Wagenweg 16,
2012 ND Harrlem-Centrum
Holland
(31 23) 421-870
catalog - rubber & plastic fashion

My Sin
Pannekoekstraat 29a
3011 LC Rotterdam
Netherlands
(31 10) 404-6568
Lingerie and SM clothes and toys

Mail & Female
PO Box 16668
NL-1001 RD Amsterdam
Holland
(31 20) 693-6074
(31 20) 668-4990 (fax)
Mail Order catalog - leather and
latex, toys, books, videos
shop:
Amstel 47 sous
NL-1001 RD Amsterdam
Holland
(31 20) 693-6074
(31 20) 668-4990 (fax)

Massad
Mathenesserweg 9A
Rotterdam, Netherlands
Catalog - SM clothes, toys,
bondage gear

Rimba
Postbox 33
4840 AA Prinsenbeek
Holland
(31) 076 414484
catalog - fetish wear

Rob Gallery
Weteringschans 253
NL 1017 XJ
Amsterdam, The Netherlands
(31 20) 625-4686
(31 20) 627-3220
Catalog: leather, SM toys, SM art

Skin Tight
Josephstraat 168
NL-3014 TX
Rotterdam, Holland
(31 10) 436-3756
shoes, boots, latex, wigs, corsets

Studio Kat
1E Jan Steenstraat 112
Third Floor
1072 NR, Amsterdam
Holland
(31 20) 662-3883
Catalog - plastic, leather, rubber
custom work

NEW ZEALAND

L'Amour
P.O. Box 5200
St Kevin's Arcade
Karangahape Road
Auckland 1, New Zealand
(64 9) 379-0497
(64 9) 480-1400
latex rubber wear, leather SM &
bondage gear
also:
270 Onewa Road, Birkenhead
Auckland 1
New Zealand
also:
518 Karangahape Road
Auckland 1
New Zealand

SWEDEN

Barbarella
Fjarde langgt 6, Andra Lang g22
41328 Goteborg
Sweden
(46) 31-147968
Rubber, leather, PVC, high heels,
piercing studio

Delta Fashion
Box 4715
S-402 59 Gothenburg, Sweden
(46 31) 481-026 Fax
Catalog- rubber and leather
fashions and masks

Foxy Lady
Lundavagen 9
212 18 Malmo
Sweden
Lingerie

SWITZERLAND

Aie Design
Segantinistr 85
8049 Zurich
Switzerland
Women's leather fashions

Arabesque
Brauerstr 31, 8004,
Zurich, Switzerland
(41) 01 242-9626
Catalog - Fetish fashions in
leather, rubber, and PVC
also:
Limmatstr. 10
CH-5432 Neuenhof
Switzerland
(41) 01 242-9626

Boutique Fancy
Elisabethenstrasse 41
CH-4056 Basel
Switzerland
(41) 061-2714656 (voice)
(41) 061-2714720 (fax)

Dana
Grossackerstr 5
CH-9006 St Gallen
Switzerland
(41) 071253195
rubber, leather, body jewelry

Eccentric Fashion
Mail order:
Postfach 1, CH 4857
Riken, Switzerland
(41 62) 44 2221
Shop:
Bernstrasse 215,
Rothrist, Switzerland.
Catalog - Fetish clothing (by
appointment)

Appendix D: SM and Fetish Magazines

This is not "the definitive list" of SM and fetish magazines, we're sure to have missed someone's favorites. However, we've enjoyed these and think you will, too.

"Artemis"
Artmis
BM Perfect
London, England
WC1N 3XX

"Bad Attitudes"
PO Box 39110
Cambridge, MA 02139

"B&D Pleasures" (also;
"LeatherLinks")
PO Box 92889
Long Beach, CA 90809-2889
310-631-1600

"Body Art"
Blake House Studios
Blake End, Rayne
Braintree, Essex
CM7 8SH

"Body Play" & "Modern Primitives
Quarterly"
Insight Books
PO Box 2575
Menlo Park, CA 94026-2575

"Bondage Photo Treasures" (also;
"Images in Restraint" and several
other bondage titles)
London Enterprises, Ltd.
Lyndon Distributors
15756 Arminta St.
Van Nuys, CA 91406

"Boudoir Noir"
Boudoir Noir Publications
Box 5, Station F
Toronto, ON
Canada, M4Y 2L4
(416) 591-2387
(416) 591-1572
email: Boudoir@the-wire.com
web home page: http://www.the-
wire.com/boudoir.noir

"Brat Attack"
PO Box 40754
San Francisco, CA 94141-0754

"Corset Newsletter"
(Ruth Johnson's newsletter)
BR Creations
PO Box 4201
Mountain View, CA 94040

"Demonia"
Comedit
15 cite Jole
75011 Paris, France

"Dominant Mystique" (also;
"Dominant Domain")
New Esoteric Press, Inc.
PO Box 30689, JFK Station
Jamaica, NY 11430

"Domination Directory
International" (also; "Stiletto",
"Mistresses of England",
"Mistresses of Germany",
"Mistresses of Holland", "Fantasy
Register" & "Fetishist")
Strictly Speaking Publishing Co.
PO Box 8006
Palm Springs, CA 92263

"Dressing For Pleasure Magazine"
Constance Enterprises, Ltd.
PO Box 43079
Upper Monclair, NJ 07043
201-746-4200

"Drummer"
Desmodus, Inc.
P.O. Box 11314
San Francisco, CA 94101
415 252-1195

"EIDOS"
PO Box 96
Boston, MA 02137-0096

"Fetish Times" (also; "Foot
Worship News", "Watersports", &
"Platinum")
Platinum
4501 Van Nuys Blvd. #215
Sherman Oaks, CA 91404

"Frighten the Horses"
Heat Seeking Publishing
41 Sutter Street #1108
San Francisco, CA 94104

"Get Kinky"
Modern Products
976 Murfreesboro Rd., Ste. 155
Nashville,TN 37217-1516

"Greenery: Lady Green's
Newsletter for Women and Men
Exploring Female Domination"
3739 Balboa Ave. #195
San Francisco, CA 94121

"Hellfire" (also: "Leather
Underground", "SMExpress",
"Dominant Men/submissive
women")
Inner Act Publications
PO Box 4244
New Winsor, NY 12553
212-647-0063

"Leather Journal"
Cedar Publishing Co.
7985 Santa Monica Bldv.
#109-368
West Hollywood, CA 90046
"Love Bondage Gallery" (Many
other bondage related
publications and videos)
Harmony Publications
Box 69976
Los Angeles, CA 90069

"O" Magazine
Una Deva
PO Box 1177
Cheddar, Somerset
England
BS27 3UQ

"On Our Backs"
526 Castro Street
San Francisco, CA 94114

"OUCH!" (also;Deviations,
Discipline Classes, Dominatrix
Domain, Fem-Dom Video,
Obeisance, Femme Fatale,
Petticoat Power, Humbly Yours,
Maitresse, Humiliated
Transvestites, and Deviation
Directory)
Matriarch Productions
PO Box 4295, Grand Central Sta.
NY, NY 10017

"Outrageous Women"
PO Box 23
Somerville, MA 02143

"PFIQ" (Piercing Fans
International Quarterly)
Gauntlet, Inc.
1201 Old Country Road, Unit #3
Belmont, CA 94002

"Quim"
BM 2182
London, England
WC1N 3XX

"Sado Maso"
Apdo. Correos, 12166
08080 Barcelona, Spain
93 419 2630

"Sandmutopia Guardian"
The Utopian Network
PO Box 1146
New York, NY 10156
(516) 842-1711 M-F 11am-8pm
(516) 842-7518 fax

"Secret"
PO Box 1400
1000 Bruxelles, Belgium

"Skin Two"
23 Grande Union Centre
Kensal Road

London, England
W1O 5AX
081 968 9692
Fax: 081 960 8404

"S&M News"
PO Box 727
Pocono Summit, PA 18346
717-839-2512

"Stand Corrected"
PO Box 1910
Studio City, CA 91614-0910

"Strap"
Thor Productions
PO Box 950, Parkchester Station
Bronx,NY 10462

"A Taste of Latex"
"Bitches with Whips"
DM International
P.O. Box16188
Seattle, WA 98116-0188

"Tied and Tickled" (Many other
bondage related publications and
videos)
HOM
PO Box 7302
Van Nuys, CA 91409-9987

"Zeitgeist"
Blue Angel Publishing Co.
27 Old Gloucester St.
London, England
WC1N 3XX

SM Friendly Book Sellers

A Different Light Review
548 Hudson St.
New York NY 10014-3233
(212) 989-4850
Fax: (212) 989-2158
MO catalog: 800-343-4002

A Different Light Review
8853 Santa Monica Blvd.
West Hollywood CA 90069
(310) 854-6601

A Different Light Review
489 Castro St.
San Fransisco CA 94114
(415) 431-0891

Alamo Square Distributors
PO Box 14543
San Francisco, CA 94114
(415) 863-7410

Alyson Publications
40 Plympton Street
Boston MA 02118
(617(524-5679

Atomic Books
229 W. Read Street
Baltimore MD 21201
(410) 728-5490

Arthur Hamilton, Inc.
695 East 132nd Street
Bronx NY 10454
(718) 585-3468

B&D Pleasures
PO Box 92889
Long Beach CA 90809
(213) 631-1600

Blowfish
2261 Market St. #284
San Francisco CA 94114
(415) 864-0880
(415) 864-1858

Blue Moon Books
Box 1040, Cooper Station
New York NY 10276
(800) 535-0000

Books Bohemian
PO Box 17218
Los Angeles CA 90017
(213) 385-6761

Borders Books & Music
1501 4th Ave.
Seattle WA 98101
(206) 622-4599

Circlet Press
P.O. Box 15143
Boston, MA 02215
ctan@world.std.com

Constance Enterprises, Ltd.
P.O. Box 43079
Upper Montclair, NJ 07043
Voice: (201) 746-4200
Fax: (201) 746-4722

Gay Pleasures Bookstore
548 Hudson St.
NYC NY 10014
(212) 645-7573

Glad Day Books
598 A Yonge Street
Toronto, Ontario
Canada M4Y 1Z3
(416) 961-4161

Marigny Bookstore
600 Frenchman St.
New Orleans LA
(504) 943-9875

QSM
PO Box 880154
San Francisco, CA 94188
(800) 537-5815
qsm@crl.com

Source Bookstore, The
958 Queen Street
Southington CT 06489
(203) 621-6255

Tower Books
383 Lafayette St.
New York NY 10003
(212) 228-5100

Wooden Shoe Bookstore, The
112 South 20th Street
Phila. PA 19103
(215) 569-2477

Appendix E: Recommended Reading

Many of these are the books that we read, adored, re-read, slept with, bought copies of for friends, tearfully gave away, or lent against our better judgement to worthless scourges who never returned them (you know who you are!). Among these pages are ideas that shaped our experience in our exploration of sexuality and SM and, in many cases, helped us stay out of trouble. Other books come highly recommended by friends or people we admire so much we would like to be adopted by them.

Non-fiction

Anand, Margo. The Art of Sexual Ecstasy ; the path of sacred sexuality for western lovers, 1st ed. / J.P. Tarcher, c1989

Antoniou, Laura - Looking for Mr. Preston / Masquerade Books, 1995
   Some Women / Rhinoceros Books, 1995

Baldwin, Guy - Ties That Bind; The SM/Leather/Fetish Erotic Style; Issues, Commentaries, and Advice/ Daedalus Pub. Co., c1993

Bannon, Race - Learning the Ropes ; a basic guide to safe and fun S/M lovemaking / Daedalus Pub. Co., c1992.

Bean, Joseph W. - Leathersex : a guide for the curious outsider and the serious player / The Haworth Press, 1994.

Brame, G.; Brame, W. & Jacobs, J. - Different Loving ; an exploration of the world of sexual dominance and submission, 1st ed. / Villard Books, 1993

Califia, Pat - Sensuous Magic ; A Guide for Adventurous Couples / Masquerade Books, 1993.
   The Lesbian S/M Safety Manual / Alyson Publications

Camphausen, Rufus C. - The Encyclopedia of Erotic Wisdom ; A reference Guide to the Symbolism, Techniques, Rituals, Sacred Texts, Psychology, Anatomy, and History of Sexuality / Inner Traditions International, 1991

Green, Lady - The Sexually Dominant Woman ; A Workbook for Nervous Beginners / available from the author: 3739 Balboa Ave. #195, San Francisco, CA 94121

Herrman, Jack - Trust / Alamo Square

Institute for Advanced Study of Human Sexuality, The - The Complete Guide to Safe Sex / Barricade Books

Jacque, Trever; Dale; Hamilton; & Sniffer - On the Safe Edge / WholeSM Publishing, Toronto 1993

Liszt, C. & Easton, D. - The Bottoming Book; Or, How To Get Terrible Things Done to You By Wonderful People / Published by Lady Green, 3739 Balboa Ave. #195, San Francisco, CA 94121

Mains, Geoff - Urban Aboriginals / Gay Sunshine Press

Piselli, Morrocchi, Giovanni, and Stanton - Sophisticated Bondage; The Art of John Willie, an Illustrated Biography / Glittering Images, available from Constance Enterprises, Ltd.,

Rosen, Michael A. - Sexual Magic; the S/M photographs / Shaynew Press, c1986.

SAMOIS - Coming to Power; Writings and Graphics on Lesbian S/M ; S/M, a form of eroticism based on a consensual exchange of power / Alyson Publications, 1987

Scott, Gini Graham, Ph.D. - Erotic Power; An Exploration of Dominance and Submission / Carol Publishing Group, 1983

Steinberg, David - The Erotic Impulse; Honoring the Sensual Self / Tarcher, Perigee Books, 1992

Thompson, Mark (edited by) - <u>Leatherfolk</u> : radical sex, people, politics, and practice, 1st ed. / Alyson Publications, c1991.

Townsend, Larry - <u>The Leatherman's Handbook</u> / Other Traveller, c1972
<u>The Leatherman's Handbook II</u> / Carlyle Communications, c1989

Warren, John, Ph.D. - <u>The Loving Dominant</u> / Masquerade Books, 1994

Wiseman, Jay - <u>SM101: A Realistic Introduction</u> / available from the author: P.O. Box 1261, Berkeley, CA 94701

Fiction

Antoniou, Laura - <u>Leather Women</u>, <u>Leather Women II</u>,<u>No Other Tribute</u>, <u>By Her Subdued</u>, (as Sara Adamson) - <u>The Marketplace</u>, <u>The Catalyst</u>, <u>The Trainer</u>, <u>The Slave</u> / Masquerade Books

Antrews, Grant - <u>My Darling Dominatrix</u> / Rhinoseros Books

Califia, Pat - books of fiction: <u>Doc & Fluff</u>, <u>Melting Point</u>, <u>Macho Sluts</u> / New York, Masquerade Books

Dante, Robert - <u>Silent Command; Poems from the S&M Scene</u> / Houston, Wings Press, 1992

De Sade, The Marquis - <u>The 120 Days of Sodom</u> / Grove Weidenfeld, New York, 1987

McNeill, Elizabeth - <u>Nine and a Half Weeks; A memoir of a love affair</u> / New York, Dutton, c1978

Nin, Anais - <u>Delta of Venus</u> / Harcourt Brace Jovanovich, New York, 1969

Preston, John - <u>The Love of a Master</u> / Alyson Publications, 1987, also: <u>Mr. Benson</u>

Reage, Pauline - <u>The Story of O</u> / Grove Press, 1965

Rice, Anne - A trilogy written as A.N. Roquelaure: <u>The Claiming of Sleeping Beauty</u>, <u>Beauty's Punishment</u>, and <u>Beauty's Release</u> / E.F. Dutton, also: writing as Anne Rampling, <u>Exit to Eden</u> / Arbor House, c1985

Tan, Cecilia - <u>Telepaths Don't Need Safewords; And Other Stories from the Erotic Edge of Science Fiction and Fantasy</u>, <u>SexMagick; Women Conjuring Erotic Fantasy</u> / Circlet Press

Townsend, Larry - <u>Dream Master and Other SM Stories</u>/ Beverly Hills, CA : LT Publications, c1992

Von Sacher-Masoch, Leopold - <u>Venus in Furs</u>

Several of the book dealers that carry titles that cannot be found elsewhere are listed on page 270. It would be very much worth your while to write them to ask for their catalog of offerings:

We don't know anything about this one, but it sounds like a fun book to schlepp along with you on those lonely trips to the video rental store. Allen Marburger - <u>Bondage Fantasies in Popular Entertainment</u> ; an annotated listing of sequences from movies and television / A. Marburger, c1980

In our research we stumbled across this one. We haven't read it yet and it might be a real dog, but, dear lord, this title is intriguing! We're going to hunt it down, so to speak, how about you? Robert Eisler (1882-1949) - <u>Man Into Wolf; An anthropological interpretation of sadism, masochism, and lycanthropy; a lecture delivered at a meeting of the Royal Society of Medicine</u>. New York, Greenwood Press [1969, c1951] also: Santa Barbara, CA, Ross-Erikson, 1978

Statement on Domestic Violence

The National Leather Association:International has called on the Leather SM Fetish community to take the lead in reducing domestic violence through education.

No group is free of domestic battering and abuse, but fear, denial, and lack of knowledge have slowed public response to this serious problem.

The NLA is committed to reducing this violence by attempting:

1. to show that **community action can reduce domestic violence**;

2. **to hold batterers accountable for choosing to be violent**; to encourage victims to take legal action; to deny that drug and alcohol abuse alone excuse battering; and to encourage the batterer to seek treatment and the victim to seek support;

3. **to listen and support** those who have the courage to tell us -- to help them end their shame and isolation;

4. **to educate** the legal and social service systems about the difference between consensual SM and domestic violence and to encourage their appropriate intervention;

5. **to take the responsibility for educating our community** about the forms of domestic abuse and their extent and severity; and

6. **to promote information** about where to go for help.

Domestic violence takes many forms: physical abuse, isolation, outright or subtle psychological and emotional abuse, economic control, sexual abuse and the destruction of personal property. Non-consensual manipulation, terror and assault are not part of SM.

The National Leather Association advocates relationships and friendships based on responsibility, honesty and integrity in which power and pleasure derive from mutual respect.

Dhampir, Child of The Blood

Vampyres walk amongst us. Here, for perhaps the first time in this century, a vampyre of the Clan of Lilith invites us into her life through letters to her newly made "cub" and to those she calls her "food." In **Dhampir; Child of The Blood**, the myths come alive, but they are not as one expects from the myriad fictional accounts. You will see what it means to become Vampyre, what they endure, what they sacrifice and why, how a vampyre feeds, hunts and how they feel when the "beast" is upon them. Courageously, Johnson uses her real name, discusses real people and events and passes on to us the history, legends and wisdom of The Clan of Lilith handed down by her sire when he made her.

Frank, explicit letters from a mother to a daughter about life and survival as one of the newest members of the vampyre Clan of Lilith.

It is time for me to speak to you of The Blood.

The Blood is the bond between our clan and our vessels. It is more than just sustenance, more than need, more than hunger; it is what makes us Vampyre. It is life.

The Blood draws us and drives our very existence. Just as a drowning man needs air, and a thirsting man needs water, we must drink the blood of others to exist. There is no way to describe how quickly The hunger turns to bloodlust when left unheeded, just as there are no words to adequately portray, nor any drug to comparably simulate the ecstacy we feel when The Blood flows into and courses through our bodies.

Some clans call it their curse, but we of The Clan of Lilith know vampyrism as a devine gift. If you live within our laws, you will never regret your transformation, nor will you ever have cause to mourn those who become your food. But following The Law will not always be easy for you.

You must always master The Blood. It must never master you. You must always be on guard. This is how we protect our vessels. If you do not pay heed to the hunger it will quickly make you a dangerous predator, seeing only food and not friend. This is not our clan's way. The hunger comes on in stages. I must teach you to know them, for each stage is more dangerous than the one before it.

You have tasted The Blood and it has nourished you. Nourishment creates need, the first stage of your hunger. Your body will tell you when it needs to feed. LISTEN TO IT!

A VAMPYRE's Babybook by V. M. JOHNSON

Dhampir
Child of The Blood

$ 8.95 US ISBN 0 - 9645960 - 1- 0

by V.M. Johnson

Cover design by Andrea LaBruno

Illustration by Molly Devon

Mystic Rose Books

P.O. Box 1036/SMS
Fairfield, CT 0643

Phone: (203) 371-6912
Fax: (203) 371-4843
email: mystrose@palace.com
Web page: http://palace.com/rose/mystic1.htm

Mystic Rose

Mystic Rose Books

Quantity discounts are available on bulk purchases of **Dhampir, Child of the Blood** and **Screw the Roses, Send Me the Thorns** for educational purposes, fund raising, or gift giving. Special books, booklets, or book excerpts can also be created to fit your specific needs. Contact us for more information.

Phone: (203) 371-6912
Fax: (203) 371-4843
email: mystrose@palace.com
Web page: http://palace.com/rose/mystic1.htm

To order **Dhampir, Child of The Blood** or **Screw the Roses, Send Me the Thorns**, fill out the form below and send it with your payment to:

Mysic Rose Books
P.O. Box 1036/SMS
Fairfield, CT 06432

Name: _____

Address: _____

City, State, Zip: _____

Country: _____

Number of copies of **Screw the Roses, Send Me the Thorns**
at $24.95: _____

Number of copies of **Dhampir, Child of The Blood**
at $8.95 _____

Sub-total: _____

Shipping: _____

Total: _____

USA Shipping: $3.75 for the 1st book , $2.00 for each additional book.
Canada and Mexico Shipping $5.00, Other countries $12.00

Mystic Rose